BA 304
MANAGEMENT
AND
ORGANIZATION

PENNSTATE
1855

SMEAL College of Business

KENDALL/HUNT PUBLISHING COMPANY
4050 Westmark Drive   Dubuque, Iowa 52002

CONTENTS

UNDERSTANDING THE MANAGER'S JOB

OPENING INCIDENT

When Leslie Wexner opened the first The Limited clothing store in an Ohio shopping mall in 1963, he had no idea that his fledgling business would grow to include thousands of specialty stores comprised of such well-known brands as Express, Abercrombie & Fitch, and Victoria's Secret. But by 1993 his firm was running out of steam, and rivals like Gap and J. Crew were attracting more and more attention. Now, though, The Limited seems to have righted itself and is again moving toward the forefront of the specialty retailing industry. The reasons for the decline and rebirth of The Limited underscore the importance of maintaining compatibility between a manager's style and the organization's situation.

When Wexner started The Limited, he was clearly an entrepreneur, and his focus was primarily on business growth and expansion. He pursued this growth in two ways. First, he continually looked for ways to branch out and systematically launched several different chains. Second, he grew each chain rapidly by opening new stores at a breakneck pace. Part of Wexner's strategy was to place his stores adjacent to one another in large shopping malls. Thus customers might walk from The Limited to Express to Lerner, buying clothes at each without realizing that they were actually buying from the same company.

Wexner created or bought several major chains, including The Limited, Express, Lerner New York,

Lane Bryant, Henri Bendel, Victoria's Secret, Bath & Body Works, Structure, and Abercrombie & Fitch. Wexner himself also jumped from business to business, leaving the day-to-day operations in the hands of others. His focus, meanwhile, continued to be on growth and expansion as he continued to buy other chains, retool his existing chains, and build more and more stores. In some malls, for instance, The Limited stores might comprise as much as 25 percent of total square footage.

But in the early 1990s troubles began to surface. Sales declined in some markets, for example, and costs and operating expenses began to creep up. Moreover, competitors such as Gap and Old Navy started attracting more customers and increasingly became the stores of choice for hip young consumers. Investors also began to get nervous, and the company's stock price plummeted. And some experts openly questioned whether or not The Limited could be turned around.

Wexner recognized that he had a problem, but he also didn't know quite how to define it. So, starting in the mid-1990s he began to visit several of the very best managers in the United States, including such luminaries as Sam Walton (founder of Wal-Mart), Jack Welch (CEO of General Electric), and Wayne Calloway (former CEO of PepsiCo). And he gradually began to recognize the problem: The Limited had stopped being an entrepreneurial startup operation and had evolved into a mature major business oper-

> **"I was an entrepreneur . . . I think what went wrong was the . . . entrepreneurial style wasn't working."**
>
> —Leslie Wexner,
> founder and CEO of The Limited

ation, yet he was still trying to run it using the same managerial style he had used when he had only a few dozen stores. Clearly, he realized, running a global company with more than 5,000 stores, generating annual revenues of $9.3 billion, and employing 127,000 people required a different approach than the one he had been using.

So Wexner immersed himself in a crash course on how to manage a mature business. He learned about operations and financial control, revamped the firm's organization design, and implemented a more professional approach to human resource management. He also began to focus more on profit margins and acknowledged that sometimes you have to close or sell underperforming stores and businesses. And he learned the difference between competitive strategy and growth strategy.

By the end of the decade, signs were clearly pointing to a resurgence at The Limited. For example, same-store sales are again increasing, and the firm's stock price reached a record high in mid-2000. But Wexner is quick to point out that, even though he has helped reinvent his company, he doesn't want to make the same mistake again. He has committed himself to staying abreast of modern management techniques and contemporary management thought.

This book is about managers like Leslie Wexner and the work they do. In Chapter 1 we examine the nature of management, its dimensions, and its challenges, the concepts of management and managers, discuss the management process, and summarize the origins of contemporary management thought. We conclude by introducing critical contemporary challenges and issues.

An Introduction to Management

management A set of functions directed at the efficient and effective utilization of resources in the pursuit of organizational goals

efficient Using resources wisely and in a cost-effective way

effective Making the right decisions and successfully implementing them

Management is the set of functions directed at the efficient and effective utilization of resources in the pursuit of organizational goals. By **efficient,** we mean using resources wisely and in a cost-effective way. By **effective,** we mean making the right decisions and successfully implementing them. In general, successful organizations are both efficient and effective.

Today's managers face a variety of interesting and challenging situations. The average executive works 60 hours a week, has enormous demands placed on his or her time, and faces increased complexities posed by globalization, domestic competition, government regulation, and shareholder pressure. The task is further complicated by rapid change, unexpected disruptions, and both minor and major crises. The manager's job is unpredictable and fraught with challenges, but it is also filled with opportunities to make a difference.

Kinds of Managers

Many different kinds of managers are at work in organizations today. Figure 1.1 shows how managers within an organization can be differentiated by level and area.

Levels of Management. One way to differentiate managers is by their level in the organization. **Top managers** make up the relatively small group of executives who manage the overall organization. Titles found in this group include president, vice president, and chief executive officer (CEO). Top managers create the organization's goals, overall strategy, and operating policies. They also officially represent the organization to the external environment by meeting with government officials, executives of other organizations, and other individuals and groups.

Howard Schultz, CEO of Starbucks, is a top manager, as is Deidra Wager, the firm's senior vice president for retail operations. Top managers make decisions about such activities as acquiring other companies, investing in research and development, entering or abandoning various markets, and building new plants and office facilities. They often work long hours and spend much of their time in meetings or on the telephone. In most cases, top managers are also very well paid. In fact, the elite top managers of very large firms sometimes make several million dollars a year in salary, bonuses, and stock.

Middle management is probably the largest group of managers in most organizations. Common middle-management titles include plant manager, operations manager, and division head. **Middle managers** are primarily responsible for implementing the policies and plans developed by top managers and for supervising and coordinating the activities of lower-level managers. Plant managers, for example, handle inventory management, quality control, equipment failures, and minor union problems. They also coordinate the work of supervisors within the plant.

top managers The relatively small set of senior executives who manage the overall organization

middle managers The relatively large set of managers responsible for implementing the policies and plans developed by top managers and for supervising and coordinating the activities of first-line managers

FIGURE 1.1
Kinds of Managers by Level and Area

Organizations generally have three levels of management, represented by top managers, middle managers, and first-line managers. Regardless of level, managers are also usually associated with a specific area within the organization, such as marketing, finance, operations, human resources, or administration.

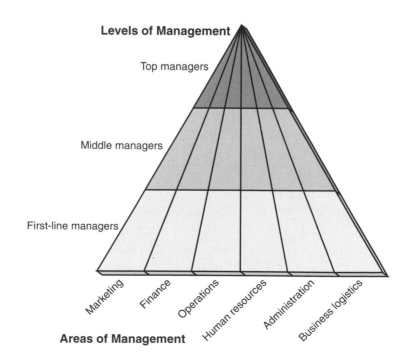

Jason Hernandez, a regional manager at Starbucks responsible for the firm's operations in three eastern states, is a middle manager.

First-line managers supervise and coordinate the activities of operating employees. Common titles for first-line managers are supervisor, coordinator, and office manager. Positions like these are often the first held by employees who enter management from the ranks of operating personnel. Wayne Maxwell and Jenny Wagner, managers of Starbucks coffee shops in Texas, are first-line managers. They oversee the day-to-day operations of their respective stores, hire operating employees to staff them, and handle other routine administrative duties required of them by the parent corporation. In contrast with top and middle managers, first-line managers typically spend a large proportion of their time supervising the work of subordinates.

first-line managers
Managers who supervise and coordinate the activities of operating employees

Areas of Management. Regardless of their level, managers may work in various areas within an organization. In any given firm, for example, areas of management may include marketing, finance, operations, human resources, administration, and other areas.

Marketing managers work in areas related to the marketing function—getting consumers and clients to buy the organization's products or services, be they Nokia digital cell phones, Ford automobiles, *Newsweek* magazines, Associated Press news reports, flights on Southwest Airlines, or cups of latte at Starbucks. These areas include new product development, promotion, and distribution.

Financial managers deal primarily with an organization's financial resources. They are responsible for activities such as accounting, cash management, and investments.

Operations managers are concerned with creating and managing the systems that create an organization's products and services. Typical responsibilities of operations managers include production control, inventory control, quality control, plant layout, and site selection.

Human resource managers are responsible for hiring and developing employees. They are typically involved in human resource planning, recruiting and selecting employees, training and development, designing compensation and benefit systems, formulating performance appraisal systems, and discharging low-performing and problem employees.

Administrative managers are not associated with any particular management specialty. Probably the best example of an administrative management position is that of a hospital or clinic administrator. Administrative managers tend to be generalists; they have some basic familiarity with all functional areas of management rather than specialized training in any one area.

Basic Management Functions

Regardless of level or area, management involves the four basic functions of planning and decision making, organizing, leading, and controlling. This book is organized around these basic functions, as shown in Figure 1.2.

planning Setting an organization's goals and deciding how best to achieve them

decision making Part of the planning process that involves selecting a course of action from a set of alternatives

Planning and Decision Making. In its simplest form, **planning** means setting an organization's goals and deciding how best to achieve them. **Decision making,** a part of the planning process, involves selecting a course of action from a set of

FIGURE 1.2

The Management Process

Management involves four basic activities—planning and decision making, organizing, leading, and controlling. Although there is a basic logic for describing these activities in this sequence (as indicated by the solid arrows), most managers engage in more than one activity at a time and often move between the activities in unpredictable ways (as shown by the dotted arrows).

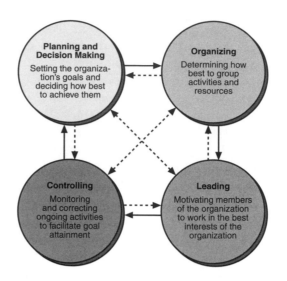

alternatives. Planning and decision making help maintain managerial effectiveness by serving as guides for future activities. Part II of this text is devoted to planning and decision making.

organizing Grouping activities and resources in a logical fashion

Organizing. Once a manager has set goals and developed a workable plan, the next management function is to organize people and the other resources necessary to carry out the plan. Specifically, **organizing** involves determining how activities and resources are to be grouped. Although some people equate this function with the creation of an organization chart, we will see in Part III that it is actually much more.

leading The set of processes used to get members of the organization to work together to further the interests of the organization

Leading. The basic managerial function is leading. Some people consider leading to be both the most important and the most challenging of all managerial activities. **Leading** is the set of processes used to get people to work together to advance the interests of the organization.

controlling Monitoring organizational progress toward goal attainment

Controlling The final phase of the management process is **controlling,** or monitoring the organization's progress toward its goals. As the organization moves toward its goals, managers must monitor progress to ensure that it is performing in such a way as to arrive at its "destination" at the appointed time.

Fundamental Management Skills

To carry out these management functions properly, managers rely on a number of specific skills. The most important management skills are technical, interpersonal, conceptual, diagnostic, communication, decision-making, and time management skills.

technical skills The skills necessary to accomplish or understand tasks relevant to the organization

Technical Skills. **Technical skills** are the skills necessary to accomplish or understand the specific kind of work being done in an organization. Technical skills are especially important for first-line managers. These managers spend much of their time training subordinates and answering questions about work-related problems. They must know how to perform the tasks assigned to those they supervise if they are to be effective managers.

Interpersonal Skills. Managers spend considerable time interacting with people both inside and outside the organization. For obvious reasons, then, the manager also needs **interpersonal skills**—the ability to communicate with, understand, and motivate individuals and groups. As a manager climbs the organizational ladder, he or she must be able to get along with subordinates, peers, and those at higher levels of the organization. Because of the multitude of roles managers must play, a manager must also be able to work with suppliers, customers, investors, and others outside of the organization.

Conceptual Skills. **Conceptual skills** depend on the manager's ability to think in the abstract. Managers need the mental capacity to understand the overall workings of the organization and its environment, to grasp how all the parts of the organization fit together, and to view the organization in a holistic manner. This allows them to think strategically, to see the "big picture," and to make broad-based decisions that serve the overall organization.

Diagnostic Skills. Successful managers also possess **diagnostic skills,** or skills that enable a manager to visualize the most appropriate response to a situation. A physician diagnoses a patient's illness by analyzing symptoms and determining their probable cause. Similarly, a manager can diagnose and analyze a problem in the organization by studying its symptoms and then developing a solution.

Communication Skills. **Communication skills** refer to the manager's abilities to effectively convey ideas and information to others and to effectively receive ideas and information from others. These skills enable a manager to transmit ideas to subordinates so that they know what is expected, to coordinate work with peers and colleagues so that they work well together properly, and to keep higher-level managers informed about what is going on. In addition, they help the manager listen to what others say and to understand the real meaning behind letters, reports, and other written communication.

Decision-making Skills. Effective managers also have good decision-making skills. **Decision-making skills** refer to the manager's ability to correctly recognize and define-problems and opportunities and to then select an appropriate course of action to solve problems and capitalize on opportunities. No manager makes the right decision all the time. However, effective managers make good decisions most of the time. And, when they do make a bad decision, they usually recognize their mistake quickly and then make good decisions to recover with as little cost or damage to their organization as possible.

Time Management Skills. Finally, effective managers usually have good time management skills. **Time management skills** refer to the manager's ability to prioritize work, to work efficiently, and to delegate appropriately. As already noted, managers face many different pressures and challenges. It is all too easy for a manager to get bogged down doing work that can easily be postponed or delegated to

interpersonal skills The ability to communicate with, understand, and motivate both individuals and groups

conceptual skills The manager's ability to think in the abstract

diagnostic skills The manager's ability to visualize the most appropriate response to a situation

communication skills The manager's abilities to both effectively convey ideas and information to others and to effectively receive ideas and information from others

decision-making skills The manager's ability to correctly recognize and define problems and opportunities, and then to select an appropriate course of action to solve problems and capitalize on opportunities

time management skills The manager's ability to prioritize work, to work efficiently, and to delegate appropriately

others. When this happens, unfortunately, more pressing and higher-priority work may get neglected.

The Science and the Art of Management

Given the complexity inherent in the manager's job, a reasonable question relates to whether management is a science or an art. In fact, effective management is a blend of both science and art. And successful executives recognize the importance of combining both the science and the art of management as they practice their craft.

The Science of Management. Many management problems and issues can be approached in ways that are rational, logical, objective, and systematic. Managers can gather data, facts, and objective information. They can use quantitative models and decision-making techniques to arrive at "correct" decisions. And they need to take such a scientific approach to solving problems whenever possible, especially when they are dealing with relatively routine and straightforward issues. When Starbucks considers entering a new market, its managers look closely at a wide variety of objective details as they formulate their plans. Technical, diagnostic, and decision-making skills are especially important when practicing the science of management.

The Art of Management. Even though managers may try to be scientific as much as possible, they must often make decisions and solve problems on the basis of intuition, experience, instinct, and personal insights. Relying heavily on conceptual, communication, interpersonal, and time management skills, for example, a manager may have to decide between multiple courses of action that look equally attractive. Further, at any given time, as illustrated in the cartoon, a manager is likely to be engaged in several different activities simultaneously. And even "objective facts" may prove to be wrong. When Starbucks was planning its first store in New York, market research clearly showed that New Yorkers preferred drip coffee to more exotic espresso-style coffees. After first installing more drip coffee makers and fewer espresso makers than in their other stores, managers had to backtrack when New Yorkers lined up clamoring for espresso. Starbucks now introduces a standard menu and layout in all its stores, regardless of presumed market differences, and then makes necessary adjustments later. Thus managers must blend an element of intuition and personal insight with hard data and objective facts.

The Evolution of Management

Most managers today recognize the importance of history and theory in their work. For example, knowing the origins of their organization and the kinds of practices that have led to success—or failure—can be an indispensable tool in managing the contemporary organization. Thus in our next section we briefly trace the history of management thought. Then we move forward to the present day by introducing contemporary management issues and challenges.

The Importance of Theory and History

Some people question the value of history and theory. Their arguments are usually based on the assumptions that history has no relevance to contemporary society and that theory is abstract and of no practical use. In reality, however, both theory and history are important to all managers today.

A theory is simply a conceptual framework for organizing knowledge and providing a blueprint for action. Although some theories seem abstract and irrelevant, others appear very simple and practical. Management theories, used to build organizations and guide them toward their goals, are grounded in reality. In addition, most managers develop and refine their own theories of how they should run their organization and manage the behavior of their employees.

An awareness and understanding of important historical developments are also important to contemporary managers. Understanding the historical context of management provides a sense of heritage and can help managers avoid the mistakes of others. Most courses in U.S. history devote time to business and economic developments in this country, including the Industrial Revolution, the early labor movement, and the Great Depression, and to such captains of U.S. industry as Cornelius Vanderbilt (railroads), John D. Rockefeller (oil), and Andrew Carnegie (steel). The contributions of these and other industrialists left a profound imprint on contemporary culture. And in recent years, new business history books have appeared that are directed more toward women managers and the lessons they can learn from the past. Wells Fargo & Company, Polaroid, Shell Oil, Levi Strauss, Ford, Lloyd's of London, Disney, Honda, and Unilever all maintain significant archives about their past and frequently evoke images from that past in their orientation and training programs, advertising campaigns, and other public relations activities.

The Historical Context of Management

The practice of management can be traced back thousands of years. The Egyptians used the management functions of planning, organizing, and controlling when they constructed the great pyramids. Alexander the Great employed a staff organization to coordinate activities during his military campaigns. The Roman Empire developed a well-defined organizational structure that greatly facilitated communication and control.

In spite of this history, however, the study of management did not begin until the nineteenth century. Two of its first true pioneers were Robert Owen and Charles Babbage. Owen (1771–1858), a British industrialist and reformer, was one of the first managers to recognize the importance of an organization's human resources and the welfare of workers. Babbage (1792–1871), an English mathematician, focused his attention on efficiencies of production. He placed great faith in the division of labor and advocated the application of mathematics to problems such as the efficient use of facilities and materials.

The Classical Management Perspective

At the dawn of the twentieth century, the preliminary ideas and writings of these and other managers and theorists converged with the emergence and evolution of large-scale businesses and management practices to create interest and focus attention on how businesses should be operated. The first important ideas to emerge are now called the **classical management perspective**. This perspective actually includes two different viewpoints: scientific management and administrative management.

classical management perspective Consists of two distinct branches: scientific management and administrative management

Scientific Management. Productivity emerged as a serious business problem during the first few years of the twentieth century. Business was expanding and capital was readily available, but labor was in short supply. Hence, managers began to search for ways to use existing labor more efficiently. In response to this need, experts began to focus on ways to improve the performance of individual workers. Their work led to the development of **scientific management.** Some of the earliest advocates of scientific management included Frederick W. Taylor (1856–1915), Frank Gilbreth (1868–1924), and Lillian Gilbreth (1878–1972).

scientific management Concerned with improving the performance of individual workers

One of Taylor's first jobs was as a foreman at the Midvale Steel Company in Philadelphia. It was there that he observed what he called **soldiering**—employees' deliberately working at a pace slower than their capabilities. Taylor studied and timed each element of the steelworkers' jobs. He determined what each worker should be producing, and then he designed the most efficient way to do each part of the overall task. Next, he implemented a piecework pay system. Rather than paying all employees the same wage, he began increasing the pay of each worker who met and exceeded the target level of output set for his or her job.

soldiering Employees' deliberately working at a slow pace

After Taylor left Midvale, he worked as a consultant for several companies, including Simonds Rolling Machine Company and Bethlehem Steel. At Simonds he studied and redesigned jobs, introduced rest periods to reduce fatigue, and implemented a piecework pay system. The results were higher quality and quantity of output, and improved morale. At Bethlehem Steel, Taylor studied efficient ways of loading and unloading rail cars and applied his conclusions with equally impressive results. During these experiences, he formulated the basic ideas that he called "scientific management." Figure 1.3 illustrates the basic steps Taylor suggested. He believed that managers who followed his guidelines would improve the efficiency of their workers.

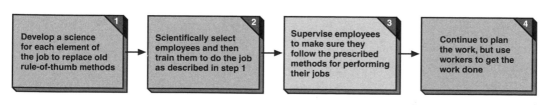

FIGURE 1.3

Steps in Scientific Management

Frederick Taylor developed this system of scientific management, which he believed would lead to a more efficient and productive workforce. Bethlehem Steel was among the first organizations to profit from scientific management and still practices some parts of it today.

Taylor's work had a major impact on U.S. industry. By applying his principles, many organizations achieved major gains in efficiency. Taylor did have his critics, however. For instance, organized labor argued that scientific management was just a device to get more work from each employee and to reduce the total number of workers needed by a firm. There was a congressional investigation into Taylor's ideas, and evidence suggests that he falsified some of his findings. Nevertheless, Taylor's work left a lasting imprint on business.

Frank and Lillian Gilbreth, contemporaries of Taylor, were a husband-and-wife team of industrial engineers. One of Frank Gilbreth's most interesting contributions was to the craft of bricklaying. After studying bricklayers at work, he developed several procedures for doing the job more efficiently. For example, he specified standard materials and techniques, including the positioning of the bricklayer, the bricks, and the mortar at different levels. The results of these changes were a reduction from 18 separate physical movements to 5 and an increase in output of about 200 percent. Lillian Gilbreth made equally important contributions to several different areas of work, helped shape the field of industrial psychology, and made substantive contributions to the field of personnel management. Working individually and together, the Gilbreths developed numerous techniques and strategies for eliminating inefficiency. They applied many of their ideas to their family and documented their experiences raising 12 children in the book and movie *Cheaper by the Dozen.*

Administrative Management. Whereas scientific management deals with the jobs of individual employees, **administrative management** focuses on managing the total organization. The primary contributors to administrative management were Henri Fayol (1841–1925), Lyndall Urwick (1891–1983), and Max Weber (1864–1920).

administrative management Focuses on managing the total organization

Henri Fayol was administrative management's most articulate spokesperson. A French industrialist, Fayol was unknown to U.S. managers and scholars until his most important work, *General and Industrial Management,* was translated into English in 1930. Drawing on his own managerial experience, he attempted to systematize the practice of management to provide guidance and direction to other managers. Fayol also was the first to identify the specific managerial functions of planning, organizing, leading, and controlling. He believed that these functions accurately reflect the core of the management process. Most contemporary management books (including this one) still use this framework, and practicing managers agree that these functions are a critical part of their job.

After a career as a British army officer, Lyndall Urwick became a noted management theorist and consultant. He integrated scientific management with the work of Fayol and other administrative management theorists. He also advanced modern thinking about the functions of planning, organizing, and controlling. Like Fayol, he developed a list of guidelines for improving managerial effectiveness. Urwick is noted not so much for his own contributions as for his synthesis and integration of the work of others.

Although Max Weber lived and worked at the same time as Fayol and Taylor, his contributions were not recognized until some years had passed. Weber was a German sociologist, and his most important work was not translated into English until 1947. Weber's work on bureaucracy laid the foundation for contemporary organization theory. The concept of bureaucracy is based on a rational set of guidelines for structuring organizations in the most efficient manner.

The Classical Perspective Today. The classical management perspective provides many techniques and approaches to management that are still relevant today. For example, thoroughly understanding the nature of the work being performed, selecting the right people for that work, and approaching decisions rationally are all useful ideas—and each was developed during this period. Similarly, some of the core concepts from Weber's bureaucratic model can still be used in the design of modern organizations, as long as their limitations are recognized. Managers should also recognize that efficiency and productivity can indeed be measured and controlled in many situations. On the other hand, managers must also recognize the limitations of the classical perspective and avoid its narrow focus on efficiency to the exclusion of other important perspectives.

The Behavioral Management Perspective

Early advocates of the classical management perspective essentially viewed organizations and jobs from a mechanistic point of view; that is, they essentially sought to conceptualize organizations as machines and workers as cogs within those machines. Even though many early writers recognized the role of individuals, their focus tended to be on how managers could control and standardize the behavior of their employees. In contrast, the **behavioral management perspective** placed much more emphasis on individual attitudes and behaviors and on group processes, and recognized the importance of behavioral processes in the workplace.

behavioral management perspective
Emphasizes individual attitudes and behaviors and group processes

The behavioral management perspective was stimulated by a number of writers and theoretical movements. One of those movements was industrial psychology, the practice of applying psychological concepts to industrial settings. Hugo Munsterberg (1863–1916), a noted German psychologist, is recognized as the father of industrial psychology. Munsterberg suggested that psychologists could make valuable contributions to managers in the areas of employee selection and motivation. Industrial psychology is still a major course of study at many colleges and universities.

Another early advocate of the behavioral approach to management was Mary Parker Follett (1868–1933) Follett worked during the scientific management era but quickly came to recognize the human element in the workplace. Indeed, her work clearly anticipated the behavioral management perspective, and she appreciated the need to understand the role of behavior in organizations.

The Hawthorne Studies. Although Munsterberg and Follett made major contributions to the development of the behavioral approach to management, its primary catalyst was a series of studies conducted near Chicago at Western Electric's Hawthorne plant between 1927 and 1932. The research, originally sponsored by General Electric, was conducted by Elton Mayo and his associates. The first study involved manipulating illumination for one group of workers and comparing their subsequent productivity with the productivity of another group whose illumination was not changed. Surprisingly, when illumination was increased for the experimental group, productivity went up in both groups. Productivity continued to increase in both groups, even when the lighting for the experimental group was decreased. Not until the lighting was reduced to the level of moonlight did productivity begin to decline (and General Electric withdrew its sponsorship).

Another experiment established a piecework incentive pay plan for a group of nine men assembling terminal banks for telephone exchanges. Scientific management would have predicted that each man would try to maximize his pay by producing as many units as possible. Mayo and his associates, however, found that the group itself informally established an acceptable level of output for its members. Workers who overproduced were branded "rate busters," and underproducers were labeled "chiselers." To be accepted by the group, workers produced at the accepted level. As they approached this acceptable level of output, workers slacked off to avoid overproducing.

Other studies, including an interview program involving several thousand workers, led Mayo and his associates to conclude that human behavior was much more important in the workplace than had been previously believed. In the lighting experiment, for example, the results were attributed to the fact that both groups received special attention and sympathetic supervision for perhaps the first time. The incentive pay plans did not work because wage incentives were less important to the individual workers in determining output than was social acceptance. In short, individual and social processes played a major role in shaping worker attitudes and behavior.

human relations movement Argued that workers respond primarily to the social context of the workplace

Human Relations. The **human relations movement**, which grew from the Hawthorne studies and was a popular approach to management for many years, proposed that workers respond primarily to the social context of the workplace, including social conditioning, group norms, and interpersonal dynamics. A basic assumption of the human relations movement was that the manager's concern for workers would lead to increased satisfaction, which would in turn result in improved performance. Two writers who helped advance the human relations movement were Abraham Maslow and Douglas McGregor.

In 1943 Maslow advanced a theory suggesting that people are motivated by a hierarchy of reds, including monetary incentives and social acceptance. Maslow's hierarchy is perhaps the best-known human relations theory. Meanwhile, Douglas McGregor's Theory X and Theory Y model best represents the essence of the human relations movement. According to McGregor, Theory X and Theory Y reflect two extreme belief sets that different managers have about their workers. **Theory X** is a relatively negative view of workers, consistent with the views of scientific management. **Theory Y** is more positive and represents the assumptions that human relations advocates make. In McGregor's view, Theory Y was a more appropriate philosophy for managers. Both Maslow and McGregor notably influenced the thinking of many practicing managers.

Theory X A pessimistic and negative view of workers consistent with the views of scientific management

Theory Y A positive view of workers, representing the assumptions that human relations advocates make

organizational behavior Contemporary field focusing on behavioral perspectives on management

Contemporary Behavioral Science in Management. Munsterberg, Mayo, Maslow, McGregor, and others have made valuable contributions to management. Contemporary theorists, however, have noted that many assertions of the human relationists were simplistic and inadequate descriptions of work behavior. Current behavioral perspectives on management, best reflected by the field of **organizational behavior**, acknowledge that human behavior in organizations is much more complex than the human relationists realized. The field of organizational behavior draws from a broad, interdisciplinary base of psychology, sociology, anthropology, economics, and medicine.

Organizational behavior theory takes a holistic view of behavior and addresses individual, group, and organizational processes. These processes are major elements in contemporary management theory. Important topics in this field include job satisfaction, stress, motivation, leadership, group dynamics, organizational politics, interpersonal conflict, and the structure and design of organizations contingency orientation also characterizes the field (discussed more fully later in this chapter).

The Behavioral Perspective Today. The primary contributions of the behavioral perspective relate to ways in which this approach has changed managerial thinking. Managers are now more likely to recognize the importance of behavioral processes and to view employees as valuable resources instead of mere tools. On the other hand, organizational behavior theory is still imprecise in its ability to predict behavior. It is not always accepted or understood by practicing managers. Hence, the contributions of the behavioral school have yet to be fully realized.

The Quantitative Management Perspective

The third major school of management thought began to emerge during World War II. During the war, government officials and scientists in England and the United States worked to help the military deploy its resources more efficiently and effectively. These groups took some of the mathematical approaches to management developed decades earlier by Taylor and Gantt, and applied them to logistical problems during the war. They learned that problems regarding troop, equipment, and submarine deployment, for example, could all be solved through mathematical analysis. After the war, companies such as Du Pont and General Electric began to use the same techniques for deploying employees, choosing plant locations, and planning warehouses. Basically, then, this perspective is concerned with applying quantitative techniques to management. More specifically, the **quantitative management perspective** focuses on decision making, economic effectiveness, mathematical models, and the use of computers. There are two branches of the quantitative approach: management science and operations management.

Management Science. Unfortunately, the term management science appears to be related to scientific management, the approach developed by Taylor and others early in the twentieth century. But the two have little in common and should not be confused. **Management science** focuses specifically on the development of mathematical models. A mathematical model is a simplified representation of a system, process, or relationship.

At its most basic level, management science focuses on models, equations, and similar representations of reality. For example, managers at Detroit Edison use mathematical models to determine how best to route repair crews during blackouts. The Bank of New England uses models to figure out how many tellers need to be on duty at each location at various times throughout the day. In recent years, paralleling the advent of the personal computer, management science techniques have become increasingly sophisticated. For example, automobile manu-

quantitative management perspective
Applies quantitative techniques to management

management science
Focuses specifically on the development of mathematical models

facturer DaimlerChrysler uses realistic computer simulations to study collision damage to cars. These simulations give them precise information and avoid the costs of crashing so many test cars.

operations management Concerned with helping the organization more efficiently produce its products or services

Operations Management. Operations management is somewhat less mathematical and statistically sophisticated than management science and can be applied more directly to managerial situations. Indeed, we can think of **operations management** as a form of applied management science. Operations management techniques are generally concerned with helping the organization produce its products or services more efficiently and can be applied to a wide range of problems.

For example, Rubbermaid and Home Depot use operations management techniques to manage their inventories. (Inventory management is concerned with specific inventory problems, such as balancing carrying costs and ordering costs, and determining the optimal order quantity.) Linear programming (which involves computing simultaneous solutions to a set of linear equations) helps United Air Lines to plan its flight schedules, Consolidated Freightways to develop its shipping routes, and General Instrument Corporation to plan what instruments to produce at various times. Other operations management techniques include queuing theory, breakeven analysis, and simulation. All of these techniques and procedures apply directly to operations, but they are also helpful in such areas as finance, marketing, and human resource management.

The Quantitative Perspective Today. Like the other management perspectives, the quantitative management perspective has made important contributions and has certain limitations. It has provided managers with an abundance of decision-making tools and techniques, and has increased understanding of overall organizational processes. It has been particularly useful in the areas of planning and controlling. On the other hand, mathematical models cannot fully account for individual behaviors and attitudes. Some believe that the time needed to develop competence in quantitative techniques retards the development of other managerial skills. Finally, mathematical models typically require a set of assumptions that may not be realistic.

Contemporary Management Thought _____

It is important to recognize that the classical, behavioral, and quantitative approaches to management are not necessarily contradictory or mutually exclusive. Even though each of the three perspectives makes very different assumptions and predictions, each can also complement the others. Indeed, a complete understanding of management requires an appreciation of all three perspectives. The systems and contingency perspectives can help us integrate the earlier approaches and enlarge our understanding of all three.

The Systems Perspective

system An interrelated set of elements functioning as a whole

open system An organizational system that interacts with its environment

closed system An organizational system that does not interact with its environment

subsystem A system within another system

synergy Two or more subsystems working together to produce more than the total of what they might produce working alone

The systems perspective is one important contemporary management theory. A **system** is an interrelated set of elements functioning as a whole. As shown in Figure 1.4, by viewing an organization as a system, we can identify four basic elements: inputs, transformation processes, outputs, and feedback. First, inputs are the material, human, financial, and information resources the organization gets from its environment. Next, through technological and managerial processes, inputs are transformed into outputs. Outputs include products, services, or both (tangible and intangible); profits, losses, or both (even not-for-profit organizations must operate within their budgets); employee behaviors; and information. Finally, the environment reacts to these outputs and provides feedback to the system.

Thinking of organizations as systems provides us with a variety of important viewpoints on organizations, such as the concepts of open systems, subsystems, synergy, and entropy. **Open systems** are systems that interact with their environment, whereas **closed systems** do not interact with their environment. Although organizations are open systems, some make the mistake of ignoring their environment and behaving as though their environment is not important.

The systems perspective also stresses the importance of **subsystems**—systems within a broader system. For example, the marketing, production, and finance functions within Mattel are systems in their own right but also subsystems within the overall organization. Because they are interdependent, a change in one subsystem can affect other subsystems as well. If the production department at Mattel lowers the quality of the toys being made (by buying lower-quality materials, for example), the effects are felt in finance (improved cash flow in the short run owing to lower costs) and marketing (decreased sales in the long run because of customer dissatisfaction). Managers must therefore remember that, although organizational subsystems can be managed with some degree of autonomy, their interdependence should not be overlooked.

Synergy suggests that organizational units (or subsystems) may often be more successful working together than working alone. The Walt Disney Company, for example, benefits greatly from synergy. The company's movies, theme parks, television programs, and merchandise licensing programs all benefit one another. Children who enjoy a Disney movie like *Tarzan* want to go to Disney World, see the Tarzan show there, and buy stuffed animals of the film's characters. Music from the film generates additional revenues for the firm, as do computer games and other licensing arrangements for lunchboxes, clothing, and so forth. Synergy

FIGURE 1.4
The Systems Perspective of Organizations

By viewing organizations as systems, managers can better understand the importance of their environment and the level of interdependence among subsystems within the organization. Managers must also understand how their decisions affect and are affected by other subsystems within the organization.

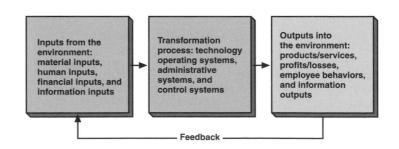

entropy A normal process leading to system decline

is an important concept for managers because it emphasizes the importance of working together in a cooperative and coordinated fashion.

Finally, **entropy** is a normal process that leads to system decline. When an organization does not monitor feedback from its environment and make appropriate adjustments, it may fail. For example, witness the problems of Studebaker (an automobile manufacturer) and Montgomery Ward (a major retailer). Each of these organizations went bankrupt because it failed to revitalize itself and keep pace with changes in its environment. A primary objective of management, from a systems perspective, is to continually re-energize the organization to avoid entropy.

The Contingency Perspective

universal perspective An attempt to identify the "one best way" to do something

contingency perspective Suggests that appropriate managerial behavior in a given situation depends on, or is contingent on, a wide variety of elements

Another recent noteworthy addition to management thinking is the contingency perspective. The classical, behavioral, and quantitative approaches are considered **universal perspectives,** because they tried to identify the "one best way" to manage organizations. The **contingency perspective,** in contrast, suggests that universal theories cannot be applied to organizations, because each organization is unique. Instead, the contingency perspective suggests that appropriate managerial behavior in a given situation depends on, or is contingent on, unique elements in that situation.

Stated differently, effective managerial behavior in one situation cannot always be generalized to other situations. Recall, for example, that Frederick Taylor assumed that all workers would generate the highest possible level of output to maximize their own personal economic gain. We can imagine some people being motivated primarily by money—but we can just as easily imagine other people being motivated by the desire for leisure time, status, social acceptance, or any combination of these (as Mayo found at the Hawthorne plant). This perspective relates perfectly to Leslie Wexner and The Limited, featured in the opening incident. His managerial style worked perfectly when his firm was small and rapidly growing but did not match as well when The Limited became a huge, mature enterprise. Thus Wexner had to alter his style at that point to better fit the changing needs of his business.

Contemporary Management Issues and Challenges

Managers today also face an imposing set of challenges as they guide and direct the fortunes of their companies. Coverage of each topic, introduced next, is thoroughly integrated throughout this book.

One of the most critical challenges facing managers in 1999 and 2000 was a labor shortage in the high-tech sector. This pattern manifests itself in several ways. First, companies in high-tech markets have found that they must offer lavish benefits and high salaries to attract talented and motivated employees. And, even though they continue to provide an ever-growing array of benefits, many of these same employees still move on to other—and more lucrative—jobs more quickly than at any other time in recent memory. This trend has also trickled down to lower-skills jobs as well. Many hotels and restaurants, for example, are having difficulties in maintaining an adequate staff of house cleaners and dishwashers because of the abundance of more attractive jobs available today.

But the economic slowdown in 2001 decreased the demand for some workers and at least temporarily curtailed this management challenge.

A second important challenge today is the management of diversity. Diversity refers to differences among people. Although diversity may be reflected along numerous dimensions, most managers tend to focus on age, gender, ethnicity, and physical abilities or disabilities. The internationalization of businesses has also increased diversity in many organizations, carrying with it additional challenges as well as new opportunities.

Aside from demographic composition, the workforce today is also changing in other ways. It seems as if the values, goals, and ideals of each succeeding generation differ from those of their parents. Today's young workers, for example, are sometimes stereotyped as being less devoted to long-term career prospects and less willing to conform to a corporate mindset that stresses conformity and uniformity. Thus managers are increasingly faced with the challenge of first creating an environment that will be attractive to today's worker. And they must address the challenge of providing new and different incentives to keep people motivated and interested in their work. Finally, they must incorporate sufficient flexibility in the organization to accommodate an ever-changing set of lifestyles and preferences.

Another management challenge that managers must be prepared to address is change. Although organizations have always had to be concerned with managing change, the rapid and constant environmental change faced by businesses today has made change management even more critical. Simply put, an organization that fails to monitor its environment and to change to keep pace with that environment is doomed to failure. But more and more managers are seeing change as an opportunity, not as a cause for alarm. Indeed, some managers think that, if things get too calm in an organization and people start to become complacent, managers should shake things up to get everyone energized.

New technology, especially as it relates to information, also poses an increasingly important management challenge. The Internet and the increased use of e-mail and voice-mail systems are among the most recent technological changes in this area. Among the key issues associated with information technology are employee privacy, decision-making quality, and optimizing a firm's investments in new forms of technology as they continue to emerge. A related issue confronting managers has to do with the increased capabilities this technology provides for people to work at places other than their office. Finally, the appropriate role of the Internet in business strategy is also a complex arena for managers. That is, managers must make decisions regarding the role of the Internet throughout their operations, including purchasing, marketing, and human resources.

Another important management challenge today is the complex array of new ways of organizing which managers can consider. Many organizations are seeking greater flexibility and the ability to respond more quickly to their environment by adopting flat structures. These flat structures are characterized by few levels of management; broad, wide spans of management (the number of individuals reporting to a specific manager); and fewer rules and regulations. The increased use of work teams also goes hand in hand with this new approach to organizing.

Globalization is yet another significant contemporary challenge for managers. Managing in a global economy poses many different challenges and opportunities. For example, at a macro level, property ownership arrangements vary widely.

So does the availability of natural resources and components of the infrastructure, as well as the role of government in business. But, for our purposes, a very important consideration is how behavioral processes vary widely across cultural and national boundaries. For example, values, symbols, and beliefs differ sharply among cultures. Different work norms and the role work plays in a person's life, for example, influence patterns of both work-related behavior and attitudes toward work. They also affect the nature of supervisory relationships, decision-making styles and processes, and organizational configurations.

Another management challenge that has taken on renewed importance is the area of ethics and social responsibility. Unfortunately, business scandals have become almost commonplace today. From the social responsibility angle, increasing attention has been focused on pollution and business's obligation to help clean up our environment, business contributions to social causes, and so forth.

Quality also continues to pose an important management challenge today. Quality is an important issue for several reasons. First, more and more organizations are using quality as a basis for competition. Continental Airlines, for example, stresses its high rankings in the J. D. Powers survey of customer satisfaction with print advertising. Second, improving quality tends to increase productivity, because making higher-quality products generally results in less waste and rework. Third, enhancing quality lowers costs. Whistler Corporation once found that it was using 100 of its 250 employees to repair defective radar detectors that were built incorrectly the first time. Quality is also important because of its relationship to productivity.

Finally, the shift toward a service economy also continues to be important. Traditionally, most businesses were manufacturers—they used tangible resources like raw materials and machinery to create tangible products like automobiles and steel. In the last few decades, however, the service sector of the economy has become much more important. Indeed, services now account for well over half of the gross domestic product (GDP) in the United States and play a similarly important role in many other industrialized nations. Service technology involves the use of both tangible resources (such as machinery) and intangible resources (such as intellectual property) to create intangible services (such as a haircut, insurance protection, or transportation between two cities). Although there are obviously many similarities between managing in a manufacturing and in a service organization, there are also many fundamental differences.

Summary of Key Points

Management is a set of functions directed at achieving organizational goals in an efficient and effective manner. A manager is someone whose primary responsibility is to carry out the management process within an organization. Managers can be differentiated by level and by area. By level, we can identify top, middle, and first-line managers. Kinds of managers by area include marketing, financial, operations, human resource, administrative, and specialized managers.

The basic activities that comprise the management process are planning and decision making, organizing, leading, and controlling. These activities are not performed on a systematic and predictable schedule. Effective managers also tend to have technical, interpersonal, conceptual, diagnostic, communication, decision-making, and time management skills. The effective practice of management requires a synthesis of science and art; that is, a blend of rational objectivity and intuitive insight.

Theories are important as organizers of knowledge and as roadmaps for action. Understanding the historical context and precursors of management and organizations provides a sense of heritage and can also help managers avoid repeating the mistakes of others. Evidence suggests that interest in management dates back thousands of years, but a scientific approach to management has emerged only in the last hundred years.

The classical management perspective had two major branches: scientific management and administrative management. Scientific management was concerned with improving efficiency and work methods for individual workers. Administrative management was more concerned with how organizations themselves should be structured and arranged for efficient operations. Both branches paid little attention to the role of the worker.

The behavioral management perspective, characterized by a concern for individual and group behavior, emerged primarily as a result of the Hawthorne studies. The human relations movement recognized the importance and potential of behavioral processes in organizations but made many overly simplistic assumptions about those processes. Organizational behavior, a more realistic outgrowth of the behavioral perspective, is of interest to many contemporary managers.

The quantitative management perspective and its two components, management science and operations management, attempt to apply quantitative techniques to decision making and problem solving. These areas are also of considerable importance to contemporary managers. The contributions of quantitative management have been facilitated by the tremendous increase in the use of personal computers and integrated information networks.

Two relatively recent additions to management theory, the systems and contingency perspectives, appear to have great potential both as approaches to management and as frameworks for integrating the other perspectives. Challenges facing managers today include a high-tech labor shortage, diversity and the new work force, change, information technology, new ways of organizing, globalization, ethics and social responsibility; the importance of quality, and the continued shift toward a service economy.

◎ Discussion Questions _____

Questions for Review

1. What are the four basic functions that comprise the management process? How are they related to one another?
2. Identify different kinds of managers by both level and area in the organization.
3. Identify the different important skills that help managers succeed. Give an example of each.
4. Briefly summarize the classical and behavioral management perspectives and identify the most important contributors to each.
5. Describe the contingency perspective and outline its usefulness to the study and practice of management.

Questions for Review

6. The text notes that management is both a science and an art. Is one of these aspects more important than the other? Under what circumstances might one ingredient be more important than the other?
7. Recall a recent group project or task in which you have participated. Explain how the four basic management functions were performed.
8. Some people argue that CEOs in the United States are paid too much. Find out the pay for a CEO and discuss whether you think he or she is overpaid.
9. Explain how a manager can use tools and techniques from each major management perspective in a complementary fashion.
10. Which of the contemporary management challenges do you think will have the greatest impact on you and your career? Which will have the least?

Building Effective Technical Skills

Exercise Overview

Technical skills refer to the manager's abilities to accomplish or understand work done in an organization. More and more managers today are realizing that having the technical ability to use the Internet is an important part of communication, decision making, and other facets of their work. This exercise introduces you to the Internet and provides some practice in using it.

Exercise Background

The so-called information highway, or the Internet, refers to an interconnected network of information-based resources using computers and computer systems. Whereas electronic mail was perhaps the first widespread application of the Internet, increasingly popular applications are based on home pages and search engines.

A *home page* is a file (or set of files) created by an individual, business, or other entity. It contains whatever information its creator chooses to include. For example, a company might create a home page for itself that includes its logo, its address and telephone number, information about its products and services, and so forth. An individual seeking employment might create a home page that includes a resume and a statement of career interests. Home pages are indexed by key words chosen by their creators.

A *search engine* is a system through which an Internet user can search for home pages according to their indexed key words. For example, suppose an individual is interested in knowing more about art collecting. Key words that might logically be linked to home pages related to this interest include art, artists, galleries, and framing. A search engine will take these key words and provide a listing of all home pages that are indexed to them. The user can then browse each page to see what information they contain. Popular search engines include Yahoo!, Lycos, and Webcrawler.

Exercise Task

1. Visit your computer center and learn how to get access to the Internet.
2. Use a search engine to conduct a search for three or four terms related to general management (for example, management, organization, business).
3. Now select a more specific management topic and search for two or three topics (if you cannot think of any terms, scan the margin notes in this book).
4. Finally, select three or four companies and search for their home pages.

Building Effective Diagnostic Skills

Exercise Overview

Diagnostic skills enable a manager to visualize the most appropriate response to a situation. This exercise encourages you to apply your diagnostic skills to a real business problem and to assess the possible consequences of various courses of action.

Exercise Background

For some time now, college textbook publishers have been struggling with a significant problem. The subject matter that constitutes a particular field, such as management, chemistry, or history, continues to increase in size, scope, and complexity. Thus authors feel compelled to add more and more information to new editions of their textbooks. Publishers have also sought to increase the visual sophistication of their texts by adding more color and photographs. At the same time, some instructors don't have time to cover the material in longer textbooks. Moreover, longer and more attractive textbooks cost more money to produce, resulting in higher selling prices to students.

Publishers have considered a variety of options to confront this situation. One option is to work with authors to produce briefer and more economical books (such as this one). Another option is to cut back on the complimentary supplements that publishers provide to instructors (such as videos and color transparencies) as a way of lowering the overall cost of producing a book. Another option is to eliminate traditional publishing altogether and provide educational resources via CD-ROM, the Internet, or other new media.

Confounding the situation, of course, is cost. Profit margins in the industry are such that managers feel the need to be cautious and conservative. That is, they cannot do everything and must not risk alienating their users by taking too radical a step. Remember, too, that publishers must consider the concerns of three different sets of customers: the instructors who make adoption decisions, the bookstores that buy educational materials for resale (at a retail markup), and students who buy the books for classroom use and then often resell them back to the bookstore.

Exercise Task

With this background in mind, respond to the following:

1. Discuss the pros and cons of each option currently being considered by text-book publishers.
2. Identify the likely consequences of each option.
3. Can you think of other alternatives that publishers in the industry should consider?
4. What specific recommendations would you make to an executive in a publishing company regarding this set of issues?

Building Effective Communication & Interpersonal Skills

Exercise Overview

Communication skills refer to the manager's abilities both to effectively convey ideas and information to others and to effectively receive ideas and information from others. Interpersonal skills refer to the ability to communicate with, understand, and motivate individuals and groups. This exercise applies these skills from a contingency perspective in selecting modes of communication to convey various kinds of news.

Exercise Background

You are the regional branch manager for a large insurance company. For the last week, you have been so tied up in meetings that you have had little opportunity to communicate with any of your subordinates. You have now caught up on things, however, and have a lot of information to convey. Specifically, here are the things that people need to know or that you need to do:

1. Three people need to be told that they are getting a pay raise of 10 percent.
2. One person needs to be told that she has been placed on probation and will lose her job if her excessive absenteeism problem isn't corrected.
3. One person needs to be congratulated for receiving his master's degree.
4. Everyone needs to be informed about the schedule for the next cycle of performance reviews.
5. Two people need to be informed that their requests for transfers have been approved, whereas a third was denied. In addition, one other person is being transferred even though she did not submit a transfer request. You know that she will be unhappy.

You can convey this information via telephone calls during regular office hours, a cell phone call as you're driving home this evening, a formal written letter, a handwritten memo, a face-to-face meeting, or e-mail.

Exercise Task

With this background in mind, respond to the following:
1. Choose a communication mode for each message you need to convey.
2. What factors went into your decision about each situation?
3. What would be the least appropriate communication mode for each message?
4. What would be the likely consequences for each inappropriate choice?

Experiential Exercise

Johari Window

Purpose: This exercise has two purposes: to encourage you to analyze yourself more accurately and to start you working on small-group cohesiveness. This exercise encourages you to share data about yourself and then to assimilate and process feedback. Small groups are typically more trusting and work better together, as you will be able to see after this exercise has been completed. The Johari Window is a particularly good model for understanding the perceptual process in interpersonal relationships.

This skill builder focuses on the *human resources model* and will help you develop your *mentor role*. One of the skills of a mentor is self-awareness.

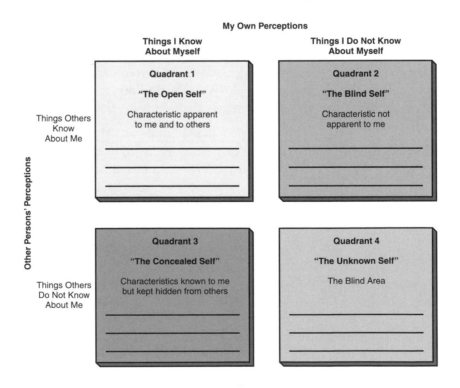

SOURCES: Adapted from Joseph Luft, *Group Processes: An Introduction to Group Dynamics* (Palo Alto, CA: Mayfield, 1970), 10–11; William C. Morris and Marshall Sashkin, *Organizational Behavior in Action* (St. Paul, MN: West, 1976), 56.

Introduction: Each individual has four sets of personality characteristics. One set, which includes such characteristics as working hard, is well known to the individual and to others. A second set is unknown to the individual but obvious to others. For example, in a working situation, a peer might observe that your jumping in to get the group moving off dead center is appropriate. At other times, you jump in when the group is not really finished, and you seem to interrupt. A third set is known to the individual but not to others. These are situations that you have elected not to share, perhaps because of a lack of trust. Finally, there is a fourth set, which is not known to the individual or to others, such as why you are uncomfortable at office parties.

Instructions: Look at the Johari Window on page 24. In quadrant 1, list three things that you know about yourself and that you think others know. List three things in quadrant 3 that others do not know about you. Finally, in quadrant 2, list three things that you did not know about yourself last semester that you learned from others.

CLOSING CASE

Managing in a Wired World

Although Amazon.com is not yet a decade old, it's already a case study in Internet success. Founded by Jeff Bezos in 1995 as an online bookstore, Seattle-based Amazon rings up more than $1.6 billion in e-commerce sales every year. First books, then music and videos, and now software, screwdrivers, and sofas—Amazon has grown into a virtual department store for its 17 million online customers worldwide. Even as successful chains such as Barnes & Noble and Wal-Mart try to grab a larger piece of the online retailing pie, CEO Bezos has maintained Amazon's market leadership and customer loyalty through constant innovation.

Nothing like Amazon existed when Bezos was researching software and the Internet for a New York City firm in 1994. He became intrigued by the business possibilities of selling books on the World Wide Web in much the same way that mail-order firms sell books by mail. This idea proved so compelling that Bezos quickly quit his job, raised money from family and friends, wrote a business plan, and moved out to Seattle to locate near a major book wholesaler. One year later, Amazon.com was open for business. In its first month, without advertising or public relations, the site attracted customers from every state in the Union and more than 40 other countries.

In those early days, the giant bookstore chains paid little attention to Amazon. Within two years, however, Amazon's discount prices, free e-mail book reviews, and easy search capabilities had attracted so many shoppers and so much media coverage that competitors started scrambling to open their own Internet bookstores. But Amazon's established reputation and loyal customer following were major hurdles for rivals to overcome. In fact, despite aggressive promotions and pricing, Barnesandnoble.com is still trying to catch up to Amazon's online sales and sizable customer base.

Meanwhile, Bezos has expanded into all kinds of products by buying stakes in e-commerce companies such as drugstore.com and pets.com. He's also set up an auction section on Amazon to tap the excitement generated by the success of eBay, the first Internet auction site. In addition, he made room on the Amazon site for zShops, an area where smaller businesses can, for a fee, sell products.

One reason for Amazon's success is founder Bezos's action-oriented management style. Although he carefully plans his company's future moves, he also wants to avoid the paralysis that can come from endless analysis and deliberation. As an e-commerce pioneer, Bezos is accustomed to making speedy decisions to take advantage of unexpected or fleeting opportunities. He encourages everyone at Amazon to do the same, even if that means an occasional misstep. Working on Internet time, Bezos would rather lead his troops into the unknown, and fix problems later, than slow down now.

To continue growing and innovating, Amazon must keep recruiting, training, and motivating good managers and employees. Bezos gets personally involved with hiring decisions about top managers, whom he trusts to hire the people who will work under them. Because he knows that a skilled workforce is critical to Amazon's success, Bezos asks probing questions about hiring techniques when he interviews top-management candidates.

Still, Bezos carves out precious time from his hectic management schedule to surf the Web, click around the Amazon site, and, on occasion, wander through shopping malls in search of new ideas. To stay in touch, he goes out of his way to thank specific employees for their efforts, and he reads e-mail messages from customers to find out what they like and don't like. About one-third of the CEO's time is devoted to visiting Amazon's national network of distribution centers, where he answers employee questions and reinforces the company's six "core values." These values include customer obsession, ownership, bias for action, frugality, high hiring bar, and innovation.

Every December, Bezos and his entire management team pitch in to meet the holiday rush. By wrapping packages for customer shipments or answering customer service phone calls, they all get a better sense of what Amazon's first-line managers and employees face—and what their customers want. This yearly tradition of hands-on experience also rekindles the managers' sense of purpose—no small consideration in an industry where change is the only constant.

Case Questions

1. Which managerial skills does Jeff Bezos appear to be emphasizing at Amazon?
2. How does Bezos carry out his interpersonal, informational, and decisional roles at Amazon?
3. Why are communication skills particularly vital for managers at a fast-growing firm like Amazon?

Case References

"Can Amazon Make It?" *Business Week,* July 11, 2000, pp. 38ff.; Miguel Helft, "Poster Boy Grows Up," *the standard.com,* April 24, 2000, http://www.the standard.com/article/display/0,1151,14264,00.html, June 2, 2000; George Anders, "Taming the Out-of-Control In-Box," *Wall Street Journal,* February 4, 2000, pp. B1, B4; Michael Krantz, "Cruising Inside Amazon," *Time,* December 27, 1999, pp. 68ff.; Joshua Cooper Ramo, "Jeffrey Preston Bezos: 1999 Person of the Year," *Time,* December 27, 1999, pp. 50ff.; and Joshua Quittner, "An Eye on the Future: Jeff Bezos Merely Wants Amazon.com to Be Earth's Biggest Seller of Every-thing," *Time,* December 27, 1999, pp. 56ff.

APPENDIX TO CHAPTER 1

MANAGEMENT YESTERDAY AND TODAY

A MANAGER'S DILEMMA

"You rarely see anything original anymore in this industry.

Usually, everybody copies everybody else's ideas." This harsh assessment of the toy industry by an industry analyst might surprise you. Yet, when Ivy Ross, senior vice president of worldwide girls' design at Mattel Toys, needed a new hit toy, *she* was determined to do something original.

Mattel's most popular products include Barbies for girls and Hot Wheels for boys. When Ivy and Adrienne Fontanella (president of the girls' division) wanted to develop a new hit in a new market, they didn't want just another doll. They knew from market research that sewing and jewelry kits were popular with girls, but that "Legolike construction sets" were more popular with boys. They also knew that the reason wasn't that girls didn't like to build things; it was that girls build differently from boys. The challenge was to innovate a building toy that would appeal to girls.

To inspire innovative thinking, Ross put together a team from various departments to collaborate on this new product. Outside experts and Mattel's own child psychology expert schooled the team in architecture and play patterns. The team also watched groups of girls play. Ivy dubbed the team's innovation process Project Platypus. She said, "Why a platypus? When I looked up the definition, it said an uncommon mix of different species." And, that's a good description of what it takes to be innovative.

One of the hardest adjustments for the team initially was the lack of structure. Ivy let the team organize itself and encouraged members to align themselves with whatever tasks they were passionate about—toy design, package design, marketing, and so forth. What did the platypi come up with? A toy for 5- to 10-year-old girls called the Elio Creation System that consisted of colorful, easy-to-use plastic pieces and reusable stickers designed for the open-ended, creative way girls play—an innovative toy developed in an innovative way. (You can see it at *www.mattel.com*.)

Put yourself in Ivy's position. What can she learn from Project Platypus to help her better manage innovation throughout her division?

What would you do?

Mattel's push to come up with something innovative for the marketplace isn't all that unusual today. Many organizations both large and small have made similar commitments to pursuing innovation with all its challenges and rewards. Why? Global competition and general competitive pressures reflect today's reality: Innovate or lose. Although Ivy Ross was innovative in how she inspired her employees in thinking about this new toy, she recognized that it's not always easy to implement new ideas. In fact, the history of management is filled with evolutions and revolutions in implementing new ideas.

Looking at management history can help us understand today's management theory and practice. It can help us see what worked and what didn't work. In this chapter, we'll introduce you to the origins of many contemporary management concepts and show how they have evolved to reflect the changing needs of organizations and society as a whole. We'll also introduce important trends and issues that managers currently face, in order to link the past with the future and demonstrate that the field of management is still evolving.

Historical Background of Management

Organized endeavors directed by people responsible for planning, organizing, leading, and controlling activities have existed for thousands of years. The Egyptian pyramids and the Great Wall of China, for instance, are tangible evidence that projects of tremendous scope, employing tens of thousands of people, were undertaken well before modern times. The pyramids are a particularly interesting example. The construction of a single pyramid occupied more than 100,000 workers for 20 years. Who told each worker what to do? Who ensured that there would be enough stones at the site to keep workers busy? The answer to such questions is *managers*. Regardless of what managers were called at the time, someone had to plan what was to be done, organize people and materials to do it, lead and direct the workers, and impose some controls to ensure that everything was done as planned.

Another example of early management can be seen during the 1400s in the city of Venice, Italy, a major economic and trade center. The Venetians developed an early form of business enterprise and engaged in many activities common to today's organizations. For instance, at the arsenal of Venice, warships were floated along the canals, and at each stop materials and riggings were added to the ship. Doesn't that sound a lot like a car "floating" along an automobile assembly line while components are added to it? In addition to this assembly line, the Venetians also used warehouse and inventory systems to keep track of materials, human resource management functions to manage the labor force, and an accounting system to keep track of revenues and costs.

These examples demonstrate that organizations and managers have been around for thousands of years. However, two pre-twentieth-century events are particularly significant to the study of management.

First, in 1776, Adam Smith published *The Wealth of Nations,* in which he argued for the economic advantages that organizations and society would gain

division of labor The breakdown of jobs into narrow and repetitive tasks

Industrial Revolution The advent of machine power, mass production, and efficient transportation

from the **division of labor,** the breakdown of jobs into narrow and repetitive tasks. Using the pin industry as an example, Smith claimed that 10 individuals, each doing a specialized task, could together produce about 48,000 pins a day. However, if each person worked alone performing each task separately, it would be quite an accomplishment to produce even 10 pins a day! Smith concluded that division of labor increased productivity by increasing each worker's skill and dexterity, by saving time lost in changing tasks, and by creating labor-saving inventions and machinery. The continued popularity of job specialization—for example, specific tasks performed by members of a hospital surgery team, specific meal preparation tasks done by workers in restaurant kitchens, or specific positions played by players on a football team—is undoubtedly due to the economic advantages cited by Adam Smith.

The second important pre-twentieth-century influence on management is the **Industrial Revolution.** Starting in the eighteenth century in Great Britain, the revolution had crossed the Atlantic to America by the end of the Civil War. What the Industrial Revolution did was substitute machine power for human power, which, in turn, made it more economical to manufacture goods in factories rather than at home. These large, efficient factories required managerial skills. Why? Managers were needed to forecast demand, ensure that enough material was on hand to make products, assign tasks to people, direct daily activities, and so forth. The need for a formal theory to guide managers in running these large organizations had arrived. However, it wasn't until the early 1900s that the first major step toward developing such a theory was taken.

In the next sections we present the six major approaches to management: scientific management, general administative theory, quantitative, organizational behavior, systems, and contingency. (See Figure 1.1a.) Keep in mind that each approach is concerned with the same "animal"; the differences reflect the backgrounds and interests of the writer. A relevant analogy is the classic story of the blind men and the elephant, in which each man declares the elephant to be like the part he is feeling: The first man touching the side declares that the elephant is like a wall; the second touches the trunk and says the elephant is like a snake; the

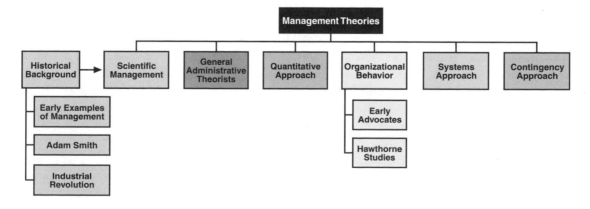

FIGURE 1.1a
Development of Major Management Theories

third feels one of the elephant's tusks and believes it to be like a spear; the fourth grabs a leg and says an elephant is like a tree; and the fifth touches the elephant's tail and concludes that the animal is like a rope. Each is encountering the same elephant, but what each observes depends on where he stands. Similarly, each of the six perspectives is correct and contributes to our overall understanding of management. However, each is also a limited view of a larger animal. We'll begin our journey into management's past by looking at the first major theory of management—scientific management.

Scientific Management

scientific management
The use of the scientific method to determine the "one best way" for a job to be done

If you had to pinpoint the year modern management theory was born, 1911 might be a logical choice. That was the year Frederick Winslow Taylor's *Principles of Scientific Management* was published. Its contents became widely accepted by managers around the world. The book described the theory of **scientific management:** the use of scientific methods to define the "one best way" for a job to be done.

Important Contributions

Important contributions to scientific management theory were made by Frederick W. Taylor and Frank and Lillian Gilbreth. Let's look at what they did.

Frederick W. Taylor. Taylor did most of his work at the Midvale and Bethlehem Steel Companies in Pennsylvania. As a mechanical engineer with a Quaker and Puritan background, he was continually appalled by workers' inefficiencies. Employees used vastly different techniques to do the same job. They were inclined to "take it easy" on the job, and Taylor believed that worker output was only about one-third of what was possible. Virtually no work standards existed. Workers were placed in jobs with little or no concern for matching their abilities and aptitudes with the tasks they were required to do. Taylor set out to correct the situation by applying the scientific method to shop-floor jobs and spent more than two decades passionately pursuing the "one best way" for each job to be done.

Taylor's experiences at Midvale led him to define clear guidelines for improving production efficiency. He argued that these four principles of management (see Figure 1.2a) would result in prosperity for both workers and managers. How did these scientific principles really work? Let's look at an example.

Probably the best known example of Taylor's scientific management was the pig iron experiment. Workers loaded "pigs" of iron (each weighing 92 lbs) onto rail cars. Their daily average output was 12.5 tons. However, Taylor believed that by scientifically analyzing the job to determine the "one best way" to load pig iron, output could be increased to 47 or 48 tons per day. After scientifically applying different combinations of procedures, techniques, and tools, Taylor succeeded in getting that level of productivity. How? He put the right person on the job with the correct tools and equipment, had the worker follow his instructions exactly, and motivated the worker with an economic incentive of a signifi-

1. Develop a science for each element of an individual's work, which will replace the old rule-of-thumb method.
2. Scientifically select and then train, teach, and develop the worker.
3. Heartily cooperate with the workers so as to ensure that all work is done in accordance with the principles of the science that has been developed.
4. Divide work and responsibility almost equally between management and workers. Management takes over all work for which it is better fitted than the workers.

FIGURE 1.2a
Taylor's Four Principles of Management

cantly higher daily wage. Using similar approaches to other jobs, Taylor was able to define the "one best way" to do each job. Overall, Taylor achieved consistent productivity improvements in the range of 200 percent or more. Through his groundbreaking studies of manual work using scientific principles, Taylor became known as the "father" of scientific management. His ideas spread in the United States, France, Germany, Russia, and Japan, and inspired others to study and develop methods of scientific management. His most prominent followers were Frank and Lillian Gilbreth.

Frank and Lillian Gilbreth. A construction contractor by trade, Frank Gilbreth gave up that career to study scientific management after hearing Taylor speak at a professional meeting. Frank and his wife Lillian, a psychologist, studied work to eliminate wasteful hand-and-body motions. The Gilbreths also experimented with the design and use of the proper tools and equipment for optimizing work performance.

Frank is probably best known for his experiments in bricklaying. By carefully analyzing the bricklayer's job, he reduced the number of motions in laying exterior brick from 18 to about 5, and on laying interior brick the motions were reduced from 18 to 2. Using Gilbreth's techniques, the bricklayer could be more productive and less fatigued at the end of the day.

The Gilbreths were among the first researchers to use motion pictures to study hand-and-body motions. They invented a device called a microchronometer, which recorded a worker's motions and the amount of time spent doing each motion. Wasted motions missed by the naked eye could be identified and eliminated. The Gilbreths also devised a classification scheme to label 17 basic hand motions (such as search, grasp, hold) which they called **therbligs** (Gilbreth spelled backward with the *th* transposed). This scheme allowed the Gilbreths a more precise way of analyzing a worker's exact hand movements.

therbligs A classification scheme for labeling 17 basic hand motions

How Do Today's Managers Use Scientific Management?

The guidelines that Taylor and others devised for improving production efficiency are still used in organizations today. When managers analyze the basic work tasks that must be performed, use time-and-motion study to eliminate wasted motions, hire the best qualified workers for a job, and design incentive systems based on output, they're using the principles of scientific management. But current management practice isn't restricted to scientific management. In fact, we can see ideas from the next major approach—general administrative theory—being used as well.

General Administrative Theorists

general administrative theorists Writers who developed general theories of what managers do and what constitutes good management practice

Another group of writers looked at the subject of management but focused on the entire organization. These were the **general administrative theorists** who developed more general theories of what managers do and what constituted good management practice. Let's look at some important contributions that grew out of this perspective.

Important Contributions

The two most prominent theorists behind the general administrative approach were Henri Fayol and Max Weber.

Henri Fayol. We mentioned Fayol in Chapter 1 because he described management as a universal set of functions that included planning, organizing, commanding, coordinating, and controlling. Because his ideas were important, let's look more closely at what he had to say.

Fayol wrote during the same time period as Taylor. While Taylor was concerned with first-line managers and the scientific method, Fayol's attention was directed at the activities of *all* managers. He wrote from personal experience as he was the managing director of a large French coal-mining firm.

Fayol described the practice of management as something distinct from accounting, finance, production, distribution, and other typical business functions. His belief that management was an activity common to all human endeavors in business, government, and even in the home led him to develop 14 **principles of management**—fundamental rules of management that could be taught in schools and applied in all organizational situations. These principles are shown in Figure 1.3a.

principles of management Fundamental rules of management that could be taught in schools and applied in all organizational situations

bureaucracy A form of organization characterized by division of labor, a clearly defined hierarchy, detailed rules and regulations, and impersonal relationships

Max Weber. Weber (pronounced VAY-ber) was a German sociologist who studied organizational activity. Writing in the early 1900s, he developed a theory of authority structures and relation Weber described an ideal type of organization which he called a **bureaucracy**—a form of organization characterized by division of labor, a clearly defined hierarchy, detailed rules and regulations, and impersonal relationships. Weber recognized that this "ideal bureaucracy didn't exist in reality. Instead he intended it as a basis for theorizing about how work could be done in large groups. His theory became the model structural design for many of today's large organizations. The features of Weber's ideal bureaucratic structure are outlined in Figure 1.4a.

1. *Division of work.* Specialization increases output by making employees more efficient.
2. *Authority.* Managers must be able to give orders and authority gives them this right.
3. *Discipline.* Employees must obey and respect the rules that govern the organization.
4. *Unity of command.* Every employee should receive orders from only one superior.
5. *Unity of direction.* The organization should have a single plan of action to guide managers and workers.
6. *Subordination of individual interests to the general interest.* The interests of any one employee or group of employees should not take precedence over the interests of the organization as a whole.
7. *Remuneration.* Workers must be paid a fair wage for their services.
8. *Centralization.* This term refers to the degree to which subordinates are involved in decision making.
9. *Scalar chain.* The line of authority from top management to the lowest ranks is the scalar chain.
10. *Order.* People and materials should be in the right place at the right time.
11. *Equity.* Managers should be kind and fair to their subordinates.
12. *Stability of tenure of personnel.* Management should provide orderly personnel planning and ensure that replacements are available to fill vacancies.
13. *Initiative.* Employees who are allowed to originate and carry out plans will exert high levels of effort.
14. *Esprit de corps.* Promoting team spirit will build harmony and unity within the organization.

FIGURE 1.3a
Fayol's 14 Principles of Management

FIGURE 1.4a
Weber's Ideal Bureaucracy

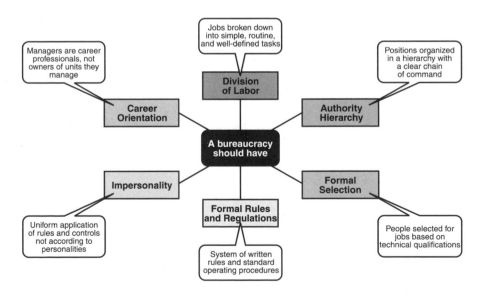

Bureaucracy, as described by Weber, is a lot like scientific management in its ideology. Both emphasize rationality, predictability, impersonality, technical competence, and authoritarianism. Although Weber's writings were less operational than Taylor's, the fact that his "ideal type" still describes many contemporary organizations attests to the importance of his work.

How Do Today's Managers Use General Administrative Theories?

Some of our current management ideas and practices can be directly traced to the contributions of the general administrative theorists. For instance, the functional view of the manager's job can be attributed to Fayol. In addition, his 14 principles serve as a frame of reference from which many current management concepts have evolved.

Weber's bureaucracy was an attempt to formulate an ideal prototype for organizations. Although many characteristics of Weber's bureaucracy are still evident in large organizations, his model isn't as popular today as it was in the twentieth century. Many contemporary managers feel that bureaucracy's emphasis on strict division of labor, adherence to formal rules and regulations, and impersonal application of rules and controls takes away the individual employee's creativity and the organization's ability to respond quickly to an increasingly dynamic environment. However, even in highly flexible organizations of talented professionals—such as Mattel, General Electric, or Cisco Systems—some bureaucratic mechanisms are necessary to ensure that resources are used efficiently and effectively.

Quantitative Approach to Management

quantitative approach
The use of quantitative techniques to improve decision making

The **quantitative approach** involves the use of quantitative techniques to improve decision making. This approach also has been called *operations research* or *management science*.

Important Contributions

The quantitative approach evolved out of the development of mathematical and statistical solutions to military problems during World War II. After the war was over, many of the techniques that had been used to solve military problems were applied to businesses. One group of military officers, nicknamed the Whiz Kids, joined Ford Motor Company in the mid-1940s and immediately began using statistical methods and quantitative models to improve decision making. Two of these individuals whose names you might recognize are Robert McNamara (who went on to become president of Ford, U.S. Secretary of Defense, and head of the World Bank) and Charles "Tex" Thornton (who founded Litton Industries).

What exactly does the quantitative approach do? It involves applications of statistics, optimization models, information models, and computer simulations to management activities. Linear programming, for instance, is a technique that managers use to improve resource allocation decisions. Work scheduling can be more efficient as a result of critical-path scheduling analysis. The economic order quantity model helps managers determine optimum inventory levels. Each of these is an example of quantitative techniques being applied to improve managerial decision making.

How Do Today's Managers Use the Quantitative Approach?

At Circuit City's some 626 locations, everything from the clothes the floor salespeople wear to how long zero percent financing should be offered has been studied by statisticians. They found, for instance, that flat commissions worked better than the product-based commission that had been used for 48-plus years. This and other findings from two studies in early 2000 and 2001 led to company changes that contributed an estimated $300 million in sales for 2002.

The quantitative approach contributes directly to management decision making in the areas of planning and control. For instance, when managers make budgeting, scheduling, quality control, and similar decisions, they typically rely on quantitative techniques. The availability of software programs has made the use of quantitative techniques somewhat less intimidating for managers, although they must still be able to interpret the results.

The quantitative approach hasn't influenced management practice as much as the next one we're going to discuss—organizational behavior—for a number of reasons. These include the fact that many managers are unfamiliar with and intimidated by the quantitative tools, behavioral problems are more widespread and visible, and it is easier for most students and managers to relate to real, day-to-day people problems than to the more abstract activity of constructing quantitative models.

Toward Understanding Organizational Behavior _____

organizational behavior (OB) The field of study concerned with the actions (behavior) of people at work

As we know, managers get things done by working with people. This explains why some writers have chosen to look at management by focusing on the organization's human resources. The field of study concerned with the actions (behavior) of people at work is called **organizational behavior (OB)**. Much of what currently makes up the field of human resource management, as well as contemporary views on motivation, leadership, trust, teamwork, and conflict management, has come out of organizational behavior research.

Early Advocates

Although a number of people in the late 1800s and early 1900s recognized the importance of the human factor to an organization's success, four stand out as early advocates of the OB approach: Robert Owen, Hugo Munsterberg, Mary Parker Follett, and Chester Barnard. The contributions of these individuals were varied and distinct, yet they all believed that people were the most important asset of the organization and should be managed accordingly. Their ideas provided the foundation for such management practices as employee selection procedures, employee motivation programs, employee work teams, and organization-environment management techniques. Figure 1.5a summarizes the most important ideas of these early advocates.

FIGURE 1.5a
Early Advocates of OB

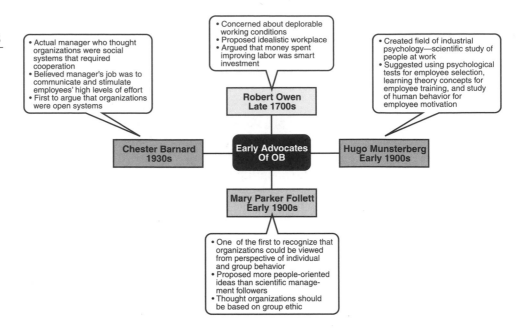

- Actual manager who thought organizations were social systems that required cooperation
- Believed manager's job was to communicate and stimulate employees' high levels of effort
- First to argue that organizations were open systems

- Concerned about deplorable working conditions
- Proposed idealistic workplace
- Argued that money spent improving labor was smart investment

- Created field of industrial psychology—scientific study of people at work
- Suggested using psychological tests for employee selection, learning theory concepts for employee training, and study of human behavior for employee motivation

Chester Barnard 1930s

Early Advocates Of OB

Robert Owen Late 1700s

Hugo Munsterberg Early 1900s

Mary Parker Follett Early 1900s

- One of the first to recognize that organizations could be viewed from perspective of individual and group behavior
- Proposed more people-oriented ideas than scientific management followers
- Thought organizations should be based on group ethic

The Hawthorne Studies

Hawthorne Studies A series of studies during the 1920s and 1930s that provided new insights into individual and group behavior

Without question, the most important contribution to the developing OB field came out of the **Hawthorne Studies,** a series of studies conducted at the Western Electric Company Works in Cicero, Illinois. These studies, which started in 1924, were initially designed by Western Electric industrial engineers as a scientific management experiment. They wanted to examine the effect of various illumination levels on worker productivity. Like any good scientific experiment, control and experimental groups were set up with the experimental group being exposed to various lighting intensities, and the control group working under a constant intensity. If you were the industrial engineers in charge of this experiment, what would you have expected to happen? It's logical to think that individual output in the experimental group would be directly related to the intensity of the light. However, they found that as the level of light was increased in the experimental group, output for both groups increased. Then, much to the surprise of the engineers, as the light level was decreased in the experimental group, productivity continued to increase in both groups. In fact, a productivity decrease was observed in the experimental group *only* when the level of light was reduced to that of a moonlit night. What would explain these unexpected results? The engineers weren't sure, but concluded that illumination intensity was not directly related to group productivity, and that something else must have contributed to the results. They weren't able to pinpoint what that "something else" was, though.

In 1927, the Western Electric engineers asked Harvard professor Elton Mayo and his associates to join the study as consultants. Thus began a relationship that would last through 1932 and encompass numerous experiments in the redesign of jobs, changes in workday and workweek length, introduction of rest periods, and individual versus group wage plans. For example, one experiment was designed to evaluate the effect of a group piecework incentive pay system on group productivity. The results indicated that the incentive plan had less effect on a worker's output than did group pressure, acceptance, and security. The researchers concluded that social norms or group standards were the key determinants of individual work behavior.

Scholars generally agree that the Hawthorne Studies had a dramatic impact on management beliefs about the role of human behavior in organizations. Mayo concluded that behavior and attitudes are closely related, that group influences significantly affect individual behavior, that group standards establish individual worker output, and that money is less a factor in determining output than are group standards, group attitudes, and security. These conclusions led to a new emphasis on the human behavior factor in the management of organizations and the attainment of goals.

However, these conclusions were criticized. Critics attacked the research procedures, analyses of findings, and conclusions. From a historical standpoint, it's of little importance whether the studies were academically sound or their conclusions justified. What *is* important is that they stimulated an interest in human behavior in organizations.

How Do Today's Managers Use the Behavioral Approach?

The behavioral approach has largely shaped today's organizations. From the way managers design motivating jobs to the way they work with employee teams to the way they use open communication, we can see elements of the behavioral approach. Much of what the early OB advocates proposed and the conclusions from the Hawthorne Studies provided the foundation for our current theories of motivation, leadership, group behavior and development, and numerous other behavioral topics which we'll address fully in later chapters.

The Systems Approach

system A set of interrelated and interdependent parts arranged in a manner that produces a unified wholes

closed systems Systems that are not influenced by or do not interact with their environment

open systems Systems that dynamically interact with their environment

During the 1960s, researchers began to analyze organizations from a systems perspective, a concept taken from the physical sciences. A **system** is a set of interrelated and interdependent parts arranged in a manner that produces a unified whole. The two basic types of systems are closed and open. **Closed systems** are not influenced by and do not interact with their environment. In contrast, **open systems** dynamically interact with their environment. Today, when we describe organizations as systems, we mean open systems. Figure 1.6a shows a diagram of an organization from an open systems perspective. As you can see, an organization takes in inputs (resources) from the environment and transforms or processes these resources into outputs that are distributed into the environment. The organization is "open" to its environment and interacts with that environment.

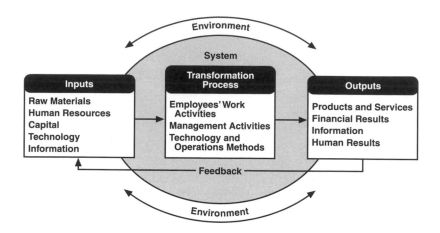

FIGURE 1.6a

The Organization as an Open System

The Systems Approach and Managers

How does the systems approach contribute to our understanding of management thinking? Systems researchers envisioned an organization as being made up of "interdependent factors, including individuals, groups, attitudes, motives, formal structure, interactions, goals, status, and authority. What this means is that managers coordinate the work activities of the various parts of the organization and ensure that all the interdependent parts of the organization are working together so that the organization's goals can be achieved. For example, the systems approach would recognize that, no matter how efficient the production department might be, if the marketing department doesn't anticipate changes in customer tastes and work with the product development department in creating products customers want, the organization's overall performance will suffer.

In addition, the systems approach implies that decisions and actions taken in one organizational area will affect others and vice versa. For example, if the purchasing department doesn't acquire the right quantity and quality of inputs, the production department will not be able to do its job effectively.

Finally, the systems approach recognizes that organizations are not self-contained. They rely on their environments for essential inputs and as sources to absorb their outputs. No organization can survive for long if it ignores government regulations, supplier relations, or the varied external constituencies upon which it depends.

How relevant is the systems approach to management? Quite relevant. Think, for example, of a day-shift manager at a local Wendy's restaurant who every day must coordinate the work of employees filling customer orders at the front counter and the drive-through windows, direct the delivery and unloading of food supplies, and address any customer concerns that come up. This manager "manages" all parts of the "system" so that the restaurant meets its daily sales goals.

The Contingency Approach

contingency approach
An approach that says that organizations are different, face different situations (contingencies), and require different ways of managing

Early management thinkers such as Taylor, Fayol, and Weber gave us principles of management that they generally assumed to be universally applicable. Later research found exceptions to many of their principles. For example, division of labor is valuable and widely used, but jobs can become *too* specialized. Bureaucracy is desirable in many situations, but in other circumstances, other structural designs are *more* effective. Management is not (and cannot be) based on simplistic principles to be applied in all situations. Different and changing situations require managers to use different approaches and techniques. The **contingency approach** (sometimes called the situational approach) says that organizations are different, face different situations (contingencies), and require different ways of managing.

The Contingency Approach and Managers

A contingency approach to management is intuitively logical because organizations and even units within the same organization are diverse—in size, goals, work, and the like. It would be surprising to find universally applicable management rules that would work in all situations. But, of course, it's one thing to say that the method of managing "depends on the situation" and another to say what the situation is. Management researchers have been working to identify these "what" variables. Figure 1.7a describes four popular contingency variables. The list is by no means comprehensive—more than 100 different "what" variables have been identified—but it represents those most widely used and gives you an idea of what we mean by the term contingency variable. As you can see, the contingency variables can have a significant impact on managers. The primary value of the contingency approach is that it stresses there are no simplistic or universal rules for managers to follow

---

Organization Size. As size increases, so do the problems of coordination. For instance, the type of organization structure appropriate for an organization of 50,000 employees is likely to be inefficient for an organization of 50 employees.

Routineness of Task Technology. To achieve its purpose, an organization uses technology. Routine technologies require organizational structures, leadership styles, and control systems that differ from those required by customized or nonroutine technologies.

Environmental Uncertainty. The degree of uncertainty caused by environmental changes influences the management process. What works best in a stable and predictable environment may be totally inappropriate in a rapidly changing and unpredictable environment.

Individual Differences. Individuals differ in terms of their desire for growth, autonomy, tolerance of ambiguity, and expectations. These and other individual differences are particularly important when managers select motivation techniques, leadership styles, and job designs.

FIGURE 1.7a
Popular Contingency Variables

Current Trends and Issues

Where are we today? What current management concepts and practices are shaping "tomorrow's history"? We'll now examine trends including globalization, ethics, workforce diversity, entrepreneurship, e-business, knowledge management and learning organizations, and quality management.

Globalization

Management is no longer constrained by national borders. BMW, a German firm, builds cars in South Carolina. McDonald's, a U.S. firm, sells hamburgers in China. Toyota, a Japanese firm, makes cars in Kentucky. Australia's leading real estate company, Lend Lease Corporation, built the Bluewater shopping complex in Kent, England, and has contracts with Coca-Cola to build all the soft-drink maker's bottling plants in Southeast Asia. Swiss company ABB Ltd. has constructed power generating plants in Malaysia, South Korea, China, and Indonesia. There are significant opportunities from globalization, and the world has definitely become a global village! Yet, globalization can be controversial. After the terrorist attacks on the United States on 9/11, some have questioned whether the "openness" of globalization has made countries more vulnerable to conflicts over political and cultural differences. Regardless of the controversy, managers in organizations of all sizes and types around the world have to confront the challenges of operating in a global market.

Ethics

$299,150,992. That's the value of the stock cashed in by now-resigned or fired top managers Ken Lay of Enron, Sam Waksal of ImClone, Gary Winnick of Global Crossing, and Dennis Kozlowski of Tyco International as they sold shares at close to the firms' peak stock price. The tragedy is that while these executives walked away with nearly $300 million, their companies lay in ruins and the jobs and retirement savings of thousands of their employees had vanished.

During the summer of 2002, it seemed as if every day brought to light another case of corporate lying, misrepresentations, and financial manipulations. What happened to managerial ethics? This important aspect of managerial behavior seems to have been forgotten or ignored as these managers put their self-interest ahead of others who might be affected by their decisions. Take, for example, the "Enron Three" (former chairman Ken Lay, former CEO Jeff Skilling, and former CFO Andy Fastow). All behaved as if the laws and accounting rules didn't apply to them. They used greed, manipulation, and collusion to deceive their board of directors, employees, stockholders, and others about Enron's worsening financial condition. Because of these managers' unethical actions, thousands of Enron employees lost their jobs and the company stock set aside in their retirement savings became worthless. Although Enron seemed to be the pivotal event in this corporate ethics crisis, executives at a number of other large companies were engaging in similar kinds of unethical acts.

What would you have done had you been a manager in these organizations? How would you have reacted? One thing we know is that ethical issues aren't simple or easy! Make one decision and someone will be affected; make another, and someone else is likely to be affected. In today's changing workplace, managers need an approach to deal with the complexities and uncertainties associated with the ethical dilemmas that arise. We propose a process as outlined in Figure 1.8a. What does this process entail? First, managers need to make sure they understand the ethical dilemma they're facing. They need to step back and think about what issue (or issues) is at stake here. Next, it's important to identify the stakeholders that would be affected by the decision. What individuals or groups are likely to be impacted by my decision? Third, managers should identify the factors that are important to the decision. These include personal, organizational, and possibly external factors. Next, managers should identify and evaluate possible courses of action, keeping in mind that each alternative will impact affected stakeholders differently. Then, it's time to make a decision and act. As today's managers manage, they can use this process to help them assess those ethical dilemmas they face and to develop appropriate courses of action.

While most managers continue to behave in a highly ethical manner, the ethical abuses that were so widely publicized indicated a need to "upgrade" ethical standards. This is being addressed at two levels. First, ethics education is being widely emphasized in college curriculums. Second, organizations themselves are taking a more active role in creating *and using* codes of ethics, providing ethics training programs, and hiring ethics officers.

Workforce Diversity

workforce diversity
A workforce that's more heterogeneous in terms of gender, race, ethnicity, age, and other characteristics that reflect differences

Another issue facing managers in the twenty-first century is coordinating work efforts of diverse organizational members in accomplishing organizational goals. Today's organizations are characterized by **workforce diversity**—a workforce that's more heterogeneous in terms of gender, race, ethnicity, age, and other characteristics that reflect differences. How diverse is the workforce? A report on work and workers in the twenty-first century, called *Workforce 2020*, stated that the U.S. labor force would continue its ethnic diversification, although at a fairly slow pace. Throughout the early years of the twenty-first century, minorities will account for slightly more than one-half of net new entrants to the U.S. workforce. The fastest growth will be Asian and Hispanic workers. In fact, Hispanics have now surpassed African Americans as the largest minority group in the United States. However, this report also stated that a more significant demographic force affecting work-force diversity during the next decade will be the aging of the population.

Step 1: What is the *ethical dilemma?*

Step 2: Who are the *affected stakeholders?*

Step 3: What *personal, organizational,* and *external factors* are important to my decision?

Step 4: What are *possible alternatives?*

Step 5: Make a *decision* and act on it.

FIGURE 1.8a
A Process for Addressing Ethical Dilemmas

This trend is likely to affect the U.S. workforce in three ways. First, aging individuals will choose to work full-time, work part-time, or retire completely. Because of the negative performance of the stock market and its effect on many retirement investment accounts, many older employees may be forced to continue working. Think of the implications for an organization when older workers can't afford to retire and block career opportunities for younger employees, or if longtime employees with their vast wealth of knowledge, experience, and skills do choose to retire. Second, aging individuals typically begin to receive public entitlements. Having sufficient tax rates to sustain these programs has serious implications for organizations and younger workers since there will be more individuals demanding entitlements and a smaller base of workers contributing dollars to the program budgets. Finally, the aging population will become a powerful consumer force driving demand for certain types of products and services. Organizations in industries of potentially high market demand (such as entertainment, travel, specialized health care, financial planning, etc.) will require larger workforces to meet that demand while organizations in industries where market demand faces potential declines (such as singles bars, ski resorts, etc.) may have to make adjustments in their workforces through layoffs and downsizing.

Workforce diversity isn't a managerial issue only in the United States. It's an issue facing managers of organizations in Japan, Australia, Germany, Italy, and other developed countries. For instance, as the level of immigration increases in Italy, the number of women entering the workforce rises in Japan, and the population ages in Germany, managers are finding they need to effectively manage diversity.

Does the fact that workforce diversity is an issue today mean that organizations weren't diverse before? No. They were, but diverse individuals made up a small percentage of the workforce, and organizations, for the most part, ignored the issue. Before the early 1980s, people took a "melting pot" approach to differences in organizations. We assumed that people who were "different" would want to assimilate. But we now recognize that employees don't set aside their cultural values and lifestyle preferences when they come to work. The challenge for managers, therefore, is to make their organizations more accommodating to diverse groups of people by addressing different lifestyles, family needs, and work styles. The melting pot assumption has been replaced by the recognition and celebration of differences. Smart managers recognize that diversity can be an asset because it brings a broad range of viewpoints and problem-solving skills to a company, and additionally helps organizations better understand a diverse customer base. Many companies such as Levi Strauss, Advantica, McDonald's, Dole Food, Avis Rent A Car, SBC Communications, Avon Products, and Xerox have strong diversity management programs.

Entrepreneurship

entrepreneurship The process whereby an individual or group of individuals uses organized efforts to pursue opportunities to create value and grow by fulfilling wants and needs through innovations and uniqueness, no matter what resources the entrepreneur currently has

Entrepreneurship is a growing activity. But what exactly is **entrepreneurship?** It's the process whereby an individual or group of individuals uses organized efforts to pursue opportunities to create value and grow by fulfilling wants and needs through innovation and uniqueness, no matter what resources the entrepreneur currently has. It involves the discovery of opportunities and the resources to exploit them. Three important themes can be seen in this definition of entrepreneurship. First is the pursuit of opportunities. Entrepreneurship is about pursuing environmental trends and changes that no one else has seen or paid attention to. For example, Jeff Bezos, founder of Amazon.com, was a successful programmer at an investment firm on Wall Street in the mid-1990s. However, statistics on the explosive growth in the use of the Internet and World Wide Web (at that time, it was growing about 2,300% a month) kept nagging at him. He decided to quit his job and pursue what he felt were going to be enormous retailing opportunities on the Internet. Today, Amazon sells books, music, cars, furniture, jewelry, and numerous other items from its Web site.

The second important theme in entrepreneurship is innovation. Entrepreneurship involves changing, revolutionizing, transforming, or introducing new products or services or new ways of doing business. Dineh Mohajer is a prime example. As a fashion-conscious young woman, she hated the brilliant and bright nail polishes sold in stores. The bright colors clashed with her trendy pastel-colored clothing. She wanted pastel nail colors that would match what she was wearing. When she couldn't find them, Mohajer decided to mix her own. When her friends raved over her homemade colors, she decided to take samples of her nail polish to exclusive stores in Los Angeles. They were an instant hit! Today, her company, Hard Candy, sells a complete line of cosmetics in trendy stores across the United States—all the result of Mohajer's innovative ideas.

The final important theme in entrepreneurship is growth. Entrepreneurs pursue growth. They are not content for their organizations to stay small or to stay the same size. Entrepreneurs want their businesses to grow and work very hard to pursue growth as they continually look for trends and continue to innovate new products and new approaches.

Managing in an E-Business World

Do you use e-mail to communicate? Can you find an advertisement that doesn't have a Web address in it somewhere? Today's managers function in an e-business world. In fact, as a student, your learning may increasingly be taking place in an electronic environment. While critics have questioned the viability of Internet-based companies (dot-coms), especially after the high-tech implosion in 2000 and 2001, e-business is here for the long term. E-business offers many advantages to organizations—small to large, profit or not-for-profit, global and domestic, and in all industries.

e-business (electronic business) A comprehensive term describing the way an organization does its work by using electronic (Internet-based) linkages with its key constituencies in order to efficiently and effectively achieve its goals

e-commerce (electronic commerce) The sales and marketing component of e-business

E-business (electronic business) is a comprehensive term describing the way an organization does its work by using electronic (Internet-based) linkages with its key constituencies (employees, managers, customers, clients, suppliers, and partners) in order to efficiently and effectively achieve its goals. It includes **e-commerce**, which is essentially the sales and marketing component of e-business. Firms such as Dell (computers) and Varsitybooks (textbooks) are engaged in e-commerce because they sell items over the Internet.

Not every organization is, or needs to be, a total e-business. Figure 1.9a illustrates three categories of e-business involvement. The first type is an e-business *enhanced* organization, a traditional organization that sets up e-business capabilities, usually e-commerce, while maintaining its traditional structure. Many *Fortune* 500-type organizations have evolved into e-businesses using this approach. They

FIGURE 1.9a

Categories of E-Business Involvement

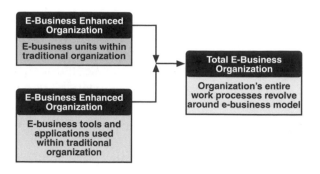

use the Internet to *enhance* (not to replace) their traditional ways of doing business. For instance, the Internet division of Sears, a traditional bricks-and-mortar retailer with thousands of physical stores worldwide, is intended to expand, not replace, the company's main source of revenue.

Another category of e-business involvement is an e-business *enabled* organization, which uses the Internet to perform its traditional business functions better, but not to sell anything. In other words, the Internet *enables* organizational members to do their work more efficiently and effectively. Numerous organizations use electronic linkages to communicate with employees, customers, or suppliers, and to support them with information. For instance, Levi Strauss uses its Web site to interact with customers, providing them the latest information about the company and its products, but not to sell the jeans. It also uses an **intranet,** an internal organizational communication system that uses Internet technology and is accessible only to organizational employees, to communicate with its global workforce.

The last category of e-business involvement is when an organization becomes a total e-business. Organizations such as Amazon.com, Yahoo!, E*TRADE, and eBay are total e-business organizations. Their whole existence revolves around the Internet. Other organizations, like Charles Schwab & Company, have evolved into e-business organizations that seamlessly integrate traditional and e-business functions. When an organization becomes a total e-business, there's a complete transformation in the way it does its work. For instance, when managers at Schwab decided to merge its traditional and e-business operations, it had to reprice its core products, retrain all of its employees, and renovate all of its systems.

Knowledge Management and Learning Organizations

Today's managers confront an environment in which change takes place at an unprecedented rate. As a result, many past management approaches and principles—created for a world that was more stable and predictable—no longer apply.

Organizations of the twenty-first century must be able to learn and respond quickly. These organizations will be led by managers who can effectively challenge conventional wisdom, manage the organization's knowledge base, and make needed changes. These organizations will need to be **learning organizations**— that is, ones that have developed the capacity to continuously learn, adapt, and change. Figure 1.10a clarifies how a learning organization is different from a traditional organization.

intranet An internal organizational communication system that uses Internet technology and is accessible only by organizational employees

learning organization An organization that has developed the capacity to continuously learn, adapt, and change

	Traditional Organization	Learning Organization
Attitude toward change	If it's working, don't change it.	If you aren't changing, it won't be working for long.
Attitude toward new ideas	If it wasn't invented here, reject it.	If it was invented or reinvented here, reject it.
Who's responsible for innovation?	Traditional areas such as R&D	Everyone in organization
Main fear	Making mistakes	Not learning; not adapting
Competitive advantage	Products and service	Ability to learn, knowledge and expertise
Manager's job	Control others	Enable others

FIGURE 1.10a

Learning Organization versus Traditional Organization

knowledge management Cultivating a learning culture where organizational members systematically gather knowledge and share it with others in the organization so as to achieve better performance

Part of a manager's responsibility is to create learning capabilities throughout the organization—from lowest level to highest level and in all areas. How? An important step is understanding the value of knowledge as an important resource, just like cash, raw materials, or office equipment. To illustrate the value of knowledge, think about how you register for college classes. Do you talk to others who have had a certain professor? Do you listen to their experiences with this individual and make your decision based on what they have to say (their knowledge about the situation)? If you do, you're tapping into the value of knowledge. But in an organization, just recognizing the value of accumulated knowledge or wisdom isn't enough. Managers must deliberately manage that base of knowledge. **Knowledge management** involves cultivating a learning culture where organizational

Thinking Critically About Ethics

Information is power—those who have information have power. Because information gives them power, it's human nature to want to keep that information, not share it. Knowledge hoarding is a business habit that's hard to break. In fact, it's an attitude that still characterizes many businesses. In a learning organization, however, we're asking people to share information.

Getting people to share information may turn out to be one of the key challenges facing managers. Is it ethical to ask people to share information that they've worked hard to obtain? What if performance evaluations are based on how well individuals do their jobs, and how well they do their jobs is dependent on the special knowledge that they have? Is it ethical to ask them to share that information? What ethical implications are inherent in creating an organizational environment that promotes learning and knowledge sharing?

members systematically gather knowledge and share it with others in the organization so as to achieve better performance. For instance, accountants and consultants at Ernst & Young, a professional-services firm, document best practices they have developed, unusual problems they have dealt with, and other work information. This "knowledge" is then shared with all employees through computer-based applications and through COIN (community of interest) teams that meet regularly throughout the company. Many other organizations—General Electric, Toyota, Hewlett Packard, Buckman Laboratories—have recognized the importance of knowledge management to being a learning organization.

Quality Management

A quality revolution swept through both the business and public sectors during the 1980s and 1990s. The generic term used to describe this revolution was total quality management, or TQM. It was inspired by a small group of quality experts, the most famous of whom were W. Edwards Deming and Joseph M. Juran. The ideas and techniques espoused by these two men in the 1950s had few supporters in the United States but were enthusiastically embraced by Japanese organizations. As Japanese manufacturers began beating out U.S. competitors in quality comparisons, Western managers soon took a more serious look at TQM. Deming's and Juran's ideas became the basis for today's quality management programs.

quality management
A philosophy of management that is driven by continual improvement and responding to customer needs and expectations

Quality management is a philosophy of management driven by continual improvement and responding to customer needs and expectations. (See Figure 1.11a) The term *customer* has expanded beyond the original definition of the purchaser outside the organization to include anyone who interacts with the organization's product or services internally or externally. It encompasses employees and suppliers as well as the people who purchase the organization's goods or services. The objective is to create an organization committed to continuous improvement in work processes.

---

1. Intense focus on the *customer*. The customer includes not only outsiders who buy the organization's products or services but also internal customers who interact with and serve others in the organization.

2. Concern for *continual improvement*. Quality management is a commitment to never being satisfied. "Very good" is not good enough. Quality can always be improved.

3. *Process-focused*. Quality management focuses on work processes as the quality of goods and services is continually improved.

4. Improvement in the *quality of everything* the organization does. Quality management uses a very broad definition of quality. It relates not only to the final product but also to how the organization handles deliveries, how rapidly it responds to complaints, how politely the phones are answered, and the like.

5. *Accurate measurement*. Quality management uses statistical techniques to measure every critical variable in the organization's operations. These are compared against standards or benchmarks to identify problems, trace them to their roots, and eliminate their causes.

6. *Empowerment of employees*. Quality management involves the people on the line in the improvement process. Teams are widely used in quality management programs as empowerment vehicles for finding and solving problems.

FIGURE 1.11a
What Is Quality Management?

Quality management is a departure from earlier management theories that were based on the belief that low costs were the only road to increased productivity. The U.S. car industry is often used as a classic example of what can go wrong when managers focus solely on trying to keep costs clown. In the late 1970s, GM, Ford, and Chrysler built products that many consumers rejected. Your second author remembers vividly purchasing a new Pontiac Grand Prix in 1978, driving it off the lot, pulling up to a gas pump, filling the gas tank, and watching gas pour out on the ground because of a hole in the car's gas tank! When you consider the costs of rejects, repairing shoddy work, product recalls, and expensive controls to identify quality problems, U.S. manufacturers actually were *less* productive than many foreign competitors. The Japanese demonstrated that it *was* possible for the highest-quality manufacturers to be among the lowest cost producers. American manufacturers in the car and other industries soon realized the importance of quality management and implemented many of its basic components. Quality management is important, and we'll discuss it throughout this book.

⊚ Learning Summary

After reading and studying this chapter, you should be able to:

- Explain why studying management history is important.
- Describe some early evidences of management practice.
- Describe the important contributions made by Frederick W. Taylor and Frank and Lillian Gilbreth.
- Explain how today's managers use scientific management.
- Discuss Fayol's 14 management principles.
- Describe Max Weber's contributions to the general administrative theory of management.
- Explain how today's managers use general administrative theories of management.
- Explain what the quantitative approach has contributed to the field of management.
- Discuss how today's managers use the quantitative approach.
- Describe the contributions of the early advocates of OB.
- Explain the contributions of the Hawthorne Studies to the field of management.
- Discuss how today's managers use the behavioral approach.
- Describe an organization using the systems approach.
- Discuss how the systems approach is appropriate for understanding management.
- Explain how the contingency approach differs from the early theories of management.
- Discuss how the contingency approach is appropriate for studying management.
- Explain why we need to look at the current trends and issues facing managers.
- Describe the current trends and issues facing managers.

Thinking About Management Issues

1. What kind of workplace would Henri Fayol create? How about Mary Parker Follett? How about Frederick W. Taylor?
2. Can a mathematical (quantitative) technique help a manager solve a "people" problem such as how to motivate employees or how to distribute work equitably? Explain.
3. Is globalization an issue for e-businesses? Explain.
4. "Entrepreneurship is only for small, start-up businesses." Do you agree or disagree with this statement? Explain.
5. How do societal trends influence the practice of management? What are the implications for someone studying management?
6. Would you feel more comfortable in a learning organization or in a traditional organization? Why?

Working Together: Team-Based Exercise

Building a base of knowledge that others in an organization can tap into and use to help do their jobs better is a bottom-line goal of knowledge management. Form groups of three or four class members. Your task is to do some preliminary work on creating a knowledge base for your college. Think about what organizational members could learn from each other in this organization. What common tasks might they perform that would help them learn from each other about how best to do those tasks? What unique tasks do they perform that others might learn something from? After discussing these issues, come up with an outline of major areas of important knowledge for this organization. (Here are a couple of hints that might help you get started—using technology in classrooms, keeping in touch with former students and alumni.) As a group, be prepared to share your outline with the class and to explain your choices.

THE EXTERNAL ENVIRONMENT

TELECOMS FACE EXTERNAL PRESSURES

While there was plenty of blame to go around after the dot-com meltdown in the early 2000s, from poor strategy to corporate greed, another factor played a role in the failure of many firms: government regulations. A lawyer for Global Crossing, which filed for bankruptcy after falling from its exalted position as one of the top-earning telecom firms, likened the fees demanded by all levels of government to robbery, saying, "They're being held up."

Local, state, and government agencies demanded excessive fees or free services from firms before granting them rights-of-way for cables. Moreover, breaking through the red tape some-times took years before access was approved as the firms' requests worked their way through bureaucracies and legal hurdles. The results for consumers were delays in service, limited providers, and higher prices when the excessive fees were passed on to them.

For example, although Global Crossing had been told that it needed only a routine permit to finish its trans-Pacific fiber-optic cable over the final 60 miles to Seattle, the federal National Oceanic and Atmos-pheric Administration (NOAA) then required $5 million from the firm as a fee for laying the cable within a federal marine sanctuary. The permit fees included $3.9 million to monitor the effects of the cable on the sanctuary's starfish, coral, sponges, and other sea life over 10 years and $500,000 to finance a visitors-center exhibit about the ocean floor. A separate $7.2 million easement fee was charged by NOAA for the fair market value of the ocean property easement.

Other telecom participants, such as phone providers, complain that the cable systems receive exclusive franchises while they must compete with each other (as well as with the cable systems). Government agencies are allowed by law to seek only "fair and reasonable compensation" for rights-of-way, which the agencies feel means the equivalent of market rents, while the firms feel they should not have to pay for more than the impact of their work. "If we cut up the street, we believe we should have to restore it, but when we see fees based on my gross operating revenues, I have a problem tying that to the city's costs," says Williams Communications's Rick Wolfe.

Examples of the barriers faced by telecom firms:

- *High fees.* For the right to run wires in White Plains, New York, to provide fast data services to businesses, AT&T was asked to pay 5 percent not only of the local phone-service revenue but also of long-distance, wireless, and cable-service income from the town. Eugene, Oregon, charges 9 percent of basic phone revenue.
- *Demands for free service.* When Williams wanted to lay 10 miles of cable along Maryland highways, that state's department of transportation required Williams to provide free fiber-optic cable that monitors the temperature of state roads and links computers so that citizens can apply for state licenses online, in addition to $780,000 a year in right-of-way fees.
- *Red tape.* When Qwest installed less than a mile of wire for broadband service for its one business customer, Berkeley, California, the city charged it for excessive information, such as business plans, application fees, and underground maps, which Qwest called "intrusive and a tremendous amount of work." (A court struck down many of the paperwork rules.)
- *Delays.* After 10 months of repeatedly contacting Shreveport, Louisiana, as it tried to finalize a franchise, Adelphia dropped its plans. Culver City, California, forced Adelphia, Level 3 Communications, and Metromedia Fiber Network to wait nearly two years while it debated a right-of-way ordinance.

Federal Communications Commission Chairman Michael Powell noted his agency's "growing concern about rights-of-way as a barrier." Texas, Florida, Michigan, and Kansas recently limited the fees cities can charge, and a bill has been introduced in Congress to curb the right-of-way fees levied by federal agencies such as NOAA.

SOURCE: Adapted from Paul Davidson "Cities, Feds Force Firms to Pay for Rights-of-Way," *USA Today*, July 2, 2002.

Besides problems of their own making, telecom firms were beset by government fees and restrictions—factors of the external environment—that affected their ability to compete effectively. This chapter discusses how pressures from outside organizations create the external context in which organizations operate.

As you learned in the first chapter, organizations are open systems that are affected by, and in turn affect, their external environments. By **external environment,** we mean all relevant forces outside the organization's boundaries. By *relevant*, we mean factors to which managers must pay attention to help their organizations compete effectively and survive.

external environment
All relevant forces outside a firm's boundaries, such as competitors, customers, the government, and the economy

Many of these factors are uncontrollable. Companies large and small are buffeted or battered by recession, government interference, competitors' actions, and so forth. But their lack of control does not mean that managers can ignore such forces, use them as excuses for poor performance, and try to just get by. Managers must stay abreast of external developments and react accordingly. Moreover, as we will discuss later in this chapter, it sometimes is possible to influence components of the external environment. We will examine ways in which organizations can do just that.

competitive environment The immediate environment surrounding a firm; includes suppliers, customers, competitors, and the like

Figure 2.1 shows the external environment of a firm. The firm exists in its **competitive environment**, which is composed of the firm and competitors,

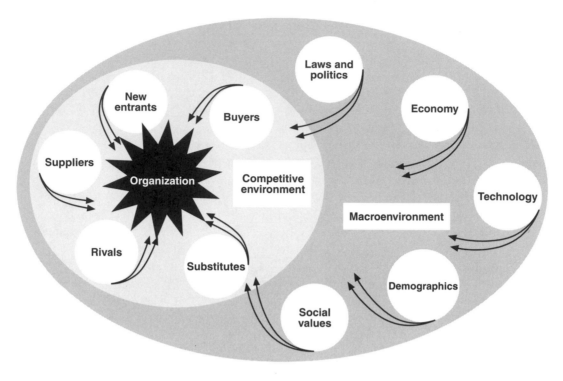

FIGURE 2.1
The External Environment

suppliers, customers, new entrants, and substitutes. At the more general level is the **macroenvironment,** which includes legal, political, economic, technological, demographic, and social and natural factors that generally affect all organizations.

Laws and Regulations

U.S. government policies both impose strategic constraints and provide opportunities. The government can affect business opportunities through tax laws, economic policies and international trade rulings. An example of restraint on business action is the U.S. government's standards regarding bribery. In some countries, bribes and kickbacks art common and expected ways of doing business, but for U.S. firms these are illegal practices. Indeed, some U.S. businesses have been fined for using bribery when competing internationally.

Regulators are specific government organizations in a firm's more immediate task environment. Regulatory agencies such as the Occupational Safety and Health Administration (OSHA), the Interstate Commerce Commission (ICC), the Federal Aviation Administration (FAA), the Equal Employment Opportunity Commission (EEOC), the National Labor Relations Board (NLRB), the Office of Federal Contract Compliance Programs (OFCCP), and the Environmental Protection Agency (EPA) have the power to investigate company practices and take legal action to ensure compliance with the laws.

For example, the Securities and Exchange Commission (SEC) regulates U.S. financial markets; since the insider-trading scandals, the SEC has changed investment houses' policies and practices dramatically. And the Food and Drug Administration (FDA) can prevent a company from selling an unsafe or ineffective product to the public.

Publicly traded pharmaceutical firms, for example, face regulation both from the FDA and from the SEC. When the FDA declined to review IMClone's application for the approval of Erbitux, a new cancer-fighting drug, the firm's stock price plummeted and the SEC opened an investigation into whether the firm misled investors and was involved in insider trading. Bristol-Myers Squibb, which had invested $2 billion for a 20 percent stake in IMClone Systems, lost $875 million and faced a separate SEC investigation into its accounting practices.

The Economy

Although most Americans are used to thinking in terms of the U.S. economy, the economic environment is created by complex interconnections among the economies of different countries. Wall Street investment analysts begin their workday thinking not just about what the Dow Jones did yesterday but also about how the London and Tokyo exchanges did overnight. Growth and recessions occur worldwide as well as domestically.

The economic environment dramatically affects companies' ability to function effectively and influences their strategic choices. Interest and inflation rates affect the availability and cost of capital, the ability to expand, prices, costs, and consumer demand for products. Unemployment rates affect labor availability and the wages the firm must pay, as well as product demand.

An important economic influence has centered on the stock market. Individuals and institutions looking for good returns had invested in promising companies, including start-ups and dot-coms. When technology-based firms during the 1990s provided better than 20 percent returns to investors, more individuals entered the capital markets (Figure 2.2). With the slide in technology stocks and the mistrust of corporate accounting, the returns fell to negative numbers in the early 2000s, although other economic indicators remained strong.

Economic conditions change over time and are difficult to predict. Bull and bear markets come and go. Periods of dramatic growth may be followed by a recession. Every trend undoubtedly will end—but when? Even when times seem good, budget deficits or other considerations create concern about the future.

FIGURE 2.2
Twelve-Month Comparison of Stock Markets

SOURCE: www.nasdaq.com.

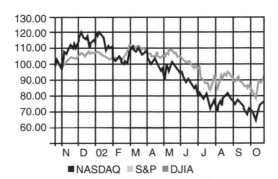

Technology

Today a company cannot succeed without incorporating into its strategy the astonishing technologies that exist and continue to evolve. Technological advances create new products, advanced production techniques, and better ways of managing and communicating. In addition, as technology evolves, new industries, markets, and competitive niches develop. For example, the advent of computers created a huge industry. Early entrants in biotechnology are trying to establish dominant positions, while later entrants work on technological advances that will give them a competitive niche.

New technologies also provide new production techniques. In manufacturing, sophisticated robots perform jobs without suffering fatigue, requiring vacations or weekends off, or demanding wage increases. Until the U.S. steel industry began modernizing its plants, its productivity lagged far behind that of the technologically superior Japanese plants.

New technologies also provide new ways to manage and communicate. Computerized management information systems (MIS) make information available when needed. Computers monitor productivity and note performance deficiencies. Telecommunications allow conferences to take place without requiring people to travel to the same location. Consider the following discussion of changes in the field of retail sporting goods. As you can see, technological advances create innovations in business. Strategies developed around the cutting edge of technological advances create a competitive advantage; strategies that ignore or lag behind competitors in considering technology lead to obsolescence and extinction.

Demographics

demographics
Measures of various characteristics of the people who comprise groups or other social units

Demographics are measures of various characteristics of the people comprising groups or other social units. Work groups, organizations, countries, markets, and societies can be described statistically by referring to their members' age, gender, family size, income, education, occupation, and so forth.

Companies must consider workforce demographics in formulating their human resources strategies. Population growth influences the size and composition of the labor force. By 2010, the U.S. civilian labor force, growing at a rate of 1.1 percent annually, is expected to reach approximately 158 million. Fluctuations in the birthrate influence population trends somewhat. In past years, the number of younger workers (16 to 24 years of age) has declined, but now that children of the baby-boom generation are entering the workforce, this age group is expected to grow 16.8 percent by 2010. At the same time, baby boomers themselves are reaching retirement age, and so the number of older workers (55 and above) will rise to about 15 percent of the labor force. Eventually, declining participation in work of older persons will largely offset the increase in the number of persons in this population group.

Immigration is also a factor that significantly influences the U.S. population and labor force. Over the last decade immigrants have accounted for approximately 40 percent of the U.S. population growth, a trend that has an important impact on the labor force. Immigrants are frequently of working age but have different educational and occupational backgrounds from the rest of the labor force. By 2010, the labor force will be even more diverse than it is today. White males will constitute approximately 39 percent of the labor force, African-Americans 13 percent, Hispanics 13 percent, and Asians and others 6 percent.

Women continue to join the U.S. labor force in record numbers. In 1970, women made up only about one-third of the labor force. By 2010 women are expected to account for over 51.9 percent, a trend that provides companies with more talent from which to choose.

A more diverse workforce has its advantages, but managers have to make certain they provide equality for women and minorities with respect to employment, advancement opportunities, and compensation. Strategic plans must be made for recruiting, retaining, training, motivating, and effectively utilizing people of diverse demographic backgrounds with the skills needed to achieve the company's mission.

Social Issues and the Natural Environment

Societal trends regarding how people think and behave have major implications for management of the labor force, corporate social actions, and strategic decisions about products and markets.

During the 1980s and 1990s women in the workforce often chose to delay having children as they focused on their careers, but today more working women are having children and then returning to the workforce. As a result, companies have introduced more supportive policies, including family leave, flexible working hours, and child care assistance. Many firms also extend these benefits to all employees or allow them to design their own benefits packages, where they can choose from a menu of available benefits that suit their individual situations. Domestic partners, whether they are in a marital relationship or not, also are covered by many employee benefit programs. Firms provide these benefits as a way of increasing a source of competitive advantage: an experienced workforce.

A prominent issue today pertains to natural resources: drilling for oil in formerly protected areas in the United States. Firms in the oil industry face considerable public opinion both in favor of preserving the natural environment, and against the country's dependence on other countries for fuel. Automakers face similar concerns about air quality as they strive to create more fuel-efficient cars.

The Competitive Environment

All organizations are affected by the general components of the macroenvironment we have just discussed. Each organization also functions in a closer, more immediate competitive environment. The competitive environment includes the specific organizations with which the organization interacts. As shown in Figure 2.3, the competitive environment includes rivalry among current competitors, threat of new entrants, threat of substitutes, power of suppliers, and power of customers. This model was originally developed by Michael Porter, a Harvard professor and a noted authority on strategic management. According to Porter, successful managers do more than simply react to the environment; they act in ways that actually

FIGURE 2.3
The Competitive Environment

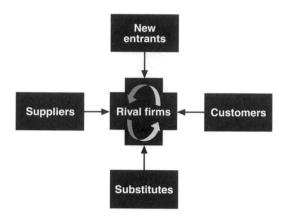

shape or change the organization's environment. In strategic decision making, Porter's model is an excellent method for analyzing the competitive environment in order to adapt to or influence the nature of competition.

Competitors

Among the various components of the competitive environment, competitors within the industry must first deal with one another. When organizations compete for the same customers and try to win market share at the others' expense, all must react to and anticipate their competitors' actions.

The first question to consider is: Who is the competition? Sometimes answers are obvious. Coca-Cola and PepsiCo are competitors, as are the Big Three automakers: General Motors, Ford, and DaimlerChrysler. But sometimes organizations focus too exclusively on traditional rivalries and miss the emerging ones. Historically, Sears & Roebuck focused on its competition with J.C. Penney. However, Sears' real competitors are Kmart and Wal-Mart at the low end; Target in the middle; Nordstrom at the high end; and a variety of catalogers, such as L.L. Bean, and Eddie Bauer. Similarly, United Airlines, Delta, American, and U.S. Airways have focused their attention on a battle over long haul and international routes. In the process, they all but ignored smaller carriers such as Southwest, Alaska Air, and Jet Blue that have grown and succeeded in regional markets.

Thus, as a first step in understanding their competitive environment, organizations must identify their competitors. Competitors may include (1) small domestic firms, especially their entry into tiny, premium markets; (2) overseas firms, especially their efforts to solidify positions in small niches (a traditional Japanese tactic); (3) big, new domestic companies exploring new markets; (4) strong regional competitors; and (5) unusual entries such as Internet shopping.

Once competitors have been identified, the next step is to analyze how they compete. Competitors use tactics such as price reductions, new-product introductions, and advertising campaigns to gain advantage over their rivals. It's essential to understand what competitors are doing when you are honing your own strategy. Competition is most intense when there are many direct competitors (including foreign contenders), when industry growth is slow, and when the product or service cannot be differentiated in some way.

New, high-growth industries offer enormous opportunities for profits. When an industry matures and growth slows, profits drop. Then, intense competition causes an industry shakeout: Weaker companies are eliminated, and the strong companies survive.

Threat of New Entrants

barriers to entry
Conditions that prevent new companies from entering an industry

New entrants into an industry compete with established companies. If many factors prevent new companies from entering the industry, the threat to established firms is less serious. If there are few such **barriers to entry,** the threat of new entrants is more serious. Some major barriers to entry are government policy, capital requirements, brand identification, cost disadvantages, and distribution channels. The government can limit or prevent entry, as occurs when the FDA forbids a new drug entrant. Some industries, such as trucking and liquor retailing, are regulated; more subtle government controls operate in fields such as mining and ski area development. Patents are also entry barriers. When a patent expires, other companies can then enter the market. For example, when the pharmaceutical firm Eli Lilly and Co.'s patent on its antidepressant drug Prozac expired, it lost its U.S. monopoly on the drug and its sales plunged. Barr Laboratories Inc. won the right to be the exclusive seller of a generic version of Prozac for six months. After that period other copycats flooded the market, eroding Barr's sales of the drug.

Other barriers are less formal but can have the same effect. Capital requirements may be so high that companies won't risk or try to raise such large amounts of money. Brand identification forces new entrants to spend heavily to overcome customer loyalty. The cost advantages established companies hold—due to large size, favorable locations, existing assets, and so forth—also can be formidable entry barriers.

Finally, existing competitors may have such tight distribution channels that new entrants have difficulty getting their products or services to customers. For example, established food products already have supermarket shelf space. New entrants must displace existing products with promotions, price breaks, intensive selling, and other tactics.

Threat of Substitutes

Technological advances and economic efficiencies are among the ways that firms can develop substitutes for existing products. For example, although Southwest Airlines has developed strong rivalries with other airlines, it also competes—as a substitute—with bus companies such as Greyhound and rental car companies such as Avis. Southwest has gotten its cost base down to such a low point that it is now cheaper to fly from Los Angeles to Phoenix than it is to take a bus or rent a car. This particular example shows that substitute products or services can limit another industry's revenue potential. Companies in those industries are likely to suffer growth and earnings problems unless they improve quality or launch aggressive marketing campaigns.

In addition to current substitutes, companies need to think about potential substitutes that may be viable in the near future. For example, as alternatives to fossil fuels, experts suggest that nuclear fusion, solar power, and wind energy may prove useful one day. The advantages promised by each of these technologies are many: inexhaustible fuel supplies, electricity "too cheap to meter," zero emissions, universal public acceptance, and so on. Yet while they may look good on paper (and give us a warm, fuzzy feeling inside), they often come up short in terms of economics and/or technical viability. Table 2.1 shows a list of products and potential substitutes.

Suppliers

Recall from our discussion of open systems that organizations must acquire resources from their environment and convert those resources into products or services to sell. Suppliers provide the resources needed for production and may come in the form of people (supplied by trade schools and universities), raw materials (supplied by producers, wholesalers, and distributors), information (supplied by researchers and consulting firms), and financial capital (supplied by banks and other sources). But suppliers are important to an organization for reasons that go beyond the resources they provide. Suppliers can raise their prices or provide poor-quality goods and services. Labor unions can go on strike or demand higher wages. Workers may produce defective work. Powerful suppliers, then, can reduce an organization's profits, particularly if the organization cannot pass on price increases to its customers.

One particularly noteworthy set of suppliers to some industries is the international labor unions. Although unionization in the United States has dropped to about 10 percent of the private labor force, labor unions are still particularly powerful in industries such as steel, autos, and transportation. Even the Screen Actors Guild, the union representing workers in the entertainment industry, exerts considerable power on behalf of its members. For example, Tiger Woods was fined $100,000 for making a nonunion Buick commercial during a strike by the American Federation of Television and Radio Artists. Labor unions represent and protect the interests of their members with respect to hiring, wages, working conditions, job security, and due process appeals. Historically, the relationship between management and labor unions has been adversarial; however, both sides

TABLE 2.1 Potential Substitutes for Products	
If the Product Is . . .	The Substitute Might Be . . .
Cotton	Polyester
Coffee	Soft drinks
Fossil fuels	Solar fusion
Movie theater	Home video/DVD
Music CD	Radio/MP3
Automobile	Train, bus, bicycle
Personal computer	Personal Digital Assistant (PDA)
Sugar	Nutrasweet
House	Apartment, condo, mobile home
Bricks	Aluminum siding
Trashy magazine	Internet
Local telephone	Cellular phone, pager

seem to realize that to increase productivity and competitiveness, management and labor must work together in collaborative relationships. Troubled labor relations can create higher costs and productivity declines and eventually lead to layoffs.

Organizations are at a disadvantage if they become overly dependent on any powerful supplier. A supplier is powerful if the buyer has few other sources of supply or if the supplier has many other buyers. For example, if computer companies can go only to Microsoft for software or only to Intel for microchips, those suppliers can exert a great deal of pressure. In many cases, companies build up switching costs. **Switching costs** are fixed costs buyers face if they change suppliers. For example, once a buyer learns how to operate a supplier's equipment, such as computer software, the buyer faces both economic and psychological costs in changing to a new supplier.

switching costs Fixed costs buyers face when they change suppliers

Choosing the right supplier is an important strategic decision. Suppliers can affect manufacturing time, product quality, and inventory levels. The relationship between suppliers and the organization is changing in some companies. The close supplier relationship has become a new model for many organizations, such a Ford Motor, that are using a just-in-time manufacturing approach.

Customers

Customers purchase the products or services an organization offers. Without customers, a company won't survive. You are a **final consumer** when you buy a McDonald's hamburger or a pair of jeans from a retailer at the mall. **Intermediate consumers** buy raw materials or wholesale products and then sell to final consumers. Intermediate customers actually make more purchases than individual final consumers do. Examples of intermediate customers include retailers, who buy clothes from wholesalers and manufacturers' representatives before selling them to their customers, and industrial buyers, who buy raw materials (such as chemicals) before converting them into final products.

final consumer Those who purchase products in their finished form

intermediate consumer A customer who purchases raw materials or wholesale products before selling them to final customers

Like suppliers, customers are important to organizations for reasons other than the money they provide for goods and services. Customers can demand lower prices, higher quality, unique product specifications, or better service. They also can play competitors against one another, as occurs when a car customer (or a purchasing agent) collects different offers and negotiates for the best price.

customer service The speed and dependability with which an organization can deliver what customers want

Customer service means giving customers what they want or need, the way they want it, the first time. This usually depends on the speed and dependability with which an organization can deliver its products or services. Actions and attitudes that mean excellent customer service include the following:

- Speed of filling and delivering normal orders.
- Willingness to meet emergency needs.
- Merchandise delivered in good condition.
- Readiness to take back defective goods and resupply quickly.
- Availability of installation and repair services and parts.
- Service charges (that is, whether services are "free" or priced separately).

In all businesses—services as well as manufacturing—strategies that emphasize good customer service provide a critical competitive advantage. The organization is at a disadvantage if it depends too heavily on powerful customers.

Customers are powerful if they make large purchases or if they can easily find alternative places to buy. If you are the largest customer of a firm and there are other firms from which you can buy, you have power over that firm, and you are likely to be able to negotiate with it successfully. Your firm's biggest customers—especially if they can buy from other sources—will have the greatest negotiating power over you.

Environmental Analysis

If managers do not understand how the environment affects their organizations or cannot identify opportunities and threats that are likely to be important, their ability to make decisions and execute plans will be severely limited. For example, if little is known about customer likes and dislikes, organizations will have a difficult time designing new products, scheduling production, developing marketing plans, and the like. In short, timely and accurate environmental information is critical for running a business.

environmental uncertainty Lack of information needed to understand or predict the future

But information about the environment is not always readily available. **Environmental uncertainty** means that managers do not have enough information about the environment to understand or predict the future. Uncertainty arises from two related factors: (1) complexity and (2) dynamism. Environmental *complexity* refers to the number of issues to which a manager must attend as well as their interconnectedness. For example, industries that have many different firms that compete in vastly different ways tend to be more complex—and uncertain—than industries with only a few key competitors. Similarly, environmental *dynamism* refers to the degree of discontinuous change that occurs within the industry. For example, high-growth industries with products and technologies that change rapidly tend to be more uncertain than stable industries where change is less dramatic and more predictable.

As environmental uncertainty increases, managers must develop techniques and methods for collecting, sorting through, and interpreting information about the environment. By analyzing environmental forces—in both the macroenvironment and the competitive environment—managers can identify opportunities and threats that might affect the organization.

Environmental Scanning

Perhaps the first step in coping with uncertainty in the environment is pinning down what might be of importance. It is frequently the case that organizations (and individuals) act out of ignorance, only to regret those actions in the future. IBM, for example, had the opportunity to purchase the technology behind xerography but turned it down. Xerox saw the potential, and the rest is history. However, Xerox researchers later developed the technology for the original computer mouse, but not seeing the potential, the company missed an important market opportunity.

environmental scanning Searching for and sorting through information about the environment

To understand and predict changes, opportunities, and threats, organizations such as Monsanto, Weyerhaeuser, and Union Carbide spend a good deal of time and money monitoring events in the environment. **Environmental scanning** means both searching out information that is unavailable to most people and sorting through that information to interpret what is important and what is not. Managers can ask questions such as

- Who are our current competitors?
- Are there few or many entry barriers to our industry?
- What substitutes exist for our product or service?
- Is the company too dependent on powerful suppliers?
- Is the company too dependent on powerful customers?

competitive intelligence Information that helps managers determine how to compete better

Answers to these questions help managers develop **competitive intelligence,** the information necessary to decide how best to manage in the competitive environment they have identified. Porter's competitive analysis, discussed earlier, can guide environmental scanning and help managers evaluate the competitive potential of different environments. Table 2.2 describes two extreme environments: an attractive environment, which gives a firm a competitive advantage, and an unattractive environment, which puts a firm at a competitive disadvantage.

Scenario Development

scenario A narrative that describes a particular set of future conditions

As managers attempt to determine the effect of environmental forces on their organizations, they frequently develop **scenarios** of the future. Scenarios combine alternative combinations of different factors into a total picture of the environment and the firm. For example, as Congress and the president try to work toward a balanced budget and eventually reduce the federal debt, they have developed several different scenarios about what the economy is likely to do over the next decade or so. Frequently, organizations develop a *best-case scenario* (i.e., if events occur that are favorable to the firm), a *worst-case scenario* (i.e., if events are all unfavorable), and some middle-ground alternatives. The value of scenario development is that it helps managers develop contingency plans for what they might do given different outcomes.

TABLE 2.2 Attractive and Unattractive Environments		
Environmental Factor	Unattractive	Attractive
Competitors	Many; low industry growth; equal size; commodity	Few, high industry growth; unequal size differentiated
Threat of entry	High threat; few entry barriers	Low threat; many barriers
Substitutes	Many	Few
Suppliers	Few, high bargaining power	Many; low bargaining power
Customers	Few, high bargaining power	Many; low bargaining power

Forecasting

forecasting Method for predicting how variables will change the future

Whereas environmental scanning is used to identify important factors and scenario development is used to develop alternative pictures of the future, **forecasting** is used to predict exactly how some variable or variables will change in the future. For example, in making capital investments, firms may try to forecast how interest rates will change. In deciding to expand or downsize a business, firms may try to forecast the demand for goods and services or forecast the supply and demand of labor they probably would use. Available publications such as *Business Week's Business Outlook* provide forecasts to businesses both large and small.

Although forecasts are designed to help executives make predictions about the future, their accuracy varies from application to application. Because they extrapolate from the past to project the future, forecasts tend to be most accurate when the future ends up looking a lot like the past. Of course, we don't need sophisticated forecasts in those instances. Forecasts are most useful when the future will look radically different from the past. Unfortunately, that is when forecasts tend not to be so accurate. The more things change, the less confidence we tend to have in our forecasts. The best advice for using forecasts might include the following:

- Use multiple forecasts and perhaps average their predictions.
- Remember that accuracy decreases the farther into the future you are trying to predict.
- Forecasts are no better than the data used to construct them.
- Use simple forecasts (rather than complicated ones) where possible.
- Important events often are surprises and represent a departure from predictions.

Benchmarking

benchmarking The process of comparing an organization's practices and technologies with those of other companies

In addition to trying to predict changes in the environment, firms can undertake intensive study of the best practices of various firms to understand their sources of competitive advantage. **Benchmarking** means identifying the best-in-class performance by a company in a given area, say, product development or customer service, and then comparing your processes to theirs. To accomplish this, a benchmarking team would collect information on its own company's operations and those of the other firm in order to determine gaps. These gaps serve as a point of entry to learn the underlying causes of performance differences. Ultimately, the team would map out a set of best practices that lead to world-class performance.

Responding to the Environment

Organizations have a number of options for responding to the environment. In general, these options can be grouped into three categories: (1) adapting to the environment, (2) influencing the environment, and (3) selecting a new environment.

Adapting to the Environment: Changing Yourself

To cope with environmental uncertainty, organizations frequently make adjustments in their structures and work processes. In the case of uncertainty arising from environmental complexity, we can say that organizations tend to adapt by *decentralizing* decision making. For example, if a company faces a growing number of competitors in various markets, if different customers want different things, if the characteristics of different products keep increasing, and if production facilities are being built in different regions of the world, it may be impossible for the chief executive (or a small group of top executives) to keep abreast of all activities and understand all the operational details of a business. In these cases, the top management team is likely to give authority to lower-level managers to make decisions that benefit the firm. The term **empowerment** is used frequently today to talk about this type of decentralized authority.

In response to uncertainty caused by change (dynamism) in the environment, organizations tend to establish more flexible structures. In today's business world, it is commonplace for the term *bureaucracy* to take on a bad connotation. Most of us recognize that bureaucratic organizations tend to be formalized and very stable; frequently they are unable to adjust to change or exceptional circumstances that "don't fit the rules." And while bureaucratic organizations may be efficient and controlled if the environment is stable, they tend to be slow-moving and plodding when products, technologies, customers, competitors, and the like start changing over time. In these cases, more *organic* structures tend to have the flexibility needed to adjust to change. Here, organic structure are less formal than bureaucratic organizations, and so decisions tend to be made more through interaction and mutual adjustment among individuals rather than via a set of predefined rules. Table 2.3 shows four different approaches that organizations can take in adapting to environmental uncertainty.

Adapting at the Boundaries. From the standpoint of an open system, organizations create buffers on both the input and output sides of their boundaries with the environment. **Buffering** is one such approach used for adapting to uncertainty. On the input side, organizations establish relationships with employment agencies to hire part-time and temporary help during rush periods when labor demand is difficult to predict. The growth of contingent workers in the U.S. labor

empowerment The process of sharing power with employees, thereby enhancing their confidence in their ability to perform their jobs and their belief that they are influential contributors to the organization

buffering Creating supplies of excess resources in case of unpredictable needs

TABLE 2.3 Four Approaches for Managing Uncertainty		
	Stable	Dynamic
Complex	Decentralized	Decentralized
	Bureaucratic (standardized skills)	Organic (mutual adjustment)
Simple	Centralized	Centralized
	Bureaucratic (standardized work processes)	Organic (direct supervision)

force is a good indication of the popularity of this approach to buffering input uncertainties. On the output side of the system, most organizations use some type of ending inventories that allow them to keep merchandise on hand in case a rush of customers decide to buy their products. Auto dealers are a particularly common example of this use of buffers, but we can see similar use of buffer inventories in fast-food restaurants, bookstores, clothing stores, and even real estate agencies.

smoothing Leveling normal fluctuations at the boundaries of the environment

In addition to buffering, organizations may try **smoothing** or leveling normal fluctuations at the boundaries of the environment. For example, during winter months (up north) when automobile sales drop off, it is not uncommon for dealers to cut the price of their in-stock vehicles to increase demand. At the end of each clothing season, retailers discount their merchandise to clear it out in order to make room for incoming inventories. These are each examples of smoothing environmental cycles in order to level off fluctuations in demand.

flexible processes Methods for adapting the technical core to changes in the environment

Adapting at the Core. While buffering and smoothing work to manage uncertainties at the boundaries of the organization, firms also can establish **flexible processes** that allow for adaptation in their technical core. For example, firms increasingly try to customize their products and services to meet the varied and changing demands of customers. Even in manufacturing, where it is difficult to change basic core processes, firms are adopting techniques of mass customization that help them create flexible factories. Instead of mass-producing large quantities of a "one-size-fits-all" product, with mass customization organizations can produce individually customized products at an equally low cost. Whereas Henry Ford used to claim that "you could have a Model T in any color you wanted, as long as it was black," auto companies now offer a wide array of colors and trim lines, with different options and accessories. The process of mass customization involves the use of a network of independent operating units in which each performs a specific process or task such as making a dashboard assembly on an automobile. When an order comes in, different modules join forces to deliver the product or service as specified by the customer.

Influencing Your Environment

In addition to adapting or reacting to the environment, organizations can develop proactive responses aimed at changing the environment. Two general types of proactive responses are independent action and cooperative action.

independent strategies Strategies that an organization acting on its own uses to change some aspect of its current environment

Independent Action. A company uses **independent strategies** when it acts on its own to change some aspect of its current environment. For example, when Southwest Airlines enters a new market, it demonstrates competitive aggression by cutting fares so that other, less-efficient airlines must follow it down. In contrast, Kellogg Company typically promotes the cereal industry as a whole, thereby demonstrating competitive pacification. Weyerhaeuser Company advertises its reforestation efforts (public relations). First Boston forgoes its Christmas party and donates thousands of dollars to the poor (voluntary action). Dow Chemical recently sued General Electric for hiring away some of its engineers (legal action). Dow Corning lobbied and recently won the right to put silicon implants back on the market (political action). Each of these examples shows how organizations—on their own—can have an impact on the environment.

Cooperative Action. In some situations, two or more organizations work together using cooperative strategies (contraction, cooptation, and coalition) to influence the environment. An example of contracting occurs when suppliers and customers, or managers and labor unions, sign formal agreements about the terms and conditions of their future relationships. These contracts are explicit attempts to make their future relationship predictable. An example of cooptation might occur when universities invite wealthy alumni to join their boards of directors.

Finally, an example of *coalition* formation might be when local businesses band together to curb the rise of employee health care costs and when organizations in the same industry form industry associations and special-interest groups. You may have seen cooperative advertising strategies, such as when dairy producers, beef producers, orange growers, and the like, jointly pay for television commercials.

At a more organizational level, organizations establish strategic alliances, partnerships, joint ventures, and mergers with competitors to deal with environmental uncertainties. Cooperative strategies such as these make most sense when (1) taking joint action will reduce the organizations' costs and risks and (2) cooperation will increase their power (that is, their ability to successfully accomplish the changes they desire).

Changing the Environment You Are In

As we noted previously, organizations can cope with environmental uncertainty by changing themselves (environmental adaptation), changing the environment, or changing the environment they are in. We refer to this last category as **strategic maneuvering.** By making a conscious effort to change the boundaries of its competitive environment, firms can maneuver around potential threats and capitalize on arising opportunities.

Organizations engage in strategic maneuvering when they move into different environments. Some companies, called **prospectors,** are more likely than others to engage in strategic maneuvering. Aggressive companies continuously change the boundaries of their competitive environments by seeking new products and markets, diversifying, and merging or acquiring new enterprises. In these and other ways, corporations put their competitors on the defensive and force them to react. **Defenders,** on the other hand, stay within a more limited, stable product domain.

---

strategic maneuvering
An organization's conscious efforts to change the boundaries of its task environment

Prospectors Companies that continuously change the boundaries for their task environments by seeking new products and markets, diversifying and merging, or acquiring new enterprises

defenders Companies that stay within a stable product domain as a strategic maneuver

---

Choosing a Response Approach

Three general considerations help guide management's response to the environment. First, organizations should attempt to *change appropriate elements of the environment.* Environmental responses are most useful when aimed at elements of the environment that (1) cause the company problems, (2) provide it with opportunities, and (3) allow the company to change successfully. Thus, automobile companies faced with intense competition from Japanese automakers successfully lobbied (along with labor) for government-imposed ceilings on Japanese imports. And one charcoal producer, hoping to increase consumers' opportunities to use its product, launched a campaign to increase daylight saving time.

Second, organizations should *choose responses that fears on pertinent elements of the environment.* If a company wants to better manage its competitive environment, competitive aggression and pacification are viable options. Political action influences the Legal environment, and contracting helps manage customers and suppliers.

Third, companies should *choose responses that offer the most benefit at the lowest cost.* Return-on-investment calculations should incorporate short-term financial considerations as well as long-term impact. Strategic managers who consider these factors carefully will guide their organizations to competitive advantage more effectively.

Learning Objectives

Now that you have studied Chapter 2, you should know:

How environmental forces influence organizations, as well as how organizations can influence their environments.

Organizations are open systems that are affected by, and in turn affect, their external environments. Organizations receive financial, human, material, and information resources from the environment; transform those resources into finished goods and services; and then send those outputs back into the environment.

How to make a distinction between the macroenvironment and the competitive environment.

The macroenvironment is composed of international, legal and political, economic, technological, and social forces that influence strategic decisions. The competitive environment is composed of forces closer to the organization, such as current competitors, threat of new entrants, threat of substitutes, suppliers, and customers. Perhaps the simplest distinction between the macroenvironment and the competitive environment is in the amount of control a firm can exert on external forces. Macroenvironmental forces such as the economy and social trends are much less controllable than are forces in the competitive environment such as suppliers and customers.

Why organizations should attend to economic and social developments in the international environment.

Developments in other countries have a profound effect on the way U.S. companies compete. European unification, for example, is creating a formidable buying and selling bloc. The North American Free Trade Agreement opened up trade among the United States, Canada, and Mexico. Managed well, the European Union and NAFTA represent opportunities for market growth, joint ventures, and the like. Managed poorly, these free trade agreements may give advantage to more competitive firms and nations.

How to analyze the competitive environment.

Environments can range from favorable to unfavorable. To determine how favorable a competitive environment is, managers should consider the nature of the competitors, potential new entrants, threat of substitutes, suppliers, and customers. Analyzing how these five forces influence the organization provides an indication of potential threats and opportunities. Attractive environments tend to be those which have high industry growth, few competitors, products that can be differentiated, few potential entrants, many barriers to entry, few substitutes, many suppliers (none with much power), and many customers. After identifying and analyzing competitive forces, managers must formulate a strategy that minimizes the power external forces have over the organization (a topic discussed more fully in Chapter 5).

How organizations respond to environmental uncertainty.

Responding effectively to the environment often involves devising proactive strategies to change the environment. Strategic maneuvering, for example, involves changing the boundaries of the competitive environment through domain selection, diversification, mergers, and the like. Independent strategies, on the other hand, do not require moving into a new environment but rather changing some aspect of the current environment through competitive aggression, public relations, legal action, and so on. Finally, cooperative strategies, such as contracting, cooptation, and coalition building, involve the working together of two or more organizations.

◎ Discussion Questions

1. This chapter's opening quote by Peter Drucker said, "The essence of a business is outside itself." What do you think this means? Do you agree?
2. What are the most important forces in the macroenvironment facing companies today?
3. Go back to the telecom example in "Setting the Stage." What other organizations have faced or are facing similar circumstances in their external environments?
4. What are the main differences between the macroenvironment and the competitive environment?
5. What kinds of changes do companies make in response to environmental uncertainty?
6. We outlined several proactive responses that organizations can make to the environment. What examples have you seen recently of an organization's responding effectively to its environment? Did the effectiveness of the response depend on whether the organization was facing a threat or an opportunity?

DECISION MAKING IN ORGANIZATIONS

THE ENRON-ARTHUR ANDERSEN SCANDAL: DECISION MAKING GONE AWRY

In July 1985, the Houston Natural Gas Company merged with InterNorth to form Enron. In the years that followed, shrewd financial dealings led the fledgling enterprise to become one of the world's richest and most powerful companies, eventually reaching number five on the *Fortune* 500. Or so it seemed. That was until December 2, 2001, when the company led for Chapter 11 bankruptcy protection—just days after announcing a $1.2 billion loss.

As the story unfolded, it became clear that the demise of Enron was no ordinary business failure. Rather, Enron's collapse was the inevitable result of a complex web of lies, deceit, and unethical decisions by company officials that led to the ongoing illusion that Enron was in excellent financial condition when the truth was quite the opposite. By way of some questionable accounting practices, actual losses were reported as profits (a jump of 37.6 percent in 2001 alone) in deals alleged to have put some $30 million in the pocket of Enron CEO Kenneth Lay. Despite Lay's obvious windfall, the company's collapse led to the loss of jobs and vaporized the pension savings of some 4,000 company employees. It also sent reverberations through the stock market amid fears that there may be "other Enrons out there."

In January 2002, the U.S. Justice Department launched an investigation of Enron that painted a picture of ongoing blatant financial mismanagement and greed that spread beyond Enron to its accounting firm, the then highly regarded firm of Arthur Andersen. As soon as it became apparent that it was going to be investigated by the Securities and Exchange Commission, Andersen officials allegedly ordered employees to destroy thousands of documents that could connect it to the questionable business practices of its client. Indicted by a federal grand jury, Andersen was cited with undermining the justice system by destroying "tons" of paperwork and by attempting to purge electronic data, even working around-the-clock to do it.

Andersen spokespersons have claimed that these actions were not directed by high-ranking officials, nor did they conform to company policy. Rather, they say that these acts stemmed from poor decisions by a few rogue employees in the Houston office, who subsequently were fired, including a partner in the firm, David Duncan, who is alleged to have spearheaded the destruction operations. Although the truth may never be known, it's clear that Andersen suffered greatly from its association with Enron. Not wanting to be linked to an accounting firm whose ethics may be questioned, major clients such as Delta Airlines and FedEx fired Andersen, leading the company to falter. In the fallout, as many as 7,000 Andersen employees have lost their jobs and the company's German operations have been purchased by competitor Ernst & Young.

> **Enron's collapse was the inevitable result of a complex web of lies, deceit, and unethical decisions by company officials.**

From *Behavior in Organizations: Understanding and Managing the Human Side of Work* by Greenberg/Baron, © 2003. Reprinted by permission of Pearson Education, Inc., Upper Saddle River. NJ.

Few cases in the annals of business have been as serious and as broad-reaching as the tales of corruption at Enron and its beleaguered accounting firm, Arthur Andersen, that unfolded on the pages of the business press in 2002. The resulting changes in accounting practices and government regulation of business are sure to be monumental. Yet, at the heart of all this lies a process that is very fundamental to human beings and of considerable concern to the field of OB—the making of *decisions*. Whether guided by greed or power, some Enron officials decided to engage in business practices that were intentionally misleading. Then, guided by the desire to protect its client, Andersen officials made decisions to cover up Enron's misdeeds. When viewed from this perspective, it's clear that understanding how people come to make decisions can be quite important.

Although the decisions you make as an individual may be less monumental than those associated with the Enron scandal, they are very important to you. For example, personal decisions about what college to go to, what classes to take, and what company to work for can have a major impact on the direction your life takes. If you think about the difficulties involved in making decisions in your own life, you surely can appreciate how complicated—and important—the process of decision making can be in organizations, where the stakes are often considerable and the impact is widespread. In both cases, however, the essential nature of **decision making** is identical. It may be defined as the process of making choices from among several alternatives.

decision making The process of making choices from among several alternatives

It is safe to say that decision making is one of the most important—if not *the* most important—of all managerial activities. Management theorists and researchers agree that decision making represents one of the most common and most crucial work roles of executives. Every day, people in organizations make decisions about a wide variety of topics ranging from the mundane to the monumental. Understanding how these decisions are made, and how they can be improved, is an important goal of the field of organizational behavior.

This chapter will examine theories, research, and practical managerial techniques concerned with decision making in organizations both by individuals and groups. Beginning with individuals, we will review various perspectives on how people go about making decisions. We then will identify factors that may adversely affect the quality of individual decisions and ways of combating them—that is, techniques for improving the quality of decisions. Then we will shift our focus to group decisions, focusing on the conditions under which individuals and groups are each better suited to making decisions. Finally, we will describe some of the factors that make group decisions imperfect and various techniques that can be used to improve the quality of group decisions. But, first, we will begin by examining the general nature of the decision-making process and the wide variety of decisions made in organizations.

The Nature of Decision Making

We begin by examining the basic nature of the decision-making process itself. With this in mind, we will present a model describing the general steps by which decisions are made. We then will consider the idea that all people don't make decisions in exactly the same manner. Specifically, we will discuss individual differences and cultural differences in the ways people go about making decisions.

A General, Analytical Model of the Decision-Making Process

Traditionally, scientists have found it useful to conceptualize the process of decision making as a series of analytical steps that groups or individuals take to solve problems. This is accomplished by the **analytical model of the decision-making process**, which can help us understand the complex nature of organizational decision making (see Figure 3.1) This approach highlights two important aspects of decision making: **formulation**, the process of understanding a problem and making a decision about it, and **implementation**, the process of carrying out the decision made. As we present this model, keep in mind that all decisions might not fully conform to the neat, eight-step pattern described (e.g., steps may be skipped and/or combined). However, for the purpose of pointing out the general way the decision-making process operates, the model is quite useful.

1. The first step is *problem identification*. To decide how to solve a problem, one must first recognize and identify the problem. For example, an executive may identify as a problem the fact that the company cannot meet its payroll obligations. This step isn't always as easy as it sounds. In fact, research has shown that people often distort, omit, ignore, and/or discount information around them that provides important cues regarding the existence of problems. It is easy to imagine that someone may fail to recognize a problem if doing so makes him or her uncomfortable. Denying a problem may be the first impediment on the road to solving it!

2. After a problem is identified, the next step is to *define the objectives to be met in solving the problem*. It is important to conceive of problems in such a way that possible solutions can be identified. The problem identified in our example may be defined as not having enough money, or in business

analytical model of the decision-making process An eight-step approach to organizational decision making that focuses on both th formulation of problems and the implementation of solutions

formulation The process of understanding a problem and making a decision about it

implementation The process of carrying out a decision

FIGURE 3.1

Overview of the Decision-Making Process

The analytical model of the decision-making process describes most decisions as following the eight steps shown here. Note how each step may be applied to a hypothetical organizational problem (in this example, not having sufficient funds to meet payroll obligations). SOURCE: Based on information in Wedley & Field, 1984; see Note 4.)

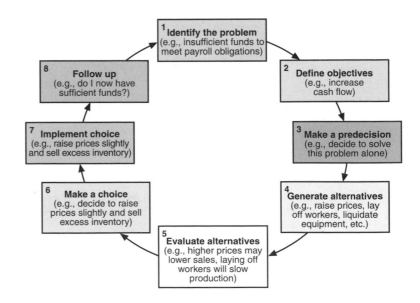

terms, "inadequate cash flow." By looking at the problem in this way, the objective is clear: increase available cash reserves. Any possible solution to the problem should be evaluated relative to this objective. A good solution is one that meets it.

3. The third step in the decision-making process is to *make a predecision*. A **predecision** is a decision about how to make a decision. By assessing the type of problem in question and other aspects of the situation, managers may opt to make a decision themselves, delegate the decision to another, or have a group make the decision. Decisions about how to make a decision should be based on research that tells us about the nature of the decisions made under different circumstances, much of which we will review later in this chapter.

   For many years, managers have been relying on their own intuition or empirically based information about organizational behavior (contained in books like this) for the guidance needed to make predecisions. Recently, however, computer programs have been developed summarizing much of this information in a form that gives managers ready access to a wealth of social science information that may help them decide how to make decisions. Such **decision support systems (DSS),** as they are called, can only be as good as the social science information that goes into developing them. Research has shown that DSS techniques are effective in helping people make decisions about solving problems. The use of decision-making technology leads to outcomes that are higher in quantity and better in quality than those made in the absence of such techniques.

4. The fourth step in the process is *alternative generation*, the stage in which possible solutions to the problem are identified. In attempting to come up with solutions, people tend to rely on previously used approaches that might provide ready-made answers for them. In our example, some possible ways of solving the revenue shortage problem would be to reduce the workforce, sell unnecessary equipment and material, and increase sales.

5. Because all these possibilities may not be equally feasible, the fifth step calls for *evaluating alternative solutions*. Which solution is considered best? What would be the most effective way of raising the revenue needed to meet the payroll? The various alternatives need to be identified. Some may be more effective than others, and some may be more difficult to implement than others. For example, although increasing sales would help solve the problem, that is much easier said than done. It is a solution, but not an immediately practical one.

6. Next, in the sixth step, a *choice is made*. After several alternatives are evaluated, one that is considered acceptable is chosen. As we will describe shortly, different approaches to decision making offer different views of how thoroughly people consider alternatives and how optimal their chosen alternatives are. Choosing which course of action to take is the step that most often comes to mind when we think about the decision-making process. However, as you can see, it is only one of several key steps.

7. The seventh step calls for *implementation of the chosen alternative*. That is, the chosen alternative is carried out.

8. The eighth and final step is *follow-up*. Monitoring the effectiveness of the decisions put into action is important to the success of organizations. Does

predecision A decision about what process to follow in making a decision

decision support systems (DSS) Computer programs in which information about organizational behavior is presented to decision makers in a manner that helps them structure their responses to decisions

the problem still exist? Have any new problems been caused by implementing the solution? In other words, it is important to seek feedback about the effectiveness of any attempted solution. For this reason, the decision-making process shown in Figure 3.1 is presented as circular in nature. If the solution works, the problem may be considered solved. If not, a new solution will have to be attempted.

It is important to reiterate that the analytical model we have been describing is a very general model of the decision-making process. Although it may not be followed exactly as specified in all circumstances, it paints a good picture of the general nature of a complex set of operations.

The Broad Spectrum of Organizational Decisions

As you might imagine, because the process of decision making is so fundamental to organizations, decisions themselves tend to be of many different kinds. Understanding the wide variety of decisions that are made in organizations is an important first step toward understanding the nature of the decision-making process. With this in mind, we will distinguish among decisions in three important ways: how routine they are, how much risk is involved, and who in the organization gets to make them.

Programmed versus Nonprogrammed Decisions. Think of a decision that is made repeatedly according to a preestablished set of alternatives. For example, a word processing operator may decide to make a backup copy of the day's work on disk, or a manager of a fast-food restaurant may decide to order hamburger buns as the supply starts to get low. Decisions such as these are known as **programmed decisions**—routine decisions, made by lower-level personnel, that rely on predetermined courses of action.

By contrast, we may identify **nonprogrammed decisions**—ones for which there are no ready-made solutions. The decision maker confronts a unique situation in which the solutions are novel. A research scientist attempting to find a cure for a rare disease faces a problem that is poorly structured. Unlike the restaurant manager, whose course of action is clear when the supply of buns runs low, the scientist in this example must rely on creativity rather than preexisting answers to solve the problem at hand.

The differences between programmed and nonprogrammed decisions can be described with respect to three important questions. First, *what type of tasks are involved?* Programmed decisions are made on tasks that are common and routine, whereas nonprogrammed decisions are made on unique and novel tasks. Second, *how much reliance is there on organizational policies?* In making programmed decisions, the decision maker can count on guidance from statements of organizational policy and procedure. However, nonprogrammed decisions require the use of creative solutions that are implemented for the first time; past solutions may provide little guidance. Finally, *who makes the decisions?* Not surprisingly, nonprogrammed decisions typically are made by upper-level organizational personnel, whereas the more routine, well-structured decisions are usually relegated to lower-level personnel. For a summary of these three distinctions between programmed and nonprogrammed decisions, see Table 3.1.

programmed decisions Highly routine decisions made by lower-level personnel following preestablished organizational routines and procedures

nonprogrammed decisions Decisions made about a highly novel problem for which there is no prespecified course of action

TABLE 3.1 Programmed and Nonprogrammed Decisions: A Comparison

The two major types of organizational decisions—programmed decisions and nonprogrammed decisions—differ regarding the types of tasks on which they are made, the degree to which solutions may be found in existing organizational policies, and the typical decision-making unit.

Variable	Type of Decision	
	Programmed Decisions	Nonprogrammed Decisions
Type of task	Simple, routine	Complex, creative
Reliance on organizational policies	Considerable guidance from past decisions	No guidance from past decisions
Typical decision maker	Lower-level workers (usually alone)	Upper-level supervisors (usually in groups)

strategic decisions
Nonprogrammed decisions typically made by high-level executives regarding the direction their organization should take to achieve its mission

Certain types of nonprogrammed decisions are known as **strategic decisions.** These decisions are typically made by coalitions of high-level executives and have important long-term implications for the organization. Strategic decisions reflect a consistent pattern for directing the organization in some specified fashion—that is, according to an underlying organizational philosophy or mission. For example, an organization may make a strategic decision to grow at a specified yearly rate or to be guided by a certain code of corporate ethics. Both of these decisions are likely to be considered "strategic" because they guide the future direction of the organization. Some excellent examples of highly successful strategic decisions made in business settings maybe found in Table 3.2.

Certain versus Uncertain Decisions. Just think of how easy it would be to make decisions if we knew what the future had in store. Making the best investments in the stock market would simply be a matter of looking up the changes in tomorrow's newspaper. Of course, we never know exactly what the future holds, but we can be more certain at some times than others. Certainty about the factors on which decisions are made is highly desired in organizational decision making.

Degrees of certainty and uncertainty are expressed as statements of *risk*. All organizational decisions involve some degree of risk—ranging from complete certainty (no risk) to complete uncertainty, "a stab in the dark" (high risk). To make the best possible decisions in organizations, people seek to "manage" the risks they take—that is, minimizing the riskiness of a decision by gaining access to information relevant to the decision.

What makes an outcome risky or not is the *probability* of obtaining the desired outcome. Decision makers attempt to obtain information about the probabilities, or odds, of certain events occurring given that other events have occurred. For example, a financial analyst may report that a certain stock has risen 80 percent of the time that the prime rate has dropped, or a meteorologist may report that the precipitation probability is 50 percent (i.e., in the past, it rained or snowed half the time certain atmospheric conditions existed). These data may be considered reports of *objective probabilities* because they are based on concrete, verifiable data.

TABLE 3.2 Strategic Decisions: Some Highly Successful Examples	
Decisions that guide the future directions of organizations are known as strategic decisions. Some of the best-known and most successful strategic decisions are shown here.	
Company	Decision Made
Toyota	In the aftermath of World War II, the company decided to emphasize high-quality manufacturing techniques.
Coca-Cola	During World War II, the company developed brand loyalty by selling bottles of Coke to members of the armed services.
IBM	In 1924, founder Thomas Watson, Sr. changed the company's name from the Computing-Tabulating-Recording Company to International Business Machines although it had no international operations at the time, boldly declaring its ambitions.
Microsoft	In 1981, Bill Gates decided to license MS-DOS to IBM, which relinquished control of the operating system for all non-IBM personal computers.
Apple	Steve Jobs decided to build his company around sales of a simple computer that could be used by individuals.
Sears	In 1905, the company decided on a way to bring its products to a wider audience by introducing a mail-order catalog.
Johnson & Johnson	In 1982, the company pulled all bottles of Tylenol capsules off store shelves after a few capsules were found to be poisoned.
Sony	In 1980, the company introduced the Walkman after officials noticed that young people like to have music with them wherever they go.
Hewlett-Packard	In 1979, the company decided to exploit an engineer's observation that metal heated in a certain way tended to splatter, resulting in the development of the ink-jet printer.

SOURCE: Based on material in Crainer, 1998; see Note 16.

Many decisions also are based on *subjective probabilities*—personal beliefs or hunches about what will happen. For example, a gambler who bets on a horse because it has a name similar to one of his children's or a person who suspects it's going to rain because he just washed his car is basing these judgments on subjective probabilities.

Obviously, uncertainty is an undesirable characteristic in decision-making situations. We may view much of what decision makers do in organizations as attempting to reduce uncertainty (i.e., putting the odds in their favor) so they can make better decisions. How do organizations respond when faced with highly uncertain conditions, when they don't know what the future holds for them? Studies have shown that decision uncertainty can be reduced by *establishing linkages with other organizations.* The more an organization knows about what another organization will do, the greater certainty it will have in making decisions. This is part of a general tendency for organizational decision makers to respond to uncertainty by reducing the unpredictability of other organizations in their business environments. Those outside organizations with which managers have the greatest contact are most likely to be the ones with whom they establish the closest connections.

In general, what reduces uncertainty in decision-making situations? The answer is *information*. Knowledge about the past and the present can be used to help make projections about the future. A modern executive's access to the data needed to make important decisions may be as close as the nearest computer terminal. Indeed, computer technology has aided greatly managers' ability to make decisions quickly, using the most accurate and thorough information available. Variety of online information services are designed to provide organizational decision makers with the latest information relevant to the decisions they are making.

Of course, not all information needed to make decisions comes from computers. Many managerial decisions also are based on the decision maker's past experiences and intuition. This is not to say that top managers rely on subjective information in making decisions (although they might), but that their history of past decisions—both successes and failures—is often given great weight in the decision-making process. In other words, when it comes to making decisions, people often rely on what has worked for them in the past. Part of the reason this strategy is often successful is because experienced decision makers tend to make better use of information relevant to the decisions they are making. Individuals who have expertise in certain subjects know what information is most relevant and also how to interpret it to make the best decisions. It is, therefore, not surprising that people seek experienced professionals, such as doctors and lawyers who are seasoned veterans in their fields, when it comes to making important decisions. With high levels of expertise comes information relevant to assessing the riskiness of decision alternatives and how to reduce it.

Top-down versus Empowered Decisions. Traditionally, in organizations the job of making all but the most menial decisions belonged to managers. In fact, organizational scientist Herbert Simon, who won a Nobel prize for his work on the economics of decision making, has gone so far as to describe decision making as synonymous with managing. Subordinates collected information and gave it to superiors, who used it to make decisions. This approach, known as **top-down decision making,** puts decision-making power in the hands of managers, leaving lower-level workers little or no opportunities to make decisions. If this sounds familiar to you, it is because it has been the way most organizations have operated for a long time.

Today, however, a new approach has come into vogue that is in many ways exactly the opposite. The idea of **empowered decision making** allows employees to make the decisions required to do their jobs without first seeking supervisory approval. As the name implies, it gives them the power to decide what they need to do in order to do their jobs effectively. The rationale for this philosophy of decision making is that the people who do the jobs know what's best, so having someone else make the decision may not make the most sense. In addition, when people are empowered to make their own decisions they are more likely to accept the consequences of those decisions. If the decision was a good one, they can feel good about it. If not, then they have learned a valuable lesson for the next time. In either case, people are more committed to courses of action based on decisions they have made themselves than ones based on decisions that others have made. And such commitment can be important to keeping the organization functioning effectively.

top-down decision making The practice of vesting decision-making power in the hands of superiors as opposed to lower-level employees

empowered decision making The practice of vesting power for making decisions in the hands of employees themselves

Many different companies today are empowering their employees to make a wide variety of decisions. As an example, the Ritz-Carlton hotel chain has empowered each of its employees to spend up to $2,000 of the company's money per day to fix whatever they find that needs to be repaired. No longer would a chambermaid who finds a broken lamp in one of the guest rooms need to fill out a form that gets passed from one person to the next. He or she is empowered to get the right person to get the job done right away. It is not only individual employees who might be empowered but work teams as well. For example, employees at the Chesapeake Packaging Company's box plant in Baltimore, Maryland are organized into eight separate internal companies. Each such unit is empowered to make its own decisions about key issues, be it ordering, purchasing new equipment, or measuring their own work.

Factors Affecting Decisions in Organizations

Given how fundamental the decision-making process is in organizations, it makes sense that it is influenced by a wide variety of factors. In fact, as we will see, organizational decisions are affected by all three levels studied in the field of OB—individuals, groups, and organizations—as well as by an even broader consideration, national culture. We will consider each of these factors here.

Decision Style: Individual Differences in Decision Making

decision style
Differences between people with respect to their orientations toward decisions

decision-style model
The conceptualization according to which people use one of four predominant decision styles: *directive*, *analytical*, *conceptual*, and *behavioral*

Do all individuals go about making decisions the same way, or are there differences in the general approaches people take? In general, research has shown that there are meaningful differences between people with respect to their orientation toward decisions—that is, their **decision style.**

Whereas some people are concerned primarily with achieving success at any cost, others are more concerned about the effects of their decisions on others. Furthermore, some individuals tend to be more logical and analytical in their approach to problems, whereas others are more intuitive and creative. Clearly, important differences exist in the approaches decision makers take to problems. The **decision-style model** identifies four major decision styles (see summary in Figure 3.2.)

1. The *directive style* is characterized by people who prefer simple, clear solutions to problems. Individuals with this style tend to make decisions rapidly because they use little information and do not consider many alternatives. They tend to rely on existing rules to make their decisions and aggressively use their status to achieve results.

2. By contrast, individuals with the *analytical style* tend to be more willing to consider complex solutions based on ambiguous information. People with this style tend to analyze their decisions carefully using as much data as possible. Such individuals tend to enjoy solving problems. They

Decision Styles

Directive	Analytical	Conceptual	Behavioral
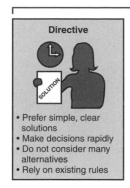	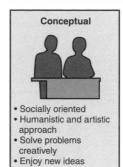	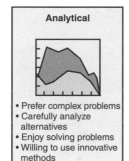	
• Prefer simple, clear solutions • Make decisions rapidly • Do not consider many alternatives • Rely on existing rules	• Prefer complex problems • Carefully analyze alternatives • Enjoy solving problems • Willing to use innovative methods	• Socially oriented • Humanistic and artistic approach • Solve problems creatively • Enjoy new ideas	• Concern for their organization • Interest in helping others • Open to suggestions • Rely on meetings

FIGURE 3.2
Decision-Style Model: A Summary

According to the decision-style model, people may be characterized as adhering to one of the four decision styles summarized here.

SOURCE: Based on information in Rowe, Boulgaides, & McGrath, 1984; see Note 26.

want the best possible answers and are willing to use innovative methods to achieve them.

3. Compared to the directive and analytical styles, people with the *conceptual style* tend to be more socially oriented in their approach to problems. Their approach is humanistic and artistic. Such individuals tend to consider many broad alternatives when dealing with problems and to solve them creatively. They have a strong future orientation and enjoy initiating new ideas.

4. Individuals with the *behavioral style* may be characterized as having a deep concern for the organizations in which they work and the personal development of their coworkers. They are highly supportive of others and very concerned about others' achievements, frequently helping them meet their goals. Such individuals tend to be open to suggestions from others and, therefore, tend to rely on meetings for making decisions.

It is important to point out that although most managers may have one dominant style, they use many different styles. In fact, those who can shift between styles—that is, those who are most flexible in their approach to decision making—have highly complex, individualistic styles of their own. Despite this, people's dominant style reveals a great deal about the way they tend to make decisions. Not surprisingly, conflicts often occur between individuals with different styles. For example, a manager with a highly directive style may have a hard time accepting the slow, deliberate actions of a subordinate with an analytical style.

Researchers have argued that being aware of people's decision styles is a potentially useful way of understanding social interactions in organizations. With this in mind, scientists have developed an instrument known as the *decision-style inventory,* a questionnaire designed to reveal the relative strength of people's decision styles. The higher an individual scores with respect to a given decision style, the more likely that style is to dominate his or her decision making.

DECISION MAKING IN ORGANIZATIONS ◎ 79

Research using the decision-style inventory has revealed some interesting findings. For example, when the inventory was given to a sample of corporate presidents, their scores on each of the four categories were found to be approximately equal. Apparently, they had no one dominant style but were able to switch back and forth between categories with ease. Further research has shown that different groups tend to have, on average, different styles that dominate their decision making. For example, military leaders tend to have high conceptual-style scores. They were not the highly domineering individuals that stereotypes suggest. Rather, they were highly conceptual and people oriented in their approach. Such findings paint a far more humanistic and less authoritarian picture of military officers than many would guess.

In conclusion, research on decision styles suggests that people tend to take very different approaches to the decisions they make. Their personalities, coupled with their interpersonal skills, lead them to approach decisions in consistently different ways—that is, using different decision styles. Although research on decision styles is relatively new, it is already clear that understanding such stylistic differences is a key factor in appreciating potential conflicts likely to arise between decision makers.

Group Influences: A Matter of Trade-Offs

As you might imagine, groups influence organizational decisions in a wide variety of ways, potentially positive and negative. We say "potentially" because the wide variety of factors influencing organizational decisions makes it difficult to predict whether anticipated benefits or problems actually will occur. Still, it is useful to understand some of the major forces that have the potential to affect the way groups make decisions in organizations.

Potential Benefits of Decision-Making Groups. There is little doubt that much can be gained by using decision-making groups. Several potential advantages of this approach may be identified. First, bringing people together may increase the amount of knowledge and information available for making good decisions. In other words, there may be a *pooling of resources*. A related benefit is that in decision-making groups there can be a *specialization of labor*. With enough people around to share the workload, individuals can perform only those tasks at which they are best, thereby potentially improving the quality of the group's efforts.

Another benefit is that group decisions are likely to enjoy *greater acceptance* than individual decisions. People involved in making decisions may be expected to understand those decisions better and be more committed to carrying them out than decisions made by someone else.

Potential Problems of Decision-Making Groups. Of course, there also are some problems associated with using decision-making groups. One obvious drawback is that groups are likely to *waste time*. The time spent socializing before getting down to business may be a drain on the group and be very costly to organizations.

Another possible problem is that potential disagreement over important matters may breed ill will and *group conflict*. Although constructive disagreement sometimes can lead to better group outcomes, highly disruptive conflict may interfere with group decisions. Indeed, with corporate power and personal pride at stake, it is not at all surprising to find that lack of agreement can cause bad feelings to develop between group members.

Finally, we may expect groups to be ineffective sometimes because of members' *intimidation by group leaders.* A group composed of several "yes" men or women trying to please a dominant leader tends to discourage open and honest discussion of solutions. In view of these problems, it is easy to understand the old adage, "A camel is a horse put together by a committee."

Groupthink: Too Much Cohesiveness Can Be a Dangerous Thing. Sometimes members of groups become so concerned about not "rocking the boat" that they are reluctant to challenge the groups' decisions. When this happens, group members tend to isolate themselves from outside information, and the process of critical thinking deteriorates. This phenomenon is referred to as **groupthink.**

groupthink The tendency for members of highly cohesive groups to so strongly conform to group pressures regarding a certain decision that they fail to think critically, rejecting the potentially correcting influences of outsiders

To illustrate the phenomenon of groupthink, consider the tragic decision to launch the space shuttle *Challenger* in January 1986. Analyses of conversations between key personnel suggested that NASA officials made the decision to launch the shuttle under freezing conditions while ignoring admonitions from engineers that this may be unsafe. Because NASA had such a successful history, the decision makers operated with a sense of invulnerability. They also worked so closely together and were under such intense pressure to launch the shuttle without further delay that they all collectively went along with the launch decision, creating the illusion of unanimous agreement. For a more precise description of groupthink and a practical guide to recognizing its symptoms, see Figure 3.3.

Groupthink doesn't occur only in governmental decision making, as you might imagine, but in the private sector as well (although, in such cases, the failures maybe less well publicized). For example, analyses of the business policies of large corporations such as British Airlines, Lockheed, and Chrysler have suggested that it was the failure of top-management teams to respond to changing market conditions that at one time led these firms to the brink of disaster. The problem is that members of very cohesive groups may have considerable confidence in their group's decisions, making them unlikely to raise doubts about these actions (i.e., "the group seems to know what it's doing"). As a result, they may suspend their own critical thinking in favor of conforming to the group. When group members become fiercely loyal to each other, they may ignore potentially useful information from other sources that challenges the group's decisions. The result of this process is

FIGURE 3.3
Groupthink: An Overview

Groupthink occurs when highly cohesive conditions in groups discourage members from challenging their group's overall decision. Poor-quality decisions result.

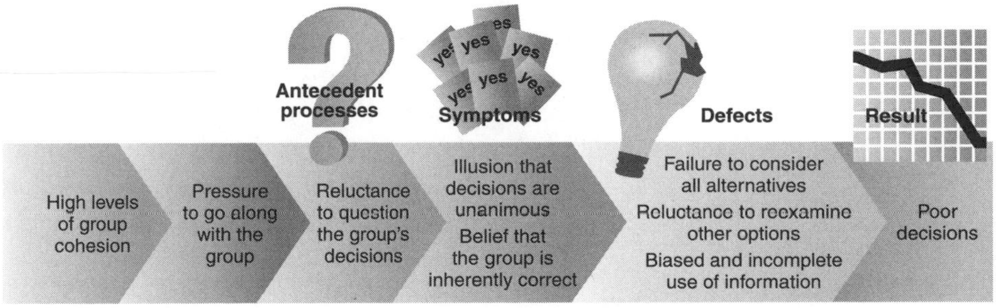
Antecedent processes
Symptoms
Defects
Result
High levels of group cohesion
Pressure to go along with the group
Reluctance to question the group's decisions
Illusion that decisions are unanimous
Belief that the group is inherently correct
Failure to consider all alternatives
Reluctance to reexamine other options
Biased and incomplete use of information
Poor decisions

that the group's decisions may be completely uninformed, irrational, or even immoral.

Organizational Barriers to Effective Decisions

Thus far we have emphasized the human cognitive shortcomings and biases that limit effective decision making. However, we must not ignore several important organizational factors that also interfere with rational decisions. Indeed, the situations faced by many organizational decision makers cannot help but interfere with their capacity to make decisions.

One obvious factor is *time constraints*. Many important organizational decisions are made under severe time pressure. Under such circumstances, it is often impossible for exhaustive decision making to occur. This is particularly the case when organizations face crisis situations requiring immediate decisions. Under such conditions, when decision makers feel "rushed into" taking action, they frequently restrict their search for information and consideration of alternatives that may otherwise help them make effective decisions.

The quality of many organizational decisions also may be limited by *political "face-saving" pressure*. In other words, decision makers may make decisions that help them look good to others, although the resulting decisions might not be in the best interest of their organizations. Imagine, for example, how an employee might distort the available information needed to make a decision if the correct decision would jeopardize his job. Unfortunately, such misuses of information to support desired decisions are all too common.

A study on the topic of political face-saving found that a group of business-people working on a group decision-making problem opted for an adequate—although less than optimal—decision rather than risk generating serious conflicts with their fellow group members in an actual case, a proponent of medical inoculation for the flu was so interested in advancing his pro-inoculation position that he proceeded with the inoculation program although there was only a 2 percent chance of an epidemic. Apparently, people often make the decisions they need to make to cultivate the best impressions although these may not be the best ones for their organizations.

Cultural Differences in Decision Making

People are people, and the process of decision making is essentially the same all over the world—right? Not exactly. Even if people were to follow the same basic steps when making decisions, there exist widespread differences in the *way* people from various cultures may go about doing so. Because we tend to take for granted the way we do things in our own country, especially such basic tasks as making decisions, some of these differences may seem quite surprising.

For example, suppose you are managing a large construction project when you discover that one of your most important suppliers will be several months late in delivering the necessary materials. What would you do? You're probably thinking, "This is a silly question; I'd simply try to get another supplier." If you're from the United States, this is probably just what you'd do. But if you're from Thailand,

Indonesia, or Malaysia, chances are good that you'd simply accept the situation as fate and allow the project to be delayed.

In other words, to the American, Canadian, or Western European manager, the situation may be perceived as a problem in need of a decision, whereas no such problem would be recognized by Thai, Indonesian, or Malaysian managers. Thus, as basic as it seems that decision making begins with recognizing that a problem exists, it is important to note that not all people are likely to perceive the same situations as problems.

Cultures also differ with respect to the nature of the decision-making unit they typically employ. In the United States, for example, where people tend to be highly individualistic, individual decisions are commonly made. However, in more collectivist cultures, such as Japan, it would be considered inconceivable for someone to make a decision without first gaining the acceptance of his or her immediate colleagues.

Similarly, there exist cultural differences with respect to *who* is expected to make decisions. In Sweden, for example, it is traditional for employees at all levels to be involved in the decisions affecting them. This is so much the case, in fact, that Swedes may totally ignore an organizational hierarchy and contact whomever is needed to make a decision, however high-ranking that individual may be. However, in India, where autocratic decision making is expected, it would he considered a sign of weakness for a manager to consult a subordinate about a decision.

Another cultural difference in decision making has to do with the amount of time taken to make a decision. For example, in the United States, one mark of a good decision maker is that he or she is "decisive," willing to take on an important decision and make it without delay. However, in some other cultures, time urgency is downplayed. In Egypt, for example, the more important the matter, the more time the decision maker is expected to take in reaching a decision. Throughout the Middle East, reaching a decision quickly would be perceived as overly hasty.

As these examples illustrate, there exist some interesting differences in the ways people from various countries go about formulating and implementing decisions. Understanding such differences is an important first step toward developing appropriate strategies for conducting business at a global level.

Time Pressure: Making Decisions in Emergencies

An unavoidable fact of life in contemporary organizations is that people often have only limited amounts of time to make important decisions. The rapid pace with which businesses operate these days results in severe pressures to make decisions almost immediately. Among firefighters, emergency room doctors, and fighter pilots, it's clear that time is of the essence. But even those of us who toil in less dramatic settings also face the need to make good decisions quickly. The practice of thoroughly collecting information, carefully analyzing it, and then leisurely reviewing the alternatives is a luxury few modern decision makers can afford. In a recent survey, 77 percent of a broad cross section of managers polled felt that the number of decisions they were required to make each day has increased, and 43 percent reported that the time they can devote to making decisions has decreased. Often the result is that bad—and inevitably, costly—decisions are made.

Highly experienced experts, psychologists tell us, are able to make good decisions quickly because they draw on a wealth of experiences collected over the years. Whereas novices are very deliberate in their decision making, considering one option at a time, experts are able to make decisions quickly because they are able to assess the situations they face and compare them to experiences they have had earlier in their careers. They know what matters, what to look for, and what pitfalls to avoid. What is so often considered "gut instinct" is really nothing more than the wealth of accumulated experiences. The more experiences a person has from which to draw, the more effectively he or she can "size up" a situation and take appropriate action.

"Fine, but I'm not yet an expert," you may he thinking, "so what can I do to make good decisions under pressure?" The answer lies in emulating some of the things that experts do. These are as follows:

1. *Recognize your prime objectives.* Many organizations have cardinal rules by which they must live. Relying on these can help you make decisions quickly. Take the job of a newspaper editor, for example. The news has to get out quickly, but it also has to be right. With this in mind, editors at the *Washington Post* follow a "when in doubt, leave it out" policy. According to Mary Hadar, an assistant managing editor, "With that firmly in mind, my decision to run or not run a story becomes much easier."

2. *Rely on experts.* Although you might not be an expert, chances are good that your organization has an expert available to you to whom you can look for decisions. Tina Carlstrom is an institutional sales trader for Merrill Lynch. She's worked for eight years on the New York trading floor, where quick decisions often can mean the difference between making and losing millions of dollars. What does she do when a buying opportunity comes along for a company she doesn't know well? The key, she says, is knowing where to turn for quick answers. Fortunately, the large brokerage firm has experts on staff on whom she can rely for the information she needs to make quick decisions.

3. *Anticipate crises.* If you want to avoid crisis situations, anticipate them in advance. This way, should they occur, you already have an idea of how to respond. In other words, if you don't have the luxury of having experienced a situation from which you were able to learn, it's a good idea to anticipate and prepare for those situations in advance. For example, psychologists tell us that you can prepare for situations by rehearsing in advance. Imagine, for example, that you are a manager who has never had an encounter with a hostile employee. By practicing how to respond should you ever have to deal with a hostile employee, it becomes easier for you to jump into action if you ever confront one.

4. *Learn from mistakes.* The one thing on which you can count for sure is making mistakes. We all make mistakes at one time or another (often, far too many). Although they are inevitable, mistakes should not be dismissed. Rather, it's essential to learn from them. One thing that makes experts so effective is that they have made many mistakes from which they have learned valuable lessons. The key is to think of each poor decision you make as training for the next time.

Commercial airline pilots used to be taught to respond to crisis situations by following a "STAR" approach—**s**top, **t**hink, **a**nalyze, **r**espond. We now know better. Whether you are a pilot, a professor, or a president, you will have to make split-second decisions at one time or another, and these cannot be made in such a deliberate fashion. By following the suggestions we've outlined here, you will be better prepared to face whatever quick decisions you have to make.

How Are Individual Decisions Made?

Now that we have identified the types of decisions people make in organizations, we are prepared to consider the matter of how people go about making them. Perhaps you are thinking, "What do you mean? You just think things over and do what you think is best." Although this maybe true, you will see that there's a lot more to decision making than meets the eye. In fact, scientists have considered several different approaches to how individuals make decisions. Here we will review three of the most important ones.

The Rational-Economic Model: In Search of the Ideal Decision

rational decisions
Decisions that maximize the chance of attaining an individual's, group's, or organization's goals

rational-economic model The model of decision making according to which decision makers consider all possible alternatives to problems before selecting the optimal solution

We all like to think that we are "rational" people who make the best possible decisions. But what exactly does it mean to make a *rational* decision? Organizational scientists view **rational decisions** as ones that maximize the attainment of goals, whether they are the goals of a person, a group, or an entire organization. What would be the most rational way for an individual to go about making a decision? Economists interested in predicting market conditions and prices have relied on a **rational-economic model** of decision making, which assumes that decisions are optimal in every way. An economically rational decision maker will attempt to maximize his or her profits by systematically searching for the *optimal* solution to a problem. For this to occur, the decision maker must have complete and perfect information and be able to process all this information in an accurate and unbiased fashion.

In many respects, rational-economic decisions follow the same steps outlined in the analytical model of decision making presented earlier (see Figure 3.1). However, what makes the rational-economic approach special is that it calls for the decision maker to recognize *all* alternative courses of action (step 4) and to accurately and completely evaluate each one (step 5). It views decision makers as attempting to make *optimal* decisions.

Of course, the rational-economic approach to decision making does not fully appreciate the fallibility of the human decision maker. Based on the assumption that people have access to complete and perfect information and use it to make perfect decisions, the model can be considered a *normative* (also called *prescriptive*) approach—one that describes how decision makers ideally ought to behave so as to make the best possible decisions. It does not describe how decision makers actually behave in most circumstances. This task is undertaken by the next major approach to individual decision making, the *administrative model*.

The Administrative Model: The Limits of Human Rationality

As you know from your own experience, people generally do not act in a completely rational-economic manner. To illustrate this point, consider how a personnel department might select a new receptionist. After several applicants are interviewed, the personnel manager might choose the best candidate seen so far and stop interviewing. Had the manager been following a rational-economic model, he or she would have had to interview all possible candidates before deciding on the best one. However, by ending the search after finding a candidate who was good enough to do the job, the manager is using a much simpler approach.

The process used in this example characterizes an approach to decision making known as the **administrative model.** This conceptualization recognizes that decision makers may have a limited view of the problems confronting them. The number of solutions that can be recognized or implemented is limited by the capabilities of the decision maker and the available resources of the organization. Also, decision makers do not have perfect information about the consequences of their decisions, so they cannot tell which one is best.

How are decisions made according to the administrative model? Instead of considering all possible solutions, decision makers consider solutions as they become available. Then they decide on the first alternative that meets their criteria for acceptability. Thus, the decision maker selects a solution that may be just good enough, although not optimal. Such decisions are referred to as **satisficing decisions.** Of course, a satisficing decision is much easier to make than an optimal decision. In most decision-making situations, satisficing decisions are acceptable and are more likely to be made than optimal ones. The following analogy is used to compare the two types of decisions: *Making an optimal decision is like searching a haystack for the sharpest needle but making a satisficing decision is like searching a haystack for a needle just sharp enough with which to sew.*

As we have noted, it is often impractical for people to make completely optimal rational decisions. The administrative model recognizes the **bounded rationality** under which most organizational decision makers must operate. The idea is that people lack the cognitive skills required to formulate and solve highly complex business problems in a completely objective, rational way. In addition, decision makers limit their actions to those that fall within the bounds of current moral and ethical standards—that is, they use **bounded discretion.** So, although engaging in illegal activities, such as stealing, may optimize an organization's profits (at least in the short run), ethical considerations strongly discourage such actions.

It should not be surprising that the administrative model does a better job than the rational-economic model of describing how decision makers actually behave. The approach is said to be *descriptive* (also called *proscriptive*) in nature. This interest in examining the actual, imperfect behavior of decision makers, rather than specifying the ideal, economically rational behaviors that decision makers ought to engage in, lies at the heart of the distinction between the administrative and rational-economic models. Our point is not that decision makers do not want to behave rationally but that restrictions posed by the innate capabilities of the decision makers preclude making "perfect" decisions.

administrative model
A model of decision making that recognizes the *bounded rationality* that limits the making of optimally rational-economic decisions

satisficing decisions
Decisions made by selecting the first minimally acceptable alternative as it becomes available

bounded rationality
The major assumption of the administrative model that organizational, social, and human limitations lead to the making of *satisficing* rather than optimal decisions

bounded discretion
The tendency to restrict decision alternatives to those that fall within prevailing ethical standards

Image Theory: An Intuitive Approach to Decision Making

If you think about it, you'll probably realize that some, but certainly not all, decisions are made following the logical steps of the analytical model of decision making. Consider Elizabeth Barrett Browning's poetic question, "How do I love thee? Let me count the ways." It's unlikely that anyone would ultimately answer the question by carefully counting what one loves about another (although many such characteristics can be enumerated). Instead, a more intuitive-based decision making is likely, not only for matters of the heart but for a variety of important organizational decisions as well.

The point is that selecting the best alternative by weighing all the options is not always a major concern when making a decision. People also consider how various decision alternatives fit with their personal standards as well as their personal goals and plans. The best decision for one person might not be the best for someone else. In other words, people may make decisions in a more automatic, *intuitive* fashion than is traditionally recognized. Representative of this approach is **image theory.** This approach to decision making is summarized in Figure 3.4.

Image theory deals primarily with decisions about adopting a certain course of action (e.g., should the company develop a new product line?) or changing a current course of action (e.g., should the company drop a present product line?). According to the theory, people make adoption decisions on the basis of a simple two-step process. The first step is the *compatibility test,* a comparison of the degree to which a particular course of action is consistent with various images—particularly individual principles, current goals, and plans for the future. If any lack of compatibility exists with respect to these considerations, a rejection decision is made. If the compatibility test is passed, then the *profitability test* is carried out. That is, people consider the extent to which using various alternatives best fits their values, goals, and plans. The decision is then made to accept the best candidate. These tests are used within a certain *decision frame*—that is, with consideration of meaningful information about the decision context (such as past experiences). The

image theory A theory of decision making that recognizes that decisions are made in an automatic, intuitive fashion based on actions that best fit a person's individual principles, current goals, and plans for the future

FIGURE 3.4

Image Theory: An Overview and Example

According to image theory, decisions are made in a relatively automatic, intuitive fashion following the two steps outlined here.

SOURCE: Adapted from Beach & Mitchell, 1990; see Note 54.

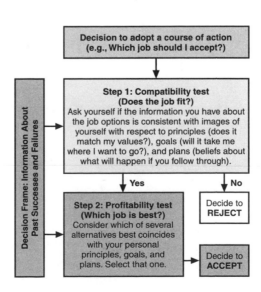

basic idea is that we learn from the past and are guided by it when making decisions. The example shown in Figure 3.4 highlights this contemporary approach to decision making.

According to image theory, the decision-making process is very rapid and simple. The theory suggests that people do not ponder and labor over decisions, but make them using an intuitive process with minimal cognitive processing. If you've ever found yourself saying that something "seemed like the right thing to do" or that something "doesn't feel right," you're probably well aware of the kind of intuitive thinking that goes on in a great deal of decision making. Recent research suggests that when it comes to making relatively simple decisions, people tend to behave as suggested by image theory. For example, it has been found that people decide against various options when past evidence suggests that these decisions may be incompatible with their images of the future.

To summarize, we have described three major approaches to decision making. The rational-economic approach represents the ideal way optimal decisions are made. However, the administrative model and image theory represent ways that people actually go about making decisions. Both approaches have received support, and neither should be seen as a replacement for the other. Instead, several different processes may be involved in decision making. Not all decision making is carried out the same way: Sometimes decision making might be analytical, and sometimes it might be more intuitive. Modern organizational behavior scholars recognize the value of both approaches. Something both approaches have in common is that they recognize the fallibility of the human decision maker. With this in mind, we will now turn our attention to the imperfect nature of individual decisions.

Imperfections in Individual Decisions

Let's face it, as a whole, people are less than perfect when it comes to making decisions. Mistakes are made all the time. Obviously, people have limited capacities to process information accurately and thoroughly like a computer. For example, we often focus on irrelevant information in making decisions. We also fail to use all the information made available to us, in part because we may forget some of it. Beyond these general limitations in human information-processing capacity, we may note several systematic biases—factors that contribute to the imperfect nature of people's decisions. These variables reside not only within individuals themselves but also the organizations within which we operate. We will now examine several major factors contributing to the imperfect nature of individual decisions.

Framing Effects

framing The tendency for people to make different decisions based on how the problem is presented to them

Have you ever found yourself changing your mind about something because of how someone explained it to you? If so, you might have said something such as, "Now that you put it that way. I agree." This may sound familiar to you because it describes a well-established decision-making bias known as **framing**—the tendency for people to make different decisions based on how the problem is presented to them. Scientists have identified three different forms of framing effects that occur when people make decisions.

Risky Choice Frames. For many years, scientists have noted that when problems are framed in a manner that emphasizes the positive gains to be received, people tend to shy away from taking risks and go for the sure thing (i.e., decision makers are said to be *risk averse*). However, when problems are framed in a manner that emphasizes the potential losses to be suffered, people are more willing to take risks so as to avoid those losses (i.e., decision makers are said to make *risk-seeking* decisions). This is known as the **risky choice framing effect**. To illustrate this phenomenon consider the following example:

> The government is preparing to combat a rare disease expected to take 600 lives. Two alternative programs to combat the disease have been proposed, each of which, scientists believe, will have certain consequences. *Program A* will save 200 people if adopted. *Program B* has a one-third chance of saving all 600 people, but a two-thirds chance of saving no one. Which program do you prefer?

When such a problem was presented to people, 72 percent expressed a preference for Program A and 28 percent for Program B. In other words, they preferred the "sure thing" of saving 200 people over the one-third possibility of saving them all. However, a curious thing happened when the description of the programs was framed in negative terms. Specifically:

> *Program C* was described as allowing 400 people to die if adopted. *Program D* was described as allowing a one-third probability that no one would die, and a two-thirds probability that all 600 would die. Now, which program would you prefer?

Compare these four programs. Program C is just another way of stating the outcomes of Program A, and Program D is just another way of stating the outcomes of Program B. However, Programs C and D are framed in negative terms, which led to opposite preferences: 22 percent favored Program C and 78 percent favored Program D. In other words, people tended to avoid risk when the problem was framed in terms of "lives saved" (i.e., in positive terms) but to seek risk when the problem was framed in terms of "lives lost" (i.e., in negative terms). This classic effect has been replicated in several studies.

Attribute Framing. Risky choice frames involve making decisions about which course of action is preferred. However, the same basic idea applies to situations not involving risk but involving evaluations. Suppose, for example, you're walking down the meat aisle of your local supermarket when you spot a package of ground beef labeled "75% lean." Of course, if the same package were to say "25% fat," you would know exactly the same thing. However, you probably wouldn't perceive that to be the case. In fact, consumer marketing research has shown that people rated the same sample of ground beef as being better tasting and less greasy when it was framed with respect to a positive attribute (i.e., 75% lean) than when it was framed with respect to a negative attribute (i.e., 25% fat).

Although this example is easy to relate to, its generalizability goes way beyond product evaluation situations. In fact, the **attribute framing effect** occurs in a

risky choice framing effect The tendency for people to avoid risks when situations are presented in a way that emphasizes positive gains and to take risks when situations are presented in a way that emphasizes potential losses that may be suffered

attribute framing effect The tendency for people to evaluate a characteristic more positively when it is presented in positive terms than when it is presented in negative terms

wide variety of organizational settings. In other words, people evaluate the same characteristic more positively when it is described in positive terms than when it is described in negative terms. Take performance evaluation, for example. In this context, people whose performance is framed in positive terms (e.g., percentage of shots made by a basketball player) tend to be evaluated more positively than those whose identical performance is framed in negative terms (e.g., percentage of shots missed by that same basketball player).

Goal Framing. A third type of framing, goal framing, focuses on an important question: When attempting to persuade someone to do something, is it more effective to focus on the positive consequences of doing it or the negative consequences of not doing it? For example, suppose you are attempting to get women to engage in self-examination of their breasts to check for signs of cancer. You may frame the desired behavior in positive terms:

> "Research shows that women who *do* breast self-examinations have an *increased* chance of finding a tumor in the early, more treatable stages of the disease."

Or you may frame it in negative terms:

> "Research shows that women who *do not* do breast self-examinations have a *decreased* chance of finding a tumor in the early, more treatable stages of the disease."

Which approach is more effective? Research has shown that women are more likely to engage in breast self-examination when presented with the consequences of not doing it rather than the benefits of doing it. This is an example of the **goal framing effect** in action. According to this phenomenon, people are more strongly persuaded by the negatively framed information than by the positively framed information.

A General Note about Framing. The three kinds of framing we have described here, although similar in several key ways, are also quite different. Specifically they focus on different types of behavior preferences for risk in the case of *risky choice framing,* evaluations of characteristics in the case of *attribute framing,* and taking behavioral action in the case of *goal framing.* For a summary of these three effects, see Figure 3.5.

Scientists believe that framing effects are due to the tendency for people to perceive equivalent situations framed differently as not really equivalent. In other words, focusing on the glass as "half full" leads people to think about it differently than when it is presented as being "half empty," although they might recognize intellectually that the two are really the same. Such findings illustrate our point that people are not completely rational decision makers, but are systematically biased by the cognitive distortions created by simple differences in the way situations are framed.

Reliance on Heuristics

Framing effects are not the only cognitive biases to which decision makers are subjected. It also has been established that people often attempt to simplify the complex decisions they face by using **heuristics**—simple rules of thumb that guide them through a complex array of decision alternatives. Although heuristics

goal framing effect The tendency for people to be more strongly persuaded by information that is framed in negative terms than information that is framed in positive terms

heuristics Simple decision rules (rules of thumb) used to make quick decisions about complex problems (see *availability heuristic* and *representativeness heuristic*)

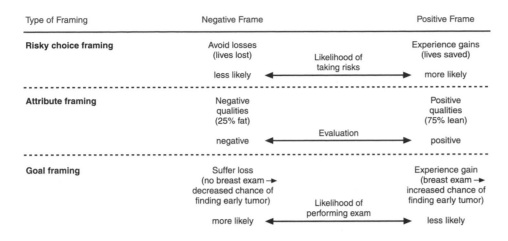

Type of Framing	Negative Frame		Positive Frame
Risky choice framing	Avoid losses (lives lost)	Likelihood of taking risks	Experience gains (lives saved)
	less likely	←————————→	more likely
Attribute framing	Negative qualities (25% fat)	Evaluation	Positive qualities (75% lean)
	negative	←————————→	positive
Goal framing	Suffer loss (no breast exam → decreased chance of finding early tumor)	Likelihood of performing exam	Experience gain (breast exam → increased chance of finding early tumor)
	more likely	←————————→	less likely

FIGURE 3.5
Framing Effects: A Summary of Three Types

Information presented (i.e., framed) negatively is perceived differently than the same information presented positively. This takes the three different forms summarized here—*risky choice framing, attribute framing,* and *goal framing.*

SOURCE: Based on suggestions by Levin et al., 1998; see Note 59.

are potentially useful to decision makers, they represent potential impediments to decision making. Two very common types of heuristics may be identified.

availability heuristic
The tendency for people to base their judgments on information that is readily available to them although it may be potentially inaccurate, thereby adversely affecting decision quality

The Availability Heuristic. The **availability heuristic** refers to the tendency for people to base judgments on information that is readily available to them—even though it might not be accurate. Suppose, for example, that an executive needs to know the percentage of entering college freshmen who go on to graduate. There is not enough time to gather the appropriate statistics, so she bases her judgments on her own recollections of when she was a college student. If the percentage she recalls graduating, based on her own experiences, is higher or lower than the usual number, her estimate will be off accordingly. In other words, basing judgments solely on information that is conveniently available increases the possibility of making inaccurate decisions. Yet, the availability heuristic is often used when making decisions.

representativeness heuristic The tendency to perceive others in stereotypical ways if they appear to be typical representatives of the category to which they belong

The Representativeness Heuristic. The **representativeness heuristic** refers to the tendency to perceive others in stereotypical ways if they appear to be typical representatives of the category to which they belong. For example, suppose you believe that accountants are bright, mild-mannered individuals, whereas salespeople are less intelligent but much more extroverted. Furthermore, imagine that there are twice as many salespeople as accountants at a party. You meet someone at the party who is bright and mild-mannered. Although mathematically the odds are two-to-one that this person is a salesperson rather than an accountant, you are likely to guess that the individual is an accountant because she possesses the traits you associate with accountants. In other words, you believe this person to be representative of accountants in general—so much so that you would knowingly go against the mathematical odds in making your judgment. Research consistently has found that people tend to make this type of error in judgment, thereby providing good support for the existence of the representativeness heuristic.

The Helpful Side of Heuristics. It is important to note that heuristics do not *always* deteriorate the quality of decisions made. In fact, they can be quite helpful. People often use rules of thumb to help simplify the complex decisions they face. For example, management scientists employ many useful heuristics to aid decisions regarding such matters as where to locate warehouses or how to compose an investment portfolio. We also use heuristics in our everyday lives, such as when we play chess ("control the center of the board") or blackjack ("hit on 16, stick on 17").

However, the representativeness heuristic and the availability heuristic may be recognized as impediments to superior decisions because they discourage people from collecting and processing as much information as they should. Making judgments on the basis of only readily available information or on stereotypical beliefs, although making things simple for the decision maker, does so at the potentially high cost of poor decisions. Thus, these systematic biases represent potentially serious impediments to individual decision making.

The Inherently Biased Nature of Individual Decisions

As individuals, we make imperfect decisions not only because of our overreliance on heuristics but also because of certain inherent biases we bring to the various decision-making situations we face. Among the several biases people have when making decisions, four have received special attention by OB scientists—the *bias toward implicit favorites,* the *hindsight bias,* the *person sensitivity bias,* and the *escalation of commitment bias.*

Bias Toward Implicit Favorites

Don was about to receive his M.B.A. This was going to be his big chance to move to San Francisco, the city by the bay. Don had long dreamed of living there, and his first "real" job, he hoped, was going to he his ticket. As the corporate recruiters made their annual migration to campus, Don eagerly signed up for several interviews. One of the first was Baxter, Marsh, and Hidalgo, a medium-size consulting firm in San Francisco. The salary was right and the people seemed pleasant, a combination that excited Don very much. Apparently the interest was mutual; soon Don was offered a position.

Does the story end here? Not quite. It was only March, and Don felt he shouldn't jump at the first job to come along, even though he really wanted it. So, to do "the sensible thing," he signed up for more interviews. Shortly thereafter, Sping and Feu, a local firm, made Don a more attractive offer. Not only was the salary higher but also there was every indication that the job promised a much brighter future than the one in San Francisco.

What would he do? Actually, Don didn't consider it much of a dilemma. After thinking it over, he came to the conclusion that the work at Sping and Feu was much too low level—not enough exciting clients to challenge him. And the starting salary wasn't really all *that* much better than it was at Baxter, Marsh, and Hidalgo. The day after graduation, Don was packing for his new office overlooking the Golden Gate Bridge.

Do you think the way Don made his decision was atypical? He seemed to have his mind made up in advance about the job in San Francisco and didn't really give the other one a chance. Research suggests that people make decisions in this way all the time. That is, people tend to pick an **implicit favorite** option (i.e., a preferred alternative) very early in the decision-making process. Then, the other options they consider subsequently are not given serious consideration. Rather, the other options are merely used to convince themselves that the implicit favorite is indeed the best choice. An alternative considered for this purpose is known as a **confirmation candidate.** It is not unusual to find that people psychologically distort their beliefs about confirmation candidates so as to justify selecting their implicit favorites. Don did this when he convinced himself that the job offered by the local firm really wasn't as good as it seemed.

Research has shown that people make decisions very early in the decision process. For example, in one study of the job recruitment process, investigators found that they could predict 87 percent of the jobs that students would take as early as two months before the students acknowledged that they actually had made a decision. Apparently, people's decisions are biased by the tendency for them to not consider all the relevant information available to them. In fact, they tend to bias their judgments of the strengths and weaknesses of various alternatives so as to make them fit their already-made decision, their implicit favorite. This phenomenon clearly suggests that people not only fail to consider all possible alternatives when making decisions but also that they even fail to consider all readily available alternatives. Instead, they tend to make up their minds very early and convince themselves that they are right. As you might imagine, this bias toward implicit favorites is likely to severely limit the quality of decisions that are made.

Hindsight Bias

"Hindsight is 20-20" is a phrase commonly heard. It means that when we look back on decisions that already were made, we know better what we should have done. Indeed, research has revealed that this phenomenon is quite pervasive. For example, studies have shown that people tend to distort the way they see things so as to conform to what they already know about the past. This effect, known as the **hindsight bias,** refers to the tendency for people to perceive outcomes as more inevitable after they occurred (i.e., in hindsight) than they did before they occurred (i.e., in foresight). Hindsight bias occurs when people believe that they could have predicted past events better than they actually did—that is, when they say they "knew it all along."

The hindsight bias occurs because people feel good about being able to judge things accurately. As such, we may expect that people will be more willing to say that they expected events from the past to have occurred whenever these are positive about themselves or their work team but not when these events are negative. After all, we look good when we can take credit for predicting successes, but we

implicit favorite One's preferred decision alternative, selected even before all options have been considered

confirmation candidate A decision alternative considered only for purposes of convincing oneself of the wisdom of selecting the *implicit favorite*

hindsight bias The tendency for people to perceive outcomes as more inevitable after they have occurred (i.e., in hindsight) than they did before they occurred (i.e., in foresight)

look bad when we anticipated negative outcomes without doing anything to stop them. Indeed, recent research has shown precisely this. This qualification of the hindsight bias may have important effects on the way people make decisions.

Let's consider an example. During the 1970s, a group of public utilities known as the Washington Public Power Supply System (WPPSS) made plans to build seven nuclear power plants in an effort to meet the need for energy, estimated as growing by 7 percent each year. Through the early 1980s, 27,000 investors bought bonds to support this project. As things worked out, however, consumers found ways to conserve energy as energy prices rose, resulting in far smaller increases in energy demands than anticipated. As a result, only one of the seven planned power plants was ever completed, and in 1983, the WPPSS defaulted on bonds valued at $2.25 billion. When investors sued, they claimed that the WPPSS "should have known" that the demand for energy was going to change, thereby precluding the need for the power plants. In other words, they were biased such that they saw the decision to invest in ways that made themselves look good and the WPSS look bad. Likewise, officials from the WPPSS claimed that they had no way of anticipating the changes the future was going to bring, therefore justifying their decision to raise money and build power plants as a wise one.

Person Sensitivity Bias

person sensitivity bias
The tendency for people to give others too little credit when things are going poorly and too much credit when things are going well

When President George W. Bush first took office in January 2001, it followed a highly controversial election that some don't believe he won fairly and squarely. Many disapproved of his foreign policy, claiming that he was ill-suited to the position. Then, only eight months later, following the terrorist attacks on New York and Washington, DC, President Bush unified the country with impassioned speeches that sent his approval ratings into the stratosphere. His stance with respect to foreign policy was now widely praised. This mini history lesson nicely illustrates an interesting aspect of human nature (beyond the fickle nature of politics, that is): When things are going poorly, nobody likes you, but when things are going well, everyone's your friend. Scientists refer to this as **person sensitivity bias.** Formally, this refers to the tendency for people to blame others too much when things are going poorly and to give them too much credit when things are going well.

Evidence for the person sensitivity bias has been reported in an interesting experiment that was conducted recently. Participants in the study were people asked to judge the performance of either individuals who staffed an assembly line or machines that performed the same assembly task. The people or the machines also were described either as exceeding the company standards or not meeting them. When people were said to be responsible for exceeding the standards, they were perceived more positively than machines that also exceeded the standard. However, when the standards were not met, participants judged other people more harshly than the machines (see Figure 3.6). These findings are in keeping with both the positive and negative aspects of the person sensitivity bias.

The person sensitivity bias is important insofar as it suggests that the decisions we make about others are not likely to be completely objective. As people, we need to understand others and it makes things easier for us if we keep our perceptions consistent: What's good is very good; what's bad is very bad. With such a bias underlying our judgments of others, it's little wonder that the decisions we

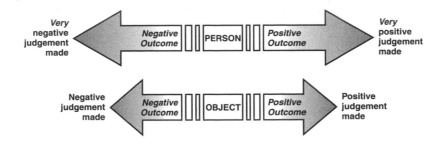

FIGURE 3.6
Person Sensitivity Bias: An Overview

According to the person sensitivity bias, we are likely to blame people too much when things are going poorly and to give them too much credit when thing are going well. Accordingly, the same positive decision outcomes are perceived as being more positive when caused by people than by objects, such as machines. Likewise, equally negative decision outcomes are perceived as being more negative when caused by people than by objects.

SOURCE: Based on suggestions by Moon & Conlon, 2002; see Note 74.

make about them may be highly imperfect. After all, to the extent that effective decisions rely on accurate information, biases such as the person sensitivity bias predispose us to perceive others in less than objective ways.

Escalation of Commitment Bias

Because decisions are made all the time in organizations, some of these inevitably will be unsuccessful. What would you say is the rational thing to do when a poor decision has been made? Obviously, the ineffective action should be stopped or reversed. In other words, it would make sense to "cut your losses and run." However, people don't always respond in this manner. In fact, it is not unusual to find that ineffective decisions are sometimes followed up with still further ineffective decisions.

Imagine, for example, that you have invested money in a company, but the company appears to be failing. Rather than lose your initial investment, you may invest still more money in the hope of salvaging your first investment. The more you invest, the more you may be tempted to protect those earlier investments by making later investments. That is to say, people sometimes may be found "throwing good money after bad" because they have "too much invested to quit." This is known as the **escalation of commitment phenomenon**—the tendency for people to continue to support previously unsuccessful courses of action because they have sunk costs invested in them.

escalation of commitment phenomenon The tendency for individuals to continue to support previously unsuccessful courses of action

Although this might not seem like a rational thing to do, this strategy is frequently followed. For example, Motorola has invested over $1.3 billion in its Iridium Satellite System, a network of 66 low-orbiting communication satellites that make it possible to make wireless telephone calls from anywhere on earth. In recent years, however, it has become clear that the system has serious technical limitations. Moreover, the service has failed to attract as many subscribers as expected. And now Motorola is beginning to face competition from other major companies. Instead of accepting its losses and walking away from the project,

Motorola officials are investing still more in the Iridium project, hoping that each successive dollar invested will be the one needed to turn the project around to make it profitable.

Why do people do this? If you think about it, you may realize that the failure to back your own previous courses of action in an organization would be taken as an admission of failure—a politically difficult act to face in an organization. In other words, people may be very concerned about "saving face"—looking good in the eyes of others and oneself. Researchers have recognized that this tendency for *self-justification* is primarily responsible for people's inclination to protect their beliefs about themselves as rational, competent decision makers by convincing themselves and others that they made the right decision all along and are willing to back it up. Although there are other possible reasons for the escalation of commitment phenomenon, research supports the self-justification explanation. For a summary of the escalation of commitment phenomenon, see Figure 3.7.

Researchers have noted several conditions under which people will refrain from escalating their commitment to a failing course of action. Notably, it has been found that people will stop making failing investments under conditions in which the *available fiords for making further investments are limited* and when the *threat of failure is overwhelmingly obvious.* For example, when the Long Island Lighting Company decided in 1989 to abandon plans to operate a nuclear power plant in Shoreham, New York, it was in the face of 23 years' worth of intense political and financial pressure (a strong antinuclear movement and billions of dollars of cost overruns).

It also has been found that people will refrain from escalating commitment when they can *diffuse their responsibility for the earlier failing actions.* That is, the more people feel they are just one of several individuals responsible for a failing course of action, the less likely they are to commit to further failing actions. In other words, the less one is responsible for an earlier failure, the less one may be motivated to justify those earlier failures by making further investments in them.

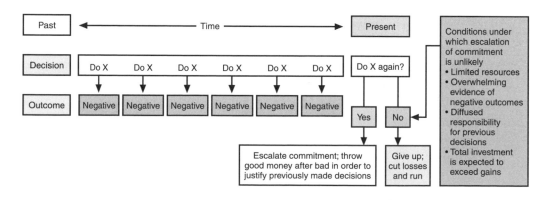

FIGURE 3.7

Escalation of Commitment: An Overview

According to the escalation of commitment phenomenon, people who have repeatedly made poor decisions continue to support those failing courses of action to justify their earlier decisions. Under some conditions, however, as summarized here, this effect will not occur.

Third, escalation of commitment toward a losing course of action will be low in organizations in which the people who have made ineffective decisions have left and are replaced by others who are not linked to those decisions. In other words, *turnover* lessens an organization's commitment to a losing course of action. Illustrating this, recent research has shown that although some banks continue to make bad (i.e., uncollectible) loans to customers to whom they have loaned money in the past, this is less likely to occur in banks whose top executives (individuals who are considered responsible for those loans) have left their posts.

Finally, it has been found that people are unwilling to escalate commitment to a course of action when it is made clear that the *total amount invested exceeds the amount expected to be gained.* Although people may wish to invest in projects that enable them to recoup their initial investments, there is little reason for them to do so when it is obvious that doing so will be a losing proposition. Under such conditions, it is difficult to justify doing so, even if one "hopes against hope" that it will work out. Indeed, research has shown that decision makers do indeed refrain from escalating commitment to decisions when it is made clear that the overall benefit to be gained is less than the overall costs to be borne. This finding was more apparent among students with accounting backgrounds than those without such backgrounds, presumably because their training predisposed them to be more sensitive to these issues.

To conclude, the escalation of commitment phenomenon represents a type of irrational decision making that has the potential to occur. However, whether or not it does occur will depend on the various circumstances that decision makers confront.

Group Decisions: Do Too Many Cooks Spoil the Broth?

Decision-making groups are a well-established fact of modern organizational life. Groups such as committees, study teams, task forces, or review panels often are charged with the responsibility for making important business decisions. They are so common, in fact, that it has been said that some administrators spend as much as 80 percent of their time in committee meetings.

In view of this, it is important to ask how well groups do at making decisions compared to individuals. Given the several advantages and disadvantages of having groups make decisions we described earlier, this question is particularly important. Specifically, we may ask: Under what conditions might individuals or groups be expected to make superior decisions? Fortunately, research provides us with some concrete answers.

When Are Groups Superior to Individuals?

Whether groups will do better than individuals or worse than individuals depends on the nature of the task. Specifically, any advantages that groups may have over individuals will depend on how complex or simple the task is.

Complex Decision Tasks. Imagine a situation in which an important decision has to be made about a complex problem—such as whether one company should merge with another. This is not the kind of problem about which any one individual working alone would be able to make a good decision. After all, its highly complex nature may overwhelm even an expert, thereby setting the stage for a group to do a better job. Naturally, groups may excel in such situations.

However, this doesn't happen automatically. In fact, for groups to outperform individuals, several conditions must exist. First, we must consider who is in the group. Successful groups tend to be composed of *heterogeneous group members with complementary skills*. So, for example, a group composed of lawyers, accountants, real estate agents, and other experts may make much better decisions on the merger problem than would a group composed of specialists in only one field. Indeed, research has shown that the diversity of opinions offered by group members is one of the major advantages of using groups to make decisions.

As you might imagine, it is not enough simply to have skills. For a group to be successful, its members also must be able to communicate their ideas to each other freely—in an open, nonhostile manner. Conditions under which one individual (or group) intimidates another from contributing his or her expertise easily can negate any potential gain associated with composing groups of heterogeneous experts. After all, having expertise and being able to make a contribution by *using* that expertise are two different things. Indeed, research has shown that only when the contributions of the most qualified group members are given the greatest weight does the group derive any benefit from that member's presence. Thus, *for groups to be superior to individuals, they must be composed of a heterogeneous collection of experts with complementary skills who can freely and openly contribute to their group's product.*

Simple Decision Tasks. In contrast to complex decision tasks, imagine a situation in which a judgement is required on a simple problem with a readily verifiable answer. For example, make believe that you are asked to translate a phrase from a relatively obscure language into English.

Groups might do better than individuals on such a task because the odds are increased that someone in the group knows the language and can perform the translation for the group. However, there is no reason to expect that even a large group will be able to perform such a task better than a single individual who has the required expertise. In fact, an expert working alone may do even better than a group. This is because an expert individual performing a simple task may be distracted by others and suffer from having to convince them of the correctness of his or her solution. For this reason, exceptional individuals tend to outperform entire committees on simple tasks. In such cases, for groups to benefit from a pooling of resources, there must be some resources to pool. The pooling of ignorance does not help.

In sum, the question, "Are two heads better than one?" can be answered this way: *On simple tasks, two heads may be better than one if at least one of those heads has in it enough of what it takes to succeed.* Thus, whether groups perform better than individuals depends on the nature of the task performed and the expertise of the people involved. We have summarized some of these key considerations in Figure 3.8.

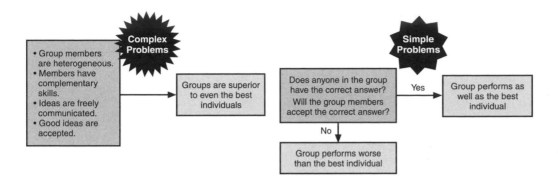

FIGURE 3.8
When Are Group Decisions Superior to Individual Decisions?

When performing complex problems, groups are superior to individuals if certain conditions prevail (e.g., when members have heterogeneous and complementary skills, when they can freely share ideas, and when their good ideas are accepted by others). However, when performing simple problems, groups perform only as well as the best individual group member—and then, only if that person has the correct answer and if that answer is accepted by others in the group.

When Are Individuals Superior to Groups?

As we have described thus far, groups may be expected to perform better than the average or even the exceptional individual under certain conditions. However, there also are conditions under which individuals are superior to groups.

Most of the problems faced by organizations require a great deal of creative thinking. For example, a company deciding how to use a newly developed adhesive in its consumer products is facing decisions on a poorly structured task. Although you would expect that the complexity of such creative problems would give groups a natural advantage, this is not the case. In fact, research has shown that *on poorly structured, creative tasks, individuals perform better than groups.*

brainstorming A technique designed to foster group productivity by encouraging interacting group members to express their ideas in a noncritical fashion

An approach to solving creative problems commonly used by groups is **brainstorming.** This technique was developed by an advertising executive as a tool for coming up with creative, new ideas. The members of brainstorming groups are encouraged to present their ideas in an uncritical way and to discuss freely and openly all ideas on the floor. Specifically, members of brainstorming groups are required to follow four main rules:

1. Avoid criticizing others' ideas.
2. Share even far-out suggestions.
3. Offer as many comments as possible.
4. Build on others' ideas to create your own.

Does brainstorming improve the quality of creative decisions? To answer this question, researchers compared the effectiveness of individuals and brainstorming groups working on creative problems. Specifically participants were given 35 minutes to consider the consequences of situations such as "What if everybody went blind?" or "What if everybody grew an extra thumb on each hand?" Clearly, the novel nature of such problems requires a great deal of creativity. Comparisons were made of the number of solutions generated by groups of four or seven people and a like number of individuals working on the same problems alone. The results were clear: Individuals were significantly more productive than groups.

In summary, groups perform worse than individuals when working on creative tasks. A great part of the problem is that some individuals feel inhibited by the presence of others even though one rule of brainstorming is that even far-out ideas may be shared. To the extent that people wish to avoid feeling foolish as a result of saying silly things, their creativity may be inhibited when in groups. Similarly, groups may inhibit creativity by slowing down the process of bringing ideas to fruition. Yet, many creative professionals strongly believe in the power of brainstorming. For some suggestions on how to reap the benefits of brainstorming, see Table 3.3.

Traditional Techniques for Improving the Effectiveness of Decisions

As we have made clear in this chapter, certain advantages can be gained from sometimes using individuals and sometimes using groups to make decisions. A decision-making technique that combines the best features of groups and individuals, while minimizing the disadvantages, would be ideal. Several techniques designed to realize the "best of both worlds" have been widely used in organizations. These include techniques that involve the structuring of group discussions in special ways. An even more basic approach to improving the effectiveness of group decisions involves training decision makers in ways of avoiding some of the pitfalls of group decision mating. We will begin this section of the chapter with a discussion of this training approach to improving group decisions and then go on to consider various ways of creating specially-structured groups.

Techniques for Improving Individual Decision Making

One of the oldest ways of improving the quality of individual decisions is by training people in specific techniques they can use to avoid some of the pitfalls inherent in decision making. Some of the most widely used techniques involve training people to improve group performance and also training them to avoid ethical pitfalls.

Training Individuals to Improve Group Performance. Earlier in this chapter we noted that how well groups solve problems depends in part on the composition of those groups. If at least one group member is capable of coming up with a solution, groups may benefit by that individual's expertise. Based on this reasoning, it follows that the more qualified individual group members are to solve problems, the better their groups as a whole will perform. What, then, might individuals do to improve the nature of the decisions they make?

TABLE 3.3 Tips for Using Brainstorming Successfully

The rules of brainstorming are simple enough, but doing it effectively is not as easy as it seems. Many brainstorming sessions fail because people don't fully appreciate the finer points of how to conduct them. Following these guidelines will help make your own brainstorming sessions more effective.

Suggestion	Explanation
Brainstorm frequently at least once per month.	Practice makes perfect. The more frequently people engage in brainstorming, the more comfortable they are with it—hence, the more effective it becomes.
Keep brainstorming sessions brief, less than an hour in length.	Brainstorming effectively can be very exhausting, so limit the time dedicated to it. After about an hour, people become too inefficient to make it worthwhile to continue.
Focus on the problem at hand.	The best brainstorming sessions begin with a clear statement of the problem at hand. These shouldn't be too broad or too narrow.
Don't forget to "build" and "jump."	The best ideas to result from brainstorming sessions are those that build on other ideas. Everyone should be strongly encouraged to jump from one idea to another as they build on the earlier one.
Prepare for the session.	Brainstorming is much more effective when people prepare in advance by reading up on the topic than when they come in "cold."
Don't limit yourself to words—use props.	Some of the most effective brainstorming sessions result when people introduce objects to help model their ideas.

SOURCE: Based on suggestions by Kelley, 2001; see Note 96.

Researchers looking into this question have found that people tend to make four types of mistakes when attempting to make creative decisions and that they make better decisions when trained to avoid these errors. Specifically, these are as follows:

hypervigilance The state in which an individual frantically searches for quick solutions to problems and goes from one idea to another out of a sense of desperation that one idea isn't working and that another needs to be considered before time runs out

1. *Hypervigilance.* The state of **hypervigilance** involves frantically searching for quick solutions to problems, going from one idea to another out of a sense of desperation that one idea isn't working and that another needs to be considered before time runs out. A poor, "last chance" solution may be adopted to relieve anxiety. This problem may be avoided by keeping in mind that it is best to stick with one suggestion and work it out thoroughly and reassuring the person solving the problem that his or her level of skill and education is adequate to perform the task at hand. In other words, a little reassurance may go a long way toward keeping individuals on the right track and avoiding the problem of hypervigilance.

unconflicted adherence The tendency for decision makers to stick to the first idea that comes to their minds without more deeply evaluating the consequences

2. *Unconflicted adherence.* Many decision makers make the mistake of sticking to the first idea that comes into their heads without more deeply evaluating the consequences, a mistake known as **unconflicted adherence.** As a result, such people are unlikely to become aware of any problems associated with their ideas or to consider other possibilities. To avoid *unconflicted adherence,* decision makers are urged (1) to think about the difficulties associated with their ideas, (2) to force themselves to consider different

unconflicted change
The tendency for people to quickly change their minds and to adopt the first new idea to come along

defensive avoidance
The tendency for decision makers to fail to solve problems because they go out of their way to avoid working on the problem at hand

ideas, and (3) to consider the special and unique characteristics of the problem they are facing and avoid carrying over assumptions from previous problems.

3. *Unconflicted change.* Sometimes people are very quick to change their minds and adopt the first new idea to come along—a problem known as **unconflicted change.** To avoid unconflicted change, decision makers are encouraged to ask themselves about (1) the risks and problems of adopting that solution, (2) the good points of the first idea, and (3) the relative strengths and weaknesses of both ideas.

4. *Defensive avoidance.* Too often, decision makers fail to solve problems effectively because they go out of their way to avoid working on the task at hand. This is known as **defensive avoidance.** People can do three things to minimize this problem. First, they should attempt to *avoid procrastination.* Don't put off the problem indefinitely just because you cannot come up with a solution right away. Continue to budget some of your time on even the most frustrating problems. Second, *avoid disowning responsibility.* It is easy to minimize the importance of a problem by saying "It doesn't matter, so who cares?" Avoid giving up so soon. Finally, *don't ignore potentially corrective information.* It is tempting to put your nagging doubts about the quality of a solution to rest in order to be finished with it. Good decision makers would not do so. Rather, they use their doubts to test and potentially improve the quality of their ideas.

It is encouraging to note that people make better-quality decisions just by merely considering these four pitfalls. How well groups perform depends to a great extent on the problem-solving skills of the individual group members. And attempting to avoid the four major pitfalls described here appears to be an effective method of improving individual decision-making skills—and, hence, the quality of group decisions.

Making Ethical Decisions. Although the suggestions we just outlined may help individuals come up with decisions that are improved in many key ways, they may not help people make decisions that are any more ethical. And this is an important consideration, too. After all, considering the Enron-Arthur Andersen scandal, it's easy to see that people often have difficulty judging what's right and behaving accordingly. Unfortunately, stealing in the workplace has become far more commonplace than we would like. However, the pursuit of quality in organizations demands that everyone adheres to the highest moral standards.

The problem with this ideal is that even those of us who subscribe to high moral values sometimes are tempted to behave unethically. If you're thinking, "other people act unethically; but not me," then ask yourself: Have you ever taken home small articles of company property (e.g., pencils, tape) for personal use? Or have you ever made personal copies on the company copier, or fudged a little on your expense account?

If the answer is yes, you may be saying, "Sure, but companies *expect* employees to do these things." And, besides, everyone does it. Although this may be true, we cannot ignore the fact that people often attempt to justify their actions by rationalizing that they are not really unethical. This is especially the case when someone does something that may be seen as unethical, except for the fact that the others with whom we work convince us that it's really okay. This kind of rationalization makes it possible for us to talk ourselves into making unethical decisions, thinking that they are really not so bad. To avoid such situations—and thereby to improve ethical decision making—it may be useful to run your contemplated decisions through an ethics test. To do so, ask yourself the following questions.

1. *Does it violate the obvious "Shall nots"?* Although many people realize that "thou shall not lie, or cheat, or steal," they do it anyway. So, instead of thinking of a way around such prohibitions (e.g., by convincing yourself that "it's acceptable in this situation'), avoid violating these well-established societal rules altogether.

2. *Will anyone get hurt?* Philosophers consider an action to be ethical to the extent that it brings the greatest good to the greatest number. Thus, if someone may be harmed in any way as a result of your actions, you should probably rethink your decision; it's probably unethical.

3. *How would you feel if your decision was reported on the front page of your newspaper?* If your decision is really ethical, you wouldn't have any reason to worry about having it made public. (In fact, you'd probably be pleased to receive the publicity.) However, if you find yourself uneasy about answering this question affirmatively, the decision you are contemplating may be unethical.

4. *What if you did it 100 times?* Sometimes an unethical action doesn't seem so bad because it's done only once. In such a case, the damage might not be so bad, although the action still might not be ethical. However, if the act you're contemplating appears to be more wrong if it were done 100 times, then it's probably also wrong the first time.

5. *How would you feel if someone did it to you?* If something you are thinking of doing to another really is ethical, you would probably find it acceptable if your situations were reversed. Thus, if you have any doubts as to how you'd feel being the person affected by your decision, you may wish to reconsider.

6. *What's your gut feeling?* Sometimes things just look bad—probably because they are. If your actions are unethical, you probably can tell by listening to that little voice inside your head. The trick is to listen to *that* voice and to silence the one that tells you to do otherwise.

Admittedly, considering these questions will not transform a devil into an angel. Moreover, they are far easier said than done. Still, they may be useful for judging how ethical the decisions are that you may be contemplating. Your answers to these six questions may help you avoid rationalizing that unethical acts are really ethical. And once we recognize that the decisions we are thinking of making may not be ethical, we are well on the way to behaving in an ethical fashion. (One factor that may influence people's perceptions of the ethical appropriateness of a decision is national culture. Indeed, people from different nations may have different views about ethical and unethical business decisions.

Techniques for Enhancing Group Decisions

Just as there are various things individuals can do to improve decision making, so too are there steps that groups can take to enhance the quality of their decisions. The basic idea underlying these techniques is identical: Structure the group experience so as to enable the many benefits of groups to occur without also experiencing the weaknesses.

The Delphi Technique: Decisions by Expert Consensus. According to Greek mythology, people interested in seeing what fate the future held for them could seek the counsel of the Delphic oracle, the ultimate authority on things to come. Today's organizational decision makers sometimes consult experts to help them make the best decisions as well. A technique developed by the Rand Corporation, known as the **Delphi technique,** represents a systematic way of collecting and organizing the opinions of several experts into a single decision. For a summary of the steps in this process, see Figure 3.9.

The Delphi process starts by enlisting the cooperation of experts and presenting the problem to them, usually in a letter or an e-mail message. Each expert then proposes what he or she believes is the most appropriate solution. The group leader compiles all of these individual responses and reproduces them so they can be shared with all the other experts in a second mailing. At this point, each expert comments on the others' ideas and proposes another solution. These individual solutions are returned to the leader, who compiles them and looks for a consensus of opinions. If a consensus is reached, the decision is made. If not, the process of sharing reactions with others is repeated until a consensus is eventually obtained.

The obvious advantage of using the Delphi technique to make decisions is that it allows the collection of expert judgments without the great costs and logistical difficulties of bringing many experts together for a face-to-face meeting. However, the technique is not without limitations. As you might imagine, the Delphi process can be very time consuming. Sending out letters or e-mail messages, waiting for everyone to respond, transcribing and disseminating the responses, and repeating the process until a consensus is reached can take quite a long time. Experts have estimated that before the advent of e-mail the minimum

Delphi technique A method of improving group decisions using the opinions of experts, which are solicited by mail and then compiled. The expert consensus of opinions is used to make a decision

FIGURE 3.9

The Delphi Technique

The Delphi technique allows decisions to be made by several experts while avoiding many of the pitfalls of face-to-face group interaction. Its general steps are outlined here.

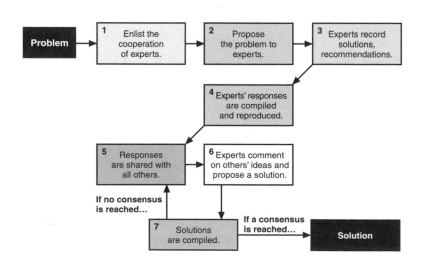

time required to use the Delphi technique would be more than 44 days. In one case, the process took five months to complete. With today's widespread use of e-mail, the Delphi approach can be sped up considerably, but it is still slow. Obviously, the Delphi approach is not appropriate for making decisions in crisis situations, or whenever time is of the essence. However, the approach has been successfully employed to make decisions requiring systematic input from several parties, such as what items to put on a conference agenda and what the potential impact of implementing new land-use policies would be.

The Nominal Group Technique: A Structured Group Meeting. When there are only a few hours available to make a decision, group discussion sessions can be held in which members interact with each other in an orderly, focused fashion aimed at solving problems. The **nominal group technique (NGT)** brings together a small number of individuals (usually about seven to ten) who systematically offer their individual solutions to a problem and share their personal reactions to others' solutions. The technique is referred to as nominal because the individuals involved form a group in name only. The participants do not attempt to agree as a group on any solution, but rather vote on all the solutions proposed. For a summary of this process, see Figure 3.10.

As shown in Figure 3.10, the nominal group process begins by gathering the group members together around a table and identifying the problem at hand. Then each member writes down his or her solutions. Next, one at a time, each member presents his or her solutions to the group and the leader writes these down on a chart. This process continues until all the ideas have been expressed. Following this, each solution is discussed, clarified, and evaluated by the group members. Each member is given a chance to voice his or her reactions to each idea. After all the ideas have been evaluated, the group members privately rank-order their preferred solutions. The idea that receives the highest rank is taken as the group's decision.

nominal group technique (NGT) A technique for improving group decisions in which small groups of individuals systematically present and discuss their ideas before privately voting on their preferred solution. The most preferred solution is accepted as the groups decision

FIGURE 3.10
The Nominal Group Technique

The nominal group technique structures face-to-face group meetings in such a way that the open expression and evaluation of ideas is encouraged. It follows the six steps summarized here.

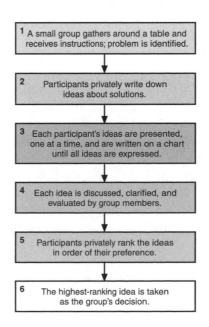

1 A small group gathers around a table and receives instructions; problem is identified.

2 Participants privately write down ideas about solutions.

3 Each participant's ideas are presented, one at a time, and are written on a chart until all ideas are expressed.

4 Each idea is discussed, clarified, and evaluated by group members.

5 Participants privately rank the ideas in order of their preference.

6 The highest-ranking idea is taken as the group's decision.

The NGT has several advantages and disadvantages. We have already noted that it can be used to arrive at group decisions in only a few hours. This can be useful for many types of decisions—but, of course, not for urgent decisions that have to be made on the spot. The benefit of the technique is that it discourages any pressure to conform to the wishes of a high-status group member because all ideas are evaluated and the preferences are expressed in private balloting. The technique must be considered limited, however, in that it requires the use of a trained group leader. In addition, using NGT successfully requires that only one narrowly defined problem he considered at a time. So, for very complex problems, many NGT sessions would have to be run—and only *if* the problem under consideration can be broken down into smaller parts.

It is important to consider the relative effectiveness of nominal groups and Delphi groups over face-to-face interacting groups. In general, research has shown the superiority of these special approaches to decision making in many ways on a variety of decision problems. Overall, members of nominal groups tend to be the most satisfied with their work and make the best-quality judgments. In addition, both nominal groups and Delphi groups are much more productive than interacting groups.

As we noted earlier, however, there is a potential benefit to be derived from face-to-face interaction that cannot be realized in nominal and Delphi groups—that is, acceptance of the decision. Groups are likely to accept their decisions and to be committed to them if members have been actively involved in making them. Thus, the more detached and impersonal atmosphere of nominal and Delphi groups sometimes makes their members less likely to accept their groups' decisions. We may conclude, then, that there is no one best type of group used to make decisions. Which type is most appropriate depends on the trade-offs decision makers are willing to make in terms of speed, quality, and commitment.

The Stepladder Technique: Systematically Incorporating New Members.
Another way of structuring group interaction is known as the **stepladder technique.** This approach minimizes the tendency for group members to be unwilling to present their ideas by adding new members to a group one at a time and requiring each to present his or her ideas independently to a group that already has discussed the problem at hand. To begin, each of two people works on a problem independently and then come together to present their ideas and discuss solutions jointly. While the two-person group is working, a third person working alone also considers the problem. Then this individual presents his or her ideas to the group and joins in a three-person discussion of a possible solution. During this period a fourth person works on the problem alone and then presents his or her ideas to the group and joins into a four-person group discussion. After each new person has been added to the group, the entire group works together at finding a solution. (For a summary of the steps in this technique, see Figure 3.11.)

In following this procedure, it is important for all individuals to be given enough time to work on the problem before they join the group. Then each person must be given enough time to present thoroughly his or her ideas to the group. Groups then must have sufficient time to discuss the problem at hand and reach a preliminary decision before the next person is added. The final decision is made only after all individuals have been added to the group.

stepladder technique
A technique for improving the quality of group decisions that minimizes the tendency for group members to be unwilling to present their ideas by adding new members to a group one at a time and requiring each to present his or her ideas independently to a group that already has discussed the problem at hand

FIGURE 3.11
The Stepladder Technique

By systematically adding new individuals into decision-making groups, the stepladder technique helps to increase the quality of the decisions made.

SOURCE: Adapted from Rogelberg & O'Conner, 1998; see Note 111.

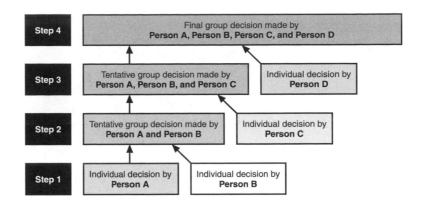

The rationale underlying this procedure is that by forcing each person to present independent ideas without knowing how the group has decided, the new person will not be influenced by the group, and the group is required to consider a constant infusion of new ideas. If this is so, then groups solving problems using the stepladder technique would be expected to make better decisions than conventional groups meeting all at once to discuss the same problem. Research has found that this is exactly what happens. Moreover, members of stepladder groups reported feeling more positive about their group experiences than their counterparts in conventional groups. Although the stepladder technique is new, evidence suggests that it holds a great deal of promise as a way of enhancing the decision-making capacity of groups.

Computer-Based Approaches to Promoting Effective Decisions

Now that we have reviewed traditional, low-tech techniques for improving decision-making effectiveness, we will move on to examining several new, technology-based approaches that have been used in recent years. Given the widespread use of computers in the workplace, it probably comes as no surprise that attempts have been made to put computers to use in improving the quality of group decisions. For the most part, these techniques are not especially sophisticated and make good use of widely available and inexpensive computer technology. As a result, they stand to be widely used to the extent that they are effective. With this in mind, we will examine three such techniques: *electronic meetings, computer-assisted communication,* and *group decision support systems.*

Electronic Meetings

Although nominal groups traditionally meet in face-to-face settings, advances in modern technology enable them to be formed even when members are in distant locations. Specifically, **electronic meetings,** as they are known, involve holding

electronic meetings
The practice of bringing individuals from different locations together for a meeting via telephone or satellite transmissions, either on television monitors or via shared space on a computer screen

DECISION MAKING IN ORGANIZATIONS 🌀 107

teleconferences in which individuals in different locations participate in group conferences by means of telephone rules or direct satellite transmissions. The messages may be sent either via characters on a computer monitor or images viewed during a teleconference. Despite their high-tech look, electronic meetings are really just nominal groups meeting in a manner that approximates face-to-face contact. And, for the most part, they have proven to be equally effective.

Insofar as electronic meetings allow for groups to assemble more conveniently than face-to-face meetings, they are growing in popularity. Presently, such companies as GE Appliances, US West, Marriott Corp., and Sun Microsystems have relied on electronic meetings, and growing numbers of companies are using them all the time.

Computer-Assisted Communication

computer-assisted communication The sharing of information, such as text messages and data relevant to the decision, over computer networks

Another way of leveraging technology to facilitate group decision making involves using **computer-assisted communication**—that is, the sharing of information, such as text messages and data relevant to the decision, over computer networks. The underlying idea of computer-assisted communication is that on-screen messages provide an effective means of sending some forms of information that can help groups make better decisions. But does it really work? In other words, does being able to communicate with other team members via computer help teams make more effective decisions than they would make without computer assistance?

Research suggests that the answer is "only sometimes." Recently, a study was conducted that compared the effectiveness of three-person groups whose members were allowed only to speak to each other (the talk-only condition) with other three-person groups whose members also were allowed to send text messages to one another over a computer network (the computer-assisted communication condition). Participants were asked to perform a task that simulated the kind of decisions made in a military "command and control" situation. This involved assessing the threat risk of aircraft spotted on a computer screen (based on such information as speed and size) after they were trained to perform this task. The teams' decisions were scored on the basis of accuracy and then were compared to one another.

The results, summarized in Figure 3.12, revealed that the effectiveness of the teams' decisions depend on another variable. Specifically teams using the computer assisted communication made better decisions than teams using verbal communication only when they were composed of individuals whose scores on a personality test indicated that they were highly open to experience. People scoring high on **openness to experience** tend to have intellectual curiosity, value learning, have an active imagination, and are intrigued by artistic endeavors. By contrast, people scoring low on this measure tend to be exactly the opposite. Apparently, because computer-assisted communication was new to many of the participants, its effectiveness was limited to those who were most accepting of the new technology and who possessed the creativity to use the technology in an efficient manner. These individuals reaped the benefits associated with the computer assistance. However, those who were less open to experience failed to perform better when using computer-assisted communication—actually, they performed slightly worse. Apparently, the computer-assisted communication was not much "assistance" to them, after all.

openness to experience A personality variable reflecting the degree to which individuals have intellectual curiosity, value learning, have an active imagination, and are intrigued by artistic endeavors

FIGURE 3.12

Computer Assisted Communication Improves Decision Making Among People Who Are Open to Experience

Computer-assisted communication involves the sharing of information (e.g., text messages and data relevant to them) over computer networks. Research simulating a military decision-making situation has shown that the effectiveness of this technique depends on peoples openness to experience. As summarized here, computer-assisted communication improved the decision-making performance of three-person teams only when they were composed of individuals who scored highly on a personality test measuring openness to experience. However, individuals who were not open to experience not helped by computer-assisted communication.

SOURCE: Based on data reported by Colquitt et al., 2002; see Note 113.

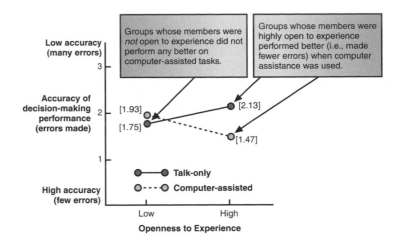

Because it provides a useful means of exchanging crucial information, one might be inclined to assume that computer-assisted communication is an effective way to improve group decision quality. And, because it can he adopted readily and inexpensively, some may be tempted to put it into practice. However, given that it appears not to be effective for everyone, implementing computer-assisted communications on a widespread basis would be unwise—at least, it may be premature. Perhaps, after such systems are in use for a while and people come to be familiar with them, even those who are not open to experiences will find them acceptable. Furthermore, training on how to integrate computer-assisted communication with more traditional forms also could compensate for any lack of openness. For the moment, however, officials implementing computer-assisted communication systems would be wise to proceed with caution.

Group Decision Support Systems

group decision support systems (GDSS)
Interactive computer-based systems that combine communication, computer, and decision technologies to improve the effectiveness of group problem-solving meetings

Another approach to using technology to improve the effectiveness of decisions that has received attention in recent years is known as **group decision support systems (GDSS).** These are interactive computer-based systems that combine communication, computer, and decision technologies to improve the effectiveness of group problem-solving meetings. They often involve having people type their ideas into a computer program and discuss these ideas anonymously with others in chat rooms. A record of these discussions is then left for all to examine as needed. Their underlying rationale is straightforward: The quality of group decisions stands to be improved insofar as this process removes some of the impediments to decision making. In this sense, just as decision support systems, described earlier can be used to identify effective ways of making decisions, so too can group decision support systems.

One of the reasons why face-to-face groups sometimes make poor decisions is that group members do not always share information they have available to them that might help the group. As we discussed earlier, in connection with the phenomenon of group-think, this may occur because people sometimes censor unpopular ideas voluntarily, even if these are good ideas that can improve the quality of group decisions. This is where GDSS can be useful. Groups using GDSS may avoid this problem insofar as the anonymous recording of ideas makes people less reluctant to share them and makes it easier than ever to have access to them. In this manner, some of the most potent impediments to group decision quality can be eliminated. Recent research has found that this is, in fact, exactly what happens in groups using GDSS. An experiment was conducted comparing the effectiveness of groups of managers asked to solve simulated management problems in face-to-face groups and using GDSS. As expected, the results showed that, compared to face-to-face groups, groups using GDSS not only shared considerably more information, but they also made far better decisions as a result.

For now, it seems that group decision support systems appear to be quite effective. However, because they are very new, we don't yet know all the conditions under which they will continue to be successful. As OB researchers conduct further research on this topic, we surely will learn more about this promising technique in the future.

⊚ Discussion Questions

1. What are the general steps in the decision-making process, and how can different types of organizational decisions be characterized?
2. How do individual decision style, group influences, and organizational influences affect decision making in organizations?
3. What are the major differences between the rational-economic model, the administrative model, and the image theory approach to individual decision making?
4. Explain how each of the following factors contributes to the imperfect nature of decisions: framing effects, reliance on heuristics, decision biases, and the tendency to escalate commitment to a losing course of action.
5. When it comes to making decisions, under what conditions are individuals superior to groups and under what conditions are groups superior to individuals?
6. What traditional techniques and computer-based techniques can be used to improve the quality of decisions made by groups or individuals?

Experiential Questions

1. Think of any decision you recently made. Would you characterize it as programmed or nonprogrammed? Highly certain or highly uncertain? Top-down or empowered? Explain your answers.
2. Identify ways in which various decisions you have made were biased by framing, heuristics, the use of implicit favorites, and the escalation of commitment.

3. Think of various decision-making groups in which you may have participated over the years. Do you think that groupthink was involved in these situations? What signs were evident?

Questions to Analyze

1. Imagine that you are a manager facing the problem of not attracting enough high-quality personnel to your organization. Would you attempt to solve this problem alone or by committee? Explain your reasoning.
2. Suppose you were on a committee charged with making an important decision and that committee was composed of people from various nations. How do you think this might make a difference in the way the group operates?
3. Argue pro or con: "All people make decisions in the same manner."

 # Group Exercise

Running a Nominal Group: Try It Yourself

A great deal can be learned about nominal groups by running one—or, at least, participating in one—yourself. Doing so will not only help illustrate the procedure but also demonstrate how effectively it works.

Directions

1. Select a topic suitable for discussion in a nominal group composed of students in your class. It should be a topic that is narrowly defined and on which people have many different opinions (these work best in nominal groups). Some possible examples include:
   ■ What should your school's student leaders be doing for you?
   ■ What can be done to improve the quality of instruction in your institution?
   ■ What can be done to improve the quality of jobs your school's students receive when graduating?
2. Divide the class into groups of approximately 10 members each. Arrange each group in a circle or around a table, if possible. In each group, select one person to serve as the group facilitator.
3. Following the steps outlined in Figure 3.10, facilitators should guide their groups in discussions regarding the focal question identified previously in step 1. Allow approximately 45 minutes to 1 hour to complete this process.
4. If time allows, select a different focal question and a different group leader, and repeat the procedure.

Questions for Discussion

1. Collectively, how did the group answer the question? Do you believe that this answer accurately reflected the feelings of the group?
2. How did the various groups' answers compare? Were they similar or different? Why?

3. What were the major problems, if any, associated with the nominal group experience? For example, were there any group members who were reluctant to wait their turns before speaking up?
4. How do you think your group experiences would have differed had you used a totally unstructured, traditional face-to-face group instead of a nominal group?

☉ Web Surfing Exercise

Decision Skills Training

In recent years, several commercial enterprises and nonprofit organizations have been created that offer services designed to help people become better decision makers. Using your favorite search engine, enter search terms such as "decision skills," "empowered decision making," or "decision training." Examine the sites that emerge from this search and answer the following questions based on what you find.

1. In what ways do these services differ from one another? Specifically, what services are being offered and to what groups?
2. How effective do you think these services may be?
3. Under what circumstances, if any, might you envision yourself using such services?

Decision Support Systems

Most companies that offer decision support systems (DSS) describe their products and services online. To get a feel for these, enter the search term "decision support systems" in your favorite search engine. Examine the sites that emerge from this search and answer the following questions based on what you find.

1. With respect to what types of decisions are DSS available? How do these differ from one another?
2. Besides software-based solutions, what other types of decision support services are available?
3. For what types of situations might you be interested in using DSS in your own work?

CLOSING CASE

Keep the New Orleans Saints Marching Down the Field

Bruce Lemmerman spends 363 days per year preparing for important decisions that have to be made in just a few minutes during the other two days. As director of college scouting for the New Orleans Saints, he visits colleges and universities throughout the United States in search of football players who are good enough to be selected for the "Big Show" (slang for the National Football League) during the NFL's two-day college draft each April.

The key to Lemmerman's mission is gathering all pertinent information so that it can be called up when Saints officials need to make decisions about which prospects to select as their draft choices. With this in mind, Lemmerman is almost always on the road, going to as many as 70 schools in four months. While there, he closely watches players during games or in practice sessions—live from the sidelines when he can but at least on videotape. He also talks to coaches and trainers, getting their slant on each athlete's strengths and weaknesses.

He routinely gathers detailed information on a player's physical qualities, such as his height, weight, speed, percentage of body fat, and height of vertical leap, but that's not all. Lemmerman also pays close attention to personal qualities and intangible characteristics, such as a player's "football intelligence," his work ethic, his competitiveness, and his workout habits during the off-season.

Traditionally, the records were written by hand and kept in folders, resulting in disarray. Player profiles were kept in blue folders in the team's conference room, medical evaluations were in the trainer's office, and scouting reports were someplace else. Getting all the critical information on a player was a hopelessly difficult task—and it was only made worse by the fact that until Lemmerman joined the Saints in 1994, much of the recruiting was outsourced. His first mission was to assist in developing a database so that anyone in the front office could access whatever information was needed at any time.

Acknowledging that such a system is only as good as the data entered into it, Lemmerman spends a great deal of time entering information about players into his notebook computer. But he can't run up and down the sidelines while typing notes into the computer. Neither is a handheld computer practical because the screen is too small. So Lemmerman prefers doing things the old-fashioned way—he takes notes on paper forms attached to a clipboard while speaking his impressions into a microcassette recorder. Then, either while on the plane or back at the hotel, he enters all of this information into the notebook computer and transmits it back to the main computer on his desktop in New Orleans.

As tedious as this process may be, Lemmerman realizes that it's necessary to enable the team to make the best possible recruiting decisions. As he puts it, "Imagine it's the fourth quarter and you're tired. You want to quit, but you suck it up and play anyway. At times like that it's easy to be less sharp and to take shortcuts." However, knowing that there are multi-million-dollar decisions at stake, Lemmerman does his part for the team by keeping the recruiting records in impeccable form.

Critical Thinking Questions

1. As an individual who is potentially overwhelmed by statistics and observations about individual players, how do you think Lemmerman's own decision processes may be biased?
2. In what ways do you think that the quality of the decisions made by officials from the New Orleans Saints is helped or harmed by the practice of making draft decisions as a group?
3. In what ways do you think that escalation of commitment may be involved in the decisions Lemmerman makes for the team?

STRATEGIC MANAGEMENT

MICHAEL DELL: FROM DORM ROOM TO PERSONAL COMPUTER KING

Over the years I've spent a fair amount of time hanging out with Michael Dell, and what I noticed during my latest visit with him in Austin is how things have changed. Yes, he is still unflappable. And yes, he greets me in his new glossy offices with the same Stepford Wife-like grin he has always had. But he appears thinner now, as if he's lost baby fat. While he's still slow-moving, as if he's conserving energy, he now cuts to the quick in conversation. And when he zeroes in on the point he wants to make, when he reiterates why Dell Computer is in a better position than any other PC maker in the world, you realize that the 36-year-old has lost what was once one of his greatest advantages: No one underestimates him any more.

Instead, Michael Dell looms over the PC landscape like a giant, casting a shadow over all his unfortunate competitors. This is a terrible time in a difficult business. PC sales were down for the first time last year. Dell's sales will be down, too, also for the first time. Yet even with that, even with recession, even with the threat of a Hewlett-Packard/Compaq Goliath, this is the only PC maker you can count on to grow and grow and grow. Almost single-handedly, Dell is forcing this industry to consolidate. Could this mean "game over" in the PC biz? Not even the ambitious CEO buys that. "Game over?" he looks back at me incredulously. "No way. We only have 14% global market share."

The Dellites may not admit to "game over" aspirations, but clearly they are thinking of a kind of domination never seen before among PC makers. "We think 40% market share is possible," says Dell's No. 2, Kevin Rollins. That's a remarkable goal; what's more remarkable is that it really is attainable. Don't look for Dell to hit that kind of number anytime soon. Rather, the company's growth will come from grinding out gains on several existing fronts, while shrewdly expanding into new target markets. But the growth will come—just ask Oracle CEO Larry Ellison, who has watched Dell take great chunks out of the market for Windows servers, which are essentially high-powered PCs that can help manage Web sites or data on corporate networks. "If you want to be in the PC business, you have to compete against Dell," says Ellison, "and that is very, very difficult."

The reason is simple: There's no better way to make, sell, and deliver PCs than the way Dell does it, and nobody executes that model better than Dell. By now most business people can recite the basic tenets of Dell's direct-sales model. Dell machines are made to order and delivered directly to the customer. There is no middle-man. The customer gets the exact machine he wants cheaper than he can get it from the competition. The company gets paid by the customer weeks before it pays suppliers. Given all that, the company that famously started in Austin out of a University of Texas dorm room now dominates the northern side of this city the way giant steelworks once lorded over old mill towns. Dell has some 24 facilities in and near Austin and employs more than 18,000 local workers. Dell did over $30 billion in sales in 2000, ranking 48th on the *Fortune* 500, ahead of names like Walt Disney, Johnson & Johnson, and Du Pont. Michael is the richest man under 40 in the world, worth $16 billion.

Two facts show how well the Dell model is working, even in tough times: Dell is on track to *earn* over $1.7 billion in 2001, taking almost every single dollar of profit among makers of Windows-based PCs. (Intel and Microsoft, of course, earn good money too—but they extract profits *from* the PC makers.) And Dell is gaining market share. That's not true for any other major PC maker.

Quite the contrary. The others are going *splat* for the same reason Dell is succeeding: commoditization. The desktop PC has become a commodity. That's great for consumers, who get standardized, easy-to-use, cheap PCs. But it's horrible for all but one manufacturer. As prices plummet, CEOs of most PC makers find it so hard to make a dime that they must justify to shareholders staying in the business at all. Commoditization relentlessly drives consolidation. And so it is no surprise when former high-flying PC makers like AST crash. Or when IBM stops selling PCs in stores. Or when Gateway pulls back from selling overseas. . . .

The economic slowdown was bad news for everyone, but Michael Dell and Kevin Rollins, who is increasingly his equal partner in running this business, made sure it was terrible news for Dell's competitors. In late 2000 they decided to slash prices. "It was advantageous for us, actually, because in periods of slow demand component prices drop, and, unlike our competition, we can pass those savings on immediately to customers," explains Rollins. . . . Dell could make more money selling more computers at lower prices than it could selling fewer computers at higher prices. The low prices wreaked havoc on competitors. Compaq, HP, and Gateway all lost market share for the 12 months ended Sept. 30, 2001, while Dell's share of the U.S. market climbed 31%. . . .

Other companies, most notably IBM, have turned to services for growth. IBM sells a wide range of hardware, but its meat and potatoes now is business services—the company's army of consultants who advise customers on how to use and implement its technology. . . .

Competitors think services are Dell's great weakness. They say that Dell, which often partners with companies like EDS, doesn't have what it takes to truly serve large corporations. As an example, they point to the fact that Dell lost a big global account with Shell. . . . Michael Dell dismisses the criticism. "Services is now a $3-billion-a-year business at Dell," he says." In the large-account space it's becoming a critical factor in many bids. We don't, however, need to copy IBM. We can keep doing it our way and win." Dell Computer will have enough of a consulting business to satisfy large customers—and no more.

That's because Michael Dell believes he can get higher margins from any number of hardware businesses. He is actively pushing the company into a wide range of peripheral products. How does he decide which products fit the bill? A few criteria must be met: The product must be (1) PC-related, (2) sizable, (3) profitable, and (4) increasingly a commodity.

Two product lines that make the list are storage and switches, and Dell is pushing like mad into those businesses. (Hey, EMC and Cisco! Guess who's coming to dinner?)

Strategic management drives the effort to succeed amid constant change, uncertainty, and obstacles. If Dell Computer stands still or rests on its remarkable accomplishments, it will fail. Thus, Michael Dell and his coworkers are constantly on the lookout both for threats to their core PC business and for potentially profitable new markets. Without the discipline of a strategic management orientation, Dell's 40,000 employees would tend to work at cross-purposes, with no unified direction. In fact, a statistical analysis of 26 published studies documented the positive impact of strategic planning on business performance.

Many people automatically assume that strategy is the exclusive domain of top-level management, but that simply is not true. Its relevance for those lower in the organization may not be as apparent, but it is equally important. A management student who is 10 to 20 years away from a top-level executive position might ask, "If top managers formulate strategies and I'm headed for a supervisory or staff position, why should I care about strategic management?" There are three good reasons why staff specialists and managers at all levels need a general understanding of strategic management.

First, in view of widespread criticism that American managers tend to be short-sighted, a strategic orientation encourages farsightedness (see Table 4.1). Second, employees who think in strategic terms tend to understand better how top managers think and why they make the decisions they do. In other words, the rationale behind executive policies and decisions is more apparent when things are put into a strategic perspective.

A third reason for promoting a broader understanding of strategic management relates to a recent planning trend. Specifically, greater teamwork and cooperation throughout the planning/control cycle are eroding the traditional distinction between those who plan and those who implement plans. There is a clear trend *away from* the command, symbolic, and rational modes and *toward* the transactive and generative modes. In other words, the traditional idea of top-management strategists as commanders, coaches, or bosses is giving way to a view of them more as participative facilitators and sponsors. In each of the traditional modes, people below the top level must be obedient, passive, and reactive.

TABLE 4.1 Key Dimensions of Strategic Farsightedness

	Shortsighted	Farsighted
1. **Organizational strategy**	No formally documented strategies.	A formally written and communicated statement of long-term organizational mission.
2. **Competitive advantage**	"Follow the leader: No attention devoted to long-term competitive edge.	"Be the leader." Emphasis an gaining and holding a strategic competitive edge.
3. **Organizational structure**	Rigid structure emphasizing status quo, downward communication, and predictability.	Flexible structure encouraging change. upward and lateral communication, adaptability, and speed.
4. **Research and development**	Emphasis on applying competitors' good ideas.	Heavy emphasis on developing new products and services and on innovations in production, marketing, and human resource management.
5. **Return**	Emphasis on short-term profits.	Emphasis on increased market share, growth, and future profit potential.
6. **Human resources**	Emphasis on stopgap hiring and training. Labor viewed as a commodity. Layoffs common.	Emphasis on long-term development of employees. Labor viewed as a valuable human resource. Layoffs seen as a last resort.
7. **Problem solving**	Emphasis on chasing symptoms and blaming scapegoats.	Emphasis on finding solutions to problems.
8. **Management style**	Emphasis on day-to-day firefighting. owing to short-term orientation.	Multilevel strategic thinking that encourages managers to consider long-term implications of their actions and decisions.

In the *transactive* strategy-making mode, continuous improvement is the order of the day, as middle- and lower-level managers and staff specialists actively participate in the process. They go a step further, becoming risk-taking entrepreneurs, in the generative mode. Here is a case in point:

> J. M. Smucker Co., the Ohio-based maker of jams and jellies, . . . enlisted a team of 140 employees—7 percent of its workforce—who devoted nearly 50 percent of their time to a major strategy exercise for more than six months. "Instead of having just 12 minds working it, we really used the team of 140 as ambassador to solicit input from all 2,000 employees," says President Richard K. Smucker. "It gave us a broader perspective, and it brought to the surface a lot of people with special talents." The company which has struggled to grow in a mature market, now has a dozen viable initiatives that could double its $635 million revenues over the next five years.

Thus, you, today's management student, are not as far away from the strategic domain as you may think. The time to start thinking strategically is now. This chapter defines strategic management, looks at ways to think strategically, explores the strategic management process, and discusses forecasting.

Strategic Management = Strategic Planning + Implementation + Control

strategic management
Seeking a competitively superior organization-environment fit

strategy Integrated, externally oriented perception of how to achieve the organization's mission

Strategic management is the ongoing process of ensuring a competitively superior fit between an organization and its changing environment. In a manner of speaking, strategic management is management on a grand scale, management of the "big picture." Accordingly, **strategy** has been defined as an integrated and externally oriented perception of how the organization will achieve its mission. The strategic management perspective is the product of a historical evolution and is now understood to include budget control, long-range planning, and strategic planning.

Significantly, strategic management does not do away with earlier, more restricted approaches. Instead, it synthesizes and coordinates them all in a more systematic fashion. For example, consider the relationship between strategic planning and strategic management. *Strategic planning* is the process of determining how to pursue the organization's long-term goals with the resources expected to be available. Notice that nothing is said in this definition about adjustment or control. But just as astronauts and space scientists need to make mid-flight corrections to ensure that space shuttles reach their distant destinations, strategic adjustment and control are necessary. The more encompassing strategic management concept is useful today because it effectively merges strategic planning, implementation, and control.

Today's competitive pressures necessitate a dynamic strategic management process. According to *Fortune*:

> The old methods won't do. At too many companies strategic planning has become overly bureaucratic, absurdly quantitative, and largely irrelevant. In executive

suites across America, countless five-year plans, updated annually and solemnly clad in three-ring binders are gathering dust—their impossibly specific prognostications about costs, prices, and market share long forgotten.

Managers who adopt a strategic management perspective appreciate that strategic plans are living documents. They require updating and fine-tuning as conditions change. They also need to draw upon all available talent in the organization.

The strategic management process is discussed in greater detail later in this chapter. But first we need to consider alternative ways to encourage strategic thinking.

Thinking Strategically (Including E-Business Strategies)

Effective strategic management involves more than just following a few easy steps. It requires *every* employee, on a daily basis, to consider the "big picture" and think strategically about gaining and keeping a competitive edge. A pair of experts on the subject recently framed the issue in terms of innovation:

> Strategy innovation is not simply about extending a product line or pouring money into long-term, theoretical R&D projects. It is about rethinking the basis of competition for any company in any industry. Innovation cannot be a one-time event in the race to the future; it must be a continuous theme that extends throughout the entire company. . . .
>
> It is a deliberate process by which daring companies question the business model that may have brought them success in the first place. Although obviously needed when the economic chips are down, this type of thinking is equally critical for companies riding a wave of success. That's precisely when they may feel exempt from the need for radical innovation. "Why tinker," the reasoning goes, "with a proven formula?" . . .
>
> What's needed is a built-in capacity to challenge orthodoxies, develop foresight, build innovation-oriented processes, and continuously regenerate the strategy.

This section presents four alternative perspectives for thinking innovatively about strategy in today's fast-paced global economy: synergies, Porter's generic strategies, business ecosystems, and e-business strategies.

Synergy

Although not necessarily a familiar term, *synergy* is a well-established and valuable concept. **Synergy** occurs when two or more variables (for example, chemicals, drugs, people, organizations) interact to produce an effect greater than the sum of the effects of any of the variables acting independently. Some call this the $1 + 1 = 3$ effect; others prefer to say that with synergy, the whole is greater than the sum of its parts. Either definition is acceptable as long as one appreciates the bonus effect

synergy The concept that the whole is greater than the sum of its parts

in synergistic relationships. In strategic management, managers are urged to achieve as much *market, cost, technology,* and *management synergy* as possible when making strategic decisions. Those decisions may involve mergers, acquisitions, new products, new technology or production processes, or executive replacement. When Germany's Daimler Benz and Detroit's Chrysler merged in 1998 to form DaimlerChrysler, executives trumpeted the potential synergies. The merger now seems to be bearing some fruit. One result is the Crossfire, a sporty two-seat coupe. According to *Business Week:* "It has a sleek Chrysler look, while many of the components under the hood are borrowed from Mercedes."

Market Synergy. When one product or service fortifies the sales of one or more other products or services, market synergy has been achieved. Examples of market synergy are common in the business press. For example, consider this scenario inspired by Vivendi Universal, the French entertainment and broadcasting giant:

> The ultimate synergistic dream is to take a hit such as *American Pie* (the movie), spin it into *American Pie* (the TV series) that runs endlessly on USA Network, and then maybe crank out several *American Pie* soundtracks and create an *American Pie* attraction at the Universal Studios theme parks.

Cost Synergy. This second type of synergy can occur in almost every dimension of organized activity. When two or more products can be designed by the same engineers, produced in the same facilities, distributed through the same channels, or sold by the same salespeople, overall costs will be lower than if each product received separate treatment. In an interesting example of cost synergy, major hotels are trying to squeeze more value from their costly real estate. "At Miami Airport, Marriott has three hotels on the same plot of land. There's the Marriott Hotel, a full-service hotel. Behind the hotel are a Courtyard by Marriott, a midprice hotel, and a Fairfield Inn, an economy brand."

Cost synergy also can be achieved by recycling by-products and hazardous wastes that would normally be thrown away. Human imagination is the only limit to creating cost synergies through recycling. For example, chicken farms in the Shenandoah valley region of Virginia annually produce half a million tons of manure. Harmony Products, in Harrisonburg, Virginia, has found a way to make high-quality fertilizer pellets for golf courses from the chicken waste. Even better, Harmony burns some of the manure to produce heat for its drying process, thereby saving $500,000 a year on natural gas. Cost synergy through waste recycling is good business ethics, too.

Technological Synergy. The third variety of synergy involves transferring technology from one application to another, thus opening up new markets. For example, Alfa-Laval, a Swedish manufacturing company specializing in centrifugal separators, broadened its market base through technological synergy.

> Alfa designed a separator to remove yeast particles from beer. Brewers were uninterested, but genetic researchers were fascinated; with some modifications, the same equipment is well-suited for preparing cells and harvesting bacteria in genetic research.

Thanks to this sort of technological synergy, profitable new markets can be tapped without the expense of developing totally new products.

Management Synergy. This fourth type of synergy occurs when a management team is more productive because its members have complementary rather than identical skills. For example, cofounder Herb Kelleher turned over the reins of Southwest Airlines in 2001 to a multitalented team. Now occupying the CEO spot is Jim Parker who, like Kelleher, is a lawyer who knows the details of airline regulations. Colleen Barrett, now president, worked her way up from the bottom and is the heartbeat of Southwest's people-friendly culture.

You may find it difficult, if not impossible, to take advantage of all four types of synergy when developing new strategies. Nonetheless, your strategies are more likely to be realistic and effective if you give due consideration to all four types of synergy as early as possible.

Porter's Generic Competitive Strategies

In 1980, Michael Porter, a Harvard University economist, developed a model of competitive strategies. During a decade of research, Porter's model evolved to encompass these four generic strategies: (1) cost leadership, (2) differentiation, (3) cost focus, and (4) focused differentiation. Porter's model combined two variables, *competitive advantage* and *competitive scope.*

On the horizontal axis is competitive advantage, which can be achieved via low costs or differentiation. A competitive advantage based on low costs, which means lower prices, is self-explanatory. **Differentiation,** according to Porter, "is the ability to provide unique and superior value to the buyer in terms of product quality, special features, or after-sale service. Differentiation helps explain why consumers willingly pay more for branded products such as Sunkist oranges or Crest toothpaste. On the vertical axis is competitive scope. Is the firm's target market broad or narrow? IBM, which sells many types of computers all around the world, serves a very broad market. A neighborhood pizza parlor offering one type of food in a small geographical area has a narrow target market.

Like the concept of synergy, Porter's model helps managers think strategically: it enables them to see the big picture as it affects the organization and its changing environment. Each of Porter's four generic strategies deserves a closer look.

Cost Leadership Strategy. Managers pursuing this strategy have an overriding concern for keeping costs, and therefore prices, lower than those of competitors. Normally, this means extensive production or service facilities with efficient economies of scale (low unit costs of making products or delivering services). Productivity improvement is a high priority for managers following the cost leadership strategy. Wal-Mart Stores, Inc., is a prime example of the cost leadership strategy.

> The Wal-Mart formula is deceptively simple: Sell good-quality, name-brand, modestly priced merchandise in a clean, no-frills setting that offers one-stop family shopping. Rather than entice shoppers with an ever-changing array of discounts and sales, Wal-Mart operates from an "everyday low price" philosophy.

differentiation Buyer perceives unique and superior value in a product

Wal-Mart's computerized warehousing network gives it an additional cost advantage over its less efficient competitors. When rival Kmart declared bankruptcy in 2002, a retail industry consultant bluntly observed: "Kmart is simply another piece of retail roadkill in Wal-Mart's march to dominance.

In manufacturing firms, the preoccupation with minimizing costs flows beyond production into virtually all areas: purchasing, wages, overhead, R&D, advertising, and selling. A relatively large market share is required to accommodate this high-volume, low-profit margin strategy.

Differentiation Strategy. For this strategy to succeed, a company's product or service must be considered unique by most of the customers in its industry. Advertising and promotion help the product to stand out from the crowd. Specialized design (BMW automobiles), a widely recognized brand (Diet Coke), leading-edge technology (Intel), or reliable service (Caterpillar) also may serve to differentiate a product in the industry. Because customers with brand loyalty will usually spend more for what they perceive to be a superior product, the differentiation strategy can yield larger profit margins than the low-cost strategy. When brand loyalty erodes, as it did in the early 1990s for Compaq Computer Corp. because clones became available for 30 percent less, prices need to be lowered to meet the competition. (Note: Compaq is now part of Hewlett-Packard.) This step necessitates a switch to a cost leadership or a cost focus strategy. For businesses sticking to a differentiation strategy, it is important to note that cost reduction is not ignored; it simply is not the highest priority.

Cost Focus Strategy. Organizations with a cost focus strategy attempt to gain a competitive edge in a narrow (or regional) market by exerting strict control. For instance, Foot Locker has become a powerhouse in athletic footwear and apparel by selling off unrelated businesses, such as San Francisco Music Box, and focusing on what it does best.

> With an 18% (and growing) share of the athletic retail market—nearly twice that of its nearest competitor—Foot Locker uses its weight to negotiate advantageous deals with manufactures like Nike and Reebok. It gets the hottest products earlier and cheaper than its peers.

Foot Locker plans to increase its 3,600-store chain by 1,000 in the years ahead.

Focused Differentiation Strategy. This generic strategy involves achieving a competitive edge by delivering a superior product and/or service to a limited audience. The Mayo Clinic's world-class health care facilties—in Rochester, Minnesota; Jacksonville, Florida; and Scottsdale, Arizona—are an expression of this strategy.

A contingency management approach is necessary for determining which of Porter's generic strategies is appropriate. Research on Porter's model indicates a positive relationship between long-term earnings growth and a good strategy/environment fit.

Business Ecosystems

Researchers recently have given new meaning to the saying, "It's a jungle out there." They have extended the concept of ecosystems from nature to business. In his bestseller *The Death of Competition: Leadership and Strategy in the Age of Business Ecosystems,* James F. Moore writes: "It is my view that executives need to think of themselves as part of organisms participating in an ecosystem in much the same way that biological organisms participate in a biological ecosystem." A **business ecosystem** is an economic community of organizations and all their stakeholders, including suppliers and customers. This evolving model makes one very important contribution to modern strategic thinking: *organizations need to be as good at cooperating as they are at competing if they are to succeed.*

A Business Ecosystem in Action. Within a dominant business ecosystem, key organizations selectively cooperate and compete to achieve both their individual and collective goals. A prime example is the relationship between Microsoft and Intel. In fact, the so-called Wintel technology (the combination of Microsoft Windows software and Intel microprocessors) dominates the personal computer market. Yet make no mistake about it—Microsoft and Intel are competitors in all other respects. In the language of business ecosystems, Microsoft and Intel have *coevolved* to a dominant position in the personal computer ecosystem (along with Dell Computer). Meanwhile, according to Moore: "Larry Ellison at Oracle is promoting $500 Internet-access devices as substitutes for personal computers, hoping to steal the future from Intel and Microsoft." The Wintel ecosystem has responded by slashing the cost of personal computers and saying PCs are not obsolete in the Internet age. In ten years, will the Wintel ecosystem, with its reliance on personal computers packed with expensive software, still be dominant? Or will Ellison be able to pull together a successful community of organizations and individuals to create a new dominant ecosystem in which inexpensive information appliances are used to pull low-cost software applications off the Internet on an as-needed basis? Only time will tell; an epic battle is on in the business jungle.

Needed: More Strategic Cooperation. Through the years, the terms *strategy* and *competition* have become synonymous. Business ecologists now call for greater cooperation, even among the toughest of competitors. Moore puts it this way: "The major factor today limiting the spread of realized innovation is not a lack of good ideas, technology, or capital. It is the inability to command cooperation across broad, diverse communities of players who must become intimate parts of a far-reaching process of coevolution." So Oracle's Ellison will need to team up with organizations that can provide high-speed, high-volume, and reliable Internet access (not yet widely available at reasonable cost) if he is to realize his vision. In ecosystem terms, he will have to coevolve with key strategic partners because his company cannot do it alone.

E-Business Strategies for the Internet

The recent boom-and-bust cycle for dot-coms, although painful for many, has been an excellent learning laboratory. We now see the Internet not as some sort of miracle but rather as a powerful business tool requiring thoughtful application. Janey Place, e-business manager for Mellon Financial Corp. in Pittsburgh, recently shared these useful lessons:

■ The Internet changes everything—but it doesn't change everything overnight. . . . *The Internet changes everything: how we get information, how we learn, how we conduct business. But I was alarmed by the hype of the late 1990s, when the mind-set was "Fire, then aim"—you didn't ever have to be ready. . . .*

- Some of the old rules still rule. . . . *Technology, in and of itself, isn't enough of a reason to invest in the Internet. There has to be a reasonable, logical business model. Either you're saving money or you're making money. . . .*
- First, we overestimated the Internet; don't underestimate it now. . . . *Looking ahead, I am convinced that the Internet will exceed our expectations.*

A broad, strategic perspective of the Internet is needed. E-business involves using the Internet to make *all* business functions—from sales to human resource management—more efficient, responsive, and speedier. The purpose of this section is to build a framework of understanding for squeezing maximum value from the Internet.

Evolving Internet Technologies. The Internet is not a fixed thing. It is a complex bundle of emerging technologies at various stages of development. Corporate strategists and entrepreneurs are challenged to build business models based on *where they expect these technologies to be* X years down the road. This exercise is akin to hitting a moving target from a moving platform—very difficult, at best.

There Is No One-Size-Fits-All Internet Strategy. Harvard's Michael Porter, whose generic competitive strategies we just covered, cautions us to avoid putting Internet strategies into one basket. Instead, he sees two major categories:

> At this critical juncture in the evolution of Internet technology, dot-coms and established companies face different strategic imperatives. Dot-coms must develop real strategies that create economic value. They must recognize that current ways of competing are destructive and futile and benefit neither themselves nor, in the end, customers. Established companies, in turn, must stop deploying the Internet on a stand-alone basis and instead rise it to enhance the distinctiveness of their strategies.

Mellon's Janey Place calls these two types of businesses dot-coms and dot-corps. Porter urges established "brick-and-mortar" businesses to weave the Internet into the very fabric of their operations—in short, to become true e-businesses. IBM, for example, is already moving in the right direction:

> [New CEO Sam] Palmissano aims to drive costs down across the board at IBM. He's hoping to do that by tapping further into the power of the Web, using it to buy and sell, link with suppliers, and develop products—saving time and money. [In 2001,] . . . IBM purchased about $45 billion of its goods and services—some 90%—over the Net, saving $400 million. But only 25% of IBM's products and services were sold online, saving $500 million. "You will see us continue to drive our productivity and effectiveness" through the Web, says [retired CEO Lou] Gerstner.

Now let us consider five additional lessons from the dot-com and dot-corp world.

There Are Lots of Ways to Make Money on the Internet. A business can make money via the Internet through one or a combination of the following revenue sources: collecting fees from subscribers (e.g., online newsletters), selling advertising space, selling goods and selling goods directly to other businesses or end consumers, collecting transaction fees (e.g., online banks and stockbrokers), and collecting commissions for bringing together buyers and sellers (e.g., auctions and real estate).

E-business strategy lesson. Different types and combinations of revenue sources will require different business models.

Customer Loyalty Is Built with Reliable Brand Names and "Sticky" Web Sites. Web surfers have proved to have very short attention spans. Seemingly attractive Web sites can have many visitors ("hits"), but few or no sales. When doing business at Internet speed, Web sites need to satisfy three criteria: (1) high-quality lay-out and graphics; (2) fast, responsive service; and (3) complete and up-to-date information. A trusted brand name can further enhance what e-business people call the *stickiness* of a Web site, that is, the ability to draw the same customer back again and again. A great deal of work is needed in this area, considering the results of a recent study: two-thirds of the visitors to online stores did not return within a year.

E-business strategy lesson. Even though a retailing might appear to be a quick-and-easy and impersonal process, loyal customers still expect a personal touch and some "hand holding" when they have questions, problems, or suggestions.

Bricks and Mortar Must Earn Their Keep. Popular accounts of e-business conjure up visions of "virtual organizations" where an entrepreneur and a handful of employees run a huge business with little more than an Internet hookup and a coffee maker. Everything including product design, production, marketing, shipping, billing, and accounting—is contracted out. These network or virtual organizations *do* exist, but they are more the exception than the rule. More typically, companies with bricks-and-mortar facilities such as factories, warehouses, retail stores, and showrooms are blending the Internet into their traditional business models. For example, some traditional retailers are using "the concept of 'three-tailing,' in which retailers such as J. C. Penney use multiple channels—stores, Web site and catalogs—to reach consumers." Expect to see many more so-called *clicks*-and mortar combinations in the future.

E-business strategy lesson. Strategists need to identify their company's core competencies to determine which assets and tasks give them a distinct competitive advantage. No one can afford the luxury of inefficient or unproductive assets in the Internet age. For example, why own a fleet of trucks and warehouses when FedEx or United Parcel Service can handle your shipments faster, better, and less expensively?

Cannibalism Can Pay. Over years, one article of faith in management classrooms and offices has been that you should never get into a line of business or sell a product that cannibalizes your present sales. One early lesson from the e-business front directly contradicts this rule. However, as David Pottruck discovered at Charles Schwab, this e-business strategy is not for the faint-hearted:

> In 1996 the co-CEO of discount broker Charles Schwab established a separate online unit, e.Schwab, with its own staff, own offices, and own sense of mission. Then he did the unthinkable: He let e.Schwab eat Schwab.
>
> The moment of truth came in late 1997, just as demand for e.Schwab's $29.95 online trades was booming beyond anyone's expectations. Problem was, customers with Charles Schwab's traditional brokerage still had to pay an average of $65 per trade. The two-tiered pricing system was clearly awkward: Some customers were keeping small sums of money with Charles Schwab to maintain access to live brokers, then executing their trades through e.Schwab. So Pottruck came to a radical decision: All trades would be priced at $29.95. In essence, all of Schwab would become e.Schwab.
>
> Employees in the company's branch offices were skittish. "All of them thought they would have no more business and were going to lose their jobs," Pottruck says. "It attacked our old business." Schwab's board had its doubts too. The price cut would shave an estimated $125 million off revenues, and the company's stock would clearly take a pummeling. Even Pottruck himself wasn't quite sure of what he was doing. "I can't tell you honestly that I didn't lose a lot of sleep abort it," he says now. . . .
>
> In January 1998 the price cut took effect. Schwab's stock lost almost a third of its value. But the short-term pain yielded outsized long-term gain: Total accounts climbed from three million to 6.2 million; the stock recovered; $51 billion in new assets poured in during the first six months of [1999].

E-business strategy lesson. E-business sometimes requires a quick revolution, rather than slow evolution. A separate e-business unit can start with a blank sheet of paper when building a new business model, as opposed to encountering the stubborn resistance to change found in existing business units. Managers and employees are typically reluctant to turn their backs on comfortably familiar assumptions, tools, techniques, facilities, and work habits.

E-Business Partnering Should Not Dilute Strategic Control or Ethical Standards. If uncompetitive assets are sold and tasks contracted out, care needs to be taken to maintain ethical and quality standards. Do both domestic and foreign subcontractors follow applicable labor laws and ethical labor practices, or do sweatshop conditions prevail? Are subcontractors ruining the natural environment to reduce costs? Is a product designed properly before it is manufactured by an outside contractor? Are product quality standards faithfully met? These ethical and technical questions can be answered only through systematic monitoring and strategic oversight. Tough sanctions are also needed.

E-business strategy lesson. Increasingly, informed consumers are holding the sellers of goods and services to higher standards. And in doing so, they include a company's entire supply chain, foreign and domestic. Sweatshop-produced goods sold via sophisticated e-business networks are still dirty business.

The Strategic Management Process

Strategic plans are formulated during an evolutionary process with identifiable steps. In line with the three-level planning pyramid, the strategic management process is broader and more general at the top and filters down to narrower and more specific terms. Figure 4.1 outlines the four major steps of the strategic management process: (1) formulation of a grand strategy, (2) formulation of strategic plans, (3) implementation of strategic plans, and (4) strategic control. Corrective action based on evaluation and feedback takes place throughout the entire strategic management process to keep things headed in the right direction.

It is important to note that this model represents an ideal approach for instructional purposes. Because of organizational politics, and different planning orientations among managers, a somewhat less systematic process typically results. Nevertheless, it is helpful to study the strategic management process as a systematic and rational sequence to better understand what it involves. Although noting that rational strategic planning models should not be taken literally, Henry Mintzberg acknowledged their profound instructional value. They teach necessary vocabulary and implant the notion that strategy represents a fundamental congruence between external opportunity and internal capability.

Formulation of a Grand Strategy

A clear statement of organizational mission serves as a focal point for the entire planning process. Key stakeholders inside and outside the organization are given a general idea of why the organization exists and where it is headed. Working from the mission statement, top management formulates the organization's **grand strategy,** a general explanation of *how* the organization's mission is to be accomplished. Grand strategies are not drawn out of thin air. They are derived from a careful *situational analysis* of the organization and its environment. A clear vision of where the organization *is* headed and where it *should be* headed is the gateway to competitive advantage.

grand strategy How the organization's mission will be accomplished

FIGURE 4.1
The Strategic Management Process

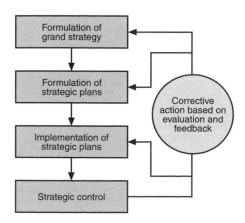

situational analysis
Finding the organization's niche by performing a SWOT analysis

Situational Analysis. A **situational analysis** is a technique for matching organizational strengths and weaknesses with environmental opportunities and threats to determine the organization's right niche (see Figure 4.2). Many strategists refer to this process as a SWOT analysis. SWOT stands for *Strengths*, *Weaknesses*, *Opportunities*, and *Threats*. (Perform an actual SWOT analysis in the Hands-On Exercise at the end of this chapter.) Every organization should be able to identify the purpose for which it is best suited. But this matching process is more difficult than it may at first appear. Strategists are faced not with snapshots of the environment and the organization but with a movie of rapidly changing events. As one researcher said: The task is to find a match between opportunities that are still unfolding and resources that are still being acquired. For example, Citibank, whose headquarters are in New York City, has set its strategic sights on a greater share of emerging Asian markets:

> . . . most foreign banks still shy away from developing countries such as India, Indonesia, and Thailand. Their rationale is that these markets are too small and that consumers lack experience in handling personal debt. . . .
>
>   Citi, however, is gambling that such Asian economies won't remain backward. Consider India, with a population of [over 1 billion]. . . . The growing middle class still rides mopeds. But within a decade, Citi bets they'll be buying BMW's. To take advantage of that possibility, Citi has positioned itself as one of the country's leading moped-loan originators.

Forecasting techniques, such as those reviewed later in this chapter, help managers cope with uncertainty about the future while conducting situational analyses.

Strategic planners, whether top managers, key operating managers, or staff planning specialists, have many ways to scan the environment for opportunities and threats. They can study telltale shifts in the economy, recent innovations, growth and movement among competitors, market trends, labor availability, and demographic shifts.

Unfortunately, according to a survey of executives at 100 U.S. corporations, not enough time is spent looking outside the organization: "Respondents said they spend less than half of their planning time (44 percent) evaluating external factors—competition and markets—compared with 48 percent on internal analysis—budget, organizational factors, human resources. 'That's the corporate equivalent of contemplating one's navel,'" says the researcher.

Environmental opportunities and threats need to be sorted out carefully. A perceived threat may turn out to be an opportunity, or vice versa. Steps can be taken to turn negatives into positives.

Capability Profile. After scanning the external environment for opportunities and threats, management's attention turns inward to identifying the organization's

FIGURE 4.2
Determining Strategic Direction
Through Situational (SWOT) Analysis

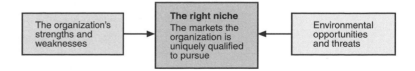

strengths and weaknesses. This subprocess is called a **capability profile**. The following are key capabilities for today's companies:

- Quick response to market trends
- Rapid product development
- Rapid production and delivery
- Continuous cost reduction
- Continuous improvement of processes, human resources, and products
- Greater flexibility of operations

Diversity initiatives are an important way to achieve continuous improvement of human resources. Also, notice the clear emphasis on *speed* in this list of key organizational capabilities.

The Strategic Need for Speed. Speed has become an important competitive advantage. Warren Holtsherg, a Motorola corporate vice president, recently offered this perspective:

> I find the impatience of the new economy refreshing. The concept that fast is better than perfect bodes well, particularly for the technology industry. At Motorola, we used to be able to introduce a cellular telephone, and it would have a life expectancy in the marketplace of about two years. Now we face cycle times of four to six mouths. People continue to demand new things. They demand change. They're impatient. Bringing that into a big corporation is invigorating.

Accordingly the new strategic emphasis on speed invokes more than doing the same old things, only faster. It calls for rethinking and radically redesigning the entire business cycle, a process called **reengineering**. The idea is to have cross-functional teams develop a whole new—and better—production process, one that does not let time-wasting mistakes occur in the first place.

Formulation of Strategic Plans

In the second major step in the strategic management process, general intentions are translated into more concrete and measurable strategic plans, policies, and budget allocations. This translation is the responsibility of top management, though input from staff planning specialists and middle managers is common. From our discussion in the last chapter we recall that a well-written plan consists of both an objective and an action statement. Plans at all levels need to specify who, what, when, and how things are to be accomplished and for how much. Many managers prefer to call these specific plans "action plans" to emphasize the need to turn good intentions into action. Even though strategic plans may have a time horizon of one or more years, they must meet the same criteria that shorter-run intermediate and operational plans meet. They should do the following:

1. Develop clear, results-oriented objectives in measurable terms.
2. Identify the particular activities required to accomplish the objectives.
3. Assign specific responsibility and authority to the appropriate personnel.
4. Estimate times to accomplish activities and their appropriate sequencing.
5. Determine resources required to accomplish the activities.
6. Communicate and coordinate the above elements and complete the action plan.

All of this does not happen in a single quick-and-easy session. Specific strategic plans usually evolve over a period of months as top management consults with key managers in all areas of the organization to gather their ideas and recommendations and, one hopes, to win their commitment.

Strategic Implementation and Control

As illustrated in Figure 4.1, the third and fourth stages of the strategic management cycle involve implementation and control. The entire process is only as strong as these two traditionally underemphasized areas.

Implementation of Strategic Plans

Because strategic plans are too often shelved without adequate attention to implementation, top managers need to do a better job of facilitating the implementation process and building middle-manager commitment.

A Systematic Filtering-Down Process. Strategic plans require further translation into successively lower-level plans. Top-management strategists can do some groundwork to ensure that the filtering-down process occurs smoothly and efficiently. Planners need answers to four questions, each tied to a different critical organizational factor:

1. *Organizational structure.* Is the organizational structure compatible with the planning process, with new managerial approaches, and with the strategy itself?
2. *People.* Are people with the right skills and abilities available for key assignments, or must attention be given to recruiting, training, management development, and similar programs?
3. *Culture.* Is the collective viewpoint on "the right way to do things" compatible with strategy, must it be modified to reflect a new perspective, or must top management learn to manage around it?
4. *Control systems.* Is the necessary apparatus in place to support the implementation of strategy and to permit top management to assess performance in meeting strategic objectives?

Strategic plans that successfully address these four questions have a much greater chance of helping the organization achieve its intended purpose than those that do not. In addition, field research indicates the need to sell strategies to all affected parties. New strategies represent change, and people tend to resist change for a variety of reasons. "The strategist thus faces a major selling job; that is, trying to build and maintain support among key constituencies for a plan that is freshly emerging." This brings us to the challenge of obtaining commitment among middle managers.

Building Middle-Manager Commitment. Resistance among middle managers can kill an otherwise excellent strategic management program. A study of

90 middle managers who wrote 330 reports about instances in which they had resisted strategic decisions documented the scope of this problem. It turned out that, to protect their own self-interests, the manager in the study frequently derailed strategies. This finding prompted the researchers to conclude as follows:

> If general management decides to go ahead and impose its decisions in spite of lack of commitment, resistance by middle management can drastically lower the efficiency with which the decisions are implemented, if it does not completely stop them from being implemented. Particularly in dynamic, competitive environments, securing commitment to the strategy is crucial because rapid implementation is so important.

Participative management and influence tactics can foster middle management commitment.

Strategic Control

Strategic plans, like our more informal daily plans, can go astray. But a formal control system helps keep strategic plans on track. Software programs (such as eWorkbench by PerformaWorks) that synchronize and track all contributors' goals in real time are indispensable today. Importantly, strategic control systems need to be carefully designed ahead of time, not merely tacked on as an afterthought. Before strategies are translated downward, planners should set up and test channels for information on progress, problems, and strategic assumptions about the environment or organization that have proved to be invalid. If a new strategy varies significantly from past ones, new production, financial, or marketing reports will probably have to be drafted and introduced.

The ultimate goal of a strategic control system is to detect and correct downstream problems in order to keep strategies updated and on target, without stifling creativity and innovation in the process. A survey of 207 planning executives found that in high-performing companies there was no tradeoff between strategic control and creativity. Both were delicately balanced.

Corrective Action Based on Evaluation and Feedback

As illustrated in Figure 4.1, corrective action makes the strategic management process a dynamic cycle. A rule of thumb is that negative feedback should prompt corrective action at the step immediately before. Should the problem turn out to be more deeply rooted, then the next earlier step also may require corrective action. The key is to detect problems and initiate corrective action, such as updating strategic assumptions, reformulating plans, rewriting policies, making personnel changes, or modifying budget allocations, as soon as possible. In the absence of prompt corrective action, problems can rapidly worsen.

Let us turn to forecasting. Without the ability to obtain or develop reliable environmental forecasts, managerial strategists have a minimal chance of successfully negotiating their way through the strategic management process.

Forecasting

forecasts Predictions, projections, or estimates of future situations

An important aspect of strategic management is anticipating what will happen. **Forecasts** may be defined as predictions, projections, or estimates of future events or conditions in the environment in which the organization operates. Forecasts may be little more than educated guesses or may be the result of highly sophisticated statistical analyses. They vary in reliability. (Consider the track record of television weather forecasters!) They may be relatively short run—a few hours to a year—or long run—five or more years. A combination of factors determines a forecast's relative sophistication, time horizon, and reliability. These factors include the type of forecast required, management's knowledge of forecasting techniques, and the money that management is willing to invest.

Types of Forecasts

There are three types of forecasts: (1) event outcome forecasts, (2) event timing forecasts, and (3) time series forecasts. Each type answers a different general question (see Table 4.2). **Event outcome forecasts** are used when strategists want to predict the outcome of highly probable future events. For example: "How will an impending strike affect output?"

event outcome forecasts Predictions of the outcome of highly probable future events

event timing forecasts Predictions of when a given event will occur

Event timing forecasts predict when, if ever, given events will occur. Strategic questions in this area might include, "When will the prime interest rate begin to fall?" or, "When will our primary competitor introduce a certain product?" Timing questions like these typically can be answered by identifying leading indicators that historically have preceded the events in question. For instance, a declining inflation rate often prompts major banks to lower their prime interest rate, or a competitor may flag the introduction of a new product by conducting market tests or ordering large quantities of a new raw material.

time series forecasts Estimates of future values in a statistical sequence

Time series forecasts seek to estimate future values in a sequence of periodically recorded statistics. A common example is the sales forecast for a business. Sales forecasts need to be as accurate as possible because they impact decisions all along the organization's supply chain. As learned the hard way by Cisco Systems, sales forecasts based on poor input can be very costly.

TABLE 4.2 Types of Forecasts		
Types of Forecast	General Question	Example
1. **Event outcome forecast**	"What will happen when a given event occurs?"	"Who will win the next World Series?"
2. **Event timing forecast**	""When will a given event occur?"	"When will a human set foot on Mars?"
3. **Time series forecast**	"What value will a series of periodic data have at a given point in time?"	"What will the closing Dow Jones Industrial Average be on January 5, 2007?"

In May 2001, Cisco Systems announced the largest inventory write-down in history: $2.2 billion erased from its balance sheet for components it ordered but couldn't use. . . .

To lock in supplies of scarce components during the [Internet] boom, Cisco ordered large quantities well in advance, based on demand projections from the company's sales force. What the forecasters didn't notice, however, was that many of their projections were inflated artificially. With network gear hard to come by, many Cisco customers also ordered similar equipment from Cisco's competitors, knowing that they'd ultimately make just one purchase—from whoever could deliver the goods first.

Forecasting Techniques

Modern managers may use one or a combination of four techniques to forecast future outcomes, timing, and values. These techniques are informed judgment, scenario analysis, surveys, and trend analysis.

Informed Judgment. Limited time and money often force strategists to rely on their own intuitive judgment when forecasting. Judgmental forecasts are both fast and inexpensive, but their accuracy depends greatly on how well informed the strategist is. Frequent visits with employees—in sales, purchasing, and public relations, for example—who regularly tap outside sources of information are a good way of staying informed. A broad reading program to stay in touch with current events and industry trends and refresher training through management development programs are also helpful. Additionally, customized news clipping services (delivered by e-mail), spreadsheet forecasting software, and a competitive intelligence-gathering operation can help keep strategic decision makers up to date.

In 1997, Nintendo of America President Minoru Arakawa made the biggest bet of his career.

> Everyone said he was nuts to import a strange Japanese video game featuring 150 tiny collectible monsters. Research showed that American kids hated it, and employees dismissed the game as too confusing. But Arakawa persisted—and hit the Pokemon jackpot.

Of course, informed judgment is no panacea. It generally needs to be balanced with data from other forecasting techniques.

scenario analysis
Preparing written descriptions of equally likely future situations

longitudinal scenarios
Describing how the future will evolve from the present

cross-sectional scenarios Describing future situations at a given point in time

Scenario Analysis. This technique also relies on informed judgment, but it is more systematic and disciplined than the approach just discussed. **Scenario analysis** (also called scenario planning) is the preparation and study of written descriptions of *alternative* but *equally likely* future conditions. Scenarios are visions of what "could be." The late futurist Herman Kahn is said to have first used the term *scenario* in conjunction with forecasting during the 1950s. The two types of scenarios are longitudinal and cross-sectional. **Longitudinal scenarios** describe how the present is expected to evolve into the future. **Cross-sectional scenarios**, the most common type, simply describe possible future situations at a given time.

While noting that *multiple forecasts* are the cornerstone of scenario analysis, one researcher offered the following perspective:

Scenario writing is a highly qualitative procedure. It proceeds more from the gut than from the computer, although it may incorporate the results of quantitative models. Scenario writing is based on the assumption that the future is not merely some mathematical manipulation of the past, but the confluence of many forces, past, present and future that can best be understood by simply thinking about the problem.

The same researcher recommends developing two to four scenarios (three being optimal) for narrowly defined topics. Likely candidates for scenario analysis are specific products, industries, or markets. For example, a grain-exporting company's strategists might look five years into the future by writing scenarios for three different likely situations: (1) above-average grain harvests, (2) average harvests, and (3) below-average harvests. These scenarios could serve as focal points for strategic plans concerning construction of facilities, staffing and training, and so on. As the future unfolds, the strategies accompanying the more realistic scenario would be followed.

This approach has been called "no surprise" strategic planning. As *Business Week* explained while offering up scenarios for the twenty-first century:

> If you envision multiple versions of the future and think through their implications, you will be better prepared for whatever ends up happening. In effect, you won't be seeing the future for the first time. You'll be remembering it. The alternative won't cut it: Those who cannot remember the future are condemned to be taken by surprise.

The key to good scenario writing is to focus on the few readily identifiable but unpredictable factors that will have the greatest impact on the topic in question. Because scenarios look far into the future, typically five or more years, they need to be written in general and rather imprecise terms.

Surveys. Surveys are a forecasting technique involving face-to-face or telephone interviews and mailed, fax, or e-mail questionnaires. They can be used to pool expert opinion or fathom consumer tastes, attitudes, and opinions. When carefully constructed and properly administered to representative samples, surveys can give management comprehensive and fresh information. They suffer the disadvantages, however, of being somewhat difficult to construct, time-consuming to administer and interpret, and expensive. Although costs can be trimmed by purchasing an off-the-shelf or "canned" survey, standardized instruments too often either fail to ask precisely the right questions or ask unnecessary questions.

trend analysis
Hypothetical extension of a past series of events into the future

Trend Analysis. Essentially, a **trend analysis** is the hypothetical extension of a past pattern of events or time series into the future. An underlying assumption of trend analysis is that past and present tendencies will continue into the future. Of course, surprise events such as the September 11, 2001, terrorist attacks can destroy that assumption. Trend analysis can be fickle and cruel to reactive companies. As a case in point, Chrysler's commitment to fuel-efficient, four-cylinder cars in the early 1980s was based on the assumption that the 1970s trend toward higher gas prices would continue. However, when the price of gasoline stabilized during the 1980s, Chrysler came up short as U.S. car buyers demanded more horsepower. By the time Chrysler had geared up its production of more powerful V-6 engines,

Iraq's 1990 invasion of Kuwait sent the price of gasoline skyward and car buyers scrambling for four-cylinder cars. Again Chrysler tripped over a faulty trend analysis. If sufficient valid historical data are readily available, trend analysis can, barring disruptive surprise events, he a reasonably accurate, fast, and inexpensive strategic forecasting tool. An unreliable or atypical database, however, can produce misleading trend projections.

Each of these forecasting techniques has inherent limitations. Consequently, strategists are advised to cross-check one source of forecast information with one or more additional sources.

Summary

1. Strategic management sets the stage for virtually all managerial activity. Managers at all levels need to think strategically and to be familiar with the strategic management process for three reasons: farsightedness is encouraged, the rationale behind top-level decisions becomes more apparent, and strategy formulation and implementation are more decentralized today. Strategic management is defined as the ongoing process of ensuring a competitively superior fit between the organization and its ever-changing environment. Strategic management effectively merges strategic planning, implementation, and control.

2. Strategic thinking, the ability to look ahead and spot key organization-environment interdependencies, is necessary for successful strategic management and planning. Four perspectives that can help managers think strategically are synergy, Porter's model of competitive strategies, the concept of business ecosystems, and e-business strategic signposts. Synergy has been called the $1 + 1 = 3$ effect because it focuses on situations where the whole is greater than the sum of its parts. Managers are challenged to achieve four types of synergy: market synergy, cost synergy, technological synergy, and management synergy.

3. According to Porter's generic competitive strategies model, four strategies are (1) cost leadership, (2) differentiation, (3) cost focus, and (4) focused differentiation. Porter's model helps managers create a profitable organization-environment "fit."

4. Contrary to the traditional assumption that strategy automatically equates to competition, the business ecosystems model emphasizes that organizations need to be as good at *cooperating* as they are at competing. By balancing competition and cooperation, competitors can *coevolve* into a dominant economic community (or business ecosystem).

5. The Internet is a disruptive technology that has managers scrambling to create successful e-business strategies. E-business pioneers have taught us these eight lessons: (1) a solid business model, not technology; should drive decisions about using the Internet; (2) evolving technologies will reshape the Internet and e-business opportunities; (3) new dot-com companies and established companies need different Internet strategies; (4) ways to make money on the web include subscriptions, advertising space, sales to business and consumers, transaction fees, and commissions; (5) reliable brand names and sticky Web sites, integrated with a personal touch and hand holding, are required to build

customer loyalty; (6) existing bricks-and-mortar assets such as factories and stores are useful in the Internet age only if they relate to core competencies that provide a competitive advantage; (7) contrary to the traditional ride against cannibalizing one's own sales, e-business sometimes requires a strategic revolution; and (8) informed consumers will not tolerate the use of sophisticated e-business partnerships, either domestic or foreign, to mask unethical labor practices and poor product quality.

6. The strategic management process consists of four major steps: (1) formulation of grand strategy, (2) formulation of strategic plans, (3) implementation of strategic plans, and (4) strategic control. Corrective action based on evaluation of progress and feedback helps keep the strategic management process on track. Results-oriented strategic plans that specify what, when, and how are then formulated and translated downward into more specific and shorter-term intermediate and operational plans. Participative management can build needed middle-manager commitment during implementation. Problems encountered along the way should be detected by the strategic control mechanism or by ongoing evaluation and subjected to corrective action.

7. Strategists formulate the organization's grand strategy after conducting a SWOT analysis. The organization's key capabilities and appropriate niche in the market-place become apparent when the organization's strengths (S) and weaknesses (W) are cross-referenced with environmental opportunities (O) and threats (T). Strategic speed has become an important capability today, sometimes necessitating radical reengineering of the entire business cycle.

8. Event outcome, event timing, and time series forecasts help strategic planners anticipate and prepare for future environmental circumstances. Popular forecasting techniques among today's managers are informed judgment, scenario analysis, surveys, and trend analysis. Each technique has its own limitations, so forecasts need to be cross-checked against one another.

⊚ Thinking Strategically: A SWOT Analysis

This exercise is suitable for either an individual or a team. First, pick an organization as the focal point of the exercise. It can be a large company, a unit of a large company, a small business, or a nonprofit organization such as a college, government agency, or religious organization. Next, look inward and list the organization's strengths and weaknesses. Turning the analysis outward, list opportunities and threats in the organization's environment. Finally, envision workable strategies for the organization by cross-referencing the two sets of factors. Be sure to emphasize organizational strengths that can exploit environmental opportunities and neutralize or overcome outside threats. Also think about what needs to be done to correct organizational weaknesses. The general idea is to create the best possible fit between the organization and its environment (the "right niche").

Note: A SWOT analysis also can be a powerful career guidance tool. Simply make *yourself* the focus of the exercise and go from there.

Organization or Unit: _____

Organization (Unit)

Strengths	Weaknesses

Environment (Unit's Situation)

Opportunities	Threats

Discussion

1. Which of the four elements—strengths, weaknesses, opportunities, threats—turned out to be the most difficult to develop? Why? Which the easiest? Why?
2. What valuable insights about your focal organization did you gain during your SWOT analysis?
3. Why should every manager know how to do a SWOT analysis?
4. What "right niche' did your SWOT analysis yield?
5. How can a personal SWOT analysis improve your career prospects?

CLOSING CASE

The Oracles of Oil

Down the hall from Ged Davis's 21st-floor office in Royal Dutch/Shell's London headquarters, there is a clear view of the enormous high-tech Ferris wheel known as the London Eve. Cantilevered out over the Thames River, the Eve is supported by two giant leaning pylons anchored, in turn, by four massive cables of braided steel. It is a spectacular feat of engineering and yet it looks as if it might topple into the river at any moment.

Sounds a lot like the oil and gas business—a vast and complex structure that appears vulnerable to disaster at many points. Upheaval appears inevitable: OPEC's reign is crumbling, new oil and gas demand is shifting to Asia, and worries about global warming are forcing hard choices on governments and businesses. And since Sept. 11, it has become impossible to ignore the deeply anti-Western psychology that festers above the world's richest oil deposits.

Davis, a soft-spoken, rapier-slim Briton with a master's in engineering from Stanford University and one in economics from the London School of Economics, is the person responsible for helping Shell managers grapple with all this uncertainty. The head of Shell's fabled scenario-planning group, Davis leads a 12-person team in developing "scenarios," or alternative visions of the future based on broad economic and political developments. Rather than making forecasts, which tend to extrapolate the future from the past, scenario planners create hypothetical stories of how the future *might* turn out. "Scenarios are plausible, pertinent, and consistent alternative stories about the future that aim at changing the policy and strategy agenda," Davis explains. If physical plant security, insurance management, and IT [information technology] safeguards are the applied mechanics of risk management, scenario planning is its quantum physics.

Many other companies, including UPS, Daimler-Chrysler, and Zurich Financial Services, now use scenario planning, but no one has practiced it longer or in a more sophisticated fashion than Shell. Every year Davis's group devises 5- to 10-year scenarios for at least a dozen countries. Every three years, they construct a pair of grand, global scenarios that trace the implications of long-term social or economic trends.

Shell's scenario movement began with a notable success. In 1972, a scenario called "Energy Crisis"—one of seven developed that year—walked through what would happen if Western oil companies lost control of world supply. When OPEC shut the spigot the next year, Shell was the only major oil company positioned to withstand the shock. The company was also prepared when prices reversed direction a decade later. "When the price collapsed in the mid-1980s," recalls Peter Schwartz, who headed Shell's scenario group during that period, "we spent $3.5 billion [buying up oil fields at depressed prices] and locked in a 20-year price advantage."

Consultants like Global Business Network, founded by Schwartz after he left Shell, . . . can help companies create scenarios without an in-house department like Shell's. Outsourced or not, scenarios must promote unconventional thinking. "A scenario practitioner has to look outside, almost with the eyes of a child, to see things anew," Davis says. To expand his own group's perspective, Davis has brought jugglers, artists, and musicians into scenario-planning workshops.

Planners say the best use of the technique is to challenge a company's strategic assumptions by pointing out that completely different outcomes are equally plausible. When scenario planning doesn't work, it's often because companies expect an immediate impact on decision-making. Shell's experience in 1972 notwithstanding, the lag between the creation of a scenario and its strategic payoff is usually years.

Shell's most recent energy scenarios, released in October [2001], show just how wide a range of outcomes planners need to assess. One, called "Dynamics as Usual," considers the implications should energy suppliers evolve gradually toward renewable forms such as solar, wind, and hydro. If this is the future, the planners conclude, oil would remain the dominant source of energy for the bulk of the 21st century. A second scenario, "Spirit of the Coming Age," envisions revolutionary technologies sparking a much faster shift toward renewable forms. In this scenario, oil is overtaken by gases, particularly hydrogen fuel cells, by 2050.

Davis's group is also putting the finishing touches on Shell's latest triennial global scenarios. . . . One premise of the scenario called "People and Connections" is that nation-states are ceding influence to networks that owe allegiance to no particular government. These include not only multinational businesses but also organized crime webs and loosely knit "communities of shared values," like the anti-globalization movement and, unfortunately, al Qaeda. Businesses and governments alike have to recognize these new constituencies, Davis warns, or they'll face consequences.

In summarizing the risks at this moment, Davis draws on a whitewater-rafting analogy that Shell planners have used before. "We are in a global 'rapids' now," he says. "With all the transitions going on— demographic, technological, geopolitical, environmental—we will be truly tested in the years ahead. Looking back, people may label this period 'childhood's end.'"

For Discussion

1. Which of Porter's four generic competitive strategies would be most profitable for Royal Dutch/Shell? Why?
2. Using your imagination and making reasonable assumptions, what opportunities and threats (the O and T portions of a SWOT analysis) can you envision for Shell?
3. Why is scenario analysis (referred to in this chapter as a "no surprise" approach to strategic planning) particularly useful for a global oil company such as Royal Dutch/Shell?
4. Which scenario do you think is more likely to come true: "Dynamics as Usual" or "Spirit of the Corning Age"? Why? (*Note:* Be sure to visit **www.shell.com** and check out the instructive and interesting material under the heading "Global Scenarios.")

ETHICS AND ORGANIZATIONAL BEHAVIOR

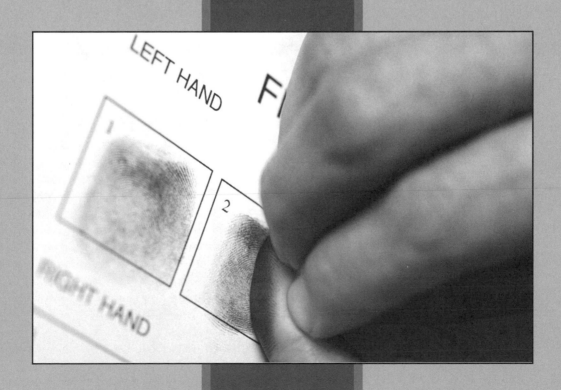

OPENING CASE

Renee Hinton says it was hard enough when she was laid off last August from Global Crossing Ltd. after 14 years with the company and its predecessor. But when the former fiber-optic darling declared bankruptcy . . . [in 2002], it dragged the systems manager into bankruptcy, too.

Like thousands of other laid-off employees, Ms. Hinton was required to take her severance package in spread-out payments rather than a lump sum. With the company's bankruptcy filing, those payments stopped. Medical benefits also were terminated. Many of the workers' 401(k) retirement plans, loaded with Global Crossing shares, became nearly worthless as the stock price plunged.

But for many Global Crossing executives, the outcome has been quite different. . . . Global Crossing's new chief executive, John Legere, received a $3.5 million signing bonus when he took the job in October [2001]—even though he was already employed as CEO of Asia Global Crossing, a separately traded affiliate. . . . At about the same time, Asia Global Crossing and Global Crossing forgave a $10 million loan to Mr. Legere, and Global Crossing eased the terms of an $8 million loan to Thomas Casey, Global's departing chief executive, according to filings the company made with the government.

The company also moved up its last pay date by a week so that executives and others still employed at Global could get paid before the company declared bankruptcy. . . . Severance payments to the already laid-off workers weren't paid.

Furthermore, in recent months Global Crossing made 11th-hour lump-sum pension payouts totaling $15 million to high-ranking executives, most of them no longer with the company.

The opening vignette highlights the relationship between decision making and ethical behavior. It also underscores the fact that top management's ethical or unethical behavior can significantly affect the lives of employees such as Renee Hinton. Ethics and ethical behavior are receiving greater attention today. This interest is partly due to reported cases of questionable or potentially unethical behavior involving companies like Global Crossing, Enron, Tyco, and Arthur Andersen and the associated costs of unethical behavior.

For instance, U.S. industries lose about $400 billion a year from unethical and criminal behavior. Another nationwide survey revealed that 20% of the respondents were asked to do something that violated their ethical standards: 41% complied. Unethical behavior is a relevant issue for all employees. It occurs from the bottom to the top of an organization. For example, a recent survey of 1000 senior-level executives revealed that as many as one-third lied on their resumes. Maybe this result should not be surprising because there are benefits to lying, such as a higher salary and stock options, and the competition for senior management positions is fierce. As you will learn, there are a variety of individual and organizational characteristics that contribute to unethical behavior. OB is an excellent vantage point for better understanding and improving workplace ethics. If OB can provide insights about managing human work behavior, then it can teach us something about avoiding *misbehavior.*

ethics Study of moral issues and choices

Ethics involves the study of moral issues and choices. It is concerned with right versus wrong, good versus bad, and the many shades of gray in supposedly black-and-white issues. Moral implications spring from virtually every decision, both on and off the job. Managers are challenged to have more imagination and the courage to do the right thing. For example, do you think credit card companies should actively inform consumers that they are charging additional fees on any international transactions? Visa and MasterCard regularly tack on a 1% fee to cover the cost of international purchases.

> Now, many of the banks that issue the cards have been quietly adding separate fees of their own. Earlier this month, First USA added a 2% surcharge to all overseas transactions for cards that didn't already have one. That means users of its popular Visa cards will pay an additional 3% on all foreign charges. . . .
>
> In many instances, the credit card fees don't show up separately on travelers' monthly credit card statements. Instead, the surcharges are folded into the cost of each item charged. The fees are disclosed only in the fine print when you first sign up for your card, or sometimes your card issuer will send you an official notice that it's raising the fee. One notable exception is Chase, which discloses the fee on the bill.

Are Visa and MasterCard engaging in sound business practices or unethical behavior? The answer will ultimately be resolved in the courts. *The Wall Street Journal* reports that these hidden charges have instigated a number of lawsuits against both Visa and MasterCard.

To enhance your understanding about ethics and organizational behavior, we discuss (1) a conceptual framework for making ethical decisions, (2) whether moral principles vary by gender, (3) general moral principles for managers, and (4) how to improve an organization's ethical climate.

A Model of Ethical Behavior

Ethical and unethical conduct is the product of a complex combination of influences (see Figure 5.1). At the center of the model in Figure 5.1 is the individual decision maker. He or she has a unique combination of personalty characteristics, values, and moral principles, leaning toward or away from ethical behavior. Personal experience with being rewarded or reinforced for certain behaviors and punished for others also shapes the individual's tendency to act ethically or unethically. Finally, gender plays an important role in explaining ethical behavior. Men and women have different moral orientations toward organizational behavior. This issue is discussed later in this section.

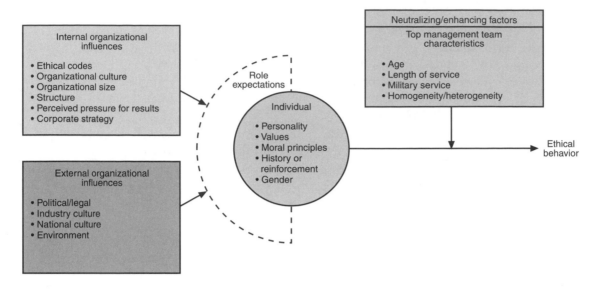

FIGURE 5.1

A Model of Ethical Behavior in the Workplace

Source: Based in part on A. J. Daboub, A. M. A. Rasheed, R. L. Priem, and D. A. Gray, "Top Management Team Characteristics and Corporate Illegal Activity." *Academy of Management Review*, January 1995, pp. 138–70.

Next, Figure 5.1 illustrates two major sources of influence on one's role expectations. People assume many roles in life, including those of employee or manager. One's expectations for how those roles should be played are shaped by a combination of internal and external organizational factors. The International OB, for example, describes how cultural differences between the United States and Europe are forcing American farmers to alter their business practices. This example illustrates how a business practice such as using genetically altered ingredients to grow crops can be viewed as ethical and unethical by people with varying cultural backgrounds. Let us now examine how various internal and external organizational influences impact ethical behavior and how these effects are neutralized or enhanced by characteristics possessed by an organization's top management team.

Internal Organizational Influences

Figure 5.1 shows six key internal organizational influences on ethical behavior. Corporate ethical codes of conduct and organizational culture clearly contribute to reducing the frequency of unethical behavior. Consider the example of Rudder Finn, the world's largest privately owned public relations agency.

> Rudder Finn established an ethics committee early on in its history because the founders maintain that public relations professionals have a special obligation to believe in what they are doing. David Finn, co-founder and CEO, chairs every ethics committee meeting to demonstrate how seriously he takes this issue. In part, these meetings perform the function of a training program in that all members of staff are invited to participate in an open forum, during which actual ethical problems are freely discussed and an outside adviser provides objectivity.

"Employees have to trust that if they go to a line manager to discuss a delicate situation or seek advice, they can do so without fear of repercussions," says Finn.

This example also illustrates the importance of top management support in creating an ethical work environment.

A number of studies have uncovered a positive relationship between organizational size and unethical behavior: Larger firms are more likely to behave illegally. Interestingly, research also reveals that managers are more likely to behave unethically in decentralized organizations. Unethical behavior is suspected to occur in this context because lower-level managers want to "look good" for the corporate office. In support of this conclusion, many studies have found a tendency among middle- and lower-level managers to act unethically in the face of perceived pressure for results. By fostering a pressure-cooker atmosphere for results, managers can unwittingly set the stage for unethical shortcuts by employees who seek to please and be loyal to the company. In contrast, consider how the organizational culture at Timberland reinforces and encourages employees to engage in socially responsible behaviors.

> Everyone gets paid for 40 hours a year of volunteer work. On Timberland's 25th anniversary, the whole place shut down so that employees could work on community projects. One employee described the event as a "religious experience."

Timberland's reward system clearly encourages ethical behavior. Individuals are more likely to behave ethically/unethically when they have incentives to do so. Managers are encouraged to examine their reward systems to ensure that the preferred types of behaviors are being reinforced.

External Organizational Influences

Figure 5.1 identifies four key external influences on role expectations and ethical behavior. The political/legal system clearly impacts ethical behavior. The United States, for example, is currently experiencing an increase in the extent to which its political/legal system is demanding and monitoring corporate ethical behavior. Treasury Secretary Paul O'Neill told reporters from *Business Week* in March 2002 that "CEOs should be held accountable not only when they intentionally mislead investors—the legal standard for taking criminal action against them—but also if they fail to stop corporate wrongdoing out of negligence." O'Neill intends to put more emphasis on investigating the ethical behavior of corporate leaders. As a case in point, the Securities and Exchange Commission announced in April 2002 that it was approving a $10 million fine against Xerox because executives led a four-year scheme to inflate revenue in order to meet Wall Street's growth targets. Past research also uncovered a tendency for firms in certain industries to commit more illegal acts. Researchers partially explained this finding by speculating that an industry's culture, defined as shared norms, values, and beliefs among firms, predisposes managers to act unethically.

Moreover, Figure 5.1 shows that national culture affects ethical behavior. This conclusion as supported in a recent multi-nation study (including United States, Great Britain, France, Germany, Spain, Switzerland, India, China, and Australia) of management ethics. Managers from each country were asked to judge the ethicality of the 12 behaviors used in the OB Exercise. Results revealed significant differences across the 10 nations. That is, managers did not agree about the ethicality of the 12 behaviors. What is your attitude toward these behaviors? Finally, the external environment influences ethical behavior. For example, unethical behavior is more likely to occur in environments that are characterized by less generosity and when industry profitability is declining.

Neutralizing/Enhancing Factors

In their search for understanding the causes of ethical behavior, OB researchers uncovered several factors that may weaken or strengthen the relationship between the internal and external influencers shown in Figure 5.1 and ethical behavior. These factors all revolve around characteristics possessed by an organization's top management team (TMT): A TMT consists of the CEO and his or her direct reports. The relationship between ethical influencers and ethical behavior is weaker with increasing average age and increasing tenure among the TMT. This result suggests that an older and more experienced group of leaders is less likely to allow unethical behavior to occur. Further, the ethical influencers are less likely to lead to unethical behavior as the number of TMT members with military experience increases and when the TMT possesses heterogenous characteristics (e.g., diverse in terms of gender, age, race, religion. etc.). This conclusion has two important implications.

First, it appears that prior military experience favorably influences the ethical behavior of executives. While OB researchers are uncertain about the cause of this relationship, it may be due to the military's practice of indoctrinating recruits to endorse the values of duty, discipline, and honor. Regardless of the cause, military experience within a TMT is positively related to ethical behavior. Organizations thus should consider the merits of including military experience as one of its selection criteria when hiring or promoting managers. Second, organizations are encouraged to increase the diversity of its TMT if they want to reduce the chances of unethical decision making.

Do Moral Principles Vary by Gender?

It is interesting to note that two women, Sherron Watkins and Maureen Castaneda, played key roles as whistle-blowers (i.e., when an employee informs others about corporate wrongdoing) in the Enron fiasco. "Watkins, Enron's vice president of corporate development, wrote the prescient memo to Enron's chief executive that warned him the company was in deep financial trouble. Castaneda, Enron's director of foreign exchange, is the one who told authorities that Enron was still shredding documents after its officials were ordered to preserve every piece of paper." Does this suggest that women are more likely to be whistle-blowers because they have different moral principles than men?

A recent study of 300 self-described whistle-blowers revealed that gender was not related to employees' reporting wrongdoing. That said, however, other research suggests that men and women view moral problems and situations differently. Carol Gilligan, a well-known psychologist, proposed one underlying cause of these gender differences. Her research revealed that men and women differed in terms of how they perceived moral problems. Males perceived moral problems in terms of a **justice perspective**, whereas women relied on a **care perspective.** The two perspectives are described as follows:

> A justice perspective draws attention to problems of inequality and oppression and holds up an ideal of reciprocal rights and equal respect for individuals. A care perspective draws attention to problems of detachment or abandonment and holds up an ideal of attention and response to need. Two moral injunctions, not to treat others unfairly and not to turn away from someone in need, capture these different concerns.

This description underscores the point that men are expected to view moral problems in terms of rights, whereas women are predicted to conceptualize moral problems as an issue of care involving empathy and compassion.

A recent meta-analysis of 113 studies tested these ideas by examining whether or not the justice and care orientations varied by gender. Results did not support the expectation that the care perspective was used predominantly by females and the justice orientation predominantly by males. The authors concluded that "although distinct moral orientations may exist, these orientations are not strongly associated with gender." This conclusion suggests that future research is needed to identify the source of moral reasoning differences between men and women, if there are gender-based differences in the first place.

justice perspective
Based on the ideal of reciprocal rights and driven by rules and regulations

care perspective
Involves compassion and an ideal of attention and response to need

General Moral Principles

Management consultant and writer Kent Hodgson has helpfully taken managers a step closer to ethical decisions by identifying seven general moral principles. Hodgson calls them "the magnificent seven" to emphasize their timeless and world-wide relevance. Both the justice and care perspectives are clearly evident in the magnificent seven, which are more detailed and, hence, more practical. Importantly, according to Hodgson, there are no absolute ethical answers for decision makers. The goal for managers should be to rely on moral principles so their decisions are *principled, appropriate,* and *defensible.* Managers require a supportive organizational climate that translates general moral principles into specific dos and don'ts and fosters ethical decisions.

How to Improve the Organization's Ethical Climate

A team of management researchers recommended the following actions for improving on-the-job ethics.

- *Behave ethically yourself.* Managers are potent role models whose habits and actual behavior send clear signals about the importance of ethical conduct. Ethical behavior is a top-to-bottom proposition.

- *Screen potential employees.* Surprisingly, employers are generally lax when it comes to checking references, credentials, transcripts, and other information on applicant résumés. More diligent action in this area can screen out those given to fraud and misrepresentation. Integrity testing is fairly valid but is no panacea.

- *Develop a meaningful code of ethics.* Codes of ethics can have a positive impact if they satisfy these four criteria:
  1. They are *distributed* to every employee.
  2. They are firmly *supported* by top management.
  3. They refer to *specific* practices and ethical dilemmas likely to be encountered by target employees (e.g., salespersons paying kickbacks, purchasing agents receiving payoffs, laboratory scientists doctoring data, or accountants "cooking the books").
  4. They are evenly *enforced* with rewards for compliance and strict penalties for noncompliance.

- *Provide ethics training.* Employees can be trained to identify and deal with ethical issues during orientation and through seminar and video training sessions.

- *Reinforce ethical behavior.* Behavior that is reinforced tends to be repeated, whereas behavior that is not reinforced tends to disappear. Ethical conduct too often is punished while unethical behavior is rewarded.

- *Create positions, units, and other structural mechanisms to deal with ethics.* Ethics needs to be an everyday affair, not a one-time announcement of a new ethical code that gets filed away and forgotten. The Raytheon Company, for example, uses an "Ethics Quick Test" that asks employees to answer a series of questions when faced with ethical dilemmas. The answers help employees determine the best course of action.

 # Group Exercise

Investigating the Difference in Moral Reasoning between Men and Women

Objectives

1. To determine if men and women resolve moral/ethical problems differently.
2. To determine if males and females use a justice and care perspective, respectively, to solve moral/ethical problems.
3. To improve your understanding about the moral reasoning used by men and women.

Introduction

Men and women view moral problems and situations dissimilarly. This is one reason men and women solve identical moral or ethical problems differently. Researchers believe that men rely on a justice perspective to solve moral problems whereas women are expected to use a care perspective. This exercise presents two scenarios that possess a moral/ethical issue. You will be asked to solve each problem and to discuss the logic behind your decision. The exercise provides you with the opportunity to hear the thought processes used by men and women to solve moral/ethical problems.

Instructions

Your instructor will divide the class into groups of four to six. (An interesting option is to use gender-based groups.) Each group member should first read the scenario alone and then make a decision about what to do. Once this is done, use the space provided to outline the rationale for your decision to this scenario. Next, read the second scenario and follow the same procedure: Make a decision and explain your rationale. Once all group members have completed their analyses for both scenarios, meet as a group to discuss the results. One at a time, each group member should present his or her final decision and the associated reasoning for the first scenario. Someone should keep a running tally of the decisions so that a summary can be turned into the professor at the end of your discussion. Follow the same procedure for the second scenario.

Scenario 1

You are the manager of a local toy store. The hottest Christmas toy of the year is the new "Peter Panda" stuffed animal. The toy is in great demand and almost impossible to find. You have received your one and only shipment of 12, and they are all promised to people who previously stopped in to place a deposit and reserve one. A woman comes by the store and pleads with you, saying that her six-year-old daughter is in the hospital very ill, and that "Peter Panda" is the one toy she has her heart set on. Would you sell her one, knowing that you will have to break your promise and refund the deposit to one of the other customers? (There is no way you will he able to get an extra toy in time.)

Your Decision: _____

	Would Sell	Would Not Sell	Unsure
Men			
Women			

Rationale for your decision:

Scenario 2

You sell corporate financial products, such as pension plans and group health insurance. You are currently negotiating with Paul Scott, treasurer of a *Fortune* 500 firm, for a sale that could be in the millions of dollars. You feel you are in a strong position to make the sale, but two competitors are also negotiating with

Scott, and it could go either way. You have become friendly with Scott, and over lunch one day he confided in you that he has recently been under treatment for manic depression. It so happens that in your office there is a staff psychologist who does employee counseling. The thought has occurred to you that such a trained professional might be able to coach you on how to act with and relate to a personality such as Scott's, so as to persuade and influence him most effectively. Would you consult the psychologist?

Your Decision: _____

	Would Consult	Would Not Consult	Unsure
Men			
Women			

Rationale for your decision:

Questions for Discussion

1. Did males and females make different decisions in response to both scenarios?
2. What was the moral reasoning used by women and men to solve the two scenarios?
3. To what extent did males and females use a justice and care perspective. respectively?
4. What useful lessons did you learn from this exercise?

MANAGING IN A GLOBAL ENVIRONMENT

THE MANAGEMENT CHALLENGE

Lincoln Electric's Global Expansion

When it comes to motivating workers, the Lincoln Electric Company of Cleveland, Ohio, is one of the most famous companies in the world. In 1934, it established its Lincoln incentive system, where Lincoln distributes much of the cash it produces each year to its employees as a bonus. Management bases the bonus on the employees' factorywide and individual performances. The plan has made Lincoln's factory workers among the highest paid in the world—many earn $80,000 or more per year.

When Lincoln decided to expand abroad in the late 1980s, its financial performance began to unravel. Lincoln's management made four basic assumptions: the incentive plan would work as well with employees abroad as it did in the United States; that with the highly motivated workforce its incentive plan produced, management would be able to control all foreign operations from the Cleveland headquarters; the company could expand abroad without a core of experienced global managers and corporate directors; and Lincoln's management systems were so good that the company's managers didn't have to study the cultures into which Lincoln was expanding.

By the early 1990s, for the first time in Lincoln's 97-year history, management had to report a multi-million dollar quarterly loss. The problem was foreign operations. Upon taking the reins as CEO, Donald Hastings needed to know the answers to these questions: Where do you think management went wrong? What would you suggest we do about it?

Globalization is a major force in business today, with exports accounting for over 11% of America's total economic activity. Some business leaders say that globalization really means "Americanization." Martin Sorrell, chairman and CEO of UK-based advertising giant WPP Group, says, "You see this in every industry: The strongest global franchises belong to companies that have strong franchises in the United States. If you're not strong in the United States, it's hard to be strong elsewhere. To dominate an industry—whatever the scale, wherever the business— you simply have to have strong representation in United States." Yet as Lincoln's experience shows, being tops in America doesn't necessarily mean you'll succeed overseas. Managing abroad brings its own special challenges. The main purpose of this chapter is to enable you to better size up the pros and cons of expanding abroad, and to better manage our global operations once you do expand. The main topics we'll cover include methods of doing business abroad; the international environment; the management team in a global business; and global management planning, organizing, leading, and controlling techniques.

Reprinted from *Management: Principles and Practices for Tomorrow's Leaders,* Third Edition, by Gary Dessler. Reprinted with permission of Relsed Publishing Co., Inc., Miami, Florida. © 2004 Relsed Publishing Co., Inc. All rights reserved.

Doing Business Abroad

Globalization is the tendency of firms to extend their sales, ownership, and/or manufacturing to new markets abroad. Globalization of *markets* is perhaps most obvious. Sony, Calvin Klein, The Gap, Nike, and Mercedes Benz are some firms that market all over the world. *Production* is global too. Toyota produces its Camry in Georgetown, Kentucky. Dell produces computers in China. In turn, the existence of globalized markets and production means that globalized *ownership* makes more sense. For example, firms outside America own four out of five American textbook publishers—Prentice Hall, Harcourt, Houghton Mifflin, and Southwestern (Britain's Pearson owns Prentice Hall). Why do managers take their firms abroad?

Companies expand abroad for several reasons. *Sales expansion* is often the goal. Thus, Lincoln Electric went abroad to open new markets in Europe and elsewhere. Wal-Mart is opening stores in South America. Dell Computer, knowing that China will soon be the world's second biggest market for PCs, is aggressively building plants and selling there.

Firms also go abroad for other reasons. Some manufacturers go seeking their foreign *products* and services to sell, and to *cut labor costs*. Thus, Florida apparel manufacturers have products assembled in Central America, where labor costs are relatively low. Sometimes, high-quality or specialized skills drive firms overseas. For example, Apple Computer enlisted Sony's aid in producing parts for a notebook computer.

The question for the manager is, "*How* should we expand abroad?" Options include exporting, licensing, franchising, foreign direct investment, joint ventures/strategic alliances, and wholly owned subsidiaries. Many things—including the company's goals and resources—determine which option is best.

Exporting

exporting Selling abroad, either directly to target customers or indirectly by retaining foreign sales agents and distributors

Exporting is often a manager's first choice when expanding abroad. Exporting is a relatively simple and easy approach. It means selling abroad, either directly to customers, or indirectly through sales agents and distributors. Agents, distributors or other intermediaries handle more than half of all exports. They are generally local people familiar with the market's customs and customers.

Carefully selecting intermediaries is important. For example, you can check business reputations via local agencies of the U.S. State Department. Then carefully draft agency and distribution agreements to ensure you have the right representatives. Bird Corporation President Fred Schweser sought out the U.S. Commerce department's trade specialist Harvey Roffman for help in generating overseas business. Roffman recommended advertising in *Commercial News USA,* a government publication designed to inform around 100,000 foreign agents, distributors, buyers, and government officials about U.S. products. The advice worked. Schweser's Elkhorn, Nebraska, Go-Cart company now boasts customers from Japan to the United Kingdom.

Exporting has pros and cons. It avoids the need to build factories in the host country, and it is a relatively quick and inexpensive way of "going international."

It's also a good way to test the waters in the host country, and to learn more about its customers' needs. However, transportation, tariff, or manufacturing costs can put the exporter at a disadvantage, as can poorly selected intermediaries. Some avoid this problem by selling direct. L.L. Bean, Lands' End, and Sharper Image all export globally via their catalogues and the Internet. Since the Internet is basically borderless, almost any company can market its products or services directly to potential customers anywhere in the world.

Licensing

licensing An arrangement whereby a firm (the licensor) grants a foreign firm the right to use intangible property

Licensing is an arrangement whereby the licensor grants a foreign firm the right to exploit intangible ("intellectual") property, such as patents, copyrights, manufacturing processes, or trade names for a specific period. The licensor usually gets royalties—a percentage of the earnings—in return. Licensing enables a firm to generate income abroad from its intellectual property without actually producing or marketing the product or service there.

For example, consider a small U.S. inventor of antipollution materials. Licensing Shell Oil to produce and sell the material in Europe lets the U.S. firm enter that market with little or no investment. However, it might not be able to control the design, manufacture, or sales of its products as well as it could if it built its own facilities there.

Franchising

franchising The granting of a right by a parent company to another firm to do business in a prescribed manner

If you've eaten in McDonald's by Rome's Spanish Steps, you know that franchising is another way to do business abroad. **Franchising** is the granting of a right by a parent company to another firm to do business in a prescribed manner.

Franchising is similar to licensing. Both involve granting rights to intellectual property. Both are quick and relatively low-cost ways to expand into other countries. However, franchising usually requires both parties to make greater commitments in time and money. A franchisee must generally follow strict guidelines in running the business. It must also make substantial investments in a physical plant (such as a fast-food restaurant). Licensing tends to be limited to manufacturers. Franchising is more common among service firms such as restaurants, hotels, and rental services. Maintaining the franchisee's quality can be a particular problem. For example, an early McDonald's franchisee in France had to close its restaurants when it failed to maintain McDonald's quality standards.

Foreign Direct Investment and the Multinational Enterprise

foreign direct investment Operations in one country by entities in a foreign country

At some point, managers find that capitalizing on international opportunities requires direct investment. **Foreign direct investment** refers to operations in one country controlled by entities in a foreign country. A foreign firm might build facilities in another country, as Toyota did when it built its Camry plant in Georgetown, Kentucky. Or a firm might acquire property or operations, as when Wal-Mart bought control of the Wertkauf stores in Germany. A foreign direct investment turns the firm into a multinational enterprise. Strictly speaking, foreign direct investment means owning more than 50% of the operation. But in practice, a firm can gain effective control by owning less than half.

Purchases like these trigger large and small changes. For example, the Italian bank UniCredito Italiano Group purchased Boston's Pioneer Group several years ago. One of its first changes was installing an Italian espresso machine in Pioneer's offices. The Milan bank also installed video cameras and screens. Now investment managers on both sides of the Atlantic can hold videoconferences. Pioneer group managers have begun learning Italian. And the companies integrated their Italian and U.S. investment teams, which then went on to launch several global funds.

Joint Ventures and Strategic Alliances

strategic alliance An agreement between potential or actual competitors to achieve common objectives

Foreign direct investments are often strategic alliances. Strictly speaking, **strategic alliances** are "cooperative agreements between potential or actual competitors." For example, Boeing partnered with several Japanese companies to produce a new commercial jet. Airline alliances, such as American Airlines' One World alliance, are also examples. The airlines don't share investments, but they do share seating on some flights, and they let passengers use alliance members' airport lounges. In practice, most managers define strategic alliances more broadly, as any agreements between firms that are of strategic importance to one or both firms. In that sense, even licensing or franchising agreements might come under the strategic alliance umbrella.

The point of the alliance is usually to quickly gain strengths that would otherwise take time to acquire. General Motors is using alliances to build its Asian presence. It has minority stakes in several Asian auto manufacturers, including Daewoo Motor Company, Suzuki Motor Ltd., Isuzu Motor Ltd., and Fuji Heavy Industries.

joint venture The participation of two or more companies in an enterprise such that each party contributes assets, owns the entity to some degree, and shares risk

A **joint venture** is "the participation of two or more companies jointly in an enterprise in which each party contributes assets, owns the entity to some degree, and shares risk." A joint venture is a special strategic alliance. Companies execute joint ventures every day. For example, the big Indian media company, Zee Telefilms, recently formed several partnerships with AOL Time Warner. The firms call their new joint venture Zee Turner. It will distribute both partners' television programs in India and neighboring countries.

A joint venture lets a firm gain useful experience in a foreign country by using the expertise and resources of a locally knowledgeable firm. Joint ventures also help both companies share the cost of starting a new operation. But as in licensing, the joint venture partners risk giving away proprietary secrets. And joint ventures usually require the partners to share control.

Joint ventures can be a necessity. In China, foreign companies that want to enter regulated industries (like telecommunications) must use joint ventures with well-connected Chinese partners. The partnership of Britain's Alcatel and Shanghai Bell to make telephone-switching equipment is an example.

Wholly Owned Subsidiaries

wholly owned subsidiary A firm that is owned 100% by a foreign firm

Some companies have the knowledge and resources to go it alone. A **wholly owned subsidiary** is one owned 100 percent by the foreign firm. In the United States, Toyota Motor Manufacturing, Inc., and its Georgetown, Kentucky, Camry facility is a wholly owned subsidiary of Japan's Toyota Motor Corporation. Toys "R" Us, Inc, was the first large U.S.-owned discount store in Japan, and it is now expanding its wholly owned subsidiary there. Wholly owned subsidiaries let the company do things exactly as it wants (subject to local laws and regulations, of course).

The Language of International Business

To do business abroad, the manager should know the vocabulary of international business. An **international business** is any firm that engages in international trade or investment. International business also refers to those activities, such as exporting goods or transferring employees, that require the movement of resources, goods, services, and skills across national boundaries. **International trade** is the export or import of goods or services to consumers in another country. **International management** is the performance of the management functions of planning, organizing, leading, and controlling across national borders. As Wal-Mart managers expand abroad, for instance, they necessarily engage in international management.

A **multinational corporation** (MNC) operates manufacturing and marketing facilities in two or more countries; managers of the parent firm, whose owners are mostly in the firm's home country, coordinate the MNC's operations. Firms like GE and GM have long been multinational corporations. However, thousands of small firms are MNCs, too.

The MNC operates in multiple countries and adapts its products and practices to each one. Sometimes, however, the MNC's behavior may still reflect its national roots. Thus, Germany's DeutscheBank recently bought a British bank, and the British managers' high incentive pay created tension between them and their new German bosses.

international business Any firm that engages in international trade or investment; also refers to business activities that involve the movement of resources, goods, services, and skills across national boundaries.

international management The performance of the management process across national boundaries

international trade The export or import of goods or services to consumers in another country

multinational corporation (MNC) A company that operates manufacturing and marketing facilities in two or more countries: managers of the parent firm, whose owners are mostly in the firm's home country, coordinate the MNC's operation

The Manager's International Environment

Tensions like these illustrate a fact of life of doing business abroad: Countries differ in terms of economic, legal, and political systems—and also in their cultures. Managers ignore such differences at their peril, since they'll shape the manager's plans, organization, leadership style, and controls.

The Economic Environment

First, managers should understand the economic environments of the countries they are thinking of entering. This includes each country's *economic system, economic development, exchange rates, trade barriers, economic integration* and *free trade.*

The Economic System. Countries differ in the extent to which they adhere to capitalistic economic ideals and policies like America's. For example, like America, Hong Kong is a *market economy.* In a pure market economy, supply and demand determine what is produced, in what quantities, and at what prices.

Managers here tend to have much flexibility to compete and set prices without government intervention.

At the other extreme, the People's Republic of China until recently was a pure *command economy* (North Korea still is). Countries like these base their yearly targets on five-year plans set by the government. Then the government establishes specific production goals and prices for each sector of the economy (for each product or group of products), as well as for each manufacturing plant. Managers from abroad usually need government approval before entering these markets and forming partnerships with local firms.

After taking over Hong Kong from Britain several years ago, China agreed to let Hong Kong keep its capitalist system for 50 years. However, Beijing now governs Hong Kong's political administration, and Hong Kong's legislature imposed limits on opposition activities. Developing lone run management plans under such circumstances can be challenging.

mixed economy An economy in which some sectors are left to private ownership and free market mechanisms, while others are largely owned and managed by the government

In a **mixed economy,** some sectors have private ownership and free market mechanisms, while others are owned and managed by the government. *Mixed* is, of course, a matter of degree. For example, France is a capitalist country. However, it has a mixed economy. The government owns shares of industries like telecommunications (France Telecom) and air travel (Air France).

Economic systems in transition can trigger social instability. This occurred several years ago in the newly capitalized Russia. Free-market economies require commercial laws, banking regulations, and an effective independent judiciary and law enforcement. Without such a political and legal infrastructure in Russia, early business owners had to cope not just with competitors but also with criminals, lax law enforcement, and the control of several industries by friends of powerful politicians. Managers taking their firms into such areas obviously can't just be concerned with running their businesses. There's the added challenge of the turbulence.

Economic Development.
Countries also differ in degree of *economic development.* For example, some countries, such as the United States, Japan, Germany, France, Italy, and Canada, have large, mature economies. They also have extensive *industrial infrastructures.* This includes telecommunications, transportation, and regulatory and judicial systems. These countries' gross domestic products range from about $700 billion for Canada to $8.5 trillion for the United States. Other countries, such as Mexico, are less developed. **Gross domestic product (GDP)** is the market value of all goods and services bought for final domestic use during a period. It is a basic measure of a nation's economic activity.

gross domestic product (GDP) The market value of all goods and services that have been brought for final use during a period of time, and, therefore, the basic measure of a nation's economic activity

Some countries are growing much faster than others. The growth rate of mature economies averages around 4% per year. On the other hand, China, India, and Taiwan are growing at about 7.5%, 5.0% and 5.2%, respectively. Many managers at firms like Wal-Mart are therefore boosting their investments in these high-growth, high-potential countries. A country's economic development level can thus be both a blessing and a curse to the manager thinking of entering it. Low economic development may suggest the potential for rapid development and growth, but it can also mean an absence of adequate roadways, communications, and regulatory and judicial infrastructure.

exchange rate The rate at which one country's currency can be exchanged for another country's currency

trade barrier A governmental influence that is usually aimed at reducing the competitiveness of imported products or services

tariff A government tax on imports

quota A legal restriction on the import of particular goods

subsidy A direct payment a country makes to support a domestic producer

free trade All trade barriers among participating countries are removed, so there is an unrestricted exchange of goods among these countries

economic integration The result of two or more nations minimizing trade restrictions to obtain the advantages of free trade

free trade area A type of economic integration in which all barriers to trade among members are removed

customs union A situation in which trade barriers among members are removed and a common trade policy exists with respect to nonmembers

common market A system in which no barriers to trade exist among member countries, and a common external trade policy is in force that governs trade with nonmembers; factors of production, such as labor capital, and technology, more freely among members

Exchange Rates. Managers engaged in international business must also juggle exchange rates. The **exchange rate** for one country's currency is the rate at which someone can exchange it for another country's currency. A dramatic drop in the value of the dollar relative to the pound could have a devastating effect on a small U.S. company that suddenly found it needed 30% more dollars than planned to build a factory in Scotland.

Trade Barriers. The Gap store in Paris's Passy area sells jeans that you could buy for two-thirds the price in midtown Manhattan. How call this be? The answer is that trade barriers distort the prices companies must charge for their products. **Trade barriers** are governmental influences aimed at reducing the competitiveness of imported products or services. **Tariffs,** the most common trade barrier, are governmental taxes levied on goods shipped internationally. The exporting country collects export tariffs. Importing countries collect import tariffs. Countries through which the goods pass collect transit tariffs. Other countries impose **quotas**—legal restrictions on the import of specific goods. Managers thinking of doing business abroad ignore taxes like these at their peril.

Nontariff trade barriers exist too. For example, cars imported to Japan must meet a complex set of regulations and equipment modifications. Side mirrors must snap off easily if they contact a pedestrian, for example. Some countries make payments called **subsidies** to domestic producers. These are government payments that can make inefficient domestic producers more competitive.

Economic Integration and Free Trade. Free trade agreements among countries are a big part of the economic situation international managers face. **Free trade** means all trade barriers among participating countries are removed. Free trade occurs when two or more countries agree to allow the free now of goods and services. This means trade is unimpeded by trade barriers such as tariffs. **Economic integration** occurs when two or more nations obtain the advantages of free trade by minimizing trade restrictions.

Economic integration occurs on several levels. In a **free trade area**, member countries remove all barriers to trade among them so that they can freely trade goods and services among member countries. A **customs union** is the next higher level of economic integration. Here, members dismantle trade barriers among themselves while establishing a common trade policy with respect to nonmembers. In a **common market,** no barriers to trade exist among members, and a common external trade policy is in force. In addition, factors of production, such as labor, capital, and technology, move freely between member countries, as shown in Figure 6.1.

Economic integration is happening around the world. Back in 1957, founding members France, West Germany, Italy, Belgium, the Netherlands, and Luxembourg established the European Economic Community (now called the European Union, or EU). They signed the Treaty of Rome. It called for the formation of a free trade area, the gradual elimination of tariffs and other barriers to trade, and the formation of a customs union and (eventually) a common market. By 1987, the renamed European Community had added six other countries (Great Britain, Ireland, Denmark, Greece, Spain, and Portugal) and signed the Single Europe Act. This act "envisages a true common market where goods, people, and money move among

FIGURE 6.1
Levels of Economic Integration

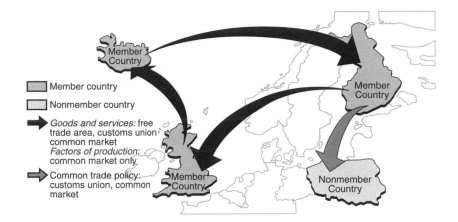

the twelve EC countries with the same case that they move between Wisconsin and Illinois." In 1995, Austria, Finland, and Sweden became the 13th, 14th, and 15th members of the EU. The EU admitted 10 more countries in 2002.

On January 1, 1999, 11 EU countries formed a European Economic and Monetary Union (EMU). On January 1, 2002, the Union's new currency, the Euro, went into circulation. Within two to three months, it entirely replaced these 11 countries' local currencies. Now companies in these countries deal with just one currency within the EU; and companies from other countries, like the United States, deal with just two currencies (theirs and the Euro) and with one exchange rate rather than several.

In 1967, Brunei, Indonesia, Malaysia, the Philippines, Singapore, Thailand, and Vietnam organized the Association of Southeast Asian Nations (ASEAN). There is also the Asia Pacific Economic Cooperation (APEC) forum. This is a loose association of 18 Pacific Rim states. Members include Australia, Chile, China, Japan, Malaysia, Mexico, Singapore, and the United States. Africa similarly has several regional trading groups, including the southern African development community, the common market for Eastern and southern Africa, and the economic community of West African states.

Canada, the United States, and Mexico established a North American Free Trade Agreement (NAFTA). NAFTA creates the world's largest free trade market, with a total output of about $6 trillion.

The WTO. Governments work together to encourage free trade in other ways. GATT—the General Agreement on Tariffs and Trade—was one example. Formed in 1947 by 23 countries, by the mid-1990s 117 countries were participating. Among other things, GATT sponsored "rounds" or sessions at which members discussed multilateral reductions in trade barriers. The World Trade Organization (WTO) replaced GATT in 1995, and it now has over 130 members. One of the WTO's important functions is granting "most favored nation" (or "normal trade relations") status for countries. This means that the WTO countries' "most favorable trade concessions must apply to all trading partners."

China recently received most favored nation status and joined the WTO. Joining means getting the benefits of normal trade relations with WTO partners, but it also means the new member must reduce its own trade barriers. Several

U.S. companies, including New York Life Insurance Company and Metropolitan Life Insurance Co., quickly got the green light to set up 50-50 joint ventures with Chinese partners once China joined the WTO. Even for WTO members, some trade barriers fall faster than others. With WTO membership, China will see its import duties on cars fall drastically (to about 25%). However, within China, Shanghai still has big license fees on cars from neighboring provinces so that Shanghai can protect its locally built Volkswagen.

Economic integration has a big effect on managers. By removing trade barriers (such as tariffs), it promotes regional trade and thus boosts competition. Thus, in Europe, airlines (like British Airways) and telecommunications firms (like France Telecom) had relatively little competition 10 years ago. Now they face new competition from firms like Air France and DeutscheTelecom within their EU trading bloc. Establishing free trade zones also put firms from nonmember countries at a disadvantage. Many U.S. managers are forming joint ventures with European partners to make it easier for them to sell in the EU.

Legal and Political Environment

Global political and legal differences can blindside even the most sophisticated companies. After spending billions of dollars expanding into Germany, for instance, Wal-Mart managers were surprised to learn that Germany's commercial laws discourage advertising or promotions that involve competitive price comparisons.

Legal considerations influence how managers expand abroad. In India, for instance, a foreign investor may own only up to 40% of an Indian industrial company, whereas in Japan, up to 100% of foreign ownership is allowed. Some managers go global by appointing sales agents or representatives in other countries. But in Algeria, for instance, agents can't represent foreign setters. Other countries view agents as employees subject to those countries' employment laws.

Legal Systems. Countries also differ fundamentally in their approaches to the law. England and the United States use *common law* legal systems. Here, tradition and precedent—not written statutes—govern legal decisions. Other countries, like France, follow a *code law system,* or a comprehensive set of written statutes. A businessperson accused of a crime there might also be surprised to find he or she is "guilty till proven innocent," while the U.S. system assumes the accused is innocent. Some countries use a combination of common law and code law. The United States adheres to a system of common law in criminal proceedings but to a written Uniform Commercial Code for governing business activities.

International law is another consideration when expanding abroad. *International law* is less an enforceable body of law than it is agreements embodied in treaties and other types of agreements. International law governs things like intellectual property rights, such as whether someone in Japan can reproduce Motown's music without its permission. Intellectual property piracy (fake brands) can be a big problem where the legal system is inadequate or inadequately enforced. For example, P&G reportedly estimates that about 20 percent of all its products sold in China are fake.

Political System. Going abroad also means sizing up the political systems and risks with which you'll have to cope. Thus, democratic countries will usually provide a more open environment in which to establish and manage businesses than will dictatorships. Sometimes, the company's fate can change unexpectedly as the political winds shift. For example, in the mid-1990s, the Coca-Cola Company was very successful with its bottling plant in Uzbekistan. One reason, apparently, was that it opened the plant in partnership with the Uzbekistan president's son-in-law. Recently, when the president's daughter separated from her husband, the bottling company's Uzbek fortunes abruptly took a turn for the worse.

The Sociocultural Environment

People around the world react to events in characteristic ways. For example, a researcher at Georgetown University found that Japanese, German, and U.S. managers tended to take different approaches when resolving workplace conflict. The Japanese prefer the power approach, tending to defer to the party with the most power. Germans tend to emphasize a more legalistic, sticking-to-the-rules approach. U.S. managers tend to try to take into account all parties' interests and to work out a solution that maximizes the benefits for everyone.

Cultural differences like these should influence how managers conduct business abroad. When it opened its new production plant in Valenciennes, France, Toyota had to explain to the French Labor Ministry why management banned the traditional red wine at lunchtime in the company cafeteria. (The reasons given were health and working conditions.)

On the other hand, Starbucks broke some traditions when it opened its first Tokyo store, and it now has over 300 stores in Japan. Starbucks (pronounced "STAH-buks-zu" in Japanese) accomplished this by redefining (not adapting to) the way the Japanese drink coffee. Its nonsmoking, bright, sofa-filled stores are in marked contrast to the dimly lit, smoke-filled stores where many Japanese traditionally drink their coffee from tiny cups. It turned out that Japanese girls preferred Starbucks' nonsmoking stores, and the boys were soon following them there to socialize. We'll look more closely at multicultural issues in management later in this chapter.

The Technological Environment

technology transfer
The transfer, often to another country, of systematic knowledge for the manufacturing of a product, for the application of a process, or for the rendering of a service; it does not extend to the mere sales or lease of goods

Doing business abroad often requires **technology transfer,** which is the "transfer of systematic knowledge for the manufacture of a product, for the application of a process, or for the rendering of a service, and [it] does not extend to the mere sale or lease of goods." When Dell builds a computer factory in China, the plant's success depends on Dell's ability to successfully transfer to local managers knowledge of its sophisticated manufacturing processes.

Successful technology transfer depends on several things. It depends on having a needed and suitable technology. Social and economic conditions must favor the transfer. (Pollution-reducing technology might be economically useless in a country where pollution reduction is not a priority.) Finally, technology transfer depends on the willingness and ability of the receiving party to use and adapt the technology: Opening a new plant or franchising a process require an acceptable level of technical expertise in the receiving country. Without it, the expansion may well fail.

Distance and Global Management

As you can see, geographic distance was just one of the barriers managers like Lincoln Electric's new CEO Donald Hastings faced when Lincoln expanded abroad. They also faced economic, legal/political, sociocultural, and technological barriers.

Studies of international trade show that factors like these are actually more important than geographic distance in explaining a foreign venture's success. For example, studies show that international trade is much more likely among countries that share a common language and that belong to a common regional trading bloc. International trade is greater among countries that formerly shared a colony-colonizer relationship (as between England and Australia). Similarly, common political systems and a common currency translate into less troublesome—and thus greater—trade.

One researcher says (see Figure 6.2) that managers like Donald Hastings should consider at least four factors before expanding abroad: (1) *cultural distance* (such as languages and religions), (2) *administrative distance* (such as absence of shared monetary or political associations), (3) *geographic distance* (such as physical remoteness), and (4) *economic distance* (such as differences in consumer incomes).

His point is that some cross-border business initiatives are more likely to succeed than are others. Figure 6.3 summarizes this. For example, in the textile industry, geographic distance isn't nearly as important as administrative distance. That's because preferential trading agreements and tariffs determine whether textiles from one country are salable in another. If you're a manager in a textile firm, you'd best take preferential trading agreements into account. Similarly, managers at Campbell Soup should consider cultural distance when launching products abroad (for instance, the Japanese tend to have soup for breakfast).

ATTRIBUTES OF CREATING DISTANCE			
Cultural Distance	**Administrative Distance**	**Geographic Distance**	**Economic Distance**
Different languages	Absence of colonial ties	Physical remoteness	Differences in consumer incomes
Different ethnicities; lack of connective ethnic or social networks	Absence of shared monetary or political association	Lack of a common border	Differences in costs and quality of:
Different religions	Political hostility	Lack of sea or river access	• natural resources
Different social norms	Government policies	Size of country	• financial resources
	Institutional weakness	Weak transportation or communication links	• human resources
		Differences in climates	• infrastructure
			• intermediate inputs
			• information or knowledge

FIGURE 6.2
Determinants of Global Distance

SOURCE: Adapted from Pankaj Ghemawat, "Distance Still Matters," *Harvard Business Review,* September, 2001, p. 140.

ATTRIBUTES OF CREATING DISTANCE			
Cultural Distance	**Administrative Distance**	**Geographic Distance**	**Economic Distance**
Linguistic Ties	Preferential Trading Agreement	Physical Remoteness	Wealth Differences
MORE SENSITIVE			
Meat and meat preparations	Gold, nonmonetary	Electricity current	*(economic distance decreases trade)*
Cereals and cereal preparations	Electricity current	Gas, natural and manufactured	Nonferrous metals
Miscellaneous edible products and preparations	Coffee, tea, cocoa, spices	Paper, paperboard	Manufactured fertilizers
Tobacco and tobacco products	Textile fibers	Live animals	Meat and meat preparations
Office machines and automatic data processing equipment	Sugar, sugar preparations, and honey	Sugar, sugar preparations, and honey	Iron and steel
			Pulp and waste paper
LESS SENSITIVE			
Photographic apparatuses, optical goods, watches	Gas, natural and manufactured	Pulp and waste paper	*(economic distance increases trade)*
Road vehicles	Travel goods, handbags	Photographic apparatuses, optical goods, watches	Coffee, tea, cocoa, spices
Cork and wood	Footwear	Telecommunications and sound-recording apparatuses	Animal oils and fats
Metalworking machinery	Sanitary, plumbing, heating, and lighting fixtures	Coffee, tea, cocoa, spices	Office machines and automatic data-processing equipment
Electricity current	Furniture and furniture parts	Gold, nonmonetary	Power-generating machinery and equipment
			Photographic apparatuses, optical goods, watches

more sensitive ← ──────────────────────────────── → *less sensitive*

FIGURE 6.3

Industry Sensitivity to Distance

The various types of distance affect different industries in different ways.

Source: Pankaj Ghemawat, "Distance Still Matters," *Harvard Business Review*, September, 2001, pp. 142–143.

The Management Team in a Global Business

Globalizing is a two-edged sword from the point of view of the manager. On the one hand, it opens up new markets and productive capabilities. On the other hand, the distances involved as well as factors like legal and cultural differences complicate marketing, producing, and staffing decisions abroad. Let's look at some examples.

Global Marketing

Expanding into markets abroad is often a matter of survival. As one expert says, "Even the biggest companies in the bigger countries cannot survive on their domestic markets if they an in global industries." In the late 1990s, Wal-Mart's total company sales rose by 16 percent, but its international sales jumped by 26 percent.

About 10 percent—or 135,000—of Wal-Mart's employees are outside the United States. Its Web site (**www.walmart.com**) shows how giants like Wal-Mart (or tiny firms), can market globally, sometimes without even leaving their home countries.

Yet we've seen that expanding abroad confronts marketing managers with many challenges. For some products, like Benetton clothes, consumer preferences in different countries are similar. However, even global firms that emphasize standardized products, like McDonald's, must still fine-tune their products when they go abroad. You won't find beef in McDonald's India restaurants, and you'll find sparkling water on sale on the Champs Elysees. Marketing managers expanding abroad, therefore, can't simply use their domestic marketing and advertising plans. They'll need local market research and analysis before creating new marketing plans.

Globalization of Production

Globalizing production means dispersing components of a firm's production process to locations around the globe. One aim may be to support local markets abroad. Another may be to capitalize on national differences in the cost and quality of production—it might be cheaper to produce in Peru, for instance.

Sometimes, the best strategy is to integrate global production operations into a unified and efficient system of manufacturing facilities around the world. For example why ship supplies from the United States to Spain, when it's possible to support the Spanish factory with supplies from the south of France? Thus, Toyota recently reorganized its global production facilities into several regional centers. Xerox is another example.

Management in Action

XEROX

In the 1980s, each Xerox subsidiary in each country had its own suppliers, assembly plants, and distribution channels. Each country's plant managers gave little thought to how their plans fit with Xerox's global needs. This approach became untenable as Canon, Minolta, and Ricoh penetrated Xerox's U.S. and European markets with low-cost copiers.

The competitive threat prompted Xerox's senior managers to coordinate their global production processes. They organized a new central purchasing group to consolidate raw materials purchases, and they, thereby, cut worldwide manufacturing costs. They instituted a "leadership through quality" program to improve product quality, streamline and standardize manufacturing processes, and cut costs. Xerox managers also eliminated over $1 billion of inventory costs with computer systems that linked customer orders from one region more closely with production capabilities in other regions.

Schlumberger integrated its global production facilities using the Internet, as the Managing @ the Speed of Thought feature illustrates.

Using the Internet as a Global Production Management Tool

Managing a global production operation is always a challenge. The distances involved are usually enormous, and its easy for home-office managers to lose track of what's going on in the field, especially when the field is 8,000 miles away. If that happens, the benefits of efficiency sought by firms like Xerox in the earlier example will not materialize.

Production managers today are therefore using the Internet to monitor their global operations. Schlumberger Ltd. is a good example. Schlumberger, which manufactures oil-drilling equipment and electronics, has headquarters in New York and Paris. The company operates in 85 countries, and in most of them, employees are in remote locations. How do the company's managers maintain control over so many far-flung locations? Here's how experts describe the company's system:

> To install their own network for so few people at each remote location would have been prohibitively expensive. Using the Internet, Schlumberger engineers in Dubai (on the Persian Gulf) can check e-mail and effectively stay in close contact with management at a very low cost. In addition, the field staff is able to follow research projects as easily as can personnel within the United States. Schlumberger has found that since it converted to the Internet from its own network, its overall communications costs are down 2% despite a major increase in network and information technology infrastructure spending. The main reason for the savings is the dramatic drop in voice traffic and in overnight delivery service charges ([since employees] attach complete documents to their e-mail messages).

At Schlumberger the Internet plays a central role in creating an efficient world-wide production system.

Global Staffing

Doing business abroad also triggers global staffing concerns. At a minimum, setting up factories abroad requires studying employment laws in the host country, establishing a recruiting office, and ensuring that the firm complies with local staffing regulations.

Global staffing is very important today. 3M produces tapes, chemicals, and electrical parts in Bangalore, India, and HP-Compaq assembles computers and designs memory boards in Guadalajara, Mexico. In Jamaica, 3,500 office workers make airline reservations, process tickets, and handle calls to toll-free numbers via satellite dishes for U.S. companies. Back in Bangalore, a skilled workforce attracted firms like Texas Instruments, Motorola, and IBM, to establish programming centers.

Even apparently minor growth abroad requires a global staffing outlook. For example, sending the company's sales manager abroad for several months to close a deal means deciding how to compensate her for her expenses abroad, what to do with her house here, and how to make sure she knows how to handle the cultural demands of her foreign assignment. And finding globally qualified managers is not easy. Companies like Motorola Inc. therefore use special programs to identify and evaluate potential global managers.

One program involves putting management candidates through two-to-three days of realistic role-playing exercises under the watchful eyes of trained psychologists. As one participant writes, ". . . the telephone calls, unexpected visitors and urgent tasks come so fast and furious that I quickly forget it is only a game." Motorola has used its new program to screen hundreds of local Chinese management candidates so far. One company, French food firm Danone reportedly reduced its expatriate failure rate from 35 percent to 3 percent in three years using similar programs. As other examples, consider the following issues managers ran into when setting up a factory in Mexico.

Management in Action

MANAGING IN MEXICO

Managers at one U.S.-owned Mexican factory discovered that they had to carefully consider the people side of managing when staffing their facility.

Workplace Harmony. The Mexican workplace has a low tolerance for adversarial relations. While getting along with others is important in U.S. factories too, Mexican employers put much more emphasis on hiring employees who have a record of working cooperatively with authority. Mexican employers, according to one expert, "tend to seek workers who are agreeable, respectful, and obedient rather than innovative and independent." This can lead to counterproductive behavior—even on the part of supervisors. For example, in attempting to preserve the appearance of harmony, supervisors may hide defective work rather than confront the problem or report it to a manager.

Role and Status. Mexican employees often put a relatively high emphasis on social order and on respecting one's status. In one factory in Chihuahua, Mexico, for instance, a U.S. manager wore jeans and insisted that everyone call him Jim. He assumed those around him would prefer that he reduce the visible status gap between himself and the workers. He was then amazed to learn that the local employees considered him "uncultured and boorish."

Exercising Authority. Mexican employees tend to have a more rigid view of authority than do their U.S. counterparts. Therefore, attempts by U.S. managers to encourage input and feedback from employees may cause confusion.

The Global Manager. Not everyone is competent to manage in a global arena. Saying you appreciate cultural differences is one thing; being able to act on it is another. Global managers therefore tend to be, first, cosmopolitan in how they view people and the world. Some define *cosmopolitan* as "belonging to the world; not limited to just one part of the political, social, commercial or intellectual spheres; free from local, provincial, or national ideas, prejudices or attachments." Global managers must be comfortable living and working anywhere in the world, and being cosmopolitan helps them to be so.

Cliff Miller is an example of how global managers operate. With his wife, he runs Mountain View Data, Inc., which produces powerful software that automatically backs up files in real time. With facilities in San Francisco and Northeast Asia, Miller likes to say that he lives in four places: "San Francisco, Beijing, Tokyo, and United Airlines." He and his wife Iris are continually on the move as they operate branches of their high-tech company in each city.

How can you tell if you're cosmopolitan? Cosmopolitan people are sensitive to what is expected of them in any context, and they have the flexibility to deal intelligently and in an unbiased way with people and situations from other cultures. You needn't have traveled extensively abroad or be multilingual to be cosmopolitan, although such experiences help. The important thing is that you are open to learning about other people's perspectives and to considering them in your own decisions.

In addition to being cosmopolitan, global managers also have what some experts call a *global brain*. They are flexible enough to accept that, at times, their own ways of doing business are not the best. For example, Volkswagen formed a partnership with Skoda, a Czech carmaker. VW trained Skoda's managers in Western management techniques. However, it followed Skoda's suggestions about how to conduct business in the Czech Republic. Being willing to apply the best solutions from different systems is what experts mean by having a global brain.

This global point of view (or its absence) tends to reflect itself in a manager's global philosophy. For example, an **ethnocentric** (home-base-oriented) management philosophy may manifest itself in an ethnocentric or home-market-oriented firm. A **polycentric** philosophy may translate into a company that is limited to several individual foreign markets. A **regiocentric** (or geocentric) philosophy may lead managers to create more of an integrated global production and marketing presence.

Would Your Company Choose You as an International Executive?

What do companies look for in their international executives? One study focused on 838 lower-, middle-, and senior-level managers from six international firms in 21 countries. The researchers studied the extent to which employers could use personal characteristics such as sensitivity to cultural differences to distinguish between managers who had high potential as international executives and those whose potential was not so high. Fourteen personal characteristics successfully distinguished those identified by their companies as having high potential from those identified as lower performing.

To get an initial impression of how you would rate, look at Table 6.1. It lists the 11 characteristics with sample items. For each, indicate (by placing a number in the space provided) whether you strongly agree (number 7), strongly disagree

ethnocentric A management philosophy that leads to the creation of home-market-oriented firms

polycentric A management philosophy oriented toward pursuing a limited number of individual foreign markets

regiocentric A management philosophy oriented toward larger areas, including the global marketplace; also called geocentric

TABLE 6.1 Characteristics of More Successful International Managers		
Scale	Score	Sample Item
Sensitive to cultural differences		When working with people from other cultures, works hard to understand their perspectives.
Business knowledge		Has a solid understanding of our products and services.
Courage to take a stand		Is willing to take a stand on issues.
Brings out the best in people		Has a special talent for dealing with people.
Acts with integrity		Can be depended on to tell the truth, regardless of circumstances.
Is insightful		Is good at identifying the most important part of a complex problem or issue.
Is committed to success		Clearly demonstrates commitment to seeing the organization succeed.
Takes risks		Takes personal as well as business risks.
Uses feedback		Has changed as a result of feedback.
Is culturally adventurous		Enjoys the challenge of working in countries other than his or her own.
Seeks opportunities to learn		Takes advantage of opportunities to do new things.
Is open to criticism		Appears brittle—as if criticism might cause him or her to break*
Seeks feedback		Pursues feedback even when others are reluctant to give it.
Is flexible		Doesn't get so invested in things that he or she cannot change when something doesn't work.

*Reverse scored, so 1 is "strongly agree" for this item.

(number 1), or fall somewhere in between. The higher you score, the more likely you would have scored high as a potential global executive in this study.

Planning, Organizing, and Controlling in a Global Environment

Managing globally also complicates the management process. *International management* means carrying out the four management functions we discuss in this book—planning, organizing, leading, and controlling—on an international scale.

Planning in a Global Environment

planning The process of setting goals and courses of action, developing rules and procedures, and forecasting future outcomes

Planning means setting goals and identifying the courses of action for achieving those goals. Since much of what the manager does—the firm's structure, and its marketing, staffing, and production policies, for instance—will stem from his or her basic global strategy, choosing that strategy is usually of paramount concern.

With respect to global strategy, one thorny question is whether to emphasize standardized versus customized products worldwide. Specifically, managers like Donald Hastings must decide, "How should we balance (1) the need to provide customized products to each country in which we do business with (2) the need to maintain standardized products worldwide so as to exploit economies of scale?" Answering that question requires choosing a global strategy. As in any strategic planning this involves defining the mission of the business and laying out the broad strategies or courses of action the firm will use to achieve that mission. Central to this agenda is deciding what products to sell.

Global Strategic Planning. With respect to the products it sells, the company can pursue one of three basic global strategies. One is the **global integration strategy.** "To capitalize on the economics of scale and to take advantage of the diverse opportunities for cost reduction that the global market provides, the [best] choice of strategy is global integration." This strategy means taking a centralized, integrated view of where to design and produce the company's product or service. The emphasis here is on producing, say, a standardized "world car" as efficiently as possible. The company then just fine-tunes this standard car for slight differences in national tastes. Managers make production decisions in a globally integrated manner. (For instance, Xerox centralized its global purchasing decisions to minimize costs.) The organization structure delegates less decision-making authority to local managers.

Global integration assumes that market similarities and the need to be efficient trump the differences among the markets. U.S. automakers generally take this approach. They build "globalizable" cars and components in different countries (an integrated production strategy). Then they sell more or less the same cars in different countries, with different nameplates.

At the other extreme, the manager may decide that the differences among markets are too numerous to allow them to take this standardized approach. If so, they may choose to pursue a *host country focus strategy*. Each market needs its own autonomous subsidiary. The managers in each country are relatively free to adapt their products or services to local tastes as they see fit. The multinational company's headquarters provides overall coordination, and perhaps tries to minimize unnecessary product duplication among country subsidiaries. Some food companies, like Kellogg's, take this approach.

Many global managers try to get the best of both global strategy worlds. They pursue a *hybrid international strategy*. Here, the manager tries to blend (1) the efficiencies that come from integrating global production with (2) the ability to provide each country with specialized products or services (the host country focus strategy). The trick here is to minimize excessive duplication among country units and to maximize the firm's ability to quickly transfer product innovations from one locale to another. ABB Group Ltd. takes this hybrid approach.

Figure 6.4 can help managers decide if global integration, host country focus, or hybrid is best. For example, where the forces for local responsiveness are weak and the forces for global integration strong, global integration is best. All countries here get more-or-less undifferentiated products. Industries fitting here include construction and mining machinery, and industrial chemicals. At the other extreme, where the forces for integration are weak and the forces for local responsiveness

FIGURE 6.4
Environmental Influences and Global Strategy

SOURCE: Adapted from Figures 2 and 5 and discussion in Sumantra Ghoshal and Nitin Nohria. Reprinted from John Daniels and Lee Radebaugh, *International Business* (Upper Saddle River, NJ: Prentice Hall, 2001), p. 529. "Horses for Courses: Organizational Forms for Multinational Corporation," *Sloan Management Review,* Winter 1993, pp. 23–36.

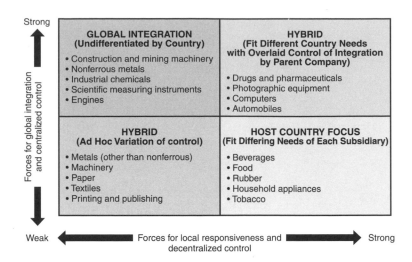

Management in Action

ABB GROUP

Local ABB units have great autonomy. However, ABB also uses the Internet and information technology to make sure good ideas get fast approval and distribution. For example, if several engineers in France develop a good idea for a new process, they post their idea, with appropriate key-words, on ABB's Internet using a special template. The ABB system amounts to a private bulletin board. ABB managers and engineers worldwide use it to instantaneously broadcast new ideas throughout ABB. That way, they minimize the amount of time they waste "reinventing the wheel."

strong, host-country focus is best. The beverages, food, and household appliances industries are examples here.

Global Feasibility Planning. In general, "domestic and international strategic planning processes are very similar, differing only in the specifics." The main difference is that companies (like Lincoln Electric) going abroad must conduct particularly thorough feasibility studies.

The reason stems from the national differences discussed earlier. International planners must contend with a multitude of economic, political/legal, socio-cultural, and technological issues. Its easy but risky to assume that things "there" are the same as "here." Furthermore, gathering information abroad—about demographics, production levels, and so on—can be difficult, and the data are often questionable. The Carrefour and Wal-Mart experiences illustrate the problem.

French retailer Carrefour (Wal-Mart's chief worldwide rival) conducts careful feasibility studies before entering new markets. For example, it avoids entering developing markets—such as Russia—that don't have reliable legal systems. Even in more traditional markets, Carrefour won't proceed without at least a year's worth of on-site research. Carrefour doesn't make many mistakes when it enters a new market. In China, for instance, "Carrefour takes care to chop vegetables vertically—not laterally—so as not to bring bad luck to superstitious shoppers."

With less experience in the international arena, Wal-Mart's first expansions abroad did not go so smoothly. For example, when it opened stores in Argentina, its hardware departments offered tools and appliances wired for 110 volts, although Argentina uses 220. Similarly, "only by trial and error did Wal-Mart learn that far more Argentine customers than Americans were in the habit of shopping at a store each day. The greater traffic meant that aisles always seemed overcrowded and floors always seemed dirty." Wal-Mart adapted by making the aisles wider and installing scuff-proof floors. Wal-Mart is huge. It could, therefore, use trial and error instead of detailed feasibility planning—and not get ruined in the process. A smaller firm (like Lincoln Electric) runs the risk of depleting its cash and having to quickly close down.

Organizing in a Global Environment

In general, the U.S. company's international organization reflects the firm's degree of globalization. Figure 6.5 presents the typical options for organizing an international business. In a *domestic organization,* each division handles its own foreign sales. In response to increasing orders from abroad, the firm may move to an *export-oriented structure.* Here, one department (often called an import-export department) coordinates all international activities such as licensing, contracting, and managing foreign sales.

In an *international organization,* management splits the company into domestic and international divisions. The international division focuses on production and sales overseas, whereas the domestic division focuses on domestic markets. Reynolds Metals, for instance, has six worldwide businesses, each with a U.S.-focused group and a separate international group. In a *multinational organization,* each country where the firm does business has its own subsidiary. The oil first Royal Dutch Shell is organized this way. It has separate subsidiaries for Shell Switzerland and Shell U.S.A. (as well as many other countries).

The organizational principles apply to organizing internationally. This includes the principle that structure follows strategy. For example, a host country focus strategy suggests having separate subsidiaries for each locale. A global integration

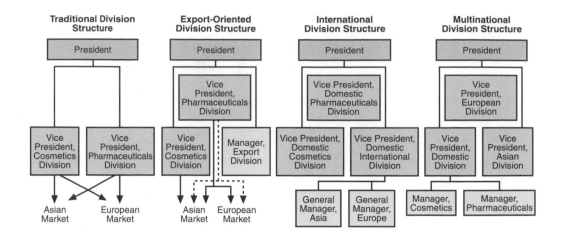

FIGURE 6.5

International Organization

As firms evolve from domestic to multinational enterprises, their increasing international operations necessitate a more globally oriented organization.

strategy suggests more emphasis on centralizing functions (such as product design and manufacturing) under a single manager.

As noted earlier, the firm's history and its stage of internationalization will also influence how it organizes its international efforts. Thus, a company at the earliest stages of internationalization (or with few globally qualified managers) will more likely opt for managing its international operations out of a headquarters import-export or international department. It's unlikely to begin its first, tentative forays into exporting abroad by reorganizing as a full-blown multinational organization. Similarly, as noted, the stage of internationalization is important. As the firm adds more foreign subsidiaries, it is more likely to move toward the multinational structure.

Top management philosophy is another consideration. For example (as noted earlier), some managers are more globally oriented, while some are more local (ethnocentric) in their philosophical outlooks. The manager who believes "my country's ways are best" is less likely to delegate much authority to remote local managers. Geographic distance is also important. Managing activities thousands of miles away is no easy matter. The manager will have to pay special attention to making sure his or her remote operations don't slip out of control.

Controlling in a Global Environment

Several years ago, Coca-Cola had a rude surprise when several European countries made it take its beverages off store shelves. Coke has high standards for product quality and integrity, but controlling what's happening at every plant worldwide is a challenge. Chemicals had seeped into the beverages at one of Coke's European plants.

Control means monitoring actual performance to ensure it is consistent with the standards that were set. This is hard enough when the people you're controlling are next door; geographic distance complicates the problem. And the other distances (socio-cultural and legal, for instance) complicate it even more. The global manager has to carefully address two things: *what to control,* and *how to control it.*

Deciding What to Control. Particularly given the geographic distances involved, the global manager has to choose the activities he or she will control with great care. The manager could, of course, try to micromanage everything—from hiring and firing to product design, sales campaigns, and cash management. However, micromanaging at long distances is less than practical. And in any case, too much control can smother the subsidiary and reduce its ability to respond quickly to customer needs.

In practice, the local manager's autonomy is *least* for financial and capital decisions, and most for personnel decisions. Production and marketing decisions tend to fall in the middle. In one study of 109 U.S., Canadian, and European multinational corporations, "these firms exercised stricter financial control, and allowed greater local freedom for labor, political, and business decisions. Also, the home office of these multinational corporations made the decisions to introduce new products and to establish R&D facilities."

Deciding How to Maintain Control. Two things characterize the methods global managers use to maintain control. One is the use of computerized information systems. For many years, Kelly Services, Inc., let its offices in each country operate with their own individual billing and accounts receivable systems. However, according to Kelly's chief technology officer, "we are consolidating our operations in all countries and subsidiaries under a standard [information system]. . . . All our customers expect us to deliver consistent practices, metrics, and measurement." Establishing global standards is an important part of meeting and exceeding that expectation.

The second characteristic of how global managers maintain control is the emphasis on self-control and employee commitment. Global managers do use financial and operating reports, visits to subsidiaries, and management performance evaluations to help control their international operations. However, supervision is limited when thousands of miles separate boss and subordinate. Furthermore, formal reports, rules, and regulations are not hard to evade. Particularly in global companies, there's wisdom in making sure employees want to do what is right—and that they know what's expected of them in terms of the company's values and goals.

In other words, global companies have to make sure their managers buy into "the way we do things around here." Companies do this in many ways: job rotation from country to country; multicountry management development programs; informal company sponsored events; and using teams from different countries to work on cross-border projects. Motivating managers and employees to do things right is especially important. We'll therefore turn to this next.

Leading and Motivating in a Multicultural Environment

Many managers are probably less adept at appreciating cultural differences than they think they are. Most would eagerly take the position that "of course, there are cultural differences among people from different cultures." Yet many, transferred abroad, would blunder into simply treating the people "there" the same as the people "here." The problem stems from what international management writers call the *universality assumption* of motivation: "These theories erroneously assume that human needs are universal." Such assumptions are certainly not uniquely American. There's often a tendency to assume that everyone everywhere thinks and feels more or less like we do. Ironically, the universality assumption seems to be universal.

Yet, for U.S. managers, the problem may be more severe. First, they don't have the same multicultural experience as people living in, say, Europe, where travel between countries is a way of life. Furthermore, U.S. researchers did much of the research on human needs and motivation using U.S. employees. The problem is that those theories and findings don't always apply to people everywhere. (You can't always generalize them to different cultures.) A Chinese believing in Confucianism's emphasis on respect and obedience may react differently to autocratic leadership than would the typical American. One of the biggest mistakes the international manager can make is to fail to see that "to understand why people do what they do, we have to understand the cultural constructs by which they interpret the world."

Values

values Basic beliefs about what is important and unimportant, and what one should and should not do

One way people around the world differ is in terms of their values. **Values** are basic beliefs we hold about what is good or bad, important or unimportant. Values (such as West Point's famous "duty, honor, country") are important because our values shape the way we behave. When Geert Hofstede studied managers around the world, he found that societies' values differ in several ways:

- *Power distance.* Power distance is the extent to which the less powerful members of institutions accept and expect that power will be distributed unequally. Hofstede concluded that acceptance of such inequality was higher in some countries (such as Mexico) than it was in others (such as Sweden).

- *Individualism versus collectivism.* In individualistic countries like Australia and the United States, "all members are expected to look after themselves and their immediate families." In collectivist countries like Indonesia and Pakistan, society expects people to care for each other more.

- *Masculinity versus femininity.* According to Hofstede, societies differ also in the extent to which they value assertiveness (which he called masculinity) or caring (femininity). Japan and Austria ranked high in masculinity; Denmark and Chile ranked lower.

- *Uncertainty avoidance.* Uncertainty avoidance refers to whether people in the society are uncomfortable with unstructured situations in which unknown, surprising, novel incidents occur. People in some countries (such as Sweden, Israel, and Great Britain) are relatively comfortable dealing with uncertainty and surprises. People living in other countries (including Greece and Portugal) tend to be uncertainty avoiders.

Leadership in a Multicultural Environment

Cultural realities like these can dramatically alter the efficacy of theories like "Leading." For example, consider the large differences Hofstede found in the "power distance" (inequality) people in different cultures will tolerate. Figure 6.6 lists countries with large and small power distance rankings.

Cultural differences have important implications for how managers apply leadership theories abroad. For example, one might assume that in societies in which large power distances (inequalities) are an accepted way of life, participative leadership may backfire. Says one expert, "For example, if a superior, in a 'large power distance society,' attempts to reduce the distance by acting more accessible and friendly, his or her subordinates may not willingly accept such openness." Indeed, studies suggest that managers in some countries (including Indonesia, Malaysia, Thailand, Turkey, and the Philippines) do prefer to use autocratic leadership; those in others such as Hong Kong prefer less autocratic styles. Table 6.2 helps to illustrate. It shows that leaders in some countries (Spain, Portugal, and Greece) tend to delegate less authority than do leaders in others (Sweden, Japan, Norway, and the United States). The point is that the indiscriminate application of leadership theories abroad can be counterproductive.

Motivation in a Multicultural Environment

Many of the motivation theories "Influencing Individual Behavior and Motivation'" make assumptions about peoples' needs. For example, the Maslow needs hierarchy assumes that peoples' needs form a five-step hierarchy from basic physiological needs, up to security, social, self-esteem, and self-actualization needs. But can the global manager act as if this assumption applies to his or her local employees?

Not always. Maslow's theory emphasizes the supremacy of self—of satisfying one's own needs and of being all you can be (self-actualization). In other societies, peoples' needs don't revolve around self as much as around social relationships. For example, one researcher concluded that we could have to rearrange the Maslow needs hierarchy to use it in China. Social needs would come first, then physiological, then security, and then, finally self-actualization—but, not to be "all you can be," but, "to serve society."

Another popular motivation theory emphasizes the importance of the need to achieve in motivating behavior. Yet an attempt by the originator of this theory to extend it to workers in India failed. Similarly, "money is not an incentive everywhere—it may be accepted gladly, but [it] will not automatically improve performance. Honor, dignity and family may be much more important. Imposing the American style of merit system may be an outrageous blow to a respected and established seniority system." Again, the indiscriminate use of familiar motivation theories abroad can backfire. The manager needs to start by understanding his or her employees and what their needs and values are.

FIGURE 6.6

FIGURE 6.6

Country Clusters Based on Power Distance

SOURCE: Adapted from G. Hofstede, *Culture's Consequences* (Beverley Hills, CA: Sage Publications, 1984).

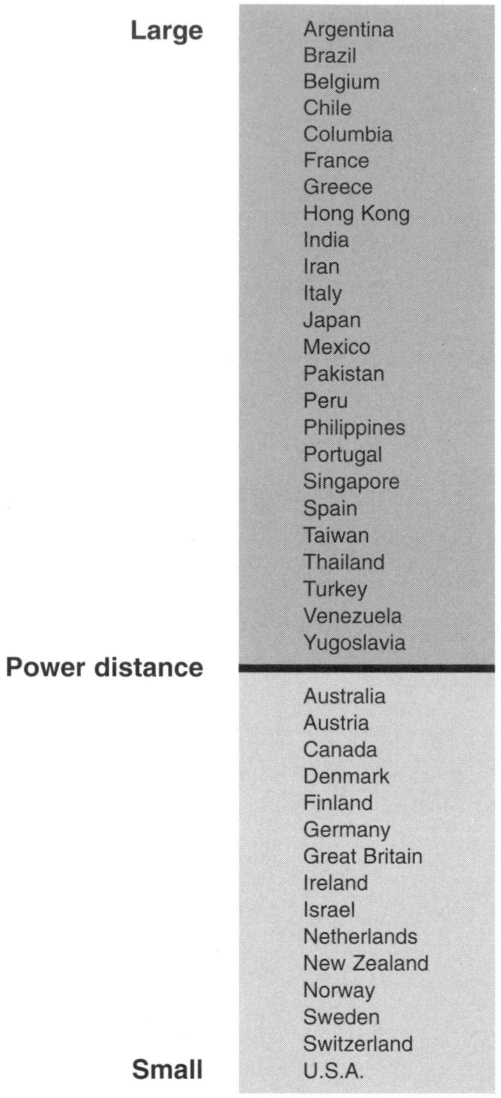

Large

Argentina
Brazil
Belgium
Chile
Columbia
France
Greece
Hong Kong
India
Iran
Italy
Japan
Mexico
Pakistan
Peru
Philippines
Portugal
Singapore
Spain
Taiwan
Thailand
Turkey
Venezuela
Yugoslavia

Power distance

Australia
Austria
Canada
Denmark
Finland
Germany
Great Britain
Ireland
Israel
Netherlands
New Zealand
Norway
Sweden
Switzerland

Small U.S.A.

TABLE 6.2 Comparative Leadership Dimensions: Participation			
Extent to Which Leaders Delegate Authority		0 = low; 100 = high	
Sweden	75.51	Germany	60.85
Japan	69.27	New Zealand	60.54
Norway	68.50	Ireland	59.53
United States	66.23	UK	58.95
Singapore	65.37	Belgium/Lux	54.55
Denmark	64.65	Austria	54.29
Canada	64.38	France	53.62
Finland	62.92	Italy	46.80
Switzerland	62.20	Spain	44.31
Netherlands	61.33	Portugal	42.56
Australia	61.22	Greece	37.95

SOURCE: C. Hampden-Turner and A. Trompenaars. *The Seven Cultures of Capitalism* (New York: Doubleday, 1993). Adapted from Helen Deresky, *International Management,* 2nd ed., NY Addison Wesley Longman, 1997, Exh 11-5, p. 402.

Communications in a Multicultural Environment

Cultural differences also influence communication in obvious and subtle ways. Language barriers are one obvious problem. An American manager negotiating a deal in England can generally make him- or herself fairly well understood using English, but he or she might need an interpreter in France. Even where the other party speaks some English, problems can arise. For example, using a colloquialism such as "you bet it is" may be incomprehensible to the person with whom you're speaking. Furthermore, as General Motors discovered to its chagrin, words that sound or look the same (such as *Nova* which means "won't go" in Spanish) may have different meanings in different countries.

The problem is not just words. Ninety percent of what people hear isn't verbal. It is nonverbal, and it is conveyed via facial expressions and signs and motions of one sort or another. Here is where the novice international manager can really get into trouble. Table 6.3 shows what some typical nonverbal behaviors mean in various countries. It's subtle differences like these that can make international management an adventure!

TABLE 6.3 Implications of Various Nonverbal Behaviors in Different Cultures

Nonverbal Behavior	Country	Meaning
Thumbs up	United States	An Approval gesture/OK/good job!
	Middle East	A gesture of insult
	Japan	A sign indicating "male"
	Germany	A sign for count of "one"
A finger circulating next to the ear	Argentina	A telephone
	United States	That is crazy!
A raised arm and waggling hand	United States	Goodbye
	India, South America	Beckoning
	Much of Europe	A signal for "no"
Showing the back of the hand in a V-sign	England	A rude sign
	Greece, Middle East	A sign for count of "two"
Showing a circle formed with index finger and thumb	United States	Very good!
	Turkey	Insult gesture/accusation of homosexuality
Eye contact, gazing	United States	A sign of attentiveness
	Japan	A rude behavior/invasion of privacy
	Most Asian countries	Sign of disrespect to senior people
Widening eye	United States	An indication of surprise
	Chinese	An indication of anger
	Hispanic	Request for help
	French	Issuance of challenge
Nodding the head up and down	Western countries	A sign for agreement/yes
	Greece, Bulgaria	A sign for disagreement/no

SOURCE: Adapted from Kamal Fatehi, *International Management* (Upper Saddle River, NJ: Prentice Hall 1996), Table 6.1, p. 194.

This chapter should help put the problems Lincoln Electric faced into perspective—and help us to understand what the company needs to do now. Donald Hastings took over as Lincoln Electric Company's CEO just after the failure of its international expansion became evident. As he says, in retrospect, it was apparent that Lincoln Electric made several bad assumptions. "For example, without truly exploring the idea, we assumed that the incentive system would be accepted abroad. We found, however, that the European culture of labor was hostile to the piecework and bonus system."

Another questionable assumption was appointing a vice president for managing the European factories who had no global management experience. In hindsight, says Hastings,

> I realize that [this vice president's] appointment reflected a broader problem: our corporate management lacked sufficient international expertise and had little experience running a complex, dispersed organization. Our managers didn't know how to run foreign operations; nor did they understand foreign cultures. Consequently; we had to rely on people in our foreign companies—people we did not know and who didn't know us.

It was soon obvious to Hastings that the whole process of control was breaking down:

> I witnessed a troubling pattern. The individual European businesses would submit extremely optimistic sales and profits estimates in their budgets. But they invariably missed the targets—often by quite a bit—and the gaps were getting bigger and bigger. Even more worrisome, nobody seemed to have a handle on why the targets were being missed or what to do about the gaps. When asked, the businesses' manager would say "We were too optimistic. The recession is worse than we thought. We'll downsize the budget."

Lincoln Electric's debt was soon soaring, and its losses were mounting. In the spring of 1993, Hastings stumbled across the reason why his European managers always missed their sales and profit targets. "The operating budget of the [headquarters] management company in Norway was funded by the individual businesses in each country, and the size of its budget was based on the forecasted, rather than the actual, sales and profits of those businesses. To inflate the management company's own operating budget its leaders had encouraged the businesses to submit optimistic—rather than realistic—forecasts." Hastings knew he had to do something—and fast. What would you have done?

In June, he handed over responsibility for North American operations to his president and moved to England to take charge of European operations himself. In Europe, some of his discoveries were even more shocking. Every factory was operating at 50% or less of capacity. As he says, "people were not working! On one visit . . . three workers were found sleeping on the job." In Germany, Hastings discovered, the average factory worker worked only about 35 hours per week, in contrast to the average Lincoln worker's 43 to 58 hours. He pushed his local managers to develop plans for boosting market share, but they said, "The only way you increase market share is to buy another company. You never take an account from a competitor, because [it] will retaliate and take one from you."

At a trade show in Germany, exhibitors traditionally spent their time entertaining customers rather than making sales, as they more often do in the United States. Hastings decided to break with tradition. He and his team did some aggressive selling. The sales gave the company a well-needed financial shot in the arm. It also proved that well-made American products would sell in Germany even if they weren't produced there.

Hastings put a turnaround plan in place. The company downsized its operations in Europe. It closed the German factory (as well as manufacturing operations in Brazil, Venezuela, and Japan). Within a year, "our new export strategy—which included selling American-made machines worldwide and rethinking which of our plants around the world could best serve a given market—was a smashing success. Moreover, in countries where we had closed operations, market share actually increased."

The only place where Lincoln was able to successfully implement its incentive system was Mexico City. There, it started small. It asked two employees to try working on the incentive system. Other workers soon asked to join the plan. In about two years; Lincoln's whole Mexico city workforce had adopted its incentive plan.

Today, with its new global integration strategy, Lincoln is thriving. Its balance sheet is strong, and revenues and profits are up. It has also added several new, internationally experienced executives to its board of directors, and it has built its international management team. In retrospect, Hastings says, "competing globally requires a lot more time, money, and management resources than we realized. At least five years before we launched our expansion program in 1987, we should have started building a management team and [board of directors] from whom we could have learned how to proceed."

◎ Summary

1. Companies can pursue several strategies when it comes to extending operations to foreign markets. Exporting is the route often chosen by manufacturers, and licensing and franchising are two popular alternatives. At some point, a firm may decide to invest funds in another country. Joint ventures and wholly owned subsidiaries are two examples of foreign direct investment.

2. An international business is any firm that engages in international trade or investment. Firms are globalizing for many reasons, the three most common being to expand sales, to acquire resources, and to diversify sources of sales and supplies. Other reasons for pursuing international business include reducing costs or improving quality by seeking products and services produced in foreign countries and smoothing out sales and profit wings.

3. Free trade means removing all barriers to trade among countries participating in the trade agreement. Its potential benefits have prompted many nations to enter into various levels of economic integration, ranging from a free trade area to a common market.

4. Globalizing production means placing parts of a firm's production process in various locations around the globe. The aim is to take advantage of national differences in the cost and quality of production and then integrate these operations in a unified system of manufacturing facilities around the world. Companies are also tapping new supplies of skilled labor in various countries. The globalization of markets, production, and labor coincides with the rise of a new type of global manager, someone who can function effectively anywhere in the world.

5. International managers must be skilled at weighing an array of environmental factors. Before doing business abroad, managers should be familiar with the economic systems, exchange rates, and level of economic development of the countries in which they plan to do business. They must be aware of import restrictions, political risks, and legal differences and restraints. Important socio-cultural differences also affect the way people in various countries act and expect to be treated. Values, languages, and customs are examples of elements that distinguish people of one culture from those of another. Finally, the relative ease with which the manager can transfer technology from one country to another is an important consideration in conducting international business.

6. With respect to the products it sells, the company can pursue one of three basic global strategies. One is the *global integration strategy*. At the other

extreme, the manager may choose to pursue a *host country focus strategy*. Many global managers try to get the best of both global strategy worlds and pursue a *hybrid international strategy.*

7. The company's international organization reflects the firm's degree of globalization. In a *domestic organization,* each division handles its own foreign sales. In response to increasing orders from abroad, the firm may move to an *export-oriented structure.* In an *international organization,* management split the company into domestic and international divisions. In a *multinational organization,* each country where the firm does business has its own subsidiary.

8. Leading, motivating, and communicating abroad is susceptible to what international management writers call the "universality assumption"—the tendency to assume that everyone everywhere thinks and feels more or less like "we" do. In fact, they do not. For one thing, people around the world hold to different values, such as power distance, individualism versus collectivism, masculinity versus femininity, and uncertainty avoidance.

Experimental Exercises

1. You have just taken an assignment to assess the feasibility of opening a branch of your company's business in Russia. Your company manufactures and sells farming equipment. Your company is located in David, California, a community known for a heavy sense of social responsibility, progressive agricultural techniques, and a liberal political atmosphere. You have a month to prepare your report. Working in teams of four or five students, prepare a detailed outline showing the main topic headings you will have in your report, including a note on the management tools you will use to get the information you need for each topic.

2. While Lincoln Electric's new strategy of exporting its welding equipment from the United States to various countries seems to be working well, management is now concerned that local competitors may start eating into its business. Furthermore, some developing countries object to having products enter that may compete with their own. Working in teams of four or five students, use the tools in this chapter, and specify the global strategy you believe Lincoln should pursue now. What global organization structure would that imply?

3. Spend several minutes using the tools and what you learned in this chapter and book to list 10 reasons "Why I would (or would not) be a good global manager."

4. Many rightfully believe that it is the business school's responsibility to familiarize business students with what it takes to be an effective global manager. In teams of four or five students, compile a list, based on this course and any others you've taken here, of what your business school is doing to cultivate a better appreciation of the challenges of doing business internationally.

CLOSING CASE

U.S. Bookseller Finds a Strong Partner in German Media Giant

When Barnes & Noble was exploring ways to become more competitive in its battle with Amazon.com, there were hundreds of U.S. companies to which it could turn. Research clearly demonstrated that the cultural differences that characterize cross-border ventures made them far more complicated than domestic ones. Yet Barnes & Noble surprised competitors when it chose to form its Internet joint venture with the German media giant Bertelsmann. Was Barnes & Noble mistaken to look abroad for a partner?

Bertelsmann is best known among college students for its record label and music club, BMG (now both owned by Universal). At the time, BMG entertainment was second in the market with $1.9 billion in sales. The BMG music club is well known to U.S. college students with its buy-one, get-10 free CD offers posted on campus bulletin boards nationwide. With $3.9 billion in sales and nearly 65,000 employees, Bertelsmann is much more than a CD club. Its holdings include Random House, the world's largest English-language book publisher, and Offset Paperback, a firm that manufactures nearly 40% of all the paperback books sold in the United States. Bertelsmann had also actively pursued e-commerce on its own. By the end of the twentieth century, Bertelsmann had quietly staked out a position as the world's third largest Internet business.

To fund **barnesandnoble.com,** the two created a separate company and conducted an initial public offering (IPO) to raise capital. The offering raised $421 million for the new venture after commissions and expenses, making it the largest e-commerce offering in history. Since launching its online business in May 1997, **barnesandnoble.com** has quickly become one of the world's largest e-commerce retailers. The company has successfully capitalized on the recognized brand value of the Barnes & Noble name to become the second largest on-line retailer of books. Yet it doesn't seem to have made as much headway as it would have liked in capturing market share from Amazon.

Discussion Questions

1. What may have motivated Barnes & Noble to partner with the German firm Bertelsmann? In general terms, what advantages would Barnes & Noble gain by having an international partner in such an endeavor? Explain the pros and cons of this partnership.
2. Specify the basic global strategy you believe **barnesandnoble.com** should pursue, and why. How, in general terms would you organize this venture?
3. With all its experience in e-commerce, why wouldn't BMG just set up its own competitor to Amazon.com?
4. List three specific planning, organizing, leading, and controlling issues Barnes & Noble's managers probably faced in establishing this new joint venture.
5. Write a one page essay on the topic "Cultural Factors our Barnes & Noble managers should keep in mind when dealing with our colleagues at Bertelsmann."

You Be the Consultant

Managing JetBlue in a Global Environment

JetBlue's route structure is basically domestic, but that doesn't mean it can ignore its global environment For one thing, its heavy flight schedule from New York already means that it is also advantageous to fly out of the continental United States—to Puerto Rico. On May 30, 2002, JetBlue, therefore, added three daily JFK-San Juan nonstop flights. Neeleman says that he has no plans to expand to Europe but that Canada, the Caribbean, and Mexico are possibilities sometime in the future.

Furthermore, JetBlue President Barger says he would sign international code-share arrangements (which would make it easier for JetBlue's domestic passengers to switch seamlessly to flights abroad on another airline), if doing so didn't interfere with JetBlue's need for quick turnarounds. (For example, having to change JetBlue's flight schedules in such a way that they had to spend more time on the ground waiting for incoming passengers from abroad might mean longer turnaround time—and, therefore, higher costs for Jetblue.)

It's not just the global aspects of its route structure that are important to JetBlue's management, but the global nature of aircraft purchases and leasing as well. Neeleman's original plan (given the $130 million or more in start-up capital) was to go directly to Airbus or Boeing to buy his firm's first aircraft. However, it turned out that neither Airbus nor Boeing could deliver all the planes the new start-up needed in the years 2000 and 2001. JetBlue therefore had to lease six Airbus A320s from a company called International Lease Finance Corp. and two more from Singapore Aircraft Leasing Enterprise. Then as JetBlue expanded (and in keeping with its desire to maintain a homogeneous fleet so that all mechanics and flight crews could more easily switch from aircraft to aircraft), JetBlue placed an order with the European aircraft manufacturer Airbus for an additional 10 A320s (the planes list to, about $54 million each, but they typically sell for less). Based on its expected needs through 2005, JetBlue will therefore end up ordering about 74 of the A320s from Europe's Airbus rather than aircraft from America's Boeing. Neeleman and his team felt that the Airbus 320 best fit their needs, given JetBlue's route structure and the Airbus's economies of operation and emphasis on technology.

Assignment

1. Other start-up airlines (not JetBlue) have made the mistake of expanding abroad too soon. Make a list of five erroneous assumptions you believe these airlines' managers made in expanding abroad.
2. Neeleman says he is only interested in expanding into Mexico, Canada, or the Caribbean in the foreseeable future. Tell him why JetBlue is (or is not) a suitable candidate for expanding into each of these three areas, based on the cultural, administrative, geographic, and economic distance between that country and his.
3. List the reasons why you think Neeleman might (or might not) be a good global manager.

4. Assuming JetBlue decides to expand outside the United States, briefly specify the basic global strategy the company should pursue, and why.
5. Draw an organization chart showing the basic global organization structure JetBlue should use if it begins flying to Canada, Mexico, and the Caribbean in addition to its current domestic U.S.A. flights.
6. What are the *noneconomic* pros and cons to a company like JetBlue in placing such a large order with a foreign rather than with a domestic supplier?

THE MAKING OF AN ENTREPRENEUR

PAVEMENT ENDS

PART I

The entrepreneur is currently a fashionable animal, so much so that entrepreneurs and "entrepreneurship" have become synonymous in the public mind with corporate success, and the epithet has become a stock in trade solution of popular writers for a variety of North America's economic woes. But what exactly IS entrepreneurship? This part is devoted to exploring the complex phenomenon of entrepreneurship.

Defining the Entrepreneur

Defining who is an entrepreneur is a difficult process. Reviewing the literature reveals that there is no generic definition of the entrepreneur. As Kets de Vries noted, there is a lack of "conceptual clarity." The term entrepreneur has never been precisely defined. Many scholars from different schools of thought have tried over the years to define this complex phenomenon. For example, economists such as Jean Baptist and J. Schumpeter view the entrepreneur as the fourth factor of production who is rewarded by profit for his innovation and risk taking activity. Sociologists on the other hand regard the entrepreneur as a deviant individual who is driven by a number of factors, such as personality, family and society, towards a particular pattern of behavior. Psychologists have turned their attention to the personal characteristics of the entrepreneur.

Kets de Vries draws a broad profile of an individual with a high need for achievements and autonomy, as might be expected. Interestingly, these qualities are frequently coupled with higher than average anxiety, a developed aesthetic sense and lower than average interpersonal skills.

There may indeed be more than one entrepreneurial archetype. Howard Stevenson and David Gumpert have shown that the popular view of the entrepreneur as a bold architect of new high technology enterprises differs from the managerial picture of a flexible, risk-taking innovator. Neither stereotype is entirely false, but entrepreneurship can be more aptly defined as a mode of behavior, a cast of mind. Box 7.1 outlines Stevenson and Gumpert's observations.

Howard Stevenson and David Gumpert believe that the entrepreneur (or "promoter") simply occupies one extreme end of a spectrum of managerial behaviour, at the opposite end is the administrator (or "trustee"). The former is concerned with locating and exploiting opportunity, the latter with exploiting the organization to its best advantage. Where the individual's self interest is concerned, the authors contend, there is an instinctive tendency toward the promoter's role, a bias that must somehow be aligned with the objectives of the corporation if both are to flourish.

The characteristics of either extreme of the spectrum are described to illustrate their point. Driven on by diminishing opportunities or an environment that is in a state of flux the entrepreneurial organization has a strategic focus on opportunity. The administrative organization is preoccupied with maintaining social contracts and an outward appearance of equilibrium, and must therefore adopt a strategic posture that is cautious, formal and oriented to a much longer planning horizon than the promoter. It is this cast of thinking that leads the trustee to overcommit resources to its enterprises, to "go first class." As the authors correctly point out however, the size of the resource commitment is of secondary importance when compared with the nature of their deployment. The promoter is forced by necessity to squeeze the most from limited resources and therefore must employ them to their best advantage. Modern history abounds with examples of the success of such Davids over corporate Goliaths.

It follows therefore that the administrator's predilection for control and longer planning horizons instills a preference for outright ownership of assets (the better to exercise control), whereas the promoter prefers to rent and thereby dispose of them easily when they are not required. For the same reasons, the trustee chooses a formal, predictable managerial structure, whereas the promoter, given the necessity of quick adaptation to changing circumstances and rapid dissemination of information, operates a fluid, informal organization.

SOURCE: H. H. Stevenson and D. E. Gumpert, "The Heart of Entrepreneurship," *Harvard Business Review* (March–April 1985), pp. 85–94.

From our perspective, an entrepreneur is defined as an individual who sees an opportunity that others do not and marshals the resources to exploit it. According to this definition, an entrepreneur is someone who introduces a new product or a process, identifies new markets or a source of supply or creates a new type of organization. In addition, he or she raises the necessary capital, creates the new venture and assumes the control and risk of the operation. The independent undertaking is emphasized throughout this process.

Therefore, we see two possible roles for the entrepreneur in the corporate world: those of the innovator/risk taker and the manager/coordinator. First, the entrepreneur is the creative wellspring for the enterprise. He or she understands its purpose and can best devise methods that are untried or unconventional. Innovation and risk taking are traits which distinguish entrepreneurs from managers. Second, he or she marshals and controls the required resources in order for the new venture to survive and grow. In this role, the entrepreneur develops his or her vision, formulates the new venture's strategy and selects the appropriate structure and management process to exploit the window of opportunity.

The critical question is: why do some individuals see opportunities while others do not? This question has intrigued academics and practitioners. In the following section we will attempt to answer this question by examining the various schools of thought on the making of an entrepreneur.

The Making of an Entrepreneur

Because of the difficulty in defining who is an entrepreneur, many scholars have turned their attention to the entrepreneurial process to provide an explanation. A number of research studies have focused on the factors that shape and influence entrepreneurs, such as individual traits, culture, family background, functions and a host of other psychological and sociological factors. As shown in Figure 7.1, these factors are grouped under four schools of thought: the traits, the environment, the behavioral, and the contingency approach.

The Traits Approach

The internal (traits) model assumes that entrepreneurs possess certain personality traits that drive them to the choice of an entrepreneurship career. Entrepreneurial characteristics and personality traits such as high need for achievement, need for independence, locus of control and risk-taking propensity have been the subject of many research studies. Figure 7.2 lists some of the characteristics found to be associated with many entrepreneurs.

The Environmental Approach

The environmental approach argues that the choice of entrepreneurship is related to external actors beyond the individual's control. In the following section, we discuss the critical role the environment plays in shaping an entrepreneur.

FIGURE 7.1

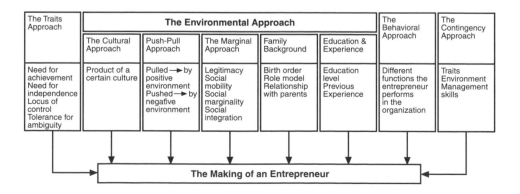

FIGURE 7.2

Characteristics—Traits Associated with Entrepreneurs

1. High Need for Achievement
2. Risk Taking Propensity
3. Tolerance for Ambiguity
4. Innovation
5. Intuition
6. High Need for Independence and Autonomy
7. Internal Locus of Control
8. Low Need for Conformity

The Role of the Culture

Why is it that some groups demonstrate more entrepreneurial characteristics than others? One obvious explanation is that entrepreneurs are products of their culture. Some cultural groups see entrepreneurship as a more desirable career opportunity than others. Indeed attitudes toward entrepreneurship affect its legitimacy in the society.

A survey of 11 nations by the Canadian Federation of Independent Business revealed that Canada has the highest percentage of entrepreneurs who were born outside the country. Indeed in both Canada and the United States there are entrepreneurs from a multitude of ethnic backgrounds and identifiable subcultures.

The "Push-Pull" Theory

The "push-pull" theory proposes that the motivation for new venture creation is not so much the result of entrepreneurial traits but rather of external factors—positive or negative. The theory argues that an individual is either pulled into an entrepreneurial career by positive elements in the environment such as new ideas and opportunities, or pushed into it by negative elements such as job dissatisfaction or being laid off from his or her job.

Some industries are more likely to act as incubators for entrepreneurs than others. They simply pull or attract entrepreneurs to create their own ventures. The computer, garment and restaurant industries are good examples. Many entrepreneurs have worked in these industries before starting their own businesses. For example, Steve Jobs, founder of the Apple Computer Company, worked at Atari while his partner, Steve Wozniak worked at Hewlett-Packard. Ken Olson, founder of Digital, worked at IBM. Push entrepreneurs, on the other hand, are driven by negative elements in the environment. For example, there is evidence of a strong relationship between a rising level of unemployment and the increase in the number of start-ups.

The Marginal/Displacement Approach

Closely associated with the negative environment is the marginal approach. Why are entrepreneurs emerging frequently from outside "mainstream" society? Some researchers suggest that marginal individuals are most likely to become entrepreneurs. On an individual level, it has been suggested that entrepreneurs are marginal individuals who are spurred on by a diverse experience in early childhood: they have become "misfits," in Kets de Vries words, who are unable to accept the authority of other individuals and to "fit into" an organizations.

On a social level, various theories about marginal individuals have been suggested to explain the entrepreneurship phenomenon. These theories are based on the concepts of social marginality, mobility, legitimacy and the social integration of individuals and groups. Individuals' perceptions that they are not part of the mainstream group drive them into an entrepreneurial career. Examples include women who face a "glass ceiling" in their organizations, and minorities who may feel that they are being discriminated against. These individuals may be driven to start their own business more out of necessity than by choice. Thus the marginal approach may explain the disproportionately large percentage of entrepreneurs who belong to ethnic or religious minorities.

Family Background

Family background has been espoused to explain the making of an entrepreneur. Research has traditionally focused on three aspects: birth order, role models and the experience of rejection in childhood.

First Born. It has been argued that entrepreneurs are often first born. The basis for this argument is simple. The first born often receives special care and more attention from his or her parents than the other siblings. This contributes to the development of traits such as self-confidence, independence and locus of control.

The Role Model. Some research suggests that individuals who come from entrepreneurial environments are more likely to start their own business. Research suggests that two thirds of entrepreneurs come from families where the father or mother is self-employed. The entrepreneurial environment and parental guidance and support appear to be conducive to fostering entrepreneurial traits such as risk-taking, independence, creativity and achievement. The self-employed parent becomes a role model and a mentor to the nascent entrepreneur and is usually inclined to encourage entrepreneurial behavior. The role model provides the potential entrepreneur with the aspiration to follow the same career choice. He or she usually identifies with the role model or mentor's life style and attitude. Mancuso wrote "Even when he is in his thirties and his dad is retired, the approval and praise of his father still provides a basis for his drive."

The Experience of Rejection. According to this approach, entrepreneurs might have experienced parental rejection early in their childhood. Kets de Vries, a noted management scholar, contends that poor and troubled family relations may explain the weak compliance motive and thus the need to be independent in order to avoid authority figures, be they parents or managers. Box 7.2 provides some interesting notes on the making of an entrepreneur.

Two Types of Entrepreneurs

What makes an entrepreneur tick? Writing in the *Journal of Management Studies*, M. F. R. Kets de Vries has attempted to answer the question. His exploration into the roots of entrepreneurship is not so much intended to plumb the depths of the entrepreneurial psyche, but to understand the forces that propel successful entrepreneurs, and the implications for the organizations that they build.

Reis de Vries joins with others before him in noting that entrepreneurs frequently emerge from an ethnic or minority background. The reasons for this are complex, as the author acknowledges. However, it is easy to appreciate that in the face of discrimination, with established avenues for achievement closed to him, the ethnic entrepreneur frequently has no choice but to follow paths that are unconventional. Although Kets de Vries provides no specific examples, it is worthwhile remembering that many of the most important figures of the industrial revolution came from backgrounds well outside the British establishment of the day—Wedgewood, Tate, Lloyd, etc. Many were drawn from the ranks of the Puritans or Presbyterians.

A second common factor is that of a self-employed father. The author suggests that turbulence associated with such an environment serves to condition the child and provide a role model for risk taking. Neither of the foregoing factors should be taken as to guarantee to produce an entrepreneur, however, only to ensure a propensity for such a career.

Family background shapes the entrepreneur in a second way. Kets de Vries notes that many report having experienced hardship during their childhood, some in the form of rejection or withdrawal of a father figure, some merely the victim of poverty (with its attendant strains on family life). Whether or not the hardship was real is irrelevant as a source of motivation, it need only be perceived. As a result, the youth passes into adulthood harbouring feelings of insecurity and possibly antipathy towards authority.

Typically the entrepreneur-to-be then passes through a period of restlessness, indecision and rejection during early adulthood. He or she fails to find a "fit" with any organization that presents itself and may appear non-conformist or inconsistent. In fact, he or she is displaying all the signs of uncertainty and lack of self-direction that a more conventional upbringing might obviate.

As the entrepreneur matures, the insecurities of childhood are manifested in the form of driving ambition and restless energy. These symptoms Kets de Vries terms a "reaction" against the stresses of childhood; where the child feels rejected, the adult removes himself from the parents' shadow. A search for quick gratification, impulsiveness and a disinclination toward analytical thinking are concomitant traits. Paradoxically success, when it arrives, serves only to heighten the entrepreneur's insecurities. The persistent belief in his or her inferiority intercedes to persuade (through guilt) that the success is undeserved, that it must be "paid for" at a later date. From the same roots spring the need for ostentatious trappings of luxury or power so often sported by successful entrepreneurs: they are physical reassurance against the anxieties harboured within, tangible evidence of accomplishment and identity.

SOURCE: M. Kets de Vries, "The Entrepreneurial Personality: A Person at the Cross Roads," *Journal of Management Studies XIV*, 1977, pp. 34–57.

THE MAKING OF AN ENTREPRENEUR ◎ 191

Education and Experience

Education. Entrepreneurs' educational levels have been explored. The myth of the uneducated entrepreneur has been challenged by many research studies. Today, according to U.S. census data, the typical entrepreneur is more educated than the person who is not self-employed. Research studies suggest that the majority of entrepreneurs have a university education. However some researchers argue that education reduces curiosity, willingness to take risk and motivation to start a business.

Experience. Research has revealed that the entrepreneur's previous experience increases the likelihood of success in the new venture. Both managerial and industry specific experience are critical in new venture creation. Thus it is no surprise that a large percentage of entrepreneurs start businesses in industries with which they are familiar. Indeed, certain industries are more likely to act as incubators than others. For example, Dan Lasater, founder of Ponderosa Restaurants, learned the restaurant business by working for McDonald's. Similarly, Bill Gates, founder of Microsoft, has worked in the computer industry since he was 14 years old. Sam Walton, founder of Wal-Mart, learned the retail business while working at J. C. Penny.

The Behavioral Approach—What the Entrepreneur Does

In this approach the entrepreneur is viewed as a critical element of the venture creation process. Karl Vesper noted that entrepreneurship is the creation of new organizations. The emphasis in this approach is placed on the organization and the different functions that the entrepreneur performs. Thus the research question shifted from who is an entrepreneur to what the entrepreneur does.

Howard Stevenson, Michael Roberts and Irving Grousbeck argue that it is not helpful to focus on certain personality traits or sociological issues, rather they view entrepreneurship as "an approach to management." Thus entrepreneurship is a way of handling key managerial functions, that is, the organization strategy, structure and management process. In other words, the entrepreneur is viewed by the behavioral approach as a person who can effectively marshal resources, pursue an appropriate strategy, structure, reward, and control systems to exploit a window of opportunity.

The Contingency Approach

A. B. Ibrahim suggests that entrepreneurship is a complex phenomenon which involves two critical elements—sensing and exploiting an opportunity. The individual's ability to sense an opportunity is the result of entrepreneurial traits such as high need for achievement, innovation, tolerance for ambiguity, risk taking and intuition. These traits allow entrepreneurs to scan the environment, recognize market gaps, develop innovative solutions to satisfy unmet customer needs. The second element is the ability to exploit the opportunity. Entrepreneurs' management skills, competencies and traits allow them to marshal the resources effectively, to develop the appropriate strategy, to work under conditions of uncertainty and to take bold actions in order to exploit the opportunity. Both the entrepreneurial traits and management skills are shaped and developed by environmental factors such as family background, culture, positive or negative environment, education and experience. Figure 7.3 depicts the contingency approach.

Summary

We have attempted in this chapter to focus on the entrepreneurial process and the making of an entrepreneur. Four different approaches were discussed, the traits, the environmental, the behavioral and the contingency approach. The traits approach emphasizes the different traits associated with entrepreneurs such as high need for achievement, risk taking propensity, tolerance for ambiguity, innovation, high need for independence, low need for conformity and internal locus of control. The environmental approach views the entrepreneur as a cultural phenomenon and that the choice of an entrepreneurial career is related to external factors beyond the individual's control. The behavioral approach focuses on what the entrepreneur does, and the different functions he or she performs in the venture creation process. Finally, the contingency approach focuses on sensing and exploiting an opportunity.

FIGURE 7.3
The Contingency Approach
to Entrepreneurship

PART II

The Entrepreneurial Traits and Motivation

Introduction

What motivates entrepreneurs? What makes them tick?

William Hewlett and David Packard started Hewlett-Packard (HP), one of the largest computer companies. Bill Gates founded one of the most successful companies in this century—Microsoft. In thinking back to all the entrepreneurs you have known, does it strike you that they share common characteristics?

The Entrepreneurial Traits

Entrepreneurial traits have been the object of much study. It has been suggested that certain traits are the driving force and motivation underlying the choice of an entrepreneurship career. Research has identified a number of entrepreneurial traits such as a high need for achievement and independence, a moderate risk-taking propensity, an internal locus of control, and tolerance for ambiguity and innovation. Figure 7.4 lists some of the traits associated with successful entrepreneurs. Understanding these traits provides some insight into entrepreneurship. Some of these traits could also serve as a benchmark to measure potential entrepreneurs' chances of success.

FIGURE 7.4
Traits Associated with Entrepreneurs

Need for Achievement
Need for Independence
Moderate risk-taking propensity
Internal locus of control
Tolerance for Ambiguity
Innovation
Proactivity
Intuition

A. K. Velan—The Successful Immigrant

At the age of 79, A. K. Velan, president and CEO of Velan Inc., has shown no sign of slowing down. He was recently named "Entrepreneur of the Year" for 1996 by Canadian Business Magazine. He has added this title to a long list of other awards for outstanding business performance.

A. K. Velan fled his native Czechoslovakia in 1949 when the Communist government took power. He came to Canada armed with his engineering know-how and a belief in his entrepreneurial drive and innovation. To him, Canada was a land of opportunity and freedom. In 1950, A. K. started a business from his house in Montreal based on his development and patenting of a device that would eliminate condensation from steam piping, the bimetallic stream trap. The company was incorporated in 1952 under the name of Velan Inc.

In the early years A. K. struggled to make his business a success. He made prototypes of his invention, and tested and modified them in his house. His first big break came when the U.S. Navy ordered the Velan bimetallic steam trap for seven of its new destroyers. These were the challenging times. He can remember working late into the night in his garage with his wife to pack the steam traps destined for the U.S. Navy. A. K. thrived on his new found success and greeted the challenges with great enthusiasm and hard work. With the development of other innovations, his business became too big for his house so he moved it to a manufacturing plant.

In the late 1950s, A. K. saw a window of opportunity developing with the birth of nuclear power. He began developing valves to be used specifically in the nuclear power industry. His products were used by the U.S. Navy and NATO for ships, nuclear submarines and aircraft carriers. Newly established nuclear power plants were also using his products.

Velan Inc. started as a small business and grew under the leadership of its founder into a multinational corporation with eight manufacturing plants in six countries and over 1,100 employees.

Velan Inc. prides itself on being a family business that is run by family members. Velan also tries to provide employment opportunities for other immigrants to North America, and has offered hundreds their all important first job.

SOURCE: Excerpt from a case study by Ingrid Sinclair, M.B.A. under the direction of Professor A. B. Ibrahim.

Need for Achievement

David McClelland's "need for achievement" first proposed in the *Achieving Society* (1961) is the best-known research associated with the traits approach. Need for achievement or n. Ach. motive seems to influence the individual to select an entrepreneurial career. A strong desire to set one's own goals and objectives and carry them out has been documented as the driving force for many entrepreneurs. The need for achievement is seldom satisfied by the traditional career path. Entrepreneurs want to take responsibility for their actions, do well in competitive situations, are result driven, take moderate risks and dislike routine activities.

The achievement motive of entrepreneurs predisposes them to perform different activities exceptionally well as a measure of their achievements. Among these is an intense preoccupation with producing high quality products or services and a desire to satisfy customer needs and wants. Bill Gates, founder of Microsoft and one of the most successful entrepreneurs of this century, is known for his long working hours, his constant demand for innovation and quality and his ability to take calculated risks.

McClelland's theory of the need for achievement identified three traits that are associated with entrepreneurs:

1. the desire to solve problems and gain satisfaction from attaining goals that they have set and prioritized themselves;
2. the ability to take moderate risks after assessing the alternatives;
3. the need for feedback as a measure of their success.

According to MacClelland, those who score highly on n. Ach were found to have a higher probability of going into business and succeeding. They also have a higher probability of benefiting from business training courses than those individuals who receive lower scores. It is interesting to note that according to research, there is a strong relation between the need for achievement in a given country and the level of economic growth in that country: the higher the need for achievement, the higher the level of the country's economic growth. Box 7.3 summarizes the results of an interesting survey.

Need for Independence and Autonomy

One of the strongest motivating factors underlying the choice of an entrepreneurial career is the need for independence. Many entrepreneurs have left successful executive careers to start their own businesses because of the strong need to work independently and be their "own boss." Jim Treybig left a well-paid position as marketing manager at Hewlett-Packard to start his own company, Tandem Computers, to satisfy his need for independence. Research has also revealed that entrepreneurs tend not to seek assistance from other people and thus tend to score low on the need for support.

New Economy Entrepreneurs

BOX 7.3

The Business Development Bank of Canada (BDC) surveyed 547 knowledge-based entrepreneurs. They reported the following interesting results. Entrepreneurs are highly motivated, full of energy and can accomplish tasks and get other people motivated. They have high level of commitment and have a different life style from the average person. They are risk takers and can work for many hours. They also sleep little and seldom have leisure time. Furthermore, they have no hobby, but are satisfied with their life.

SOURCE: Beyond Their Small Businesses: Insight Into Canada's New Economy Leaders. The Business Development Bank of Canada.

However, the need for independence might impede the firm's growth, as few entrepreneurs are willing to delegate, be it out of a perceived or a real lack of competent employees or out of an inherent reluctance to let go. Entrepreneurs' tendency to do everything themselves can prove detrimental to the company's long term survival.

Research has suggested that as the level of influence of other individuals, such as creditors or bankers, increases in relation to that of the entrepreneur, the latter begins to experience a loss of self-esteem and autonomy, which reduces the ability to manage the business effectively. If has been suggested that the entrepreneur's need for independence and autonomy could be the result of his or her resentment of authority figures, be it a parent or a bank manager.

Moderate Risk-Taking Propensity

Folklore has produced a belief that entrepreneurs are high risk takers. In the popular press, the entrepreneur is generally depicted as a dare-devil who thrives on risk and enjoys the challenge of the unknown. While this portrait may be true of some high-profile entrepreneurs, research has unveiled a different picture. Entrepreneurs take calculated risks. They do not deliberately seek out high-risk situations, nor do they strive to avoid risk altogether. In essence, they are willing to accept the risk and uncertainty inherent in new opportunities. A moderate risk-taking propensity is typical of entrepreneurs with a high need to achieve. Furthermore, they take good care to research problems and consider several alternative solutions before reaching a decision. This notion of "controlled boldness" is a key characteristic of many successful entrepreneurs. For example, in their study of an entrepreneurial firm, Henry Mintzberg and James Waters noted: "Sam Steinberg pursued what can be called a 'test-the-water' approach, always sensing an environment with minor probes before plunging in. In the earlier years at least, Steinberg never undertook a bold move until he had a pretty good idea what the consequences would be."

While it may appear to outsiders that an entrepreneur is engaging in a risky venture, the new business may in fact be considered less risky by the entrepreneur than any other available alternative. The perceived risk of losing autonomy and independence by working for someone else may outweigh the risk of being self-employed. For example, Ted Turner, founder of Turner Broadcasting System, is known for his risk-taking ability. He bought the virtually bankrupt Metro-Goldwyn-Mayer and turned it around.

Internal Locus of Control

Of all the traits generally ascribed to entrepreneurs, internal locus of control is perhaps the one that is most consistently positively related to the entrepreneurial personality. In fact, locus of control has been found to distinguish entrepreneurs from corporate executives as well as successful from less successful entrepreneurs. Locus of control refers to entrepreneurs' perception that all events in their lives are under their control and thus they are able to influence events and determine the outcome of their own actions. Internal locus of control individuals are confident that they can make things happen. They believe that they control and influence their own accomplishments and failures. They seek initiative and take responsibility for their actions. Entrepreneurs therefore feel that the results of their efforts and actions are attributable to themselves and not to such intangibles as "fate" and "luck." Internal locus of control has a direct link to the need for achievement trait, as entrepreneurs would not typically feel that they had achieved something if an outcome were not the result of their own endeavors. They therefore take responsibility for their own actions and do not blame their success or failure on the external environment. In contrast, external locus of control individuals believe that the outcome of their actions is influenced by events beyond their control, including other individuals, luck or fate.

Research has revealed that internal locus of control individuals are alert, discover opportunities and scan their environment for the information needed to ensure effective exploitation of those opportunities. Further, it has also been shown that a higher level of perceptual awareness—defined as the ability to discover new opportunities—is associated with internal locus of control. The results of a recent study suggest that internal locus of control entrepreneurs are more inclined to plan for expansion of their businesses despite an unfavourable environment such as a high interest rate and inflation. The confidence in their own ability to achieve the desired performance and to recognize new opportunities enables them to be relatively undaunted by unfavourable external events. For example, Walt Disney had to overcome many obstacles and unfavourable events before he was able to achieve profits with the introduction of *Snow White and the Seven Dwarfs* in 1937.

Tolerance for Ambiguity

David McClelland identified tolerance for ambiguity as one of the traits associated with most entrepreneurs. This trait refers to the ability of the entrepreneur to perceive ambiguous situations in a positive and challenging way. Ambiguity in this sense is defined as a lack of complete and definitive information. Tolerance for ambiguity is a definite asset to entrepreneurs, it allows them to organize their thoughts and make decisions under conditions of uncertainty. Classical economists such as Cantillon (1756) and later Knight have stressed the uncertainty aspect of the entrepreneurial action. Being an entrepreneur means that one is irresistibly drawn to a great deal of uncertainty, for many reasons. First, many start ups involve innovation and unproven concepts. Second, small businesses have very limited resources to scan the environment and to gather all relevant information. Entrepreneurs must therefore rely on their intuition and fragments of information in making their decision. Further, the lack of human resources with functional expertise dictate that entrepreneurs must make decisions in every aspect of the business. Entrepreneurs find this ambiguous and uncertain environment stimulating and challenging and usually reject the monotony and highly structured environment of a routine job. While other individuals may suffer anxiety and stress in this type of environment, entrepreneurs thrive on ambiguity and are able to identify and pursue opportunities. J. Scheré tested a sample of entrepreneurs and managers and found entrepreneurs to be more tolerant of ambiguity than managers. For example, William Hewlett and David Packard, founders of Hewlett-Packard, endured long periods of uncertainty while working in Packard's garage. They liked the challenge, and their efforts became a success story. Similarly King Camp Gillette saw a need for a razor with a throwing blade. He struggled for 6 years before he made a success of Gillette Corporation.

Innovation

In Peter Drucker's eyes, innovation, the mechanism by which entrepreneurs create or increase wealth, is an essential quality of entrepreneurship. He says it "is the effort to create purposeful, focused change in an enterprise's economic or social potential." It arises from a powerful search for opportunity in situations that may be both inside and outside the corporation. Unexpected occurrences, incongruities, process needs and industry or market changes may provoke innovation inside the firm or the industry. Economic and political trends, changes in customers' preferences and tastes and new knowledge may act as catalysts outside the firm. Drucker asserts that innovation is a skill that can be acquired and taught.

Joseph Shumpeter, the great economist, identified innovation as a key characteristic of the entrepreneur and saw the entrepreneur as a "creative destructor." In most industries, significant innovations originate from the garages and basements of entrepreneurs. Most of the Silicon Valley high-tech firms were founded by entrepreneurs such as Steve Jobs, founder of Apple computer, William Hewlett and David Packard, founders of Hewlett-Packard, and Ken Olson, founder of Digital. David McClelland's research confirmed the entrepreneur's predisposition to innovate, suggesting a strong relationship between a high need to achieve and innovation.

Proactivity

Proactivity is another prevalent trait associated with entrepreneurs: it is closely related to locus of control. Entrepreneurs have an ability to take control of events and take initiative in solving problems that arise. Further, they are able to set objectives and implement solutions effectively. Sam Walton, founder of Wal-Mart, was known for his proactive style of management.

Other Entrepreneurial Characteristics

Intuition

Much has been written about entrepreneurs' intuitive behavior. Research has revealed that the entrepreneur's intuition plays a critical role in the decision making process in small firms. In many of these firms, strategic decisions are based not on facts or complete information, but on the entrepreneur's experience, business sense and "gut feeling." Indeed, Alfred P. Sloan noted that the final act of judgement is intuitive. Pierre Péladeau, founder of Quebecor—the largest printing company in the world—was known for his intuitive behavior.

Vision

The starting point of a new venture is the entrepreneur's vision. In many respects, it is a dream of what the entrepreneur wants to achieve in the long term. This dream allows the entrepreneur to persevere. Short term failure is seen only as an obstacle that must be overcome in order to achieve the dream. Vision is a driving

THE ENTREPRENEURIAL QUIZ

The following quiz is meant to stimulate your thinking about who is an entrepreneur. It is not meant to give conclusive evidence. No statistical reliability or validity are claimed.

Answer the following questions by marking the appropriate box provided.

PART I

YES   NO

☐   ☐   1. I like to go to work at a regular time.

☐   ☐   2. I often find myself telling people what to do.

☐   ☐   3. Taking small risks makes me nervous.

☐   ☐   4. I do not like surprises.

☐   ☐   5. I like to solve problems.

☐   ☐   6. I believe you are either lucky or unlucky in this world.

☐   ☐   7. I am the first child in the family.

☐   ☐   8. I am the youngest child in the family.

☐   ☐   9. I like change.

☐   ☐   10. I am at my best when I am faced with a challenging situation.

☐   ☐   11. I always worry about my job security.

☐   ☐   12. My parents are/were self-employed.

☐   ☐   13. One of my parents are/were self-employed.

☐   ☐   14. I come from a family that always had a steady career in government or a large corporation.

PART II

15. When my boss assigns me a job, I prefer the details of the assignment to be:

☐   ☐   a. specifically spelled out

☐   ☐   b. left for me to exercise some imagination

☐   ☐   c. clear as to the objectives.

16. When my office is cluttered I feel:

☐   ☐   a. at ease and have no problem with it

☐   ☐   b. lazy and tired

☐   ☐   c. something needs to be done right away.

17. When I start a new project, I usually:

☐   ☐   a. set goals and priorities and seek feedback

☐   ☐   b. set a deadline for completion

☐   ☐   c. delegate to other people.

18. In the different jobs I have had, I:

☐   ☐   a. always introduced something different

☐   ☐   b. always followed company policy and procedure

☐   ☐   c. never deviated from what I was asked to do.

19. If I were asked to toss a coin into a bowl I would:

☐   ☐   a. stand not too far away where, with focus and persistence, I would score high.

☐   ☐   b. stand very close to score every time

☐   ☐   c. stand far away and test my chances.

20. In my job I have always liked to work:

☐   ☐   a. under close supervision

☐   ☐   b. with very little supervision

☐   ☐   c. alone so I can do things my own way.

ANSWERS: You have what it takes to be an entrepreneur if your answers are as follows: Part I: Yes: 2, 5, 7, 9, 10, 12, 13
No: 1, 3, 4, 6, 8, 11, 14; Part II: 15 (b); 16 (a); 17(a); 18 (a); 19 (a); 20 (c).

force behind the entrepreneur's success. Author Jeffrey Timmons noted that most entrepreneurs do not speak of their failures with regret, but are able to look at them as good learning experiences. Microsoft was founded in 1975 by two technology entrepreneurs, Bill Gates and Paul Allen, with a dream to develop inexpensive software that can be used by every PC user.

Summary

Entrepreneurial traits have been the object of much study. A high need for achievement and independence, a moderate risk-taking propensity, internal locus of control, and tolerance for ambiguity and innovation are traits associated with entrepreneurs. These traits have been found to be the driving force and motivation for the choice of entrepreneurship as a career. Other traits described in this chapter such as proactivity, intuition and vision are also critical for a successful entrepreneur and for venture creation.

PART III

The Successful Entrepreneur

Each year, thousands of new businesses start in the United States and Canada. The fate of these ventures is highly variable and in general is a chronology of the economic growth. Some of these small firms have evolved into corporate giants. Others have failed. It is estimated that approximately 80 percent of all start-ups fail within the first five years of operation. What does it take to succeed in venture creation? What are the characteristics of successful entrepreneurs? This chapter is devoted to exploring the critical success factors as well as causes of small business failures. Subsequent chapters will deal with these factors in more depth.

The earlier discussion on the making of an entrepreneur leads us to attempt to draw a profile of a successful entrepreneur. Studies have shown that both entrepreneurial traits and management skill are key ingredients in operating a successful venture. In part II we have focused on the entrepreneurial behaviour and traits. In this part we devote most of our discussion to the second factor, the management skills and competencies. Figure 7.5 depicts the critical factors associated with successful entrepreneurs.

The Entrepreneurial Factor—The Right Stuff

The personality traits and environmental factors that shape the entrepreneur have been examined. Research suggests that entrepreneur develops certain personality traits such as high need for achievement and independence, moderate risk-taking propensity, internal locus of control, innovation, tolerance for ambiguity, and pro-activity. Furthermore, the entrepreneur's environment seems to play a significant role in developing these entrepreneurial traits. Environmental factors such as culture and family background seem to be conducive to the development of these

FIGURE 7.5
The Successful
Entrepreneur

traits. Research studies revealed that these traits—the right stuff—are indeed associated with successful entrepreneurs.

One of the first truly objective studies that examined the characteristics of successful entrepreneurs was conducted by John Hornadey and John Aboud and was published in *Personal Psychology* in 1971. The study added much to our knowledge that entrepreneurs are driven by a greater need for achievement, independence and innovation. The study also found that successful entrepreneurs achieve above average scholastic performance. David McClelland classic study of successful entrepreneurs revealed that these individuals are achievement oriented and pro-active.

Ibrahim and Goodwin found a strong correlation between successful entrepreneurs and traits such as high need for achievement, moderate risk-taking propensity, innovation and locus of control. Finally, Charles Hofer and William Sandberg found that successful entrepreneurs exhibit a high need for achievement.

Management Skills and Competencies

The second critical success factor can be grouped under general management skills. These skills and competencies are critical to the venture creation and development stages. These skills include developing the appropriate strategy and structure for the new venture, the ability to build a network of contacts and to delegate routine activities to his/her team members small as it may be. Furthermore, effective management of various functions such as cash flow management, marketing, accounting and record keeping are critical to the venture's success. Indeed, in the beginning entrepreneurs are expected to manage the entire business. Functional expertise are usually limited due to both the small size and the scarcity of resources of the new venture. Research studies have shown that lack of these skills and competencies result in business failure. A study of bankruptcy among Canadian small firms found that small firms went bankrupt because of the lack of general management skills. According to the study failure occurs as a result of the entrepreneur's lack of both breadth and depth of knowledge including technical and general management.

Developing the New Venture's Strategy

Developing the appropriate strategy to guide the new venture is perhaps the cornerstone of a successful venture. Research studies have shown that carving a niche is the most effective type of strategy for small business. Simply, the entrepreneur must tailor the firm's product or service to meet the specific needs of a particular group of customers. The niche may be based on cost leadership or differentiation. To further understand the essence of strategy in new ventures we briefly discuss two relevant concepts—distinctive competence and industry structure.

In today's highly competitive environment only those new ventures that have established areas of distinctive competence will survive and grow. Distinctive competence refers to the unique skills and activities that a new business can offer. Distinctive competence in a specific area such as product design and quality, cost efficiency, marketing and management skills and knowledge allows the firm to build a competitive advantage.

The industry structure and the degree of attractiveness also play a significant role in determining the type of strategy the entrepreneur could pursue. Industry structure includes the industry stage of growth (growth, maturity and decline). It also includes types of competition as well as industry concepts such as entry and exit barriers. An effective strategy for the new venture must take all these factors into consideration.

Strategic Planning

An effective but simple strategic planning system is critical to new ventures' success. A strategic planning system helps the firm identify its objectives, mission, assess its internal capacity and its external environment. Internal assessment of the strengths and weaknesses and external evaluation of windows of opportunity as well as constraints give an indication of the firm's real capacity to carry out the intended mission successfully, and may suggest a more attractive and less competitive niche. Studies of successful ventures have shown that the strategic planning process should be simple and inexpensive, and focus on short and medium range planning. Box 7.4 examines the perceptual difference between loan officers and small business owners.

Perception of Success

BOX 7.4

In a study of perception of entrepreneurial success characteristics, Montagne, Kuratko and Scarcella examined the differences between loan officers and small business owners on their perception of success. Loan officers were found to perceive successful entrepreneurs in terms of managerial objectives such as goal setting, planning, organizing and problem analysis, while owners perceive success in terms of traits such as confidence, initiative, innovation, caring and encouragement.

SOURCE: R. V. Montagne, D. F. Kuratko and J. H. Scarcella, "Perception of Entrepreneurial Success Characteristics," *American Journal of Small Business,* Winter 1986, pp. 25–32.

Delegation

Many entrepreneurs attribute success to their ability to divorce themselves from the day-to-day routine activity of the business and focus on strategic type decisions. Yet studies after studies have shown that a large number of entrepreneurs are reluctant to let go of many small details that would have otherwise been handled by their staff. As a result many small firms are unable to attract competent people. Recently, however this picture of the dominant and single-handed entrepreneur has been replaced with the team entrepreneur. In most knowledge-based firms, the entrepreneur manages the team as a coach or a cheerleader. Decision making in these firms are based on consultation and consensus. Box 7.5 summarizes some of the problems facing entrepreneurs during the venture creation and development stages.

Networking

The ability to build and maintain a network of contacts is critical to the entrepreneur's success. Networking is a process that may take years before the entrepreneur can reap its benefits. Two types of contacts form the entrepreneur's network. The first is the formal type such as those contacts established with bankers; Provincial and Federal government officials, legal and financial experts. The second type is the informal type of contracts such as those established with family members, colleagues and friends. Both types are important in providing the entrepreneur with a pool of information and advice.

Effective Management of Functional Areas

In addition to the general management skills, successful entrepreneurs must be able to manage critical functions such as financial management and marketing effectively.

Financial Management Skills

Financial management skills are essential to effective decision making in any organizations large or small. Financial management are particularly crucial in the venture's start up stage. It is at this stage that the firm is most vulnerable—its resources are limited and its market position is not established yet.

Accounting techniques such as break-even, sensitivity and ratio analysis as well as cash flow projections and budgeting allow the entrepreneur to make objective decisions. Take for example two major decisions. The first is the decision to price the product or service. Here the entrepreneur has to have a basic understanding of the manufacturing cost, variable or fixed, the contribution margin, the overhead cost, the break-even point and the safety margin. He or she will then be able to set a competitive price in light of other internal and external factors.

The second decision is to determine the economic viability of the opportunity. Here again the entrepreneur is expected to have a thorough knowledge of accounting techniques such as ratio analysis to determine the expected rate of return on investment (ROI) or on equity (ROE). Cash flow projections also give an indication to when the business opportunity is expected to achieve a positive cash flow and thus, decide on the appropriate financing vehicle (short term/long term). A business opportunity that will be able to generate a positive cash flow in three or four months, for example, does not need long-term financing. The entrepreneur may also employ sensitivity analysis techniques in his or her evaluation of the economic viability of the opportunity. Sensitivity analysis provides the entrepreneur or manager with different scenarios, best guess, worst and possible scenarios and thus the ability to make a more objective decision. Box 7.6 examines the application of some of these accounting techniques in small business.

Management of Cash Flow

Effective management of cash flow is crucial to the entrepreneur's success in the early stage of the venture creation process. Profits do not guarantee a healthy cash flow situation. Therefore financial planning is a critical activity in the new venture to avoid unpleasant surprises. Its during the early venture creation that the entrepreneur face the most challenging task struggling to establish a name for himself or herself. He or she has no track record and thus it is difficult for him or her to receive a favourable line of credit from suppliers. Yet, the entrepreneur has to extend credit to the new venture's customers in order to attract them and to establish a loyal customer base. Effective management of accounts payable and receivable allows the young company to survive during this difficult stage with relatively little capital. If a proper balance is maintained between payment (90 days) and collection (30 days), the small firm can finance its needs of working capital internally. Working capital represents approximately 67 percent of the small firm's total assets. Typically, the amount of funds invested in working capital is a function of the entrepreneur's attitude toward risk. Risk in this context refers to the level of current assets considered sufficient to meet the firm's financial obligations.

Inventory Management and Control

For many young companies inventories represents a substantial investment of the firm's fund. On average, 10 percent of the firm's assets are tied up in inventory. This percentage varies from industry to industry, it could reach 55 percent in some knowledge-based companies. Effective management of inventory requires maintaining an optimal level of inventory that allows the firm to reduce its carrying and ordering costs, while avoiding stock-out. Carrying costs are the funds that the firm has invested in inventory, storage, insurance, property tax and shrinkage cost. The opportunity costs of having funds tied up in inventory (non-productive assets) may also be included under carrying costs. Stock-out costs include the cost of running short, such as the opportunity cost of lost orders and the loss of a good customer. Thus, successful entrepreneur must be able to answer two fundamental questions: when to order? and how much to order?

BOX 7.6

Why do once prosperous small companies suddenly seem to come upon hard times? Herbert N. Woodward, in his article, applies the lessons he has learned from reviving ailing firms to explore the reasons that seemingly sudden problems can develop in small businesses. His analysis is intended to help entrepreneurs improve their management skills and to steer clear of major problems before they occur.

The author's first argument is that growth in sales is seen as the cure-all solution. Accounting methods seem to associate profitability with sales volume.

The first accounting practice that the author considers is Marginal Income Accounting. Managers believe that they can add extra sales to normal sales levels for a short time period even when the new product prices do not cover a suitable percentage of fixed cost. Because new business is responsible for fixed cost just as the old one, managers must therefore develop a pricing strategy that covers all overhead costs. The next accounting practice that leads managers to make errors in judgement is break-even analysis. Entrepreneurs and small business managers believe that total cost is a static figure and that the small firm must have a larger sales volume to cover this figure. The author argues that with the exception of early stage, very little fixed costs are incurred by the small firm.

The author then turns his attention to problems of poor cost analysis. For example, he points to the fact that new product lines incur more overhead because of extra start-up costs than older product lines, yet usually the same proportionate amounts of overhead are charged to each line. The result is that managers are not fully aware of which product lines are most profitable. The author recommends that all product lines be reviewed to determine the amount to be charged to each and whether low-margin product lines should be dropped. Funds are then freed up for investments elsewhere.

The final point that the author discusses, for the entrepreneur to consider, is that the balance sheet can be a source of capital in good and bad times, and entrepreneurs should not only be concerned with the sales figures and profits on the income statement. Cash flow can be generated by collecting on late accounts receivable, by taking a loss and reducing taxes on inventory no longer worth full value, and by re-examining the fixed asset account. For example, funds may be freed up if some subcontracting is undertaken and other resources of the company can be more profitably used. Other fixed assets could be thought of as sources of capital on the balance sheet.

The author concludes by recommending that entrepreneurs should try to improve Return On Investment. If assets employed can be reduced, the Return On Investment will go up, especially if assets were previously employed inefficiently.

SOURCE: Herbert N. Woodward, *Management Strategies for Small Companies,* in David Gumpert edition, *Growing Concerns— Building and Managing the Smaller Business,* Harvard Business Review Executive Book Series, John Wiley & Sons, 1984, pp. 131–141.

Marketing Skills

The flow of goods and offering of services to fulfill the needs and desires of customers are fundamental to the successful operation of the young company. Therefore effective marketing strategy is crucial to the survival and growth of the business. Successful entrepreneurs assess the market carefully, identify the target market and design the appropriate marketing mix including the pricing and promotion strategy. David McClelland classical study of successful entrepreneurs revealed that their achievement orientation propelled them to be extremely concerned with customer needs and wants and work hard to build a solid relationship with customers.

Venture Success

Venture success has been attributed to a number of critical elements related to the entrepreneur, the venture capabilities, the industry structure and the market. Charles Hofer and William Sandberg examined critical success factors in new ventures and concluded that industry structure, business strategy and the behavior characteristics of the entrepreneur are key determinants of venture success. A. B. Ibrahim suggests that venture success is determined by four critical elements: the entrepreneur's traits and skills; the market acceptance of the product or the service innovation; the industry structure, characteristic and competitive forces and the venture capabilities as shown in Figure 7.6. The entrepreneur in this model is the cornerstone of the venture. His or her entrepreneurial traits and skills play a significant role in shaping and influencing the other three elements. First, the successful entrepreneur develops the product or service innovation based on their assessment of customer needs and the window of opportunity. Second, he or she marshals the resources and develops the capabilities needed to exploit the opportunity. Further, the successful entrepreneur develops the effective business strategy in light of the industry structure, characteristics and competitive forces.

Prediction and Development

A critical question that follows is, can we predict who will become a successful entrepreneur? And how to develop these success traits? McClelland noted that

FIGURE 7.6
<u>Key Determinants of Venture Success</u>

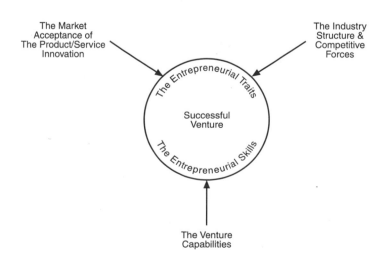

early research in the field of entrepreneurship had only uncovered lists of characteristics that entrepreneurs and experts had felt are the key personality traits for success in small business. These observations prompted McClelland to attempt to develop a test that would predict which persons show a greater or lesser probability of succeeding as an entrepreneur. He found that those who score highly on the need to achieve have a high probability of success, and are more likely to benefit from business training courses than those whose scores are lower. Box 7.7 summarizes McClelland's findings.

It is interesting to know that certain entrepreneurial traits can be predicted early. In a study by M. Kourilsky, traits such as innovation and persistence were identified in a sample of elementary school children.

Studies have also shown that experiential learning is critical in developing entrepreneurial behavior and skills. Experience-based education was found to increase entrepreneurial aspiration and behavior as well as teaching decision making skills. A. B. Ibrahim and J. R. Goodwin suggested that entrepreneurial courses should be designed to meet the psychological characteristics of budding entrepreneurs. Indeed universities are excellent training grounds for budding entrepreneurs not only for learning theories and concepts but also skills development. Individual case analysis and unstructured type courses were found to enhance entrepreneurial and managerial skills. In fact, new ventures that were started by students participating in these courses seem to live up to "prior measure of success."

Can We Predict Successful Entrepreneurs?

BOX 7.7

The first important steps in this direction were the early studies McClelland conducted that discovered that the need to achieve plays a dominant role in creating a successful entrepreneur. In a study conducted by the author and his associates, it was discovered that those who score highly on a measure of the need to achieve also have a higher probability of going into small business and succeeding. Another useful finding from the study was that those who score highly on the need to achieve benefit from business training courses more than those whose scores are lower. The persons tested were potential entrepreneurs enrolled in a small business training course. An important outcome of these results is that it may be possible to predict who will become a successful entrepreneur by measuring the need to achieve of potential entrepreneurs and enrolling those with a high need to achieve in a business training course to further enhance their chances of success in small business.

SOURCE: David McClelland, "Characteristics of Successful Entrepreneurs," *The Journal of Creative Behavior,* 21, 3, 1987, pp. 219–33.

Tom Monaghan—The Successful Entrepreneur
Domino's Pizza Inc.

Considered by many as the entrepreneurial hero of the 1980s, heading up a billion dollar a year company in Domino's Pizza Inc., and owner of the Detroit Tigers baseball team, Tom Monaghan started in the humblest of ways.

Born in 1937, Tom spent a number of years in an orphanage after the death of his father in 1941. He later saw service in the United States Marine Corps, and had an abbreviated college career at the University of Michigan. This diverse background was prior to his purchase of a pizza parlor with a $500 loan in 1960.

All was still not smooth sailing, for a co-owner kept on extracting a disproportionate amount of their modest funds.

In 1969, Monaghan lost control over Domino's growth and in the late 1970s almost lost his trademark to Amstar Corporation, makers of Domino sugar.

With the loyal support of his family, his wife and four daughters, he was able to weather yet another storm, so much so that in the spring of 1989 the company had opened more than 5,000 pizza parlors.

The company is split into three main divisions—distribution, franchises and the home offices of Domino's Pizza International Inc.

The company and its management grow ever more decentralized as the empire expands. Monaghan remains a powerful force throughout the organization, right down to monthly call-in sessions with employees. References to his growth and development seem to suggest that it really took off when he bought the Detroit Tigers baseball club, in 1983. He is reported to have said, "Even if baseball meant nothing to me—and owning the Tigers is the highest material thing that I ever aspired to—it would've made sense from a free-publicity point of view."

The company has seen the scars of many management trials and tribulations, difficulty with lenders and creditors, and lawsuits with franchisees. By the time that he took over the Tigers in late 1983 at a price of $53 million, he was considered "a successful entrepreneur." With a personal fortune estimated at $250 million, he did have control over one of the fast-food industry's most spectacular growth companies.

Second in total sales only to Pizza Hut Inc. among the national chains, Domino's excelled at doing something that nobody else did: getting orders to customers in 30 minutes or less, or the pizza came free.

In the beginning of 1984, there were 900 units, of which 300 were company-owned and two-thirds being franchised, with virtually no outstanding debt and extensive expansion plans for the forthcoming years. By the Fall of 1989 there were 5,100 units, with the saying that every 24 hours, somewhere in the world, three more Domino's delivery outlets are launched. Having risen out of obscurity, he says that "what matters is not simply the overcoming of obstacles, it is the opportunities created once those obstacles are left behind."

His frequent references to Frank Lloyd Wright, the noted architect, suggest that in many ways, he might have found a "role model."

Reports say the "Even though he never met him, Tom Monaghan obviously has a great interest, a reverence, really, for Mr. Wright's work. It may be less intellectual than instinctive, but that's the best situation to have, because [Wright] didn't necessarily create his designs for people of great wealth or intellectual accomplishment. His architecture spoke directly to the people, and obviously it spoke to Tom Monaghan a long time ago. He has a great dream and we hope that he sticks to it."

Like his fascination with Frank Lloyd Wright, his ownership of the Tigers is a hobby, not a business.

"I know more about Domino's than I ever will about running a baseball team," he says. "In fact, there aren't too many people—if any—who operate a company this size and understand it as well as I do. Its an emotional involvement, not just an intellectual one. That's why I could never be involved the same way with another company. My life is plenty exciting right now, but you know, nothing will ever compare to the years when I was in the back of my own store, making pizza, beating the rush, building something I believed in."

SOURCE: *Forbes*, October 23, 1989, pp. 30, 220; *Inc.*, February 1986, pp. 61–65.

SUMMARY

We have attempted to describe the factors contributing to successful small business. Two critical factors were described in this section, entrepreneurial traits and management skills and competence. Entrepreneurial traits include behavioral characteristics such as high need for achievement. Managerial skills and competence include management of cash flow, monitoring the inventory level, networking, strategic planning, niche strategy, systematic record keeping system, accounting and marketing skills and delegation of routine activities.

DIMENSIONS OF ORGANIZATIONAL STRUCTURE

THE · PENNSYLVANIA · STATE · UNIVERSITY

Whether you call it integration, synergy, or "convergence," AOL chairman Steve Case's favorite word, it is the driving force behind the organization structures of so-called "New Economy" firms, based on the hypothetical benefits of owning a variety of related business units. Since the future of technology remains uncertain it makes sense for firms to hedge their bets by owning many different technologies. Case, a visionary leader, says, "We are moving into an era of convergence where the lines between industries will blur." However, it is clear that owning widely diversified businesses does not yet contribute to profitability, perhaps because an overly diversified corporate structure is difficult to manage.

AOL Time Warner is struggling with this issue today. The huge firm, with $38 billion in revenue, today comprises dozens of major brands. An exhaustive, and exhausting, list of brands includes Internet businesses such as AOL, CompuServe, Road Runner, icq, Instant Messenger, Netscape, and Mapquest; cable networks HBO, Cinemax, CNN, the Cartoon Network, TNT, TBS Superstation, Turner Classic Movies, the WB; movie studios Warner Brothers, Castle Rock Entertainment, and New Line Cinema; magazines such as *Time, People, Sports Illustrated, Fortune, InStyle, Money, Entertainment Weekly, marie clarie, MAD* comics, and over one hundred other specialty titles; the Time Warner cable provider and four local TV stations; the Atlanta Braves baseball team, the Atlanta Hawks basketball team, and the Atlanta Thrashers hockey team; book publishers; the Looney Tunes animation studio; and Atlantic, Elektra, Rhino, and other recording companies.

> ## "I've always said this is a marathon, not a sprint."
> —*Steve Case, chairman of the board of AOL Time Warner*

Thus far, the much-hyped benefits have failed to materialize. According to Case, the slow start was to be expected. He says, "I've always said this is a marathon, not a sprint." The firm is effectively cross-selling products, for example, by advertising its other products on its Web portals and cable stations. But it could do more. Case maintains, "The merger was never about cross-divisional promotion. It was about cross-divisional innovation." The firm has taken the first step, adding divisions with responsibility for achieving synergies, but some obvious moves, such as offering movie sneak previews exclusively to AOL subscribers, have been widely discussed but never implemented.

The challenge for CEO Richard Parsons is to create an organization structure that will harness the power of these combined businesses, realizing synergies and sparking innovation, while also maintaining control. Parsons, who assumed the top spot in May 2002, began with a reorganization, asking some top executives who had previously reported to Case to report directly to him and changing other reporting relationships at the firm's top level. The change will give more formal authority and public visibility to several top executives, mainly those in strategic planning, external communications, and technology development. Parsons also plans to concentrate on making each business unit successful on its own, downplaying the importance of convergence. According to a senior AOL executive, Parsons feels that "if we set convergence as a dramatic target, we set ourselves up for a fall because it's clearly going to take longer than we thought." The new CEO is also attempting

SOURCE: Gregory Moorhead and Ricky Griffin: *Organizational Behavior,* Seventh Edition. Copyright © 2004 by Houghton Mifflin Company. Used with permission.

to respond to investors, who are clamoring for a simplified, more easily understood structure.

The firm's missteps, along with the slump in the technology sector, have caused the company's stock price to fall, erasing more than $100 billion of shareholder value since the 2001 merger of AOL and Time Warner. Still, Case believes that a convergence strategy will ultimately yield the best results. He points out, "The Internet phenomenon, the trend toward more of a connected society, is unabated." Now it is up to Parsons to find a way to organize the entity so as to capture Case's vision and then to make that organization profitable.

REFERENCES: "AOL Time Warner 2002 Factbook," "Corporate Information: Timeline," "Overview," AOL Time Warner website, www.aoltimewarner.com on June 5, 2002; Martin Peers, "AOL CEO Parsons Reorganizes Reporting Lines for Senior Aides," *Wall Street Journal,* May 24, 2002. online.wsj.com on June 5, 2002; Marc Gunther and Stephanie N. Mehta, "Can Steve Case Make Sense of This Beast?" *Fortune,* May 13, 2002 (quotation). www.fortune.com on April 30, 2002; Martin Peers, "In New Turn, AOL Time Warner Will De-Emphasize 'Convergence,'" *Wall Street Journal,* May 13, 2002. online.wsj. com on June 5, 2002.

AOL Time Warner is faced with developing an organization structure that allows the synergies it expected when the two companies merged yet still enables management to have some control over operations. This is not unusual in business and industry these days as companies struggle to remain competitive in a rapidly changing world. This chapter introduces many of the key concepts of organization structure and sets the stage for understanding the many aspects of developing the appropriate organization design.

The Nature of Organization Structure

organization A group of people working together to attain common goals

organization goals Objectives that management seeks to achieve in pursuing the firm's purpose

In other chapters we discuss key elements of the individual and the factors that tie the individual and the organization together. In a given organization, these factors must fit together within a common framework: the organization's structure.

Organization Defined

An **organization** is a group of people working together to achieve common goals. Top management determines the direction of the organization by defining its purpose, establishing goals to meet that purpose, and formulating strategies to achieve the goals the definition of its purpose gives the organization reason to exist, in effect, it answers the question "What business are we in?"

Establishing goals converts the defined purpose into specific, measurable performance targets. **Organizational goals** are objectives that management seeks to achieve in pursuing the purpose

> **"We needed to give people a beacon that they could follow when they were having a tough time with prioritization, leadership, where to go, what hills to take."**
>
> —Steven A. Ballmer, the new CEO of Microsoft, describing why the software giant was reorganizing

of the firm. Goals motivate people to work together. Although each individual's goals are important to the organization, it is the organization's overall goals that are most important. Goals keep the organization on track by focusing the attention and actions of the members. They also give the organization a forward-looking orientation. They do not address past success or failure; rather, they force members to think about and plan for the future.

Finally, strategies are specific action plans that enable the organization to achieve its goals and thus its purpose. Pursuing a strategy involves developing an organization structure and the processes to do the organization's work.

Organization Structure

**organizational struc-
ture** The system of task, reporting, and authority relationships within which the organization does its work

Organization structure is the system of task, reporting, and authority relationships within which the work of the organization is done. Thus, structure defines the form and function of the organization's activities. Structure also defines how the parts of an organization fit together, as is evident from an organization chart.

The purpose of an organization's structure is to order and coordinate the actions of employees to achieve organizational goals. The premise of organized effort is that people can accomplish more by working together than they can separately. The work must be coordinated properly, however, if the potential gains of collective effort are to be realized. Consider what might happen if the thousands of employees at Dell Computers worked without any kind of structure. Each person might try to build a computer that he or she thought would sell. No two computers would be alike, and each would take months or years to build. The costs of making the computers would be so high that no one would be able to afford them. To produce computers that are both competitive in the marketplace and profitable for the company, Dell must have a structure in which its employees and managers work together in a coordinated manner. DaimlerChrysler was faced with similar coordination problems following its merger, due to duplication of capabilities, facilities, and product lines, as discussed in Box 8.1.

The task of coordinating the activities of thousands of workers to produce cars or computers that do the work expected of them and that are guaranteed and easy to maintain may seem monumental. Yet whether the goal is to mass produce computers or to make soap, the requirements of organization structure are similar. First, the structure must identify the various tasks or processes necessary for the organization to reach its goals. This dividing of tasks into smaller parts is often called "division of labor." Even small organizations (those with fewer than one hundred employees) use division of labor. Second, the structure must combine and coordinate the divided tasks to achieve a desired level of output. The more interdependent the divided tasks, the more coordination is required. Every organization structure addresses these two fundamental requirements. The various ways of approaching these requirements are what make one organization structure different from another.

Organization structure can be analyzed in three ways. First, we can examine its configuration—that is, its size and shape—as depicted on an organization chart. Second, we can analyze its operational aspects or characteristics, such as separation of specialized tasks, rules and procedures, and decision making. Finally, we can examine responsibility and authority within the organization. In this chapter, we describe organization structure from all three points of view.

In 1999, German automaker Daimler, which manufactures Mercedes cars, merged with Chrysler, one of America's Big Three, and DaimlerChrysler, as the new firm is called, then purchased a 34 percent stake in Japan-based Mitsubishi Motors. Although the merger seemed like a brilliant move, combining powerhouses from three continents, the results have been weak thus far.

The German-born CEO Jurgen Schrempp is trying to combine the firm's disparate units into an integrated whole. "The chief executive should not be the one who just sort of guides the board on vision and strategy. You also have to know what you are talking about," Schrempp says. To advise him, Schrempp created a chairman's council of eleven outsiders, including IBM's Lou Gerstner. He also established an executive automotive committee whose members are the heads of Mercedes, Chrysler, and Mitsubishi; he hopes the group can improve coordination.

One problematic area is cost control. The merger resulted in duplication of capabilities, facilities, and product lines, consequently increasing expenses. Combined with the effect of slower sales and increased competition, the cost increase caused the firm to lose $589 million in 2001, compared with a 2000 gain of $7 billion. Three years after the merger, the firm is still seeking closer integration in some functions. Schrempp asks, "Why not combine parts departments, workshops and things like that?" Sharing components across the three major divisions could bring significant savings; for example, using the Mercedes gearbox in Chrysler sedans could save as much as $100 million.

> **"The chief executive should not be the one who just sort of guides the board on vision and strategy."**
> —Jurgen Schrempp, DaimlerChrysler CEO

Another problem is the potential dilution of DaimlerChrysler's brands. For example, Schrempp wants to avoid the perception that a Mercedes is just an expensive Chrysler. Garel Rhys, professor at Cardiff Business School, warns, "[Mercedes] is not doing as well as it was. It is widening its share with cars that have lower margins."

A third problem is the need to jump-start synergy and creativity across the divisions. The new Crossfire roadster is a Chrysler brand engineered by Mercedes, that shares components with both Mitsubishi and Mercedes. The innovative Pacifica station wagon/minivan hybrid is to be introduced in 2003, and Schrempp promises a pipeline of new designs through 2005. He recently announced the formulation of a ten-year plan for closer integration, but investors and customers are hoping that the merger benefits become evident long before then.

REFERENCES: Alex Taylor III, "Schrempp Shifts Gears. *Fortune,* March 18, 2002 (quotation). www.fortune.com on June 6, 2002; Christine Tierney and Joann Muller, "DaimlerChrysler's Foggy Forecast," *Business Week,* February 14, 2002. www.businessweek.com on June 6, 2002; "DaimlerChrysler Chief Seeks Greater Brand Integration," as reported in the *Financial Times,* reprinted in *Wall Street Journal Online,* May 21, 2002. online.wsj.com on June 6, 2002. Joann Muller, "Daimler and Chrysler Have a Baby," *Business Week,* January 14, 2002. www.businessweek.com on June 6, 2002.

Structural Configuration

organization chart A diagram showing all people, positions, reporting relationships, and lines of formal communication in the organization

The structure of an organization is most often described in terms of its organization chart. See Figure 8.1 for an example. A complete **organization chart** shows all people, positions, reporting relationships, and lines of form communication in the organization. (However, communication is not limited to these formal channels.) For large organizations, several charts may be necessary to show all positions. For example, one chart may show top management, including the board of directors, the chief executive officer, the president, all vice presidents, and important headquarters staff units. Subsequent charts may show the structure of each department and staff unit. Figure 8.1 depicts two organization charts for a large firm; top management is shown in the upper portion of the figure and the manufacturing department in the lower portion. Notice that the structures of the different manufacturing groups are given in separate charts.

configuration An organization's shape, which reflects the division of labor and the means of coordinating the divided tasks.

An organization chart depicts reporting relationships and work group memberships and shows how positions and small work groups are combined into departments, which together make up the **configuration,** or shape, of the organization. The configuration of organizations can be analyzed in terms of how the two basic requirements of structure—division of labor and coordination of the divided tasks—are fulfilled.

FIGURE 8.1

Examples of Organization Charts

These two charts show the similarities between a top-management chart and a department chart. In each, managers have four other managers or work groups reporting to them.

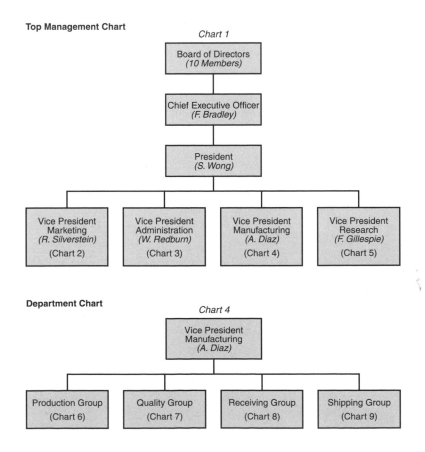

Division of Labor

division of labor The way the organization's work is divided into different jobs to be done by different people

Division of labor is the extent to which the organization's work is separated into different jobs to be done by different people. Division of labor is one of the seven primary characteristics of structuring described by Max Weber, but the concept can be traced back to the eighteenth-century economist Adam Smith. Smith used a study of pin making to promote the idea of dividing production work to increase productivity. Division of labor grew more popular as large organizations became more prevalent in a manufacturing society. This trend has continued, and most research indicates that large organizations usually have more division of labor than smaller ones.

Division of labor has been found to have both advantages and disadvantages (see Table 8.1). Modern managers and organization theorists are still struggling with the primary disadvantage: Division of labor often results in repetitive, boring jobs that undercut worker satisfaction, involvement, and commitment. In addition, extreme division of labor may be incompatible with new, integrated computerized manufacturing technologies that require reams of highly skilled workers.

However, division of labor need not result in boredom. Visualized in terms of a small organization such as a basketball team, it can be quite dynamic. A basketball team consists of five players, each of whom plays a different role on the team. In professional basketball the five positions typically are center, power forward, small forward, shooting guard, and point guard. The tasks of the players in each position are quite different, so players of different sizes and skills are on the floor at any one time. The teams that win championships, such as the Los Angeles Lakers and the Chicago Bulls, use division of labor by having players specialize in doing specified tasks, and doing them impeccably. Similarly, organizations must have specialists who are highly trained and know their specific jobs very well.

Coordinating the Divided Tasks

Three basic mechanisms are used to help coordinate the divided tasks: departmentalization, span of control, and administrative hierarchy. These mechanisms focus on grouping tasks in some meaningful manner, creating work groups of manageable size and establishing a system of reporting relationships among supervisors and managers. When companies reorganize, they are usually changing the ways in

TABLE 8.1 Advantages and Disadvantages of Division of Labor	
Advantages	Disadvantages
Efficient use of labor	Routine, repetitive jobs
Reduced training costs	Reduced job satisfaction
Increased standardization and uniformity of output	Decreased worker involvement and commitment
Increased expertise from repetition of tasks	Increased worker alienation
	Possible incompatibility with computerized manufacturing technologies

which the division of labor is coordinated. To some people affected by a reorganization, it may seem that things are still just as disorganized as they were before. But there really is a purpose for such reorganization efforts. Top management expects that the work will be better coordinated under the new system.

Departmentalization. **Departmentalization** is the manner in which divided tasks are combined and allocated to work groups. It is a consequence of the division of labor. Because employees engaged in specialized activities can lose sight of overall organizational goals, their work must be coordinated to ensure that it contributes to the welfare of the organization.

There are many possible ways to group, or departmentalize, tasks. The five groupings most often used are business function, process, product or service, customer, and geography. The first two, function and process, derive from the internal operations of the organization; the others are based on external factors. Most organizations tend to use a combination of methods, and departmentalization often changes as organizations evolve.

Departmentalization by business function is based on traditional business functions such as marketing, manufacturing, and human resource administration (see Figure 8.2). In this configuration employees most frequently associate with those engaged in the same function, a situation which helps in communication and co-operation. In a functional group, employees who do similar work can learn from one another by sharing ideas about opportunities and problems they encounter on the job. Unfortunately, functional groups lack an automatic mechanism for coordinating the flow of work through the organization. In other words, employees in a functional structure tend to associate little with those in other pans of the organization. The result can he a narrow focus that limits the coordination of work among functional groups, as when the engineering department fails to provide marketing with product information because it is too busy testing materials to think about sales.

departmentalization
The manner in which divided tasks are combined and allocated to work groups

FIGURE 8.2

Departmentalization by Business Function and by Process

These two charts compare departmentalization by business function and by process. "Functions" are the basic business function whereas "processes" are the specific categories of jobs that people do.

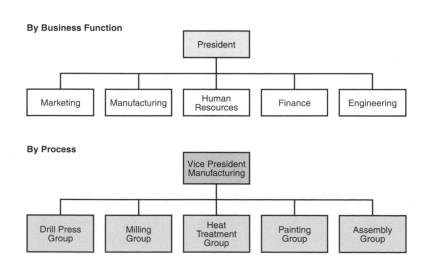

Departmentalization by process is similar to functional departmentalization except that the focus is much more on specific jobs grouped according to activity. Thus, as Figure 8.2 illustrates, the firm's manufacturing jobs are divided into certain well-defined manufacturing processes: drilling, milling, heat treatment, painting, and assembly. Hospitals often use process departmentalization, grouping the professional employees such as therapists according to the types of treatment they provide.

Process groupings encourage specialization and expertise among employees, who tend to concentrate on a single operation and share information with departmental colleagues. A process orientation may develop into an internal career path and managerial hierarchy within the department. For example, a specialist might become the "lead" person for that specialty—that is, the lead welder or lead press operator. As in functional grouping, however, narrowness of focus can be a problem. Employees in a process group may become so absorbed in the requirements and execution of their operations that they disregard broader considerations such as overall product flow.

Departmentalization by product or service occurs when employees who work on a particular product or service are members of the same department regardless of their business function or the process in which they are engaged. In the late 1980s, IBM reorganized its operations into five autonomous business units: personal computers, medium-size office systems, mainframes, communications equipment, and components. Although the reorganization worked for a while, the company took quite a downturn in the early 1990s.

Facing the Internet age at the beginning of the new century, IBM added several new divisions: a global computer services group to provide computing services; an Internet division to develop, manufacture, and distribute products for the new Internet age; and the Pervasive Computing Division to develop strategies centered on devices, software, and services that make the Internet accessible anywhere, anytime. These new divisions continued IBM's departmentalization by product or service.

Colgate-Palmolive changed its organization structure by eliminating the typical functional divisions such as basic research, processing, and packaging. Instead, employees were organized into teams based on products such as pet food, household products, and oral hygiene products. This configuration is shown in Figure 8.3. Since the reorganization, new-product development has increased significantly, and cost savings are estimated to be about $40 million.

Departmentalization according to product or service obviously enhances interaction and communication among employees who produce the same product or service and may reduce coordination problems. In this type of configuration, there may be less process specialization but more specialization in the peculiarities of the specific product or service. IBM expected that the new alignment would allow all employees, from designers to manufacturing workers to marketing experts, to become specialists in a particular product line. The disadvantage is that employees may become so interested in their particular product or service that they miss technological improvements or innovations developed in other departments.

Departmentalization by customer is often called "departmentalization by market." Many lending institutions in Texas, for example, have separate departments for retail, commercial, agriculture, and petroleum loans similar to those shown in

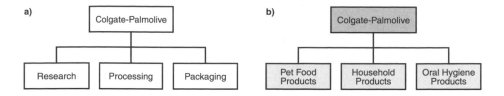

FIGURE 8.3

Departmentalization by Product or Service
a) Colgate-Palmolive's Old Functional Departmentalization
b) Colgate-Palmolive's New Product Departmentalization

Colgate-Palmolive changed its departmentalization scheme and increased its new-product development with cost savings estimated at $40 million.

Figure 8.4. When significant groups of customers differ substantially from one another, organizing along customer lines may be the most effective way to provide the best product or service possible. This is why hospital nurses often are grouped by the type of illness they handle; the various maladies demand different treatment and specialized knowledge. Deutsche Bank has recently changed its organization structure from a regional structure to one based on client groups, as discussed in the Box 8.2.

With customer departmentalization there is usually less process specialization because employees must remain flexible to do whatever is necessary to enhance the relationship with customers. This configuration offers the best coordination of the work flow to the customer; however, it may isolate employees from others in their special areas of expertise. For example, if each of a company's three metallurgical specialists is assigned to a different market-based group, these individuals are unlikely to have many opportunities to discuss the latest technological advances in metallurgy.

Departmentalization by geography means that groups are organized according to a region of the country or world. Sales or marketing groups often are arranged by geographic region. As Figure 8.4 illustrates, the marketing effort of a large

FIGURE 8.4

Departmentalization by Customer and by Geographic Region

Departmentalization by customer or by geographic region is often used in marketing or sales departments in order to focus on specific needs or locations of customers.

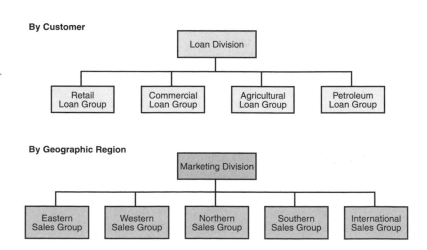

Corporate Structure Moves Deutsche Bank into the Twenty-first Century

As firms become increasingly more global, many find that their traditional, local ways of doing business no longer serve them well. This realization is apparent at German-based Deutsche Bank, which is changing its structure and management to expand its international presence and to appeal to more international investors.

German tax law and business culture favor practices that are different from those of American-style firms. Most German firms have a large management board that makes decisions based on group consensus and gets involved in a variety of issues, including some midlevel, operational ones. It is common for German corporations to have cross-shareholdings, in which firms hold each other's shares. Deutsche Bank, for example, owns a significant share of DaimlerChrysler, insurer Allianz, and other German firms. These practices can lead to problems such as inflexibility and a tendency to downplay internationalization. Some German firms also risk losing their global competitiveness.

In response, Deutsche Bank is divesting some of its nonbank holdings while restoring its focus on banking. CEO Rolf Breuer says, "The logic behind business enterprise must today be found in corporate strategy. . . . The focus is on value creation." The bank has a new organization structure built around

> **"The logic behind business enterprise must today be found in corporate strategy."**
>
> —Rolf Breur, CEO of Deutsche Bank

client groups rather than regions. Incoming CEO Josef Ackerman reduced the management board from eight to five members and increased diversity while removing the board's authority over day-to-day operations. He has created a new executive committee and given it responsibility for strategy and oversight, thus increasing the CEO's power. The appointment of Ackerman, a Swiss investment banker, signals the firm's international intentions as well as a shift toward more lucrative investment markets.

Breuer explains the impact of the changes by saying. "[They] made more of a mental difference than a change to daily operations [would have]. We [now] have another culture in the bank[,] . . . not just in the U S., but also in Europe, even in Germany." Although some of the bank's older workers are concerned that the firm will change its headquarters location or lose its German heritage, many of the younger staff and many outsiders think that this new strategy and structure will help the firm shed its "dinosaur" image and move into the top ranks of the world banking industry.

REFERENCES: "Speech by Rolf E. Breuer at the General Meeting of Deutschen Bank AG, May 22, 2002, (quotation)" "Fact Sheets," "Organizational Structure," Deutsche Bank web site. group.deutsche-bank.de on June 7, 2002; Marcus Walker, "Lean New Guard at Deutsche Bank Sets Global Agenda—But Cultural Rifts Prevent More—Aggressive Cost Cuts—The Traditionalists Haven't Gone Quietly," Wall Street Journal, February 14, 2002. www.wsj.com on April 4, 2002; Stephen Graham, "Deutsche Bank Says 2001 Profit Plummeted, Proceeds with Management Shakeup," National Business Stream, January 31, 2002; "Deutsche Bank Names Next CEO, Continuity Seen," National Business Stream, September 21, 2000.

multinational corporation can be divided according to major geographical divisions. Using a geographically based configuration may result in significant cost savings and better market coverage. On the other hand, it may isolate work groups from activities in the organization's home office or in the technological community because the focus of the work group is solely on affairs within the region. Such a regional focus may foster loyalty to the work group that exceeds commitment to the larger organization. In addition, work-related communication and coordination among groups may be somewhat inefficient.

Many large organizations use a mixed departmentalization scheme. Such organizations may have separate operating divisions based on products, but within each division, departments may be based on business function, process, customers, or geographic region (see Figure 8.5). Which methods work best depends on the organization's activities, communication needs, and coordination requirements. Another type of mixed structure often occurs in joint ventures, which are becoming increasingly popular.

span of control The number of people who report to a manager

Span of Control. The second dimension of organizational configuration, **span of control,** is the number of people reporting to a manager; thus, it defines the size of the organization's work groups. Span of control is also called "span of management." A manager who has a small span of control can maintain close control over workers and stay in contact with daily operations. If the span of control is large, close control is not possible. Figure 8.6 shows examples of small and large spans of control. Supervisors in the upper portion of the figure have a span of control of sixteen whereas in the lower portion, supervisors have a span of control of eight.

A number of formulas and rules have been offered for determining the optimal span of control in an organization, but research on the topic has not conclusively identified a foolproof method. Henry Mintzberg concluded that the optimal unit size, or span of control, depends on five conditions:

1. The coordination requirements within the unit, including factors such as the degree of job specialization
2. The similarity of the tasks in the unit

FIGURE 8.5
Mixed Departmentalization

A mixed departmentalization scheme is often used in very large organizations with more complex structures. Headquarters is organized based on products. Industrial products and consumer products are departmentalized on the basis of function. The manufacturing department is based on process. Sales is based on geographic regions.

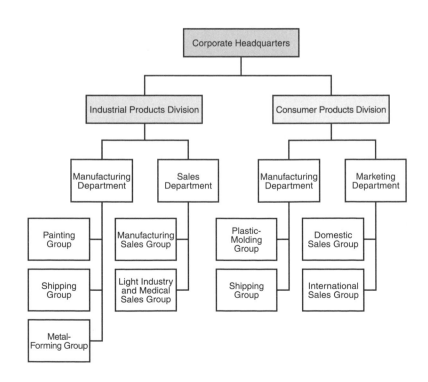

FIGURE 8.6
Span of Control and Levels in the Administrative Hierarchy

These charts show how span of control and the number of levels in the administrative hierarchy are inversely related. The thirty-two first-level employees are in two groups of sixteen in the top chart and in four groups of eight in the bottom chart. Either may be appropriate depending on the work situation.

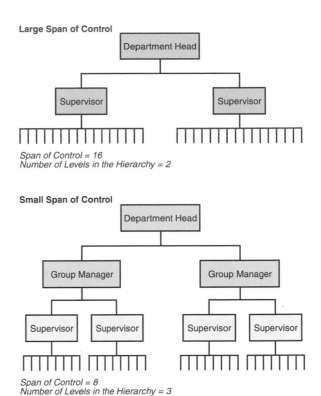

Large Span of Control

Span of Control = 16
Number of Levels in the Hierarchy = 2

Small Span of Control

Span of Control = 8
Number of Levels in the Hierarchy = 3

3. The type of information available or needed by unit members
4. Differences in the members' need for autonomy
5. The extent to which members need direct access to the supervisor

For example, a span of control of sixteen (as shown in Figure 8.6) might be appropriate for a supervisor in a typical manufacturing plant in which experienced workers do repetitive production tasks. On the other hand, a span of control of eight or fewer (as shown in Figure 8.6) might be appropriate in a job shop or custom-manufacturing facility in which workers do many different things and the tasks and problems that arise are new and unusual.

administrative hierarchy The system of reporting relationships in the organization, from the lowest to the highest managerial levels

Administrative Hierarchy. The **administrative hierarchy** is the system of reporting relationships in the organization, from the first level up through the president or CEO. It results from the need for supervisors and managers to coordinate the activities of employees. The size of the administrative hierarchy is inversely related to the span of control: Organizations with a small span of control have many managers in the hierarchy; those with a large span of control have a smaller administrative hierarchy. Companies often rearrange their administrative hierarchies to achieve more efficient operations. Gateway 2005 rearranged its management and moved the company's headquarters from South Dakota to San Diego, California, in order to develop an organization that will enable it to provide many different computer-related products and services.

Using Figure 8.6 again, we can examine the effects of small and large spans of control on the number of hierarchical levels. The smaller span of control for the supervisors in the lower portion of the figure requires that there be four supervisors rather than two. Correspondingly, another management layer is needed to keep the department head's span of control at two. Thus, when the span of control is small, the workers are under tighter supervision, and there are more administrative levels. When the span of control is large, as in the upper portion of the figure, production workers are not closely supervised, and there are fewer administrative levels. Because it measures the number of management personnel, or administrators, in the organization, the administrative hierarchy is sometimes called the "administrative component," "administrative intensity," or "administrative ratio."

The size of the administrative hierarchy also relates to the overall size of the organization. As an organization's size increases, so do its complexity and the requirements for coordination, necessitating proportionately more people to manage the business. However, this conclusion defines the administrative component as including the entire administrative hierarchy—that is, all of the support staff groups, such as personnel and financial services, legal staff, and others. Defined in this way, the administrative component in a large company may seem huge compared with the number of production workers. On the other hand, research that separates the support staff and clerical functions from the management hierarchy has found that the ratio of managers to total employees actually decreases with increases in the organization's size. Other, more recent research has shown that the size of the administrative hierarchy and the overall size of the organization are not related in a straightforward manner, especially during periods of growth and decline.

"There used to be eleven layers between me and the lowest-level employees; now there are five."

—*William Stavropoulos, CEO of Dow Chemical, describing Dow's new organization structure*

The popular movement of downsizing has been partially a reaction to the complexity that comes with increasing organization size. Much of the literature on organizational downsizing has proposed that it results in lower overhead costs, less bureaucracy, faster decision making, smoother communications, and increases in productivity.

These expectations are due to the effort to reduce the administrative hierarchy by cutting out layers of middle managers. Unfortunately, many downsizing efforts have resulted in poorer communication, reduced productivity, and lower employee morale because the downsizing is done indiscriminately, without regard for the jobs that people actually do, the coordination needs of the organization, and the additional training that may be necessary for the survivors.

Structure and Operations

Some important aspects of organization structure do not appear on the organization chart and thus are quite different from the configurational aspects discussed in the previous section. In this section, we examine the structural policies that affect operations and prescribe or restrict how employees behave in their organizational activities. The two primary aspects of these policies are centralization of decision making and formalization of rules and procedures.

Centralization

centralization A structural policy in which decision-making authority is concentrated at the top of the organizational hierarchy

The first structural policy that affects operations is **centralization,** wherein decision-making authority is concentrated at the top of the organizational hierarchy. At the opposite end of the continuum is decentralization, in which decisions are made throughout the hierarchy. Increasingly, centralization is being discussed in terms of participation in decision making: In decentralized organizations, lower-level employees participate in making decisions. The changes that Jack Smith made in 1993 and 1996 at General Motors were intended to decentralize decision making throughout the company. Smith dismantled the old divisional structure, created a single unit called North American Operations, and abolished a tangle of management committees that slowed down decision making. Managers are now encouraged to make decisions on new designs and pricing that used to take weeks to circulate through the committee structure on their way to the top.

Decision making in organizations is more complex than the simple centralized-decentralized classification indicates. One of the major distinctions we made with organizational decision making was that some decisions are relatively routine and require only the application of a decision rule. These decisions are programmed decisions whereas those that are not routine are nonprogrammed. The decision rules for programmed decisions are formalized for the organization. This difference between programmed and nonprogrammed decisions tends to cloud the distinction between centralization and decentralization. For even if decision making is decentralized, the decisions themselves may be programmed and tightly circumscribed.

> ## "Decisions weren't getting made because of structural impediments."
> —Ben Rosen, chairman of the board of Compaq, describing the reasons for Compaq's 1999 change in management

If there is little employee participation in decision making, then decision making is centralized, regardless of the nature of the decisions being made. At the other extreme, if individuals or groups participate extensively in making nonprogrammed decisions, the structure can be described as truly decentralized. If individuals or groups participate extensively in decision making but mainly in programmed decisions, the structure is called "formalized decentralization." Formalized decentralization is a common way to provide decision-making involvement for employees at many different levels in the organization while maintaining control and predictability.

Participative management has been described as a total management system in which people are involved in the daily decision making and management of the organization. As part of an organization's culture, participative management can contribute significantly to the long-term success of an organization. It has been described as effective and, in fact, morally necessary in organizations. Thus, for many people, participation in decision making has become more than a simple aspect of organization structure. Caution is required, however, because if middle managers are to make effective decisions, as participative management requires, they must have sufficient information. Honda Motor Co. originally chose a product departmentalization strategy when it introduced the Acura. Honda of America, however, later changed its structure by decentralizing and using more participation with great success. One of the highly touted benefits of the "Information Age" was that all employees throughout the organization would have more information and would therefore be able to participate more in decisions affecting their work, thus creating more decentralized organizations. However, some have suggested that all of this new information in organizations has had the opposite effect by enabling top managers to have more information about the organization's operations and to keep the decisions to themselves, thus creating more centralized organizations.

Formalization

formalization The degree to which rules and procedures shape the jobs and activities of employees

Formalization is the degree to which rules and procedures shape employees' jobs and activities. The purpose of formalization is to predict and control how employees behave on the job. Rules and procedures can be both explicit and implicit. Explicit rules are set down in job descriptions, policy and procedures manuals, or office memos. (In one large company that continually issues directives attempting to limit employee activities, workers refer to them as "Gestapo" memos because they require employees to follow harsh rules.) Implicit rules may develop as employees become accustomed to doing things in a certain way over a period of time. Though unwritten, these established ways of getting things done become standard operating procedures and have the same effect on employee behavior as written rules.

We can assess formalization in organizations by looking at the proportion of jobs that are governed by rules and procedures and the extent to which those rules permit variation. More formalized organizations have a higher proportion of rule-bound jobs and less tolerance for rule violations. Increasing formalization may affect the design of jobs throughout the organization as well as employee motivation and work group interactions. The specific effects of formalization on employees are still unclear, however.

Organizations tend to add more rules and procedures as the need for control of operations increases. Some organizations have become so formalized that they have rules for how to make new rules! One large state university created such rules in the form of a three-page document entitled "Procedures for Rule Adoption" that was added to the four-inch-thick Policy and Procedures Manual. The new policy first defines terms such as "university," "board," and "rule" and lists ten exceptions that describe when this policy on rule adoptions does not apply. It then presents a nine-step process for adopting a new rule within the university.

Other organizations are trying to become less formalized by reducing the number of rules and procedures employees must follow. In this effort, Chevron cut the number of its rules and procedures from over four hundred to eighteen. Highly detailed procedures for hiring were eliminated in favor of letting managers make hiring decisions based on common sense.

Another approach to organizational formalization attempts to describe how, when, and why good managers should bend or break a rule. Although rules exist in some form in almost every organization, how strictly they are enforced varies significantly from one organization to another and even within a single organization. Some managers argue that "a rule is a rule" and that all rules must be enforced to control employee behaviors and prevent chaos in the organization. Other managers act as if "all rules are made to be broken" and see rules as stumbling blocks on the way to effective action. Neither point of view is better for the organization; rather, a more balanced approach is recommended.

The test of a good manager in a formalized organization may be how well he or she uses appropriate judgment in making exceptions to rules. A balanced approach to making exceptions to rules should do two things. First, it should recognize that individuals are unique and that the organization can benefit from making exceptions that capitalize on exceptional capabilities. For example, suppose an engineering design department with a rule mandating equal access to tools and equipment acquires a limited amount of specialized equipment such as personal computers. The department manager decides to make an exception to the equal-access rule by assigning the computers to the designers the manager believes will use them the most and with the best results instead of making them available for use by all. Second, a balanced approach should recognize the commonalities among employees. Managers should make exceptions to rules only when there is a true and meaningful difference between individuals rather than base exceptions on features such as race, sex, appearance, or social factors.

Responsibility and Authority

Responsibility and authority are related to both configurational and operational aspects of organization structure. For example, the organization chart shows who reports to whom at all levels in the organization. From the operational perspective, the degree of centralization defines the locus of decision-making authority in the organization. However, often there is some confusion about what responsibility and authority really mean for managers and how the two terms relate to each other.

Responsibility

responsibility An obligation to do something with the expectation of achieving some act or output

Responsibility is an obligation to do something with the expectation that some act or output will result. For example, a manager may expect an employee to write and present a proposal for a new program by a certain date; thus, the employee is responsible for preparing the proposal.

Responsibility ultimately derives from the ownership of the organization. The owners hire or appoint a group, often a board of directors, to be responsible for managing the organization, making the decisions, and reaching the goals set by the owners. A downward chain of responsibility is then established. The board hires a Chief Executive Officer (CEO) or president to be responsible for running the organization. The CEO or president hires more people and holds them responsible for accomplishing designated tasks that enable her or him to produce the results expected by the board and the owners. Jack Welch became famous for the way he ran GE for twenty years. Over the years he hired many managers and delegated responsibility for running various parts of the business. However, in the end, Jack Welch was responsible for all of the activities of the organization, including the degree to which business was conducted ethically. Box 8.3 discusses how some of GE's actions have recently come under closer scrutiny.

The chain extends throughout the organization because each manager has an obligation to fulfill: to appropriately employ organizational resources (people, money, and equipment) to meet the owners' expectations. Although managers seemingly pass responsibility on to others to achieve results, each manager is still held responsible for the outputs of those to whom he or she delegates tasks.

A manager responsible for a work group assigns tasks to members of the group. Each group member is then responsible for doing his or her task, yet the manager still remains responsible for each task and for the work of the group as a whole. This means that managers can take on the responsibility of others but cannot shed their own responsibility onto those below them in the hierarchy.

> ## "I think it's a mistake to designate a No. 2 to run the business. I like a CEO who does that job himself "
>
> *—Warren Buffett, commenting on the lack of a No.2 person at Coca-Cola*

Authority

authority Power that has been legitimized within a particular social context

Authority is power that has been legitimized within a specific social context. Only when power is part of an official organizational role does it become authority. Authority includes the legitimate right to use resources to accomplish expected outcomes. As we discussed in the previous section, the authority to make decisions may be restricted to the top levels of the organization or dispersed throughout the organization.

Like responsibility, authority originates in the ownership of the organization. The owners establish a group of directors who are responsible for managing the organization's affairs. The directors, in turn, authorize people in the organization to make decisions and to use organizational resources. Thus, they delegate authority, or power in a social context, to others.

Authority is linked to responsibility because a manager responsible for accomplishing certain results must have the authority to use resources to achieve those results. The relationship between responsibility and authority must be one of parity; that is, the authority over resources must be sufficient to enable the manager to meet the output expectations of others.

But authority and responsibility differ in significant ways. Responsibility cannot be delegated down to others (as discussed in the previous section), but authority can. One complaint often heard from employees is that they have too much responsibility but not enough authority to get the job done. This indicates a lack of parity between responsibility and authority. Managers usually are quite willing to hold individuals responsible for specific tasks but are reluctant to delegate enough authority to do the job. In effect, managers try to rid themselves of responsibility for results (which they cannot do), yet they rarely like to give away their cherished authority over resources.

delegation The transfer to others of authority to make decisions and use organizational resources

Delegation is the transfer of authority to make decisions and use organizational resources to others. Delegation of authority to make decisions to lower-level managers is common in organizations today. The important thing is to give lower-level managers authority to carry out the decisions they make. Managers typically

Should GE Be a Corporate Role Model?

Few American CEOs have earned the widespread approval, even adulation, that has been garnered by General Electric's former chief executive Jack Welch, who retired in 2001. "I think history is just going to remember [that] Jack Welch was one of the greatest industrial managers of our time," says John Inch, a Bear Stearns analyst. "Every conglomerate in America wants to grow up to be GE." Under Welch's twenty-year reign, GE grew to become the sixth-largest U.S. company. However, as Welch was stepping down, several ethical issues were emerging.

First, a GE acquisition of Honeywell, which manufactures products similar to GE's, was approved by the U.S. Federal Trade Commission (the FTC), which ruled that the deal did not violate antitrust regulations. However, the acquisition was not approved by the European Competition Commission, the FTC's European equivalent. Many international firms protested to the European Commission although few firms did so in the United States, probably because the European commission's hearings are private whereas the FTC's are public. Companies were unwilling to criticize GE publicly, fearing a backlash of higher prices for their purchases.

Second, GE is involved in an ugly battle over PCB chemicals that it dumped into the Hudson River for thirty years, beginning in the 1940s. The Environmental Protection Agency (EPA)

> **"Every conglomerate in America wants to grow up to be GE."**
>
> —*John Inch, a Bear Stearns analyst*

ordered the firm to pay the $460 million cleanup cost; GE responded with an aggressive public relations campaign that spread misinformation. The EPA then directed the firm to pay an additional $37 million to cover the government's cost of conducting additional studies and publicizing their results. "This [action] is a direct message to GE that the EPA means business," claims Janet MacGillivray, senior attorney with the environmental group Riverkeeper.

Third, GE may be the victim of its own success. The firm's ability to maintain a steady 10 percent increase in earnings and always meet quarterly earnings targets is legendary—Welch missed the target only once in twenty years. But given the climate of investor distrust in the post-Enron era, GE's earnings have suddenly become questionable. Although no one suspects the firm of Enron-style fraud, Jeff Immelt, Welch's successor at GE, must now defend the company's earnings policy. He asks, "Would a miss be more honest? . . . I think that's terrible. [Should I say] 'I missed my numbers—aren't you proud of me?'" How Immelt chooses to handle these issues will reveal a lot about him, and about GE.

REFERENCES: Justin Fox, "What's So Great About GE?" *Fortune,* March 4, 2002. www.fortune.com on June 6, 2002; Dina Cappiello, "GE Ordered to Pick Up $37M Dredging-Plan Tab," *Times Union* (Albany, N.Y.), February 13, 2002. www.time-sunion.com on June 7. 2002; "Despite Failed Merger, GE's Image Still Strong," *Arizona Republic,* July 9, 2001, pp. D1, D4 (quotation p. D4). See www.azcentral.com; Philip Shiskin, "EU Makes It Official: No Honeywell for GE— Regulatory Policy Hits a Continental Divide," *Wall Street Journal,* July 4, 2001. See www.wsj.com.

have difficulty in delegating successfully. In the Self-Assessment Exercise at the end of this chapter, you will have a chance to practice delegation.

The Iran-Contra affair of 1987–1988 is a good example of the difference between authority and responsibility. Some believe the Reagan administration confused delegation of authority with abdication of responsibility. President Reagan delegated a great deal of authority to subordinates but did not require that they keep him informed, and they made no effort to do so. Hence, delegation of authority by the administration was appropriate and necessary, but its failure to require progress reports to keep informed and in control of operations resulted in the administration's trying to avoid responsibility. Although the president did hold his subordinates responsible for their actions, he ultimately—and rightfully—retained full responsibility.

An Alternative View of Authority

So far we have described authority as a "top-down" function in organizations; that is, authority originates at the top and is delegated downward as the managers at the top consider appropriate. In author Chester Barnard's alternative perspective, authority is seen as originating in the individual, who can choose whether or not to follow a directive from above. The choice of whether to comply with a directive is based on the degree to which the individual understands it, feels able to carry it out, and believes it to be in the best interests of the organization and consistent with personal values. This perspective has been called the **acceptance theory of authority** because it means that the manager's authority depends on the subordinate's acceptance of the manager's right to give the directive and to expect compliance.

For example, assume that you are a marketing analyst, and your company has a painting crew in the maintenance department. For some reason, your manager has told you to repaint your own office over the weekend. You probably would question your manager's authority to make you do this work. In fact, you would probably refuse to do it. If you received a similar request to work over the weekend to finish a report, you would be more likely to accept it and carry it out. Thus, by either accepting or rejecting the directives of a supervisor, workers can limit supervisory authority. In most organizational situations, employees accept a manager's right to expect compliance on normal, reasonable directives because of the manager's legitimate position in the organizational hierarchy or in the social context of the organization. They may choose to disobey a directive and must accept the consequences if they do not accept the manager's right.

acceptance theory of authority The authority of a manager depends on the subordinate's acceptance of the manager's right to give directives and to expect compliance with them

Classic Views of Structure

The earliest views of organization structure combined the elements of organization configuration and operation into recommendations on how organizations should be structured. These views have often been called "classical organization theory" and include Max Weber's concept of the ideal bureaucracy, the classic organizing principles of Henri Fayol, and the human organization view of Rensis Likert. Although all three are universal approaches, their concerns and structural prescriptions differ significantly.

Ideal Bureaucracy

Weber's **ideal bureaucracy** was an organizational system characterized by a hierarchy of authority and a system of rules and procedures that, if followed, would create a maximally effective system for large organizations. Weber, writing at a time when organizations were inherently inefficient, claimed that the bureaucratic form of administration is superior to other forms of management with respect to stability, control, and predictability of outcomes.

Weber's ideal bureaucracy had seven essential characteristics and utilized several of the building blocks discussed in this chapter, including the division of labor, hierarchy of authority, and rules and procedures. Weber intended these characteristics to ensure order and predictability in relationships among people and jobs in the bureaucracy. But it is easy to see how the same features can lead to sluggishness, inefficiency, and red tape. The administrative system can easily break down if any of the characteristics are carried to an extreme or are violated. For example, if endless arrays of rules and procedures bog down employees who must find the precise rule to follow every time they do something, responses to routine client or customer requests may slow to a crawl. Moreover, subsequent writers have said that Weber's view of authority is too rigid and have suggested that the bureaucratic organization may impede creativity and innovation and result in a lack of compassion for the individual in the organization. In other words, the impersonality that is supposed to foster objectivity in a bureaucracy may result in serious difficulties for both employees and the organization. However, some organizations retain some characteristics of a bureaucratic structure while remaining innovative and productive.

> "The challenge is to find ways to constantly refresh the components of bureaucracy so that it remains the healthy kind rather than the destructive kind. "
>
> —Roger R. Keene, president and COO of Mott Corporation

Paul Adler has recently countered the currently popular movements of "bureaucracy busting" by noting that large-scale, complex organizations still need some of the basic characteristics that Weber described—hierarchical structure, formalized procedures, and staff expertise—in order to avoid chaos and ensure efficiency, conformance quality, and timeliness. Adler further proposes a second type of bureaucracy that essentially serves an enabling function in organizations. The need for bureaucracy is not past. Bureaucracy, or at least some of its elements, is still critical for designing effective organizations.

The Classic Principles of Organizing

Henri Fayol, a French engineer and chief executive officer of a mining company, presented a second classic view of the organization structure at the beginning of the twentieth century. Drawing on his experience as a manager, Fayol was the first to classify the essential elements of management—now usually called **management functions**—as planning, organizing, command, coordination, and control. In addition, he presented fourteen principles of organizing that he considered an indispensable code for managers.

Fayol's principles have proved extraordinarily influential; they have served as the basis for the development of generally accepted means of organizing. For example, Fayol's "unit of command" principle means that employees should receive directions from only one person, and "unity of direction" means that tasks with the same objective should have a common supervisor. Combining these two principles with division of labor, authority, and responsibility results in a system of tasks and reporting and authority relationships that is the very essence of organizing. Fayol's principles thus provide the framework for the organization chart and the coordination of work.

The classic principles have been criticized on several counts. First, they ignore factors such as individual motivation, leadership, and informal groups—the human element in organizations. This line of criticism asserts that the classic principles result in a mechanical organization into which people must fit, regardless of their interests, abilities, or motivations. The principles have also been criticized for their lack of operational specificity in that Fayol described the principles as universal truths but did not specify the means of applying many of them. Finally, Fayol's principles have been discounted because they were not supported by scientific evidence; Fayol presented them as universal principles, backed by no evidence other than his own experience.

Human Organization

Rensis Likert's human organization approach
Based on supportive relationships, participation, and overlapping work groups

Rensis Likert called his approach to organization structure the **human organization**. Because Likert, like others, had criticized Fayol's classic principles for overlooking human factors, it is not surprising that his approach centered on the principles of supportive relationships, employee participation, and overlapping work groups.

The term "supportive relationships" suggests that in all organizational activities, individuals should be treated in such a way that they experience feelings of support, self-worth, and importance. By "employee participation," Likert meant that the work group needs to be involved in decisions that affect it, thereby enhancing the employee's sense of supportiveness and self-worth. The principle of "overlapping work groups" means that work groups are linked, with managers serving as the "linking pins." Each manager (except the highest ranking) is a member of two groups: a work group that he or she supervises and a management group composed of the manager's peers and their supervisor. Coordination and communication grow stronger when the managers perform the linking function by sharing problems, decisions, and information both upward and downward in the groups to which they belong. The human organization concept rests on the assumption that people work best in highly cohesive groups oriented toward organizational goals. Management's function is to make sure the work groups are linked for effective coordination and communication.

Likert described four systems of organizing, which he called managements steps, whose characteristics are summarized in Table 8.2. System 1, the exploitive authoritative system, can be characterized as the classic bureaucracy. System 4, the participative group, is the organization design Likert favored. System 2, the benevolent authoritative system, and system 3, the consultative system, are less extreme than either system 1 or system 4.

Characteristic	System 1: Exploitive Authoritative	System 2: Benevolent Authoritative	System 3: Consultative	System 4: Participative Group
TABLE 8.2 Characteristics of Likert's Four Management Systems				
Leadership				
• Trust in subordinates	None	None	Substantial	Complete
• Subordinates' ideas	Seldom used	Sometimes used	Usually used	Always used
Motivational Forces				
• Motives tapped	Security, status	Economic, ego	Substantial	Complete
• Level of satisfaction	Overall dissatisfaction	Some moderate satisfaction	Moderate satisfaction	High satisfaction
Communication				
• Amount	Very little	Little	Moderate	Much
• Direction	Downward	Mostly downward	Down, up	Down, up, lateral
Interaction-Influence				
• Amount	None	None	Substantial	Complete
• Cooperative teamwork	None	Virtually none	Moderate	Substantial
Decision Making				
• Locus	Top	Policy decided at top	Broad policy decided at top	All levels
• Subordinates involved	Not at all	Sometimes consulted	Usually consulted	Fully involved
Goal Setting				
• Manner	Orders	Orders with comments	Set after discussion	Group participation
• Acceptance	Covertly resisted	Frequently resisted	Sometimes resisted	Fully accepted
Control Processes				
• Level	Top	None	Some below top	All levels
• Information	Incomplete, inaccurate	Often incomplete, inaccurate	Moderately complete, accurate	Complete, accurate
Performance				
• Goals and Training	Mediocre	Fair to good	Goad	Excellent

REFERENCE: Adapted from Rensis Likert, *New Patterns of Management* (New York: McGraw-Hill, 1961), pp. 223–233; and Rensis Likert, *The Human Organization* (New York: McGraw-Hill, 1967), pp. 197, 198, 201, 203, 210, and 211.

Likert described all four systems in terms of eight organizational variables: leadership processes, motivational forces, communication processes, interaction-influence processes, decision-making processes, goal-setting processes, control processes, and performance goals and training. Likert believed that work groups should be able to overlap horizontally as well as vertically where necessary to accomplish tasks. This feature is directly contrary to the classic principle that advocates unity of command. In addition, rather than the hierarchical chain of command, Likert favored the linking-pin concept of overlapping work groups for making decisions and resolving conflicts.

Research support for Likert's human organization emanates primarily from Liken and his associates' work at the Institute for Social Research at the University of Michigan. Although their research has upheld the basic propositions of the approach, it is not entirely convincing. One review of the evidence suggested that although research has shown characteristics of system 4 to be associated with positive worker attitudes and, in some cases, increased productivity, it is not clear that the characteristics of the human organization "caused" the positive results. It may have been that positive attitudes and high productivity allowed the organization structure to be participative and provided the atmosphere for the development of supportive relationships. Likert's design has also been criticized for focusing almost exclusively on individuals and groups and not dealing extensively with structural issues. Overall, the most compelling support for this approach is at the individual and work-group levels. In some ways, Likert's system 4 is much like the team-based organization popular today.

Thus, the classic views of organization embody the key elements of organization structure. Each view, however, combined these key elements in different ways and with other management elements. These three classic views are typical of how the early writers attempted to prescribe a universal approach to organization structure that would be best in all situations. In the next chapter we describe other views of organization structure that may be effective, depending on the organizational situation.

Synopsis

The structure of an organization is the system of task, reporting, and authority relationships within which the organization does its work. The purpose of organization structure is to order and coordinate the actions of employees to achieve organizational goals. Every organization structure addresses two fundamental issues: dividing available labor according to the tasks to be performed and combining and coordinating divided tasks to ensure that tasks are accomplished.

An organization chart shows reporting relationships, work group memberships, departments, and formal lines of communication. In a broader sense, an organization chart shows the configuration, or shape, of the organization. Configuration has four dimensions: division of labor, departmentalization, span of control, and administrative hierarchy. Division of labor is the separation of work into different jobs to be done by different people. Departmentalization is the manner in which the divided tasks are combined and allocated to work groups for coordination. Tasks can be combined into departments on the basis of business function, process, product, customer, and geographic region. Span of control is the number of people reporting to a manager; it also defines the size of work groups and is inversely related to the number of hierarchical levels in the organization. The administrative hierarchy is the system of reporting relationships in the organization.

Structural policies prescribe how employees should behave in their organizational activities. Such policies include formalization of rules and procedures and centralization of decision making. Formalization is the degree to which rules and procedures shape employees' jobs and activities. The purpose of formalization is to predict and control how employees behave on the job. Explicit rules are set down in job descriptions, policy and procedures manuals, and office memos. Implicit rules develop over time as employees become accustomed to doing things in certain ways.

Centralization concentrates decision-making authority at the top of the organizational hierarchy; under decentralization, decisions are made throughout the hierarchy.

Responsibility is an obligation to do something with the expectation of achieving some output. Authority is power that has been legitimized within a specific social context. Authority includes the legitimate right to use resources to accomplish expected outcomes. The relationship between responsibility and authority needs to be one of parity; that is, employees must have enough authority over resources to meet the expectations of others.

Weber's ideal bureaucracy, Fayol's classic principles of organizing, and Likert's human organization cover many of the key features of organization structure. Weber's bureaucratic form of administration was intended to ensure stability, control, and predictable outcomes. Rules and procedures, division of labor, a hierarchy of authority, technical competence, separation of ownership, rights and property differentiation, and documentation characterize the ideal bureaucracy.

Fayol's classic principles included departmentalization, unity of command, and unity of direction; they came to be generally accepted as means of organizing. Taken together, the fourteen principles provided the basis for the modern organization chart and for coordinating work.

Likert's human organization was based on the principles of supportive relationships, employee participation, and overlapping work groups. Likert described the human organization in terms of eight variables based on the assumption that people work best in highly supportive and cohesive work groups oriented toward organization goals.

⊚ Discussion Questions

1. Define "organization structure" and explain its role in the process of managing the organization.
2. What is the purpose of organization structure? What would an organization be like without a structure?
3. In what ways are aspects of the organization structure analogous to the structural parts of the human body?
4. How is labor divided in your college or university? In what other ways could your college or university be departmentalized?
5. What types of organizations could benefit from a small span of control? What types might benefit from a large span of control?
6. Discuss how increasing formalization might affect the role conflict and role ambiguity of employees.
7. How might the impact of formalization differ for research scientists, machine operators, and bank tellers?
8. How might centralization or decentralization affect the job characteristics specified in job design?

9. When a group makes a decision, how is responsibility for the decision apportioned among the members?
10. Why do employees typically want more authority and less responsibility?
11. Consider the job you now hold or one that you held in the past. Did your boss have the authority to direct your work? Why did he or she have this authority?
12. Describe at least four features of organization structure that were important parts of the classic view of organizing.

ORGANIZATIONAL BEHAVIOR CASE FOR DISCUSSION

A Company Divided Against Itself Cannot Stand

Would you feel respect and loyalty for U.S. President George W. Bush if he held the title of co-president? Bush enjoys a high approval rating, but what if he shared power with another person? (Given Bush's perceived strengths and weaknesses, perhaps an ideal co-president would be an elderly Ph.D. holder from a northern state.) At least for Americans, a single leader is almost universally preferred. Yet several large U.S. corporations, including Southwest Airlines and SAP, are using a co-CEO structure, in which the chief executive position is jointly held by two persons.

Stuart Moore and Jerry Greenberg together founded Sapient, an Internet consultancy firm, in 1991. They come from very different backgrounds, educations, and lifestyles but function well together. In addition to having complementary skills, Moore and Greenberg possess the other two requisite qualities for sharing the CEO role—they have a long-established history of trust in each other as well as "power motivation." ("Power motivation refers not to dictatorial behavior but to a desire to have impact, to be strong and influential," say professors David McClelland and David Burnham, who coined the term. A person who has high power motivation wants to lead in order to build a great institution, not merely to exercise personal power.) Moore and Greenberg make all decisions jointly; a tie-breaking mechanism was developed, but has never been used. The two travel together, work at desks just two inches apart, and split everything 50/50, including profits, ownership, and responsibility.

One important reason to split the CEO role is to increase the skills and experiences available to the leaders. "I don't think power sharing is natural. I think its very very difficult," says professor Warren Bennis of the University of Southern California. But [with] the warp speed companies are traveling at, the amazing number of alliances that are springing up, [and] everyone's fear of being taken over by some disruptive technology—right now you need a lot of eyes. I don't think anyone can do it all."

Another valid reason is to utilize executives complementary styles. Dave Pottruck, the co-CEO of Schwab, claims he was "too competitive; too driven, making everybody around [him] uncomfortable." Sharing the CEO position with founder Charles Schwab allowed Pottruck to develop company-specific expertise and prepare for someday handling the job alone while also honing his people skills.

At Golden West Financial, founders and spouses Marion and Herbert Sandler ensure that a man's and a woman's point of view are equally represented.

Working Woman ranked the company third in the United States for supporting women, and Marion maintains that she is making the best hires. Elaborating on her hiring practices, she confidently asserts, "You're not looking for figureheads. You don't want to make any compromises."

Yet another common reason for the use of co-CEOs is to facilitate the transition after a merger, especially one of two equally powerful firms. Verizon, created by the merger of GTE and Bell Atlantic, was for a time headed by Ivan Seidenberg, co-CEO and former CEO of Bell Atlantic, and Charles R. Lee, co-CEO and former head of GTE. However, after sharing the top spot for just twenty-one months, Lee became the chairman of the board, leaving the CEO position completely to Seidenberg. Mark L. Shower, an advisor with Boston Consulting Group, notes, "The inherent instability of the co-CEO relationship makes the structure particularly problematic in mergers and acquisitions—transitory at best and downright destructive at worst."

The co-CEO relationship also went awry at Citigroup. Sanford Weill, former head of Travelers Insurance, and John Reed, former CEO of Citibank, agreed to share the top position when the two firms merged in 1998, but the structure endured less than two years. The original motivation for the arrangement was to ease the post-merger transition, but it clearly did not work out that way. Instead, as *Fortune* writer Patricia Sellers describes, "John Reed lost. Sandy Weill won." As Reed fell from power, many of his proteges left Citigroup. Although the combined firm is performing well financially, many insiders admit that the two cultures never really coalesced and that the talent drain continues today.

Although co-CEO arrangements have the potential to work in some limited circumstances—for example, in situations in which there is considerable shared history and trust—they appear risky in a merger. Sirower worries about the lack of a unified corporate culture and is quite negative about the arrangement, claiming, "If there is ever a rime when a company needs clear direction, leadership and rapid decision making, it is in the postmerger integration phase, when managers must . . . bring together two distinct organizations while protecting the day-to-day business. . . . It seems likely that the organizational disruption caused by the co-CEO model generally is not worth the perceived benefits, especially since most companies will eventually revert [back] to the single-CEO model."

> ## "[T]he co-CEO relationship [is] transitory at best and downright destructive at worst."
> *—Mark L. Sirower, corporate development advisor, Boston Consulting Group*

⊚

REFERENCES: "Corporate Information," "Following the Leader," "Golden West Financial Corporation Board of Directors," Golden West Financial web site. www.worldsavings.com on June 10, 2002; "Profile: Charles Schwab Corp." Yahoo! Finance web site. biz.yahoo.com on June 10, 2002; "Senior Leadership Profiles," Verizon web site. investor.verizon.com on June 10, 2002. "Who's Who," Schwab web site www.aboutschwab.com on June 10, 2002; Patricia Sellers, "Hubby, Wife Are Golden Duo," *Fortune*, March 4, 2002. www.fortune.com on June 10, 2002; Kathleen Melymuka, "Taking Stock," *Computerworld*, June 26, 2000. www.computerworld.com on June 10, 2002; Patricia Sellers, "CEO Deathmatch!" *Fortune*, March 20, 2000. www.fortune.com on June 10, 2002; David Whitford, "The Two-Headed Manager," *Fortune*, January 24, 2000. www.fortune.com on June 10, 2002; Mark L. Sirower, "One Head Is Better Than Two," *Wall Street Journal*, October 18, 1999 (quotation). interactive.wsj.com on October 26, 1999.

Case Questions

1. Describe ways in which a firm could use the three forms of coordination (departmentalization, span of control, and administrative hierarchy) to help manage the CEO's job when that position is being filled by two co-CEOs.
2. Would an organization that utilizes co-CEOs be more likely to be centralized or decentralized than one with a single CEO? Would it be more likely to be formal or informal? Explain your answers.

3. In your opinion, is the use of co-CEOs more likely to be successful in the long term when the two individuals have complementary skills and viewpoints, or when there is substantial similarity and agreement between them? Why?

Experiencing Organizational Behavior

Understanding Organization Structure

Purpose: This exercise will help you understand the configurational and operational aspects of organization structure.

Format: You will interview at least five employees in different parts of either the college or university you attend or a small- to medium-sized organization and analyze its structure.

Procedure: If you use a local organization, your first task is to find one with fifty to five hundred employees. The organization should have more than two hierarchical levels, but it should not be too complex to understand in a short period of study. You may want to check with your professor before contacting the company. Your initial contact should be with the highest-ranking manager, if possible. Be sure that top management is aware of your project and gives its approval.

If you use your local college or university, you could talk to professors, secretaries, and other administrative staff in the admissions office, student services department, athletic department, library, or many other areas. Be sure to represent a variety of jobs and levels in your interviews.

Using the material in this chapter, interview employees to obtain the following information on the structure of the organization.

1. The type of departmentalization (business function, process, product, customer, geographic region)
2. The typical span of control at each level of the organization
3. The number of levels in the hierarchy
4. The administrative ratio (ratio of managers to total employees and ratio of managers to production employees)
5. The degree of formalization (to what extent are rules and procedures written down in job descriptions, policy and procedures manuals, and memos?)
6. The degree of decentralization (to what extent are employees at all levels involved in making decisions?)

Interview three to five employees of the organization at different levels and in different departments. One should hold a top-level position. Be sure to ask the questions in a way that is clear to the respondents; they may not be familiar with the terminology used in this chapter.

Students should produce a report with a paragraph on each configurational and operational aspect of structure listed in this exercise as well as an organization chart of the company, a discussion of differences in responses from the employees interviewed, and any unusual structural features (for example, a situation in which employees report to more than one person or to no one). You may want to send a copy of your report to the company's top management.

1. Which aspects of structure were the hardest to obtain information about? Why?
2. If there were differences in the responses of the employees you interviewed, how do you account for them?

Self-Assessment Exercise

Making Delegation Work

Tasks and decisions must be delegated to others if what remains of middle management is to survive. With all of the recent downsizing, those who are left must do more with less time and fewer resources. In addition, the essence of total quality management is allowing others—teams and individuals—to make decisions about their work. On the other hand, many managers and supervisors complain that they do not know how to delegate effectively. The following twelve points should improve your delegation.

If you hold any type of managerial assignment or job at work or in a student club or association, you could delegate some job or task to another person. Try the following simple steps.

1. Choose a specific task and time frame. Know exactly what task is to be delegated and by when.
2. Specify in writing exactly why you are delegating this task.
3. Put down in writing exactly what you expect to be done and how it will be measured.
4. Be sure that the person or team is competent to do the task, or at least knows how to acquire the competence if they do not have it initially.
5. Be certain that those who must do the tasks really want to take on more responsibility.
6. Measure or oversee the work without being conspicuous and bothersome to those doing the task.
7. Predict how much it will cost to correct mistakes that might be made.
8. Make sure that YOUR boss knows that you are delegating this task and approves.
9. Be sure that you will be able to provide the appropriate rewards to the person or team who takes on this additional responsibility if they succeed.
10. Be ready with another task to delegate when the person or team succeeds with this one.
11. Be sure to delegate both responsibility for the task and the authority to utilize the appropriate resources to get the job done.

REFERENCES: Selwyn W. Becker, "TQM Does Work: Ten Reasons Why Misguided Attempts Fail," *Management Review,* May 1993, pp. 30–33; Janet Houser Carter, "Minimizing the Risks from Delegation," *Supervisory Management,* February 1993, pp. 1–2; John Lawrie, "Turning Around Attitudes About Delegation," *Supervisory Management,* December 1990, pp. 1–2.

Online

1. Some large, publicly traded organizations have a type of organization chart that at least shows the way that their top level is structured. Using the Internet, look up the organization charts of several organizations. You may have to go to documents that are reported to the Securities and Exchange Commission in order to find them. Pick four companies in different industries for which you can find good and recent organization charts.
2. Describe the configurational aspects of the structure of each organization.
3. By reviewing the charts and reading the annual report for each company, see if you can describe any of the operational aspects of the structure as delineated in this chapter.

Building Managerial Skills

Exercise Overview: Managers typically inherit an existing organization structure when they are promoted or hired into a position as manager. Often, however, after working with the existing structure for a while, they feel the need to rearrange the structure to increase the productivity or performance of the organization. This exercise provides you with the opportunity to restructure an existing organization.

Exercise Background: Recall the analysis you did in the "Experiencing Organizational Behavior" exercise in which you analyzed the structure of an existing organization. In that exercise you described the configurational and operational aspects of the structure of a local organization or department at your college or university.

Exercise Task: Develop a different organization structure for that organization. You may utilize any or all of the factors described in this chapter. For example, you could alter the span of control, the administrative hierarchy, and the method of departmentalization as well as the formalization and centralization of the organization. Remember, the key to structure is to develop a way to coordinate the divided tasks. You should draw a new organization chart and develop a rationale for your new design.

Conclude by addressing the following questions:

1. How difficult was it to come up with a different way of structuring the organization?
2. What would it take to convince the current head of that organization to go along with your suggested changes?

LEADERSHIP

Someone once observed that a leader is a person who finds out which way the parade is going, jumps in front of it, and yells "Follow me!" The plain fact is that this approach to leadership has little chance of working in today's rapidly changing world. Leadership involves much more than simply taking charge. Howard Lutnick not only had to deal with the emotions of losing family members and valued employees, he also needed to focus on the operational issues at hand. In short, successful leaders are those individuals who can step into a difficult situation and make a noticeable difference. But how much of a difference can leaders make in modern organizations?

OB researchers have discovered that leaders can make a difference. One study, for instance, revealed that leadership was positively associated with net profits from 167 companies over a time span of 20 years. Research also showed that a coach's leadership skills affected the success of his or her team. Specifically, teams in both Major League Baseball and college basketball won more games when players perceived the coach to be an effective leader. Rest assured, leadership makes a difference.

After formally defining the term *leadership*, this chapter focuses on the following areas: (1) trait and behavioral approaches to leadership, (2) alternative situational theories of leadership, (3) charismatic leadership, and (4) additional perspectives on leadership. Because there are many different leadership theories within each of these areas, it is impossible to discuss them all. This chapter reviews those theories with the most research support.

What Does Leadership Involve?

Because the topic of leadership has fascinated people for centuries, definitions abound. This section presents a definition of leadership and highlights the similarities and differences between leading versus managing.

What Is Leadership?

Disagreement about the definition of leadership stems from the fact that it involves a complex interaction among the leader, the followers, and the situation. For example, some researchers define leadership in terms of personality and physical traits, while others believe leadership is represented by a set of prescribed behaviors. In contrast, other researchers believe that leadership is a temporary role that can be filled by anyone. There is a common thread, however, among the different definitions of leadership. The common thread is social influence.

Within an organizational context, **leadership** is defined as "a social influence process in which the leader seeks the voluntary participation of subordinates in an effort to reach organizational goals." Tom Peters and Nancy Austin, authors of the bestseller, *A Passion for Excellence,* describe leadership in broader terms:

> Leadership means vision, cheerleading, enthusiasm, love, trust, verve, passion, obsession, consistency, the use of symbols, paying attention as illustrated by the content of one's calendar, out-and-out drama (and the management thereof), creating heroes at all levels, coaching, effectively wandering around, and numerous other things. Leadership must be present at all levels of the organization. It depends on a million little things done with obsession, consistency, and care, but all of those million little things add up to nothing if the trust, vision, and basic belief are not there.

As you can see from this definition, leadership clearly entails more than wielding power and exercising authority and is exhibited on different levels. At the individual level, for example, leadership involves mentoring, coaching, inspiring, and motivating. Leaders build teams, generate cohesion, and resolve conflicts at the group level. Finally, leaders build culture and generate change at the organizational level.

There is one component of leadership missing from the above definition: the follower's perspective. Research from this point of view reveals that people seek, admire, and respect leaders who foster three emotional responses in others. Followers want organizational leaders to create feelings of *significance* (what one does at work is important and meaningful), *community* (a sense of unity encourages people to treat others with respect and dignity and to work together in pursuit of organizational goals), and *excitement* (people are engaged and feel energy at work).

Leading versus Managing

It is important to appreciate the difference between leadership and management to fully understand what leadership is all about. Bernard Bass, a leadership expert, concluded that "leaders manage and managers lead, but the two activities are not synonymous." Bass tells us that although leadership and management overlap, each entails a unique set of activities or functions. Broadly speaking, managers typically perform functions associated with planning, investigating, organizing, and control, and leaders deal with the interpersonal aspects of a manager's job. Leaders inspire others, provide emotional support, and try to get employees to rally around a common goal. Leaders also play a key role in creating a vision and strategic plan for an organization. Managers, in turn, are charged with implementing the vision and strategic plan. Table 9.1 summarizes the key differences found between leaders and managers.

TABLE 9.1 Differences between Leaders and Managers	
Leaders	Managers
Innovate	Administer
Develop	Maintain
Inspire	Control
Long-term view	Short-term view
Ask what and why	Ask how and when
Originate	Initiate
Challenge the status quo	Accept the status quo
Do the right things	Do things right

SOURCE: Distinctions were taken from W. G. Bennis, *On Becoming a Leader* (Reading, MA: Addison-Wesley, 1989).

The distinction between leaders and managers is more than a semantic issue for four reasons:

1. It is important from a hiring standpoint. Because leaders and managers perform a subset of unique functions, it is important to recruit and select people who have the required intellectual abilities, experience, and job-relevant knowledge to perform their jobs.
2. Differences may affect group effectiveness. Work group performance can be increased by staffing a productive mix of leaders and managers.
3. Successful organizational change is highly dependent upon effective leadership throughout an organization. Senior executives cannot create change on their own. According to organizational change expert John Kotter, successful organizational transformation is 70% to 90% leadership and 10% to 30% management.
4. Distinctions between leading and managing highlight the point that leadership is not restricted to people in particular positions or roles. Anyone from the bottom to the top of an organization can be a leader. Many informal leaders have contributed to organizational effectiveness. This conclusion supports Warren Bennis's point about leaders and managers. Bennis characterized managers as people who do things right and leaders as individuals who do the right things.

Trait and Behavioral Theories of Leadership

This section examines the two earliest approaches used to explain leadership. Trait theories focused on identifying the personal traits that differentiated leaders from followers. Behavioral theorists examined leadership from a different perspective. They tried to uncover the different kinds of leader behaviors that resulted in higher work group performance. Both approaches to leadership can teach current and future managers valuable lessons about leading.

Trait Theory

leader trait Personal characteristics that differentiate leaders from followers

At the turn of the 20th century, the prevailing belief was that leaders were born, not made. Selected people were thought to possess inborn traits that made them successful leaders. A **leader trait** is a physical or personality characteristic that can be used to differentiate leaders from followers.

Before World War II, hundreds of studies were conducted to pinpoint the traits of successful leaders. Dozens of leadership traits were identified. During the postwar period, however, enthusiasm was replaced by widespread criticism. Studies conducted by Ralph Stogdill in 1948 and by Richard Mann in 1959, which sought to summarize the impact of traits on leadership, caused the trait approach to fall into disfavor.

Stogdill's and Mann's Findings. Based on his review, Stogdill concluded that five traits tended to differentiate leaders from average followers: (1) intelligence, (2) dominance, (3) self-confidence, (4) level of energy and activity, and (5) task-relevant knowledge. Among the seven categories of personality traits examined by Mann, intelligence was the best predictor of leadership. Unfortunately, the overall pattern of research findings revealed that both Stogdill's and Mann's key traits did not accurately predict which individuals became leaders in organizations. People with these traits often remained followers.

Contemporary Trait Research. Two OB researchers concluded in 1983 that past trait data may have been incorrectly analyzed. By applying modern statistical techniques to an old database, they demonstrated that the majority of a leader's behavior could be attributed to stable underlying traits. Unfortunately, their methodology did not single out specific traits.

leadership prototype Mental representation of the traits and behaviors possessed by leaders

A 1986 meta-analysis by Robert Lord and his associates remedied this shortcoming. Based on a reanalysis of past studies, Lord concluded that people have leadership *prototypes* that affect their perceptions of who is and who is not an effective leader. Your **leadership prototype** is a mental representation of the traits and behaviors that you believe are possessed by leaders. We thus tend to perceive that someone is a leader when he or she exhibits traits or behaviors that are consistent with our prototypes. Lord's research demonstrated that people are perceived as being leaders when they exhibit the traits associated with intelligence, masculinity, and dominance. More recently, a study of 6,052 middle-level managers from 22 European countries revealed that leadership prototypes are culturally based. In other words, leadership prototypes are influenced by national cultural values. Researchers have not yet identified a set of global leadership prototypes.

Another pair of leadership researchers attempted to identify key leadership traits by asking the following open-ended question to more than 20,000 people around the world: "What values (personal traits or characteristics) do you look for and admire in your superiors?" The top four traits included honesty, forward-looking, inspiring, and competent. The researchers concluded that these four traits constitute a leader's credibility. This research suggests that people want their leaders to be credible and to have a sense of direction. This conclusion is consistent with recent concerns regarding ethical and legal lapses at companies such as Enron, Tyco, and Global Crossing.

A deep cynicism has settled over corporate America as many employees in a variety of businesses wonder how much, if at all, they can trust their top bosses.

The trigger event was the Enron scandal. But while more becomes known about the energy trader's rotten numbers, and the cheating and lying that apparently prevailed in its senior ranks, accounting problems and ethical breaches are surfacing at a growing list of other companies.

The trust quotient is especially low among employees at troubled firms such as Tyco and Global Crossing, who have lost jobs and retirement savings, and feel they are bearing the brunt of their bosses' mistakes.

"Whatever company I work for in the future, I'll never again trust at face value what top executives say," say a former vice president of marketing at Global Crossing.

Gender and Leadership. The increase of women in the workforce has generated much interest in understanding the similarities and differences in female and male leaders. Three separate meta-analyses and a series of studies conducted by consultants across the country uncovered the following differences: (1) Men and women were seen as displaying more task and social leadership, respectively; (2) women used a more democratic or participative style than men, and men used a more autocratic and directive style than women; (3) men and women were equally assertive and (4) women executives, when rated by their peers, managers, and direct reports, scored higher than their male counterparts on a variety of effectiveness criteria (see Table 9.2).

In spite of these positive results, the same behavior by a male and female can be interpreted differently and lead to opposite consequences. Consider the case of Deborah Hopkins, former chief financial officer at Lucent Technologies:

Ms. Hopkins, 46 years old and widely viewed as one of America's hottest female executives, had been at the maker of phone-industry equipment just over a year. . . . Ms. Hopkins's management technique, which earned her the nickname "Hurricane Debby," fell flat at Lucent. There, she was known for unforgiving candor, in which she typically cut off colleagues in midsentence. . . . Being a woman

TABLE 9.2 A Scorecard of Male-Female Leadership Ratings Derived from 360-Degree Evaluations

Skill*	Men	Women
Motivating others		✓✓✓✓
Fostering communication		✓✓✓**
Producing high-quality work		✓✓✓✓
Strategic planning	✓✓	
Listening to others		✓✓✓✓
Analyzing issues	✓✓	✓✓**

*Each check mark denotes which group scored higher in the respective studies.
**In one study, women's and men's scores in these categories were statistically even.

SOURCE: R. Sharpe "As Leaders, Women Rule," *Business Week*, November 20, 2000, p. 75. The data came from Hagberg Consulting Group, Management Research Group, Lawrence A. Pfaff Personnel Decisions International Inc., and Advanced Teamware Inc.

didn't help, say people close to Ms. Hopkins. Indeed, she was the fourth high-ranking female executive to leave Lucent, starting with Ms. Fiorina [Carly Fiorina is CEO of Hewlett-Packard] in 1999. And while traits such as candor and abrasiveness can be considered good qualities in male chief executives in a tough turn-around situation, Ms. Hopkins was criticized for her personality.

Trait Theory in Perspective. We can no longer afford to ignore the implications of leadership traits. Traits play a central role in how we perceive leaders. Recalling social perception, it is important to determine the traits embodied in people's schemata (or mental pictures) for leaders. If those traits are inappropriate (i.e., foster discriminatory selection and invalid performance appraisals), they need to be corrected through training and development. Consider the stereotypes associated with who gets selected for corporate assignments overseas.

> While women represent about half of the global workforce, surveys indicate they count for less than 12% of the expatriate population. Why? Because many male managers still believe women aren't interested in overseas jobs or won't be effective at them. The managers cite dual-career complications, gender prejudice in many countries, and the risk of sexual harassment That's hogwash, according to researchers at Loyola University (Chicago). Their recent survey of 261 female expats and their supervisors concluded that women are just as interested as men in foreign assignments and just as effective once there. In fact, contends Linda Stroh, one of the researchers, the traits considered crucial for success overseas—knowing when to be passive, being a team player, soliciting a variety of perspectives—are more often associated with women's management styles than men's.

Managers should be careful to avoid using gender-based stereotypes when making overseas assignments. Moreover, organizations may find it beneficial to consider selected leadership traits when choosing among candidates for leadership positions. Gender should not be used as one of these traits. Consider, for example, the leadership traits that Colin Powell, Larry Bossidy, Carly Fiorina, and Jack Welch believe effective leaders need to have in the 21st century (see Table 9.3). The table reveals both agreement and disagreement in preferred traits across these leaders.

Behavioral Styles Theory

This phase of leadership research began during World War II as part of an effort to develop better military leaders. It was an outgrowth of two events: the seeming inability of trait theory to explain leadership effectiveness and the human relations movement, an outgrowth of the Hawthorne Studies. The thrust of early behavioral leadership theory was to focus on leader behavior, instead of on personality traits. It was believed that leader behavior directly affected work group effectiveness. This led researchers to identify patterns of behavior (called leadership styles) that enabled leaders to effectively influence others.

The Ohio State Studies. Researchers at Ohio State University began by generating a list of behaviors exhibited by leaders. At one point, the list contained 1,800 statements that described nine categories of leader behavior. Ultimately, the

TABLE 9.3 Leadership Traits Identified by Famous Organizational Leaders			
Colin Powell (former Chairman of the Joint Chiefs of Staff and Current Secretary of State)	Larry Bossidy (former CEO of Allied Signal)	Carly Fiorina (CEO of Hewlett-Packard Co.)	Jack Welch (former CEO of General Electric)
1. Ability to execute	1. Ability to execute	1. Self-confidence	1. Ability to execute
2. Visionary	2. Ability to professionally	2. Visionary	2. Ability to energize others
3. Proactive communicator	3. Multiple work experiences in various	3. Proactive communicator	3. The edge to make tough decisions
4. Flexible	4. A team orientation	4. Flexible	4. High energy
5. Challenges the status quo		5. A team orientation	
6. Ability to execute			

SOURCES: Derived from O. Harai, *The Leadership Secrets of Collin Powell* (New York: McGraw-Hill, 2002); L Bossidy, "The Job No CEO Should Delegate," *Harvard Business Review,* March 2001, pp. 47–49; P-W Tam, "The Chief Does Double Duty: How H-P's Fiorina Manages to Run Global Corporation while Waging Proxy Fight," *The Wall Street Journal,* February 7, 2002, pp. B1, B4; and T. A. Stewart, "The Contest for Welch's Throne Begins: Who Will Run GE?" *Fortune,* January 11, 1999, p. 27.

consideration Creating mutual respect and trust with followers

initiating structure Organizing and defining what group members should be doing

Ohio State researchers concluded there were only two independent dimensions of leader behavior: consideration and initiating structure. **Consideration** involves leader behavior associated with creating mutual respect or trust and focuses on a concern for group members' needs and desires. **Initiating structure** is leader behavior that organizes and defines what group members should be doing to maximize output. These two dimensions of leader behavior were oriented at right angles to yield four behavioral styles of leadership (see Figure 9.1).

It initially was hypothesized that a high-structure, high-consideration style would be the one best style of leadership. Through the years, the effectiveness of the high-high style has been tested many times. Overall, results have been mixed. Researchers thus concluded that there is not one best style of leadership. Rather, it is argued that effectiveness of a given leadership style depends on situational factors.

University of Michigan Studies. As in the Ohio State studies, this research sought to identify behavioral differences between effective and ineffective leaders. Researchers identified two different styles of leadership: one was employee centered, the other was job centered. These behavioral styles parallel the consideration and initiating-structure styles identified by the Ohio State group. In summarizing the results from these studies, one management expert concluded that effective leaders (1) tend to have supportive or employee-centered relationships with employees, (2) use group rather than individual methods of supervision, and (3) set high performance goals.

Blake and Mouton's Managerial/Leadership Grid. Perhaps the most widely known behavioral styles model of leadership is the Managerial Grid. Behavioral scientists Robert Blake and Jane Srygley Mouton developed and trademarked the grid. They use it to demonstrate that there is one best style of leadership. Blake

FIGURE 9.1
Four Leadership Styles Derived from the Ohio State Studies

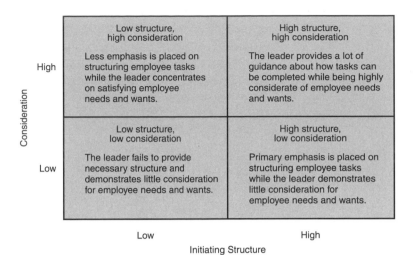

	Low structure, high consideration	High structure, high consideration
High	Less emphasis is placed on structuring employee tasks while the leader concentrates on satisfying employee needs and wants.	The leader provides a lot of guidance about how tasks can be completed while being highly considerate of employee needs and wants.
	Low structure, low consideration	High structure, low consideration
Low	The leader fails to provide necessary structure and demonstrates little consideration for employee needs and wants.	Primary emphasis is placed on structuring employee tasks while the leader demonstrates little consideration for employee needs and wants.

Consideration (vertical axis)

Low   High

Initiating Structure

leadership grid Represents four leadership styles found by crossing concern for production and concern for people

and Mouton's Managerial Grid (renamed the **Leadership Grid** in 1991) is a matrix formed by the intersection of two dimensions of leader behavior. On the horizontal axis is "concern for production." "Concern for people" is on the vertical axis.

Blake and Mouton point out that "the variables of the Managerial Grid are *attitudinal and conceptual,* with *behavior* descriptions derived from and connected with the thinking that lies behind action." In other words. concern for production and concern for people involve attitudes and patterns of thinking, as well as specific behaviors. By scaling each axis of the grid from 1 to 9, Blake and Mouton were able to plot five leadership styles. Because it emphasizes teamwork and interdependence, the 9,9 style is considered by Blake and Mouton to be the best, regardless of the situation.

In support of the 9,9 style, Blake and Mouton cite the results of a study in which 100 experienced managers were asked to select the best way of handling 12 managerial situations. Between 72% and 90% of the managers selected the 9,9 style for each of the 12 situations. Moreover, Blake and Mouton report, "The 9,9, orientation . . . leads to productivity, satisfaction, creativity, and health." Critics point out that Blake and Mouton's research may be self-serving. At issue is the grid's extensive use as a training and consulting tool for diagnosing and correcting organizational problems.

Behavioral Styles Theory in Perspective. By emphasizing leader *behavior,* something that is learned, the behavioral style approach makes it clear that leaders are made, not born. This is the opposite of the trait theorists' traditional assumption. Given what we know about behavior shaping and model-based training, leader *behaviors* can be systematically improved and developed. Consider, for example, how the U.S. Postal Service is striving to grow and develop leadership talent within the organization.

The United States Postal Service's Advanced Leadership Program was conceived and introduced in 1998. Its aim: "to develop a cadre of leaders who are prepared to take over leadership positions within the Postal Service because of the significant number of leaders that will leave over the next few years," explains Olaf Jaehnigen, ALP program manager.

The concept for ALP came out of a competency model. The model, based on information gathered by Postal Service executives and officers, was built by the service's employee development staff in conjunction with an external firm specializing in competency modeling. The competencies, 31 in all, are part cognitive and part behavioral. "The Postal Service has said that these competencies are the things that we really want our leaders to have," says Jaehnigen. "And if we see candidates that are strong in all of these competencies we can rest, relatively assured, that they will perform well."

The model became the building blocks for the ALP curriculum, delivered via four weeks of residential study over a nine-month period and a 15-semester academic component. Weeks two, three, and four comprise business foundation, business decisions, and business leadership, respectively. "We ground them in the principles of finance, strategy, and decision-making using generic models and simulations," says Dot Fisher, one of the program's three moderators. "Then we use what they learn to compare the Postal Service with its major competitors."

Behavioral styles research also revealed that there is no one best style of leadership. The effectiveness of a particular leadership style depends on the situation at hand. For instance, employees prefer structure over consideration when faced with role ambiguity. Finally, research also reveals that it is important to consider the difference between how frequently and how effectively managers exhibit various leader behaviors. For example, a manager might ineffectively display a lot of considerate leader behaviors. Such a style is likely to frustrate employees and possibly result in lowered job satisfaction and performance. Because the frequency of exhibiting leadership behaviors is secondary in importance to effectiveness, managers are encouraged to concentrate on improving the effective execution of their leader behaviors. At this time we would like you to complete the exercise on the following page.

The exercise gives you the opportunity to test the behavioral styles theory by assessing your teacher's leadership style and your associated class satisfaction and role clarity. Are you satisfied with this class? If yes, the behavioral styles approach is supported if your teacher displayed both high consideration and initiating structure. In contrast, the behavioral style approach is not supported if you are satisfied with this class and your teacher exhibits something other than the standard high-high style. Do your results support the proposition that there is one best style of leadership? Are your results consistent with past research that showed leadership behavior depends on the situation at hand? The answer is yes if you prefer initiating structure over consideration when faced with high role ambiguity. The answer also is yes if you prefer consideration over structure when role ambiguity is low. We now turn our attention to discussing alternative situational theories of leadership.

Situational Theories

situational theories
Propose that leader styles should match the situation at hand

Situational leadership theories grew out of an attempt to explain the inconsistent findings about traits and styles. **Situational theories** propose that the effectiveness of a particular style of leader behavior depends on the situation. As situations

Assessing Teacher Leadership Style, Class Satisfaction, and Student Role Clarity

Instructions: A team of researchers converted a set of leadership measures for application in the classroom. For each of the items shown here, use the following rating scale to circle the answer that best represents your feelings. Next, use the scoring key to compute scores for your teacher's leadership style and your class satisfaction and role clarity.

1 = Strongly disagree
2 = Disagree
3 = Neither agree nor disagree
4 = Agree
5 = Strongly agree

1. My instructor behaves in a manner which is thoughtful of my personal needs.   1 — 2 — 3 — 4 — 5

2. My instructor maintains a friendly working relationship with me.   1 — 2 — 3 — 4 — 5

3. My instructor looks out for my personal welfare.   1 — 2 — 3 — 4 — 5

4. My instructor gives clear explanations of what is expected of me.   1 — 2 — 3 — 4 — 5

5. My instructor tells me the performance goals for the class.   1 — 2 — 3 — 4 — 5

6. My instructor explains the level of performance that is expected of me.   1 — 2 — 3 — 4 — 5

7. I am satisfied with the variety of class assignments.   1 — 2 — 3 — 4 — 5

8. I am satisfied with the way my instructor handles the students.   1 — 2 — 3 — 4 — 5

9. I am satisfied with the spirit of cooperation among my fellow students.   1 — 2 — 3 — 4 — 5

10. I know exactly what my responsibilities are.   1 — 2 — 3 — 4 — 5

11. I am given clear explanations of what has to be done.   1 — 2 — 3 — 4 — 5

Scoring Key

Teacher consideration (1, 2, 3) _____
Teacher initiating structure (4, 5, 6) _____
Class satisfaction (7, 8, 9) _____
Role clarity (10, 11) _____

Arbitrary Norms

Low consideration = 3–8
High consideration = 9–15
Low structure = 3–8
High structure = 9–15
Low satisfaction = 3–8
High satisfaction = 9–15
Low role clarity = 2–5
High role clarity = 6–10

Source: The survey was adapted from A. J. Kinicki and C. A. Schriesheim, "Teachers as Leaders: A Moderator Variable Approach," *Journal of Educational Psychology,* 1978, pp. 928–35.

change, different styles become appropriate. This directly challenges the idea of one best style of leadership. Let us closely examine three alternative situational theories of leadership that reject the notion of one best leadership style.

Fiedler's Contingency Model

Fred Fiedler, an OB scholar, developed a situational model of leadership. It is the oldest and one of the most widely known models of situational leadership. Fiedler's model is based on the following assumption:

> The performance of a leader depends on two interrelated factors: (1) the degree to which the situation gives the leader control and influence—that is, the likelihood that [the leader] can successfully accomplish the job; and (2) the leader's basic motivation—that is, whether [the leader's] self-esteem depends primarily on accomplishing the task or on having close supportive relations with others.

With respect to a leader's basic motivation, Fiedler believes that leaders are either task motivated or relationship motivated. These basic motivations are similar to initiating structure/concern for production and consideration/concern for people. Consider the basic leadership motivation possessed by Oracle Corp. CEO Lawrence Ellison.

> Oracle Corp. CEO Lawrence J. Ellison isn't afraid to go it alone, on land or at sea. Last month, because of what he considered "prima donna" behavior, Ellison demoted one of four veteran skippers of his elite yachts, which will compete for the America's Cup this fall in New Zealand. It was the second such move in less than a year. Ellison, a respected skipper himself, says he'll pick up the slack at the helm. . . .
>
> Three years ago, rather than playing his normal big-think role, Ellison gradually took over daily management and transformed the company's internal operations using Internet technology. That ranged from centralizing data-processing operations to automating sales. Some results were positive: Oracle's operating margins doubled in two years.
>
> In other areas, Ellison has been his own enemy. His insistence on running operations led to the departure of a handful of key executives, starting with former President Raymond Lane some 21 months ago. Lane had helped lead the company to nine straight years of healthy growth. Next to go was Gary L. Bloom, who was being groomed for a top slot but left to become CEO of Veritas Software Corp. after Ellison made it clear that he would continue his tight control of Oracle.

Ellison clearly has used a task motivation style in attempting to help Oracle improve its financial performance.

Fiedler's theory also is based on the premise that leaders have one dominant leadership style that is resistant to change. He suggests that leaders must learn to manipulate or influence the leadership situation in order to create a match between their leadership style and the amount of control within the situation at hand. After discussing the components of situational control and the leadership matching process, we review relevant research and managerial implications.

Situational Control. Situational control refers to the amount of control and influence the leader has in her or his immediate work environment. Situational control ranges from high to low. High control implies that the leader's decisions will produce predictable results because the leader has the ability to influence work outcomes. Low control implies that the leader's decisions may not influence work outcomes because the leader has very little influence. There are three dimensions of situational control: leader–member relations, task structure, and position power. These dimensions vary independently, forming eight combinations of situational control (see Figure 9.2).

The three dimensions of situational control are defined as follows:

leader-member relations Extent that leader has the support, loyalty, and trust of work group

- **Leader-member relations** reflect the extent to which the leader has the support, loyalty, and trust of the work group. This dimension is the most important component of situational control. Good leader-member relations suggest that the leader can depend on the group, thus ensuring that the work group will try to meet the leader's goals and objectives.

task structure Amount of structure contained within work tasks

- **Task structure** is concerned with the amount of structure contained within tasks performed by the work group. For example, a managerial job contains less structure than that of a bank teller. Because structured tasks have guidelines for how the job should be completed, the leader has more control and influence over employees performing such tasks. This dimension is the second most important component of situational control.

position power Degree to which leader has formal power

- **Position power** refers to the degree to which the leader has formal power to reward, punish, or otherwise obtain compliance from employees.

Linking Leadership Motivation and Situational Control. Fiedler's complete contingency model is presented in Figure 9.2. The last row under the Situational Control column shows that there are eight different leadership situations. Each situation represents a unique combination of leader–member relations, task structure, and position power. Situations I, II, and III represent high control situations. Figure 9.2 shows that task-motivated leaders are hypothesized to be most effective

FIGURE 9.2
Representation of Fiedler's Contingency Model

SOURCE: Adapted from F. E. Fiedler, Situational Control and a Dynamic Theory of Leadership," in *Managerial Control and Organizational Democracy,* eds, B. King, S. Streufert, and F. E. Fiedler (New York: John Wiley & Sons. 1978), p. 114.

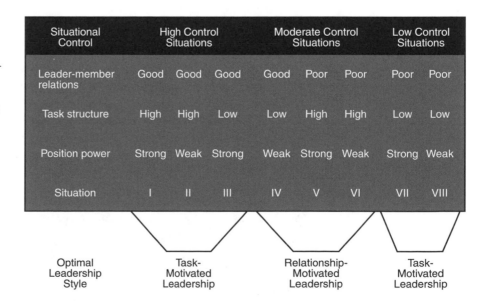

in situations of high control. Under conditions of moderate control (situations IV, V, and VI), relationship-motivated leaders are expected to be more effective. Finally, the results orientation of task-motivated leaders is predicted to be more effective under conditions of low control (situations VII and VIII).

Research and Managerial Implications. The overall accuracy of Fiedler's contingency model was tested through a meta-analysis of 35 studies containing 137 leader style-performance relations. According to the researchers' findings, (1) the contingency theory was correctly induced from studies on which it was based; (2) for laboratory studies testing the model, the theory was supported for all leadership situations except situation II; and (3) for field studies testing the model, three of the eight situations (IV, V, and VII) produced completely supportive results, and partial support was obtained for situations I, II, III, VI, and VIII. A more recent meta-analysis of data obtained from 1,282 groups also provided mixed support for the contingency model. These findings suggest that Fiedler's model needs theoretical refinement.

The major contribution of Fiedler's model is that it prompted others to examine the contingency nature of leadership. This research, in turn, reinforced the notion that there is no one best style of leadership. Leaders are advised to alter their task and relationship orientation to fit the demands of the situation at hand.

Path-Goal Theory

Path-goal theory was originally proposed by Robert House in the 1970s. It was based on the expectancy theory of motivation. Recall that expectancy theory is based on the idea that motivation to exert effort increases as one's effort→performance→outcome expectations improve. Leader behaviors thus are expected to be acceptable when employees view them as a source of satisfaction or as paving the way to future satisfaction. In addition, leader behavior is predicted to be motivational to the extent it (1) reduces roadblocks that interfere with goal accomplishment, (2) provides the guidance and support needed by employees, and (3) ties meaningful rewards to goal accomplishment.

House proposed a model that describes how leadership effectiveness is influenced by the interaction between four leadership styles (directive, supportive, participative, and achievement-oriented) and a variety of contingency factors. **Contingency factors** are situational variables that cause one style of leadership to be more effective than another. Path-goal theory has two groups of contingency variables. They are employee characteristics and environmental factors. Five important employee characteristics are locus of control, task ability, need for achievement, experience, and need for clarity. Two relevant environmental factors are task structure (independent versus interdependent tasks) and work group dynamics. In order to gain a better understanding of how these contingency factors influence leadership effectiveness, we illustratively consider locus of control, task ability and experience, and task structure.

Employees with an internal locus control are more likely to prefer participative or achievement-oriented leadership because they believe they have control over the work environment. Such individuals are unlikely to be satisfied with directive leader behaviors that exert additional control over their activities. In contrast, employees with an external locus tend to view the environment as uncon-

contingency factors
Variables that influence the appropriateness of a leadership style

trollable, thereby preferring the structure provided by supportive or directive leadership. An employee with high task ability and experience is less apt to need additional direction and thus would respond negatively to directive leadership. This person is more likely to be motivated and satisfied by participative and achievement-oriented leadership. Oppositely, an inexperienced employee would find achievement-oriented leadership overwhelming as he or she confronts challenges associated with learning a new job. Supportive and directive leadership would be helpful in this situation. Finally, directive and supportive leadership should help employees experiencing role ambiguity. However, directive leadership is likely to frustrate employees working on routine and simple tasks. Supportive leadership is most useful in this context.

There have been about 50 studies testing various predictions derived from House's original model. Results have been mixed, with some studies supporting the theory and others not. House thus proposed a new version of path-goal theory in 1996 based on these results and the accumulation of new knowledge about OB.

A Reformulated Theory. The revised theory is presented in Figure 9.3. There are three key changes in the new theory. First, House now believes that leadership is more complex and involves a greater variety of leader behavior. He thus identified eight categories of leadership styles or behavior (see Table 9.4). The need for an expanded list of leader behaviors is supported by current research and descriptions of business leaders. Consider the different leader behaviors exhibited by Dieter Zetsche. Zetsche, a German executive, was appointed CEO of the Chrysler Group shortly after Daimler and Chrysler merged into DaimlerChrysler.

> Now, Zetsche, 48, has to turn Chrysler into something it hasn't been for a while: a low-cost producer. "I'm pretty confident we'll get our act together," says Zetsche. "But it's taking longer than I thought when I first came in.". . .
>
> Along the way, the German engineer has confounded his critics in Detroit, who included almost everybody he works with, by turning out to be a decent, even likable fellow. He has spread a lot of misery, but he has done it with such sensitivity—and often in person—that potential antagonists usually decide to cooperate instead. After so many layoffs, no one expected Zetsche to address a

FIGURE 9.3
A General Representation of House's Revised Path-Goal Theory

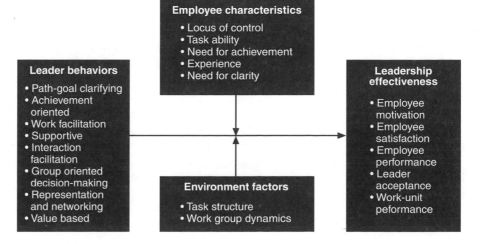

TABLE 9.4 Categories of Leader Behavior within the Revised Path-Goal Theory

Category of Leader Behavior	Description of Leader Behaviors
Path-goal clarifying behaviors	Clarifying employees' performance goals; providing guidance on how employees can complete tasks; clarifying performance standards and expectations; use of positive and negative rewards contingent on performance
Achievement-oriented behaviors	Setting challenging goals; emphasizing excellence; demonstrating confidence in employees' abilities
Work facilitation behaviors	Planning, scheduling, organizing, and coordinating work; providing mentoring coaching, counseling, and feedback to assist employees in developing their skills; eliminating roadblocks; providing resources; empowering employees to take actions and make decisions
Supportive behaviors	Showing concern for the well-being and needs of employees; being friendly and approachable; treating employees as equals
Interaction facilitation behaviors	Resolving disputes; facilitating communication; encouraging the sharing of minority opinions; emphasizing collaboration and teamwork; encouraging close relationship among employees
Group-oriented decision-making behaviors	Posing problems rather than solutions to the work group; encouraging group members to participate in decision making; providing necessary information to the group for analysis; involving knowledgeable employees in decision making
Representation and networking behaviors	Presenting the work group in a positive light to others; maintaining positive relationships with influential others; participating in organizationwide social functions and ceremonies; doing unconditional favors for others
Value-based behaviors	Establishing a vision, displaying passion for it, and supporting its accomplishment; demonstrating self-confidence; communicating high performance expectations and confidence in others' abilities to meet their goals; giving frequent positive feedback

SOURCE: Descriptions were adapted from R. J. House, "Path-Goal Theory of Leadership: Lessons, Legacy, and a Reformulated Theory," *Leadership Quarterly*, 1996, pp. 323–52.

United Auto Workers convention in Las Vegas. . . . Indeed, few CEOs have ever ventured to speak at the union's gatherings. Zetsche not only gave a speech but also mingled with the delegates for five hours. "The union and the company are working very well together," says UAW Vice President Nate Gooden, who handles relations with Chrysler. . . .

As it turned out, Zetsche had just the combination of humility and warmth to ease tensions among Chrysler's demoralized staff. He eats in the cafeteria, interrupts plant tours to talk with workers, and even promised to shave his head (he's already half-bald) if the new Dodge Ram again topped the J D Power & Associates quality survey. His town hall meetings are so popular that plant officials resort to a lottery to choose participants.

Zetsche's decisive leadership is welcome relief for an outfit that drifted aimlessly after the merger. "There's not an employee around here who didn't know this company was in trouble," says James D. Donlon III, senior vice president and controller. "They just needed somebody to get up and tell it like it is." That's true for those outside Chrysler as well. Three weeks into the job, Zetsche demanded that suppliers swallow an immediate 5% price cut. That alone should save Chrysler $2 billion this year. . . .

In terms of product development, Zetsche wants Chrysler to balance style with thrift—an approach he calls "disciplined pizzazz." He is overhauling the vehicle-development process to put more focus on the earliest stages. By pulling together teams from all areas of the company—design, engineering, marketing, manufacturing, and purchasing—Zetsche hopes to reduce waste and resolve nagging quality problems without diminishing Chrysler's creative instincts.

Dieter Zetsche exhibited path-goal clarifying behaviors, achievement-oriented behaviors, supportive behaviors, interaction facilitation behaviors, group-oriented decision-making behaviors, and representation and networking behaviors.

The second key change involves the role of intrinsic motivation and empowerment in influencing leadership effectiveness. House places much more emphasis on the need for leaders to foster intrinsic motivation through empowerment. The current list of leader behaviors shown in Table 9.4 for example, contains many of the recommendations derived from the building blocks for intrinsic motivation. Shared leadership represents the final change in the revised theory. That is, path-goal theory is based on the premise that an employee does not have to be a supervisor or manager to engage in leader behavior. Rather, House believes that leadership is shared among all employees within an organization.

Research and Managerial Implications. There are not enough direct tests of House's revised path-goal theory using appropriate research methods and statistical procedures to draw overall conclusions. Research on charismatic leadership, however, which is discussed in the next section, is supportive of the revised model: Future research is clearly needed to assess the accuracy of this model. That said, there still are two important managerial implications. First, effective leaders possess and use more than one style of leadership. Managers are encouraged to familiarize themselves with the different categories of leader behavior outlined in path-goal theory and to try new behaviors when the situation calls for them. Second, a small set of employee characteristics (i.e., ability, experience, and need for independence) and environmental factors (task characteristics of autonomy, variety, and significance) are relevant contingency factors. Managers are advised to modify their leadership style to fit these various employee and task characteristics.

Hersey and Blanchard's Situational Leadership Theory

Situational leadership theory (SLT) was developed by management writers Paul Hersey and Kenneth Blanchard. According to the theory, effective leader behavior depends on the readiness level of a leader's followers. **Readiness** is defined as the extent to which a follower possesses the ability and willingness to complete a task. Willingness is a combination of confidence, commitment, and motivation.

readiness Follower's ability and willingness to complete a task

Leaders are encouraged to use a "telling style" for followers with low readiness. This style combines high task-oriented leader behaviors, such as providing instructions, with low relationship-oriented behaviors, such as close supervision. As follower readiness increases, leaders are advised to gradually move from a telling, to a selling, to a participating, and, ultimately, to a delegating style.

Although SLT is widely used as a training tool, it is not strongly supported by scientific research. For instance, leadership effectiveness was not attributable to the predicted interaction between follower readiness and leadership style in a study of 459 salespeople. Moreover, a study of 303 teachers indicated that SLT was accurate only for employees with low readiness. This finding is consistent with a survey of 57 chief nurse executives in California. These executives did not delegate in accordance with SLT. Finally, researchers have concluded that the self-assessment instrument used to measure leadership style and follower readiness is inaccurate and should be used with caution. In summary, managers should exercise discretion when using prescriptions from SLT.

From Transactional to Charismatic Leadership

New perspectives of leadership theory have emerged in the past 15 years, variously referred to as "charismatic," "heroic," "transformational," or "visionary" leadership. These competing but related perspectives have created confusion among researchers and practicing managers. Fortunately, Robert House and Boas Shamir have given us a practical, integrated theory. It is referred to as *charismatic leadership*.

This section begins by highlighting the differences between transactional and charismatic leadership. We then discuss a model of the charismatic leadership process and its research and management implications.

What Is the Difference between Transactional and Charismatic Leadership?

transactional leadership Focuses on interpersonal interactions between managers and employees

Most of the models and theories previously discussed in this chapter represent transactional leadership. **Transactional leadership** focuses on the interpersonal transactions between managers and employees. Leaders are seen as engaging in behaviors that maintain a quality interaction between themselves and followers. The two underlying characteristics of transactional leadership are that (1) leaders use contingent rewards to motivate employees and (2) leaders exert corrective action only when subordinates fail to obtain performance goals. Rolf Stahel, CEO of Shire Pharmaceuticals, effectively uses transactional leadership to help organize and run the company.

charismatic leadership Transforms employees to pursue organizational goals over self-interests

In contrast, **charismatic leadership** emphasizes "symbolic leader behavior, visionary and inspirational messages, nonverbal communication, appeal to ideological values, intellectual stimulation of followers by the leader, display of confidence in self and followers, and leader expectations for follower self-sacrifice and for performance beyond the call of duty." Charismatic leadership can produce significant organizational change and results because it "transforms" employees to pursue organizational goals in lieu of self-interests. Charismatic leadership was instrumental for Mathew Szulik, CEO of Red Hat, a Linux operating system provider with 750 employees, as he pursued global expansion of the company's products and services.

For CEO Mathew Szulik employees of Red Hat feed off the company's rebel reputation by believing in a unified cause. "Our people believe they are changing the world of computing and reshaping its culture," he says. "And our challenge was and always will be to find people who are willing to work 24 hours a day, seven days a week not so they can drive a Porsche or BMW but because they feel they are fundamentally redefining their industry."

Let us now examine how charismatic leadership transforms followers.

How Does Charismatic Leadership Transform Followers?

Charismatic leaders transform followers by creating changes in their goals, values, needs, beliefs, and aspirations. They accomplish this transformation by appealing to followers' self-concepts—namely, their values and personal identity. Figure 9.4 presents a model of how charismatic leadership accomplishes this transformation process.

Figure 9.4 shows that organizational culture is a key precursor of charismatic leadership. You may recall, organizational cultures long-term financial performance was highest for organizations with an adaptive culture. Organizations with adaptive cultures anticipate and adapt to environmental changes and focus on leadership that emphasizes the importance of service to customers, stockholders, and employees. This type of management orientation involves the use of charismatic leadership.

Charismatic leaders first engage in three key sets of leader behavior. If done effectively, these behaviors positively affect individual followers and their work groups. These positive effects, in turn, influence a variety of outcomes. Before

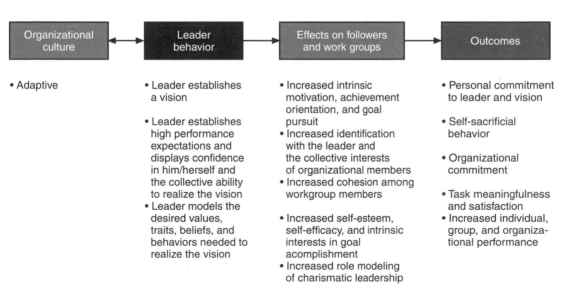

FIGURE 9.4

A Charismatic Model of Leadership

Source: Based in part on D. A. Waldman and F. J. Yammadno, "CEO Charismatic Leadership: Levels-of-Management and Levels-of-Analysis Effects," *Academy of Management Review*, April 1999, pp. 266–85; and B. Shamir, R. J. House, and M. B. Arthur, "The Motivational Effects of Charismatic Leadership: A Self-Concept Based Theory," *Organization Science*, November 1993, pp. 577–94.

discussing the model of charismatic leadership in more detail, it is important to note two general conclusions about charismatic leadership. First, the two-headed arrow between organizational culture and leader behavior in Figure 9.4 reveals that individuals with charismatic behavioral tendencies are able to influence culture. This implies that charismatic leadership reinforces the core values of an adaptive culture and helps to change dysfunctional aspects of an organization's culture that develop over time. Second, charismatic leadership has effects on multiple levels within an organization. For example, Figure 9.4 shows that charismatic leadership can positively influence individual outcomes (e.g., motivation), group outcomes (e.g., group cohesion), and organizational outcomes (e.g., financial performance). You can see that the potential for positive benefits from charismatic leadership is quite widespread.

Charismatic Leader Behavior. The first set of charismatic leader behaviors involves establishing a common vision of the future. A vision is "a realistic, credible, attractive future for your organization." According to Burt Nanus, a leadership expert, the "right" vision unleashes human potential because it serves as a beacon of hope and common purpose. It does this by attracting commitment, energizing workers, creating meaning in employees' lives, establishing a standard of excellence, promoting high ideals, and bridging the gap between an organization's present problems and its future goals and aspirations. In contrast, the "wrong" vision can be very damaging to an organization.

Consider what happened to Coastal Physician Group Inc. as it pursued the vision of its founder Dr. Steven Scott. Dr. Scott's vision was to create networks of physician practices and then sell the network services to health care providers:

> Today, his dream of a physician-led revolution has turned into a nightmare. Major clients and top executives have fled. Coastal is abandoning many of its businesses, selling clinics, and trying to resuscitate its original activity, staffing hospitals. . . .
> Dr. Scott himself, a 48-year-old workaholic obstetrician turned entrepreneur, sits in his fenced-in two-story brick home here, cooling his heels and sipping iced tea. In May, his handpicked board ousted him as chief executive officer and put him on "sabbatical." The CEO who made a practice of calling subordinates at home at night is now barred, by motion of the board, from speaking to Coastal's employees. He also can't enter its offices, even though he owns the building. . . .
> Current management describes him as an arrogant boss who ruined Coastal through a series of missteps and can't bear to let go."

As you can see, Coastal Physician Group's vision produced disastrous results. This highlights the fact that charismatic leaders do more than simply establish a vision. They also must gain input from others in developing an effective implementation plan.

The second set of leader behaviors involves two key components:

1. Charismatic leaders set high performance expectations and standards because they know challenging, attainable goals lead to greater productivity.
2. Charismatic leaders need to publicly express confidence in the followers' ability to meet high performance expectations. This is essential because employees are more likely to pursue difficult goals when they believe they can accomplish what is being asked of them.

The third and final set of leader behaviors involves being a role model. Through their actions, charismatic leaders model the desired values, traits, beliefs, and behaviors needed to realize the vision.

Motivational Mechanisms Underlying the Positive Effects of Charismatic Leadership. Charismatic leadership positively affects employee motivation (see Figure 9.4). One way in which this occurs is by increasing the intrinsic value of an employees' effort and goals. Leaders do this by emphasizing the symbolic value of effort; that is, charismatic leaders convey the message that effort reflects important organizational values and collective interests. Followers come to learn that their level of effort represents a moral statement. For example, high effort represents commitment to the organization's vision and values, whereas low effort reflects a lack of commitment

Charismatic leadership increases employees' effort→performance expectancies by positively contributing to followers' self-esteem and self-efficacy. Leaders also increase the intrinsic value of goal accomplishment by explaining the organization's vision and goals in terms of the personal values they represent. This helps employees to personally connect with the organization's vision. Charismatic leaders further increase the meaningfulness of actions aimed toward goal accomplishment by showing how goals move the organization toward its positive vision, which then gives followers a sense of growth and development, both of which are important contributors to a positive self-concept.

Research and Managerial Implications

The charismatic model of leadership presented in Figure 9.4 has been supported by research. Studies have shown that charismatic leadership was positively related to followers' self-concept, identification with and trust in the leader, positive self-sacrifice, identification with the work group, and with the work group's motivation. A meta-analysis of 54 studies further indicated that charismatic leaders were viewed as more effective leaders by both supervisors and followers and had followers who exerted more effort and reported higher levels of job satisfaction than noncharismatic leaders. Other studies revealed that charismatic leadership was positively associated with employees' safety consciousness, individual performance, and satisfaction with the leader. At the organizational level, a meta-analysis demonstrated that charismatic leadership was positively correlated with organizational measures of effectiveness. Finally, a study of 31 presidents of the United States indicated that charisma significantly predicted presidential performance.

These results underscore five important managerial implications. First, the best leaders are not just charismatic, they are both transactional and charismatic. Leaders should attempt these two types of leadership while avoiding a laissez-faire or wait-and-see style. Laissez-faire leadership is the most ineffective leadership style.

Second, charismatic leadership is not applicable in all organizational situations. According to a team of experts, charismatic leadership is most likely to be effective when

1. The situation offers opportunities for "moral" involvement.
2. Performance goals cannot be easily established and measured.
3. Extrinsic rewards cannot be clearly linked to individual performance.

4. There are few situational cues or constraints to guide behavior.
5. Exceptional effort, behavior, sacrifices, and performance are required of both leaders and followers.

Third, although it is difficult to enhance an individual's charisma, evidence suggests that employees at any level in an organization can be trained to be more transactional and charismatic. Ford Motor Company, for example, is using its Leadership Development Center to roll out a large-scale leadership development program aimed at creating transformational leaders. Fourth, charismatic leaders can be ethical or unethical. Whereas ethical charismatic leaders enable employees to enhance their self-concepts, unethical ones select or produce obedient, dependent, compliant, and dissatisfied followers. Top management can create and maintain ethical charismatic leadership by

1. Creating and enforcing a clearly stated code of ethics.
2. Recruiting, selecting, and promoting people with high morals and standards.
3. Developing performance expectations around the treatment of employees—these expectations can then be assessed in the performance appraisal process.
4. Training employees to value diversity.
5. Identifying, rewarding, and publicly praising employees who exemplify high moral conduct.

Finally, a charismatic leader's enthusiasm can lead to employment promises that cannot be met. Consider the experience of Mary Shea.

Mary Shea, an Oakland, California, lawyer specializing in employment litigation, including options litigation, says that charismatic leaders are not uncommon in the Internet world. She says that in the Internet economy there is a faction of "overzealous companies" and "true believers who made employment offers they couldn't back up." The result was that many employees "trusted these often very charismatic leaders" whose zeal outstripped—and even supplanted—their business acumen. Shea speculates that in the three California counties that form the heart of Silicon Valley and the Internet economy—Santa Clara, San Francisco, and San Mateo—there are at least 100 options-related lawsuits pending, and that more are on the way.

Organizations need to create a check-and-balance system that precludes charismatic leaders from making unrealistic or unethical employment contracts.

Additional Perspectives on Leadership

This section examines three additional approaches to leadership: leader-member exchange theory, substitutes for leadership, and servant-leadership. We spend more time discussing leader-member exchange theory and substitutes for leadership because they have been more thoroughly investigated.

The Leader-Member Exchange (LMX) Model of Leadership

The leader-member exchange model of leadership revolves around the development of dyadic relationships between managers and their direct reports. This model is quite different from those previously discussed in that it focuses on the quality of relationships between managers and subordinates as opposed to the behaviors or traits of either leaders or followers. It also is different in that it does not assume that leader behavior is characterized by a stable or average leadership style as does the Leadership Grid and Fiedler's contingency theory. In other words, these models assume a leader treats all subordinates in about the same way. This traditional approach to leadership is shown in the left side of Figure 9.5. In this case, the leader (designated by the circled L) is thought to exhibit a similar pattern of behavior toward all employees (E_1 to E_5). In contrast, the LMX model is based on the assumption that leaders develop unique one-to-one relationships with each of the people reporting to them. Behavioral scientists call this sort of relationship a *vertical dyad*. The forming of vertical dyads is said to be a naturally occurring process, resulting from the leader's attempt to delegate and assign work roles. As a result of this process, two distinct types of leader-member exchange relationships are expected to evolve.

One type of leader-member exchange is called the **in-group exchange.** In this relationship, leaders and followers develop a partnership characterized by reciprocal influence, mutual trust, respect and liking, and a sense of common fates. Figure 9.5 shows that E_1 and E_5 are members of the leader's in-group. In the second type of exchange, referred to as an **out-group exchange,** leaders are characterized as overseers who fail to create a sense of mutual trust, respect, or common fate. E_2, E_3, and E_4 are members of the out-group on the right side of Figure 9.5.

Research Findings. If the leader-member exchange model is correct, there should be a significant relationship between the type of leader-member exchange and job-related outcomes. Research supports this prediction. For example, a positive leader-member exchange was positively associated with job satisfaction, job

---

in-group exchange A partnership characterized by mutual trust, respect, and liking

out-group exchange A partnership characterized by a lack of mutual trust, respect, and liking

---

FIGURE 9.5

A Role-Making Model of Leadership

SOURCE: Adapted from F. Dansereau Jr., G. Graen, and W. J. Haga, "A Vertical Dyad Linkage Approach to Leadership within Formal Organizations," *Organizational Behavior and Human Performance,* February 1975, p. 72.

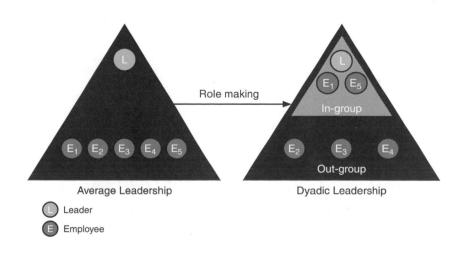

performance, goal commitment, organizational citizenship behavior, and satisfaction with leadership. The type of leader-member exchange also was found to predict not only turnover among nurses and computer analysts but also career outcomes, such as promotability, salary level, and receipt of bonuses over a seven-year period. Finally, studies also have identified a variety of variables that influence the quality of an LMX. For example, LMX was related to personality similarity and demographic similarity. Further, the quality of an LMX was positively related to the level of trust between a manager and his or her direct reports, the manager's use of positive contingent rewards, and the amount of effort the dyad partners put into the relationship.

Managerial Implications. There are four managerial implications associated with the LMX model of leadership. First, relationship building plays a key role in leadership and OB. This implies that it is important for organizations to design human resource systems and activities that proactively promote relationship building. It also suggests that managers should make it a point to focus on relationship building within their work units. Second, leaders are encouraged to establish high performance expectations for all of their direct reports because setting high performance standards fosters high-quality LMXs. Third, because personality and demographic similarity between leaders and followers is associated with higher LMXs, managers need to be careful that they don't create a homogeneous work environment in the spirit of having positive relationships with their direct reports. Diversity clearly documents that there are many positive benefits of having a diverse workforce. The fourth implication pertains to those of us who find ourselves in a poor LMX. Before providing advice about what to do in this situation, we would like you to assess the quality of your current leader-member exchange. The Exercise on the following page contains a measure of leader-member exchange that segments an LMX into our subdimensions: mutual affection, loyalty, contribution to work activities, and professional respect.

What is the overall quality of your LMX? Do you agree with this assessment? Which subdimensions are high and low? If your overall LMX and associated subdimensions are all high, you should be in a very good situation with respect to the relationship between you and your manager. Having a low LMX overall score or a low dimensional score, however, reveals that part of the relationship with your manager may need improvement. OB researcher Robert Vecchio offers the following tips to both followers and leaders for improving the quality of leader-member exchanges:

1. New employees should offer their loyalty, support, and cooperativeness to their manager.
2. If you are an out-group member, either accept the situation, try to become an in-group member by being cooperative and loyal, or quit.
3. Managers should consciously try to expand their in-groups.
4. Managers need to give employees ample opportunity to prove themselves.

Substitutes for Leadership

Virtually all leadership theories assume that some sort of formal leadership is necessary, whatever the circumstances. But that basic assumption is questioned by

Assessing Your Leader-Member Exchange

Instructions: For each of the items shown below, use the following scale and circle the answer that best represents how you feel about the relationship between you and your current manager/supervisor. If you are not currently working, complete the survey by thinking about a previous manager. Remember, there are no right or wrong answers. After circling a response for each of the 12 items, use the scoring key to compute scores for the subdimensions within your leader-member exchange.

1 = Strongly disagree
2 = Disagree
3 = Neither agree nor disagree
4 = Agree
5 = Strongly agree

1. I like my supervisor very much as a person.	1 — 2 — 3 — 4 — 5
2. My supervisor is the kind of person one would like to have as a friend.	1 — 2 — 3 — 4 — 5
3. My supervisor is a lot of fun to work with.	1 — 2 — 3 — 4 — 5
4. My supervisor defends my work actions to a superior, even without complete knowledge of the issue in question.	1 — 2 — 3 — 4 — 5
5. My supervisor would come to my defense if I were "attacked" by others.	1 — 2 — 3 — 4 — 5
6. My supervisor would defend me to others in the organization if I made an honest mistake.	1 — 2 — 3 — 4 — 5
7. I do work for my supervisor that goes beyond what is specified in my job description.	1 — 2 — 3 — 4 — 5
8. I am willing to apply extra efforts, beyond those normally required, to meet my supervisor's work goals.	1 — 2 — 3 — 4 — 5
9. I do not mind working my hardest for my supervisor.	1 — 2 — 3 — 4 — 5
10. I am impressed with my supervisor's knowledge of his/her job.	1 — 2 — 3 — 4 — 5
11. I respect my supervisor's knowledge of and competence on the job.	1 — 2 — 3 — 4 — 5
12. I admire my supervisor's professional skills.	1 — 2 — 3 — 4 — 5

Scoring Key
Mutual affection (add items 1–3) _____
Loyalty (add items 4–6) _____
Contribution to work activities (add items 7–9) _____
Professional respect (add items 10–12) _____
Overall score (all all 12 items) _____

Arbitrary Norms
Low mutual affection = 3–9
High mutual affection = 10–15
Low loyalty = 3–9
High loyalty = 10–15
Low contribution to work activities = 3–9
High contribution to work activities = 10–15
Low professional respect = 3–9
High professional respect = 10–15
Low overall leader-member exchange = 12–38
High overall leader-member exchange = 39–60

SOURCE: Survey items were taken from R. C. Liden and J. M. Maslyn, "Multidemensionality of Leader-Member Exchange: An Empirical Assessment through Scale Development," *Journal of Management,* 1998, p. 56.

substitutes for leadership Situational variables that can substitute for, neutralize, or enhance the effects of leadership

this model of leadership. Specifically, some OB scholars propose that there are a variety of situational variables that can substitute for, neutralize, or enhance the effects of leadership. These situational variables are referred to as **substitutes for leadership.** Substitutes for leadership can thus increase or diminish a leaders ability to influence the work group. For example, leader behavior that initiates structure would tend to be resisted by independent-minded employees with high ability and vast experience. Consequently, such employees would be guided more by their own initiative than by managed directives.

Kerr and Jermier's Substitutes for Leadership Model. According to Steven Ken and John Jermier, the OB researchers who developed this model, the key to improving leadership effectiveness is to identify the situational characteristics that can either substitute for, neutralize, or improve the impact of a leader's behavior. Table 9.5 lists the various substitutes for leadership. Characteristics of the subordinate, the task, and the organization can act as substitutes for traditional hierarchical leadership. Further, different characteristics are predicted to negate different types of leader behavior. For example, tasks that provide feedback concerning accomplishment, such as taking a test, tend to negate task-oriented but no relationship-oriented leader behavior (see Table 9.5). Although the list in Table 9.5 is

TABLE 9.5 Substitutes for Leadership		
Characteristic	Relationship-Oriented or Considerate Leader Behavior Is Unnecessary	Task-Oriented or Initiating Structure Leader Behavior Is Unnecessary
Of the Subordinate		
1. Ability, experience, training, knowledge		X
2. Need for independence	X	X
3. "Professional" orientation	X	X
4. Indifference toward organizational rewards	X	X
Of the Task		
5. Unambiguous and routine		X
6. Methodologically invariant		X
7. Provides its own feedback concerning accomplishment		X
8. Intrinsically satisfying	X	
Of the Organization		
9. Formalization (explicit plans, goals, and areas of responsibility)		X
10. Inflexibility (rigid, unbending rules and procedures)		X
11. Highly specified and active advisory and staff functions		X
12. Closely knit, cohesive work groups	X	X
13. Organizational rewards not within the leader's control	X	X
14. Spatial distance between superior and subordinates	X	X

SOURCE: Adapted from S. Kerr and J. M. Jermier. "Substitutes for Leadership: Their Meaning and Measurement," *Organizational Behaviour and Human Performance,* December 1978, pp. 375–403.

not all-inclusive, it shows that there are more substitutes for task-oriented leadership than for relationship-oriented leadership.

Research and Managerial Implications. Two different approaches have been used to test this model. The first is based on the idea that substitutes for leadership are contingency variables that moderate the relationship between leader behavior and employee attitudes and behavior. Recent studies have revealed that contingency relationships did not support the model. This demonstrates that substitutes for leadership do not moderate the effect of a leader's behavior as suggested by Kerr and Jermier. The second approach to test the substitutes model examined whether substitutes for leadership have a direct effect on employee attitudes and behaviors. A meta-analysis of 36 different samples revealed that the combination of substitute variables and leader behaviors significantly explained a variety of employee attitudes and behaviors. Interestingly, the substitutes for leadership were more important than leader behaviors in accounting for employee attitudes and behaviors.

The key implication is that managers should be attentive to the substitutes listed in Table 9.5 because they directly influence employee attitudes and performance. Managers can positively influence the substitutes through employee selection, job design, work group assignments, and the design of organizational processes and systems.

Servant-Leadership

Servant-leadership is more a philosophy of managing than a testable theory. The term *servant-leadership* was coined by Robert Greenleaf in 1970. Greenleaf believes that great leaders act as servants, putting the needs of others, including employees, customers, and community, as their first priority. **Servant-leadership** focuses on increased service to others rather than to oneself.

It would seem that organizations could use a dose of servant-leadership in this day and age of corporate misdoings and scandals. Consider the following examples.

> CEO L. Dennis Kozlowski of Tyco International Ltd. was indicted and Samuel D. Waksal, CEO of IMClone Systems Inc., was accused of egregious breaches of trust and abuse of power within eight days of each other. Meanwhile, in Houston, a jury deliberated on the fate of Andersen Worldwide, once one of the nation's most respected auditing firms, accused of destroying evidence in the investigation of Enron Corp. [it was later found guilty]. These scandals follow a parade of outgoing CEOs that included Kenneth L. Lay of Enron, Bernard J. Ebbers of WorldCom, and John J. Rigas of Adelphia, all forced to step down amid questions of abuse, incompetence, or both. Over the same period, other CEOs supplemented their mammoth paychecks by cashing in giant option grants just before steep stock declines.

Because the focus of servant-leadership is serving others over self-interest, servant-leaders are less likely to engage in self-serving behaviors that hurt others (e.g., stockholders and employees).

servant-leadership
Focuses on increased service to others rather than to oneself

More and more companies are trying to instill a philosophy of servant-leadership into their organizational cultures. Consider how TDI Industries is attempting to embed servant-leadership into its culture.

> A major player in the high-turnover construction industry, TDI's workforce is a loyal lot: 368 of the company's 1,413 employees have been with the Dallas-based company for more than five years, and more than 85 have been there for at least 20 years.
>
> Why? Because of TDI's commitment to the personal and professional development of each employee, which is best illustrated in the company's "People Objective." This objective promises to ensure that employees will succeed as a "total person," grow with the company, and feel important. Through extensive personal and professional training programs, TDI cultivates well-rounded employees, while simultaneously enhancing its bottom line.
>
> For TDI, creating an environment that promotes longevity begins with the concept of servant leadership. Based on Robert Greenleaf's Servant as Leader theory, the philosophy—in which managers (servants) cultivate employees (leaders) by serving and meeting the needs of others—lies at the heart of nearly all business functions.
>
> To keep servant-leadership central to TDI's corporate culture, new employees are assigned to servant-leadership discussion groups, which meet weekly for six weeks to discuss particular elements of servant-leadership and how to apply the concept to all areas of their particular job. Additionally TDI's employees who supervise at least one person must go through more extensive servant-leadership training at TDI's Leadership Institute.

This example illustrates that it takes more than words to embed servant-leadership into an organization's culture. Servant-leadership must be reinforced through organizational structure, systems, and rewards for it to take hold. At the individual level, however, managers also need to commit to a set of behaviors underlying servant-leadership.

According to Jim Stuart, co-founder of the leadership circle in Tampa, Florida, "Leadership derives naturally from a commitment to service. You know that you're practicing servant-leadership if your followers become wiser, healthier, more autonomous—and more likely to become servant-leaders themselves." Servant-leadership is not a quick-fix approach to leadership. Rather, it is a long-term, transformational approach to life and work. Table 9.6 presents 10 characteristics possessed by servant-leaders. One can hardly go wrong by trying to adopt these characteristics.

Summary of Key Concepts

1. *Define the term* leadership, *and explain the difference between leading versus managing.* Leadership is defined as a social influence process in which the leader tries to obtain the voluntary participation of employees in an effort to reach organizational objectives. Leadership entails more than having authority and power. Although leadership and management overlap, each entails a unique set of activities or functions. Managers typically perform functions associated with planning, investigating, organizing, and control, and leaders deal with the interpersonal aspects of a manager's job. Table 9.1 summarizes the differences between leading and managing.

TABLE 9.6 Characteristics of the Servant-Leader

Servant-Leader Characteristics	Description
1. Listening	Servant-leaders focus on listening to identify and clarify the needs and desires of a group.
2. Empathy	Servant-leaders try to empathize with others' feelings and emotions. An individual's good intentions are assumed even when he or she performs poorly.
3. Healing	Servant-leaders strive to make themselves and others whole in the face of failure or suffering.
4. Awareness	Servant-leaders are very self-aware of their strengths and limitations.
5. Persuasion	Servant-leaders rely more on persuasion than positional authority when making decisions and trying to influence others.
6. Conceptualization	Servant-leaders take the time and effort to develop broader based conceptual thinking. Servant-leaders seek an appropriate balance between a short-term, day-to-day focus and a long-term, conceptual orientation.
7. Foresight	Servant-leaders have the ability to foresee future outcomes associated with a current course of action or situation.
8. Stewardship	Servant-leaders assume that they are stewards of the people and resources they manage.
9. Commitment to the growth of people	Servant-leaders are committed to people beyond their immediate work role. They commit to fostering an environment that encourages personal, professional, and spiritual growth.
10. Building community	Servant-leaders strive to create a sense of community both within and outside the work organization.

SOURCE: These characteristics and descriptions were derived from L. C. Spears, "Introduction: Servant-Leadership and the Greenleaf Legacy," In *Reflections on Leadership: How Robert K. Greenleaf's Theory of Servant-Leadership Influenced Today's Top Management Thinkers*, ed. L. C. Spears (New York: John Wiley & Sons, 1995), pp. 1–14.

2. *Review trait theory research, and discuss the idea of one best style of leadership, using the Ohio State studies and the Leadership Grid as points of reference.* Historical leadership research did not support the notion that effective leaders possessed unique traits from followers. However, teams of researchers reanalyzed this historical data with modern-day statistical procedures. Results revealed that individuals tend to be perceived as leaders when they possess one or more of the following traits: intelligence, dominance, and masculinity. Another study further demonstrated that employees value credible leaders. Credible leaders are honest, forward-looking, inspiring, and competent. Research also examined the relationship between gender and leadership. Results demonstrated that (a) men and women were seen as displaying more task and social leadership, respectively, (b) leadership styles varied by gender, (c) men and women were equally assertive, and (d) women were rated as more effective than men on a variety of criteria. The Ohio State studies

revealed that there were two key independent dimensions of leadership behavior: consideration and initiating structure. Authors of the Leadership Grid proposed that leaders should adopt a style that demonstrates high concern for production and people. Research did not support the premise that there is one best style of leadership.

3. *Explain, according to Fiedler's contingency model, how leadership style interacts with situational control.* Fiedler believes leader effectiveness depends on an appropriate match between leadership style and situational control. Leaders are either task motivated or relationship motivated. Situation control is composed of leader-member relations, task structure, and position power. Task-motivated leaders are effective under situations of both high and low control. Relationship-motivated leaders are more effective when they have moderate situational control.

4. *Discuss House's revised path-goal theory and Hersey and Blanchard's situational leadership theory.* There are three key changes in the revised path-goal theory. Leaders now are viewed as exhibiting eight categories of leader behavior (see Table 9.4) instead of four. In turn, the effectiveness of these styles depends on various employee characteristics and environmental factors. Second, leaders are expected to spend more effort fostering intrinsic motivation through empowerment. Third, leadership is not limited to people in managerial roles. Rather, leadership is shared among all employees within an organization. According to situational leadership theory (SLT), effective leader behavior depends on the readiness level of a leader's followers. As follower readiness increases, leaders are advised to gradually move from a telling to a selling to a participating and, finally, to a delegating style. Research does not support SLT.

5. *Define and differentiate transactional and charismatic leadership.* There is an important difference between transactional and charismatic leadership. Transactional leaders focus on the interpersonal transactions between managers and employees. Charismatic leaders motivate employees to pursue organizational goals above their own self-interests. Both forms of leadership are important for organizational success.

6. *Explain how charismatic leadership transforms followers and work groups.* Organizational culture is a key precursor of charismatic leadership, which is composed of three sets of leader behavior. These leader behaviors, in turn, positively affect followers' and work groups' goals, values, beliefs, aspirations, and motivation. These positive effects are then associated with a host of preferred outcomes.

7. *Summarize the managerial implications of charismatic leadership.* There are five managerial implications: (1) The best leaders are both transactional and charismatic. (2) Charismatic leadership is not applicable in all organizational situations. (3) Employees at any level in an organization can be trained to be more transactional and charismatic. (4) Top management needs to promote and reinforce ethical charismatic leadership because charismatic leaders can be ethical or unethical. (5) A charismatic leader's enthusiasm can lead to employment promises that cannot be met. This can lead to costly lawsuits.

8. *Explain the leader-member exchange model of leadership.* This model revolves around the development of dyadic relationships between managers and their direct reports. These leader-member exchanges qualify as either in-group or out-group relationships. Research supports this model of leadership.

9. *Describe the substitutes for leadership, and explain how they substitute for, neutralize, or enhance the effects of leadership.* There are 14 substitutes for leadership (see Table 9.5) that can substitute for, neutralize, or enhance the effects of Leadership. These substitutes contain characteristics of the subordinates, the task, and the organization. Research shows that substitutes directly influence employee attitudes and performance.

10. *Describe servant-leadership.* Servant-leadership is more a philosophy than a testable theory. It is based on the premise that great leaders act as servants, putting the needs of others, including employees, customers and community, as their first priority.

Discussion Questions

1. Is everyone cut out to be a leader? Explain.
2. Has your college education helped you develop any of the traits that characterize leaders? Explain.
3. Should organizations change anything in response to research pertaining to gender and leadership? If yes, describe your recommendations.
4. What leadership traits and behavioral styles are possessed by the president of the United States?
5. Does it make more sense to change a person's leadership style or the situation? How would Fred Fiedler and Robert House answer this question?
6. Describe how a college professor might use House's revised path-goal theory to clarify student's path-goal perceptions.
7. Identify three charismatic leaders, and describe their leadership traits and behavioral styles.
8. Have you ever worked for a charismatic leader? Describe how he or she transformed followers.
9. Have you ever been a member of an in-group or out-group? For either situation, describe the pattern of interaction between you and your manager.
10. In your view, which leadership theory has the greatest practical application? Why?

Internet Exercise

www.leader-values.com

The topic of leadership has been important since the dawn of time. History is filled with examples of great leaders such as Mohandas Gandhi, Martin Luther King, and Bill Gates. These leaders likely possessed some of the leadership traits discussed in this chapter, and they probably used a situational approach to lead their followers. The purpose of this exercise is for you to evaluate the leadership styles of an historical figure.

Go to the Internet home page for Leadership Values (**www.leader-values.com**), and select the subheading "4 E's" on the left side of the screen. This section provides an overview of leadership and suggests four essential traits/behaviors that are exhibited by leaders: to envision, enable, empower, and energize. After reading this material, go back to the home page, and select the subheading "Historical

Leaders" from the list on the left-hand side of the page. Next, choose one of the leaders from the list of historical figures, and read the description about his or her leadership style. You may want to print all of the material you read thus far from this Web page to help you answer the following questions.

Questions

1. Describe the 4 E's of leadership.
2. To what extent do the 4 E's overlap with the theories and models of leadership discussed in this chapter?
3. Using any of the theories or models discussed in this chapter, how would you describe the leadership style of the historical figure you investigated?
4. Was this leader successful in using the 4 E's of leadership? Describe how he or she used the 4 E's.

CLOSING CASE

Successful CEOs from Genuity Inc. and Factiva Rely on Similar but Different Leadership Styles

In June 2000, Genuity CEO Paul Gudonis made Internet IPO history when the company raised nearly $2 billion in the largest US public offering. While Amazon's Jeff Bezos, Oracle's Larry Ellison, and Cisco's John Chambers grabbed magazine covers and headlines during the past three years, Gudonis—an electrical engineer equipped with a Harvard MBA and 20 years of telecommunications and technology management experience—concentrated on guiding Genuity through an extraordinary growth spun. Since 1994 with 50 employees and $5 million in revenues, it has reached 5,000 employees and revenues of $1 billion.

Gudonis' main concentration is to set corporate strategy and tightly focus the company on chief objectives. That strategy contains a handful of bold objectives: to be no. 1 in Internet traffic on Genuity's network backbone; to rank tops in network infrastructure and broadband; to be no. 1 in quality and customer satisfaction; and to be considered the company with the highest quality work/life environment.

Genuity's objectives are etched onto a plastic badge that Gudonis distributes to every new employee at the company's weekly orientation programs. "I spend a lot of my time communicating to our people, which probably contrasts with the role of Old Economy CEOs," he says, "Last year, we hired nine people a day, so I want everybody to walk around with our objectives hanging off their employee ID badge. I had one young man who stood up during orientation and said, 'Let me get this straight, if I'm working on something that's not on the card, I should stop what I'm doing?' I said, 'Exactly. That's exactly why I'm handing this out.'"

Besides establishing corporate strategy and communicating to employees, Gudonis identifies management development as a critical, and perhaps the most challenging, component of his leadership role. "When you have a company that is growing exponentially," he notes, "the pace of your employees' personal growth must remain ahead of the business growth. We cannot let their jobs out-grow their capabilities." To this end, Gudonis instituted a formal management development program and he holds senior leadership meetings twice a year for the company's top 75 managers. . . .

He also stresses the importance of training and development to his workforce, informing each orientation audience that Genuity promoted 600 employees in 2000. He also spells out specific success stories such as the temp who in four years became director of project management for Genuity's European Internet backbone, or the sales rep who in five years became a regional vice president with a 100-person team.

Gudonis cites the employee review process as another difference between New and Old Economy approaches to leadership. "Given our dynamic industry, I don't know what your objectives as an employee should be for this coming December," Gudonis explains. "While we do have an annual plan, every 90 days I lay out my objectives to my direct reports. They write down their quarterly objectives and review them with me and then with their teams throughout the organizations." Also, every 90 days each employee is eligible for a bonus, depending on overall company performance and how each individual performed against his or her quarterly objectives.

Last December, Clare Hart set some boundaries that would surprise many CEOs—not that she set them, but that it took her a year to do it. Hart's management style is decidedly open. So open, in fact, that she doesn't have an office.

But with the first year of serving as Factiva's CEO under her belt, she knew it was time to set some limits. "My leadership style is about being very approachable, and it was especially important during our first year that I spent time enabling that openness," Hart explains. Ownership also is a big piece of Hart's leadership style. Responsibilities among her leadership team are clear-cut, with no dual-ownership or dual-reporting structures. Each month, all leadership team members compile a report on their area. The reports are then combined and shared among the respective teams and condensed into Hart's report to the board of directors.

Open communication among the leadership team is further facilitated throughout the year with 10 two-day meetings in which business strategy and key issues are worked out. Team members are asked to share appropriate information from the minutes of these meetings with the managers in their areas, with the intent that all 850 employees understand what is accomplished in these meetings. "Each Factiva executive is in his or her respective role because of the intellect, skills, experience and attitude he or she brings to the job." Hart says: "I do not want to do anything that gets in the way of an individual guiding his or her team towards the achievement of our corporate goals."

Through this process, Hart believes, the company is cultivating independent, proactive leaders who aren't afraid to take charge. "I recently watched a senior manager give a presentation to the leadership team, and it was obvious just by how she presented the material that she feels as if everything she does matters to the business. That's the way I want everybody to feel."

Questions for Discussion

1. Based on the discussion of leading versus managing, did Paul Gudonis and Clare Hart exhibit more leadership or managerial behaviors? Use Table 9-1 to answer this question.
2. Citing examples, which different leadership traits and styles were displayed by Gudonis and Hart?

3. Did Gudonis and Hart display more transactional or charismatic leadership? Explain.
4. To what extent are the different styles of Gudonis and Hart consistent with research regarding gender and leadership? Discuss your rationale.
5. What did you learn about leadership from this case? Use examples to reinforce your conclusions.

Group Exercise

Exhibiting Leadership within the Context of Running a Meeting

Objectives

1. To consider the types of problems that can occur when running a meeting.
2. To identify the leadership behaviors that can be used to handle problems that occur in meetings.

Introduction

Managers often find themselves playing the role of formal or informal leader when participating in a planned meeting (e.g., committees, work groups, task forces, etc.). As a leader, individuals often must handle a number of interpersonal situations that have the potential of reducing the group's productivity. For example, if an individual has important information that is not shared with the group, the meeting will be less productive. Similarly, two or more individuals who engage in conversational asides could disrupt the normal functioning of the group. Finally, the group's productivity will also be threatened by two or more individuals who argue or engage in personal attacks on one another during a meeting. This exercise is designed to help you practice some of the behaviors necessary to overcome these problems and at the same time share in the responsibility of leading a productive group.

Instructions

Your instructor will divide the class into groups of four to six. Once the group is assembled, briefly summarize the types of problems that can occur when running a meeting—start with the material presented in the preceding introduction. Write your final list on a piece of paper. Next, for each problem on the group's list, the group should brainstorm a list of appropriate leader behaviors that can be used to handle the problem. Try to arrive at a consensus list of leadership behaviors that can be used to handle the various problems encountered in meetings.

Questions for Discussion

1. What type of problems that occur during meetings are most difficult to handle? Explain.
2. Are there any particular leader behaviors that can be used to solve multiple problems during meetings? Discuss your rationale.

How Ready Are You to Assume the Leadership Role?

Objectives: (1) To assess your readiness for the leadership role. (2) To consider the implications of the gap between your career goals and your readiness to lead.

Introduction: Leaders assume multiple roles. Roles represent the expectations that others have of occupants of a position. It is important for potential leaders to consider whether they are ready for the leadership role because mismatches in expectations or skills can derail a leader's effectiveness. This exercise assesses your readiness to assume the leadership role.

Instructions: For each statement, indicate the extent to which you agree or disagree with it by selecting one number from the scale provided. Circle your response for each statement. Remember, there are no right or wrong answers. After completing the survey, add your total score for the 20 items, and record it in the space provided.

1 = Strongly disagree		**4** = Agree	
2 = Disagree		**5** = Strongly agree	
3 = Neither agree nor disagree			

1. It is enjoyable having people count on me for ideas and suggestions.   1 — 2 — 3 — 4 — 5
2. It would be accurate to say that I have inspired other people.   1 — 2 — 3 — 4 — 5
3. It's a good practice to ask people provocative questions about their work.   1 — 2 — 3 — 4 — 5
4. It's easy for me to compliment others.   1 — 2 — 3 — 4 — 5
5. I like to cheer people up even when my own spirits are down.   1 — 2 — 3 — 4 — 5
6. What my team accomplishes is more important than my personal glory.   1 — 2 — 3 — 4 — 5
7. Many people imitate my ideas.   1 — 2 — 3 — 4 — 5
8. Building team spirit is important to me.   1 — 2 — 3 — 4 — 5
9. I would enjoy coaching other members of the team.   1 — 2 — 3 — 4 — 5
10. It is important to me to recognize others for their accomplishments.   1 — 2 — 3 — 4 — 5
11. I would enjoy entertaining visitors to my firm even it if interfered with my completing a report   1 — 2 — 3 — 4 — 5
12. It would be fun for me to represent my team at gatherings outside our department.   1 — 2 — 3 — 4 — 5
13. The problems of my teammates are my problems too.   1 — 2 — 3 — 4 — 5
14. Resolving conflict is an activity I enjoy.   1 — 2 — 3 — 4 — 5
15. I would cooperate with another unit in the organization even if I disagreed with the position taken by its members.   1 — 2 — 3 — 4 — 5
16. I am an idea generator on the job.   1 — 2 — 3 — 4 — 5
17. It's fun for me to bargain whenever I have the opportunity.   1 — 2 — 3 — 4 — 5
18. Team members listen to me when I speak.   1 — 2 — 3 — 4 — 5
19. People have asked me to assume the leadership of an activity several times in my life.   1 — 2 — 3 — 4 — 5
20. I've always been a convincing person.   1 — 2 — 3 — 4 — 5

Total score: _____

Norms for Interpreting the Total Score
90–100 = High readiness for the leadership role   40–59 = Some uneasiness with the leadership role
69–89 = Moderate readiness for the leadership role   39 or less = Low readiness for the leadership role

Questions for Discussion
1. Do you agree with the interpretation of your readiness to assume the leadership role? Explain why or why not.
2. If you scored below 60 and desire to become a leader, what might you do to increase your readiness to lead? To answer this question, we suggest that you study the statements carefully—particularly those with low responses—to determine how you might change either an attitude or a behavior so that you can realistically answer more questions with a response of "agree" or "strongly agree."
3. How might this evaluation instrument help you to become a more effective leader?

3. Was there a lot of agreement about which leader behaviors were useful for dealing with specific problems encountered in meetings? Explain.

Ethical Dilemma

Doug Durand's Staff Engages in Questionable Sales Activities

In his 20 years as a pharmaceutical salesman, Douglas Durand thought he had seen it all. Then, in 1995, he signed on as vice president for sales at TAP Pharmaceutical Products Inc. in Lake Forest, Illinois. Several months later, in disbelief, he listened to a conference call among his sales staff: They were openly discussing how to bribe urologists. Worried about a competing drug coming to market, they wanted to give a 2% "administration fee" up front to any doctor who agreed to prescribe TAP's new prostate cancer drug, Lupron. When one of Durand's regional managers fretted about getting caught, another quipped: "How do you think Doug would look in stripes?" Durand didn't say a word. "That conversation scared the heck out of me," he recalls. "I felt very vulnerable.". . .

For years, TAP sales reps had encouraged doctors to charge government medical programs full price for Lupron they received at a discount or gratis. Doing so helped TAP establish Lupron as the prostrate treatment of choice, bringing in annual sales of $800 million, about a quarter of the company's revenues. . . .

Durand grew increasingly concerned. Colleagues told him he didn't understand TAP's culture. He was excluded from top marketing and sales meetings. Then came the crack about how he would look in stripes. Durand's stomach knotted in fear that he would become the company scapegoat. Yet he left trapped: If he left within a year, he wouldn't be able to collect his bonus. He also doubted that anyone would hire him if he bolted so hastily.

What would you do if you were Doug Durand?

1. It's a tough market, and giving kickbacks is nothing more than a form of building product loyalty. I wouldn't make a big issue about this practice.
2. I wouldn't do anything because I would not receive my bonus and it wouldn't look good on my resume to leave the job within one year.
3. I would gather information about TAP and send it to a federal prosecutor. After all, TAP is giving kickbacks and it is encouraging doctors to charge full price for a drug they receive on a discount.
4. I would go to TAP's president and get his or her blessing for our sales activities.
5. Invent other options. Discuss.

MOTIVATING JOB PERFORMANCE

MEDTRONIC'S EMPLOYEES FIND FULFILLMENT IN MAKING LIFE-SAVING PRODUCTS

Visitors to corporate headquarters in Fridley, Minn., a pastel-bungalow suburb of Minneapolis, are met by a statue of Earl Bakken, the engineer who co-founded Medtronic in 1949 with his brother-in-law, Palmer Hermundslie. Bakken is depicted in late middle age, wearing a baggy suit, squinting through a pair of aviator-frame glasses, and clutching in one hand a spookily banal box with a screwed-on faceplate, an on-off switch, and a dial for revving up the pulse rate—the primitive pacemaker that made Medtronic famous. The box looks like something straight out of Dr. Frankenstein's laboratory, which is appropriate, for according to company legend, proudly recounted on the timeline in the lobby, it was the film version of *Frankenstein,* released in 1931, that awakened in young Earl Bakken a lifelong fascination with the role of electricity in medicine.

Bakken, 76, lives in Hawaii now but returns to Fridley often. He shows up at ceremonies to present new hires with their Medtronic medallions—keepsakes inscribed with an excerpt from the mission statement (ALLEVIATE PAIN, RESTORE HEALTH AND EXTEND LIFE). And he never misses the holiday party, Medtronic's annual rite of corporate renewal, where people whose bodies function thanks to Medtronic devices come to give testimonials. It's a teary, communal reminder that what goes on here day after day is not the same as making VCRs. "We have patients who come in who would be dead if it wasn't for us," says Karen McFadzen, a production supervisor. "I mean, they sit right up there and they tell us what their lives are like. You don't walk away from them not feeling anything."

If ever a company had a built-in advantage in the motivating-the-worker department, Medtronic is it. And its leaders know the power of playing to that advantage. But even making lifesaving medical devices is, ultimately, just a job. It takes constant care and feeding of corporate legend (remember *Frankenstein*) and mission (those medallions) to imbue Medtronic employees with a sense of satisfaction in their jobs day after day. In the employee surveys that help determine *Fortune's* 100 Best Companies to Work For, 86% of Medtronic employees said their work had special meaning; 94% felt pride in what they accomplished. You can get more shared satisfaction than that, but not much.

But keeping workers motivated takes much more than a mission. Spend time with people at Medtronic, and you begin to understand why people keep working at the 100 Best Companies. They don't stay for on-site gyms or free dry cleaning—although those things may have attracted them in the first place. The ones who are lucky enough to get stock options and big bonuses might stay to get a payout, but they could just as easily leave afterwards. The real reasons people stay are more personal and come down to something pretty basic: fulfillment.

motivation
Psychological process giving behavior purpose and direction

Imagine someone walking up to you and saying "Your work helped save my life." Medtronic's employees are fortunate to enjoy such gratifying feedback—as are medical doctors, firefighters, and police officers. The truth is, however, most of us are employed in far less heroic circumstances. Accordingly, the complex combinations of factors motivating our work efforts are as varied as our occupations. As used here, the term **motivation** refers to the psychological process that gives behavior purpose and direction. By appealing to this process, managers attempt to get individuals to willingly pursue organizational objectives. Motivation theories are generalizations about the the "why" and "how" of purposeful behavior.

Figure 10.1 is an overview model for this chapter. The final element in this model, job performance, is the product of a combination of an individual's motivation and ability. Both are necessary. All the motivation in the world, for example, will not enable a computer-illiterate person to sit down and create a computer spreadsheet. Ability and skills, acquired through training and/or on-the-job experience, are also required. The individual's motivational factors—needs, satisfaction, expectations, and goals—are affected by challenging work, rewards, and participation. We need to take a closer look at each key element in this model. A review of four basic motivation theories is a good starting point.

FIGURE 10.1
Individual Motivation and Job Performance

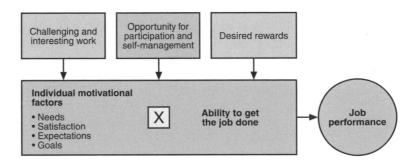

Motivation Theories

Although there are dozens of different theories of motivation, four have emerged as the most influential: Maslow's needs hierarchy theory, Herzberg's two-factor theory, expectancy theory, and goal-setting theory. Each approaches the motivation process from a different angle, each has supporters and detractors, and each teaches important lessons about motivation to work.

Maslow's Needs Hierarchy Theory

In 1943 psychologist Abraham Maslow proposed that people are motivated by a predictable five-step hierarchy of needs. Little did he realize at the time that his tentative proposal, based on an extremely limited clinical study of neurotic patients, would become one of the most influential concepts in the field of management. Perhaps because it is so straightforward and intuitively appealing, Maslow's theory has strongly influenced those interested in work behavior. Maslow's message was simply this: people always have needs, and when one need is relatively fulfilled, others emerge in a predictable sequence to take its place. From bottom to top, Maslow's needs hierarchy includes physiological, safety, love, esteem, and self-actualization needs (see Figure 10.2). According to Maslow, most individuals are not consciously aware of these needs; yet we all supposedly proceed up the hierarchy of needs, one level at a time.

Physiological Needs. At the bottom of the hierarchy are needs based on physical drives, including the need for food, water, sleep, and sex. Fulfillment of these lowest-level needs enables the individual to survive, and nothing else is important when these bodily needs have not been satisfied. As Maslow observed, "It is quite true that man lives by bread alone—when there is no bread." But today the average employee experiences little difficulty in satisfying physiological needs. Figuratively speaking, the prospect of eating more bread is not motivating when one has plenty of bread to eat.

Safety Needs. After our basic physiological needs have been relatively well satisfied, we next become concerned about our safety from the elements, enemies, and other threats. Most modern employees, by earning a living, achieve a high degree of fulfillment in this area. Unemployment assistance is a safety net for those between jobs. Insurance also helps fulfill safety needs, a point not lost on Coca-Cola Femsa, Mexico's primary bottler of Coke:

> Many of the store owners in Mexico, Coke's second-biggest market, turned out to be single mothers and retirees who couldn't afford health insurance. Armed with that intelligence, Femsa was able to create an incentive program that rewards shopkeepers who sell enough Cokes with access to group insurance—a move that helped boost Coke's sales volume in Mexico 13 percent last year.

Love Needs. A physiologically satisfied and secure person focuses next on satisfying needs for love and affection. This category is a powerful motivator of human behavior. People typically strive hard to achieve a sense of belonging with others. As with the first two levels of needs, relative satisfaction of love needs paves the way for the emergence of the next, higher level.

FIGURE 10.2
Maslow's Hierarchy of Needs Theory

SOURCE: Data for diagram drawn from A. H. Maslow, "A Theory of Human Motivation," *Psychological Review,* 50 (July 1943): 370–396.

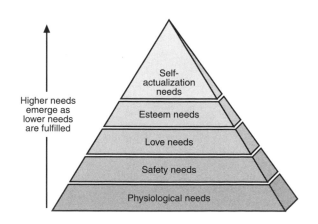

Esteem Needs. People who perceive themselves as worthwhile are said to possess high self-esteem. Self-respect is the key to esteem needs. Much of our self-respect, and therefore our esteem, comes from being accepted and respected by others. It is important for those who are expected to help achieve organizational objectives to have their esteem needs relatively well fulfilled. But esteem needs cannot emerge if lower-level needs go unattended.

Self-Actualization Needs. At the very top of Maslow's hierarchy is the open-ended category *self-actualization needs*. It is open-ended because, as Maslow pointed out, it relates to the need "to become more and more what one is, to become everything that one is capable of becoming." One may satisfy this need by striving to become a better homemaker, plumber, rock singer, or manager. According to one management writer, the self-actualizing manager has the following characteristics:

1. Has warmth, closeness, and sympathy.
2. Recognizes and shares negative information and feelings.
3. Exhibits trust, openness, and candor.
4. Does not achieve goals by power, deception, or manipulation.
5. Does not project own feelings, motivations, or blame onto others.
6. Does not limit horizons; uses and develops body, mind, and senses.
7. Is not rationalistic; can think in unconventional mays.
8. Is not conforming; regulates behavior from within.

Granted, this is a rather tall order to fill. It has been pointed out that "a truly self-actualized individual is more of an exception than the rule in the organizational context." Whether productive organizations need more self-actualized individuals is subject to debate. On the positive side, self-actualized employees might help break down barriers to creativity and steer the organization in new directions. On the negative side, too many unconventional nonconformists could wreak havoc with the typical administrative setup dedicated to predictability.

Relevance of Maslow's Theory for Managers. Behavioral scientists who have attempted to test Maslow's theory in real life claim it has some deficiencies). Even Maslow's hierarchical arrangement has been questioned. Practical evidence points toward a two-level rather than a five-level hierarchy. In this competing view, physiological and safety needs are arranged in hierarchical fashion, as Maslow contends. But beyond that point, any one of a number of needs may emerge as the single most important need, depending on the individual. Edward Lawler, a leading motivation researcher, observed, "Which higher-order needs come into play after the lower ones are satisfied and in which order they come into play cannot be predicted. If anything, it seems that most people are simultaneously motivated by several of the same-level needs."

Although Maslow's theory has not stood up well under actual testing, it teaches managers one important lesson: a *fulfilled* need does not motivate an individual. For example, the promise of unemployment benefits may partially fulfill an employee's need for economic security (the safety need). But the added security of additional unemployment benefits will probably not motivate fully employed individuals to work any harder. Effective managers anticipate each employee's personal need profile and provide opportunities to fulfill *emerging* needs. Because challenging and worthwhile jobs and meaningful recognition tend to enhance self-esteem, the esteem level presents managers with the greatest opportunity to motivate better performance.

Herzberg's Two-Factor Theory

During the 1950s, Frederick Herzberg proposed a theory of employee motivation based on satisfaction. His theory implied that a satisfied employee is motivated from within to work harder and that a dissatisfied employee is not self-motivated. Herzberg's research uncovered two classes of factors associated with employee satisfaction and dissatisfaction. As a result, his concept has come to be called Herzberg's two-factor theory.

Dissatisfiers and Satisfiers. Herzberg compiled his list of dissatisfiers by asking a sample of about 200 accountants and engineers to describe job situations in which they felt exceptionally bad about their jobs. An analysis of their responses revealed a consistent pattern. Dissatisfaction tended to be associated with complaints about the job context or factors in the immediate work environment.

Herzberg then drew up his list of satisfiers, factors responsible for self-motivation, by asking the same accountants and engineers to describe job situations in which they had felt exceptionally good about their jobs. Again, a patterned response emerged, but this time different factors were described: the opportunity to experience achievement, receive recognition, work on an interesting job, take responsibility, and experience advancement and growth. Herzberg observed that these satisfiers centered on the nature of the task itself. Employees appeared to be motivated by *job content*—that is, by what they actually did all day long. Consequently, Herzberg concluded that enriched jobs were the key to self-motivation. The work itself—not pay, supervision, or some other environmental factor—was the key to satisfaction and motivation.

Implications of Herzberg's Theory. By insisting that satisfaction is not the opposite of dissatisfaction, Herzberg encouraged managers to think carefully about what actually motivates employees. According to Herzberg, "the opposite of job satisfaction is not job dissatisfaction, but rather *no* job satisfaction; and similarly, the opposite of job dissatisfaction is not job satisfaction, but *no* dissatisfaction." Rather, the dissatisfaction-satisfaction continuum contains a zero midpoint at which both dissatisfaction and satisfaction are absent. An employee stuck on this midpoint, though not dissatisfied with pay and working conditions, is not particularly motivated to work hard because the job itself lacks challenge. Herzberg believes that the most managers can hope for when attempting to motivate employees with pay, status, working conditions, and other contextual factors is to reach the zero midpoint. But the elimination of dissatisfaction is not the same as truly motivating an employee. To satisfy and motivate employees, an additional element is required: meaningful, interesting, and challenging work. Herzberg believed that money is a weak motivational tool because, at best, it can only eliminate dissatisfaction.

Like Maslow, Herzberg triggered lively debate among motivation theorists. His assumption that job performance improves as satisfaction increases has been criticized for its weak empirical basis. For example, one researcher, after reviewing 20 studies that tested this notion, concluded that the relationship, though positive, was too weak to have any theoretical or practical significance. Others have found that one person's dissatisfier may be another's satisfier (for example, money). Nonetheless, Herzberg made a useful contribution to motivation theory by emphasizing the motivating potential of enriched work. (Job enrichment is discussed in detail in the next section.)

Expectancy Theory

Both Maslow's and Herzberg's theories have been criticized for making unsubstantiated generalizations about what motivates people. Practical experience shows that people are motivated by lots of different things. Fortunately, expectancy theory, based largely on Victor H. Vroom's 1964 classic *Work and Motivation,* effectively deals with the highly personalized rational choices individuals make when faced with the prospect of having to work to achieve rewards. Individual perception, though secondary in the Maslow and Herzberg models, is central to expectancy theory. Accordingly, **expectancy theory** is a motivation model based on the assumption that motivational strength is determined by perceived probabilities of success. The term **expectancy** refers to the subjective probability (or expectation) that one thing will lead to another. Work-related expectations, like all other expectations, are shaped by ongoing personal experience. For instance, an employee's expectation of a raise, diminished after being turned down, later rebounds when the supervisor indicates a willingness to reconsider the matter.

expectancy theory
Model that assumes motivational strength is determined by perceived probabilities of success

expectancy One's belief or expectation that one thing will lead to another

A Basic Expectancy Model. Although Vroom and other expectancy theorists developed their models in somewhat complex mathematical terms, the descriptive model in Figure 10.3 is helpful for basic understanding. In this model, one's motivational strength increases as one's perceived effort-performance and performance-reward probabilities increase. All this is not as complicated as it sounds. For example, estimate your motivation to study if you expect to do poorly on a quiz no matter how hard you study (low effort-performance probability) and you know the quiz will not be graded (low performance-reward probability). Now contrast that estimate with your motivation to study if you believe that you can do well on the quiz with minimal study (high effort-performance probability) and that by doing well on the quiz your course grade will significantly improve (high performance-reward probability). Like students, employees are motivated to expend effort when they believe it will ultimately lead to rewards they themselves value. This expectancy approach not only appeals strongly to common sense; it also has received encouraging empirical support from researchers.

FIGURE 10.3
A Basic Expectancy Model

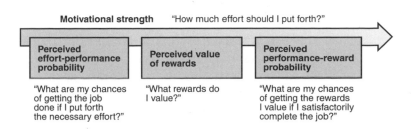

MOTIVATING JOB PERFORMANCE 285

Relevance of Expectancy Theory for Managers. According to expectancy theory, effort→performance→reward expectations determine whether motivation will be high or low. Although these expectations are in the mind of the employee, they can be influenced by managerial action and organizational experience. Training, combined with challenging but realistic objectives, helps give people the idea they can get the job done if they put forth the necessary effort. But perceived effort-performance probabilities are only half the battle. Listening skills enable managers to discover each individual's perceived performance-reward probabilities. Employees tend to work harder when they believe they have a goad chance of getting *personally meaningful* rewards. Both sets of expectations require managerial attention. Each is a potential barrier to work motivation.

Goal-Setting Theory

Think of the three or four most successful people you know personally. Their success may have come via business or professional achievement, politics, athletics, or community service. Chances are they got where they are today by being goal-oriented. In other words, they committed themselves to (and achieved) progressively more challenging goals in their professional and personal affairs. A prime example is Noël Forgeard, who has helped put France-based Airbus on an equal footing with Boeing in the commercial airliner business. According to one of his former colleagues:

> He appears low-key, but can be very tough, and when he has set a goal, nothing can distract him from it. He has an impressive ability to set priorities, to focus on his goals, and then set up a very strong team to achieve those goals.

Biographies and autobiographies of successful people in all walks of life generally attest to the virtues of goal setting. Accordingly, goal setting is acknowledged today as a respected and useful motivation theory.

goal setting Process of improving performance with objectives, dead-lines, or quality standards

Within an organizational context, **goal setting** is the process of improving individual or group job performance with formally stated objectives, deadlines, or quality standards. Management by objectives (MBO) is a specific application of goal setting that advocates participative and measurable objectives. Also, recall how managers tend to use the terms *goal* and *objective* interchangeably.

A General Goal-Setting Model. Thanks to motivation researchers such as Edwin A. Locke, there is a comprehensive body of knowledge about goal setting. Goal setting has been researched more rigorously than the three motivation theories just discussed. Important lessons from goal-setting theory and research are incorporated in the general model in Figure 10.4. This model shows how properly conceived goals trigger a motivational process that improves performance. Let us explore the key components of this goal-setting model.

Personal Ownership of Challenging Goals. MBO and writing good objectives stressed how goal effectiveness is enhanced by *specificity, difficulty,* and *participation*. Measurable and challenging goals encourage an individual or group to stretch while trying to attain progressively more difficult levels of achievement. For instance, parents who are paying a college student's tuition and expenses are

FIGURE 10.4
A Model of How Goals Can
Improve Performance

advised to specify a challenging grade point goal rather than to simply tell their son or daughter, "Just do your best." Otherwise, the student could show up at the end of the semester with two Cs and three Ds, saying, "Well, I did my best!" It is important to note that goals need to be difficult enough to be challenging but not impossible. Impossible goals hamper performance; they are a handy excuse for not even trying.

Participation in the goal-setting process gives the individual *personal owner-ship*. From the employee's viewpoint, it is "something I helped develop, not just my boss's wild idea." Feedback on performance operates in concert with well-conceived goals. Feedback lets the person or group know if things are on track or if corrective action is required to reach the goal. An otherwise excellent goal-setting program can be compromised by lack of timely and relevant feedback from managers. Researchers have documented the motivational value of matching *specific goals* with *equally specific feedback*. Sam Walton, the founder of Wal-Mart, was a master of blending goals and feedback. For example, consider this exchange between Sam Walton and an employee during one of his regular visits:

> A manager rushes up with an associate in tow.
> "Mr. Walton, I want you to meet Renee. She runs one of the top ten pet depart-ments in the country."
> "Well, Renee, bless your heart. What percentage of the store [sales] are you doing?"
> "Last year it was 3.1 percent," Renee says "but this year I'm trying for 3.3 percent."
> "Well, Renee, that's amazing," says Sam. "You know our average pet depart-ment only does about 2.4 percent. Keep up the great work."

How Do Goals Actually Motivate? Goal-setting researchers say goals perform a motivational function by doing the four things listed in the center of Figure 10.4. First, a goal is an exercise in selective perception because it directs one's attention to a specific target. Second, a goal encourages one to exert *effort* toward achieving something specific. Third, because a challenging goal requires sustained or re-peated effort, it encourages *persistence*. Fourth, because a goal creates the problem of bridging the gap between actual and desired, it fosters the creation of *strategies and action plans*. Consider, for example, how all these motivational components were activated by the following program at Marriott's hotel chain.

For years, Marriott's room-service business didn't live up to its potential. But after initiating a 15-minute-delivery guarantee for breakfast in 1985, Marriott's breakfast business—the biggest portion of its room-service revenue—jumped 25 percent. [Hotel guests got their breakfast free if it was delivered late.] Marriott got employees to devise ways to deliver the meals on time, including having deliverers carry walkie-talkies so they [could] receive instructions more quickly.

Marriott's goal, increased room-service revenue, was the focal point for this program. In effect, the service-guarantee program told Marriott employees that prompt room service was important, and they rose to the challenge with persistent and creative effort. Clear, reasonable, and challenging goals, reinforced by specific feedback and meaningful rewards, are indeed a powerful motivational tool.

Practical Implications of Goal-Setting Theory. Because the model in Figure 10.4 is a generic one, the performance environment may range from athletics to academics to the workplace. The motivational mechanics of goal setting are the same, regardless of the targeted performance. If you learn to be an effective goal setter in school, that ability will serve you faithfully throughout life.

Anyone tempted to go through life without goals should remember the smiling Cheshire Cat's good advice to Alice when she asked him to help her find her way through Wonderland:

"Would you tell me, please, which way I ought to walk from here?"
"That depends a good deal on where you want to get to," replied the Cat.
"I don't much care where—" said Alice.
"Then it doesn't matter which way you walk," said the Cat.
"—so long as I get somewhere," Alice added as an explanation.
"Oh, you're sure to do that," said the Cat, "if you only walk long enough."

Motivation Through Job Design

job design Creating task responsibilities based upon strategy, technology, and structure

A job serves two separate but related functions. It is a productive unit for the organization and a career unit for the individual. Thus **job design,** the delineation of task responsibilities as dictated by organizational strategy, technology, and structure, is a key determinant of individual motivation and ultimately of organizational success. Considering that the average adult spends about half of his or her waking life at work, jobs are a central feature of modern existence. A challenging and interesting job can add zest and meaning to one's life. Boring and tedious jobs, on the other hand, can become a serious threat to one's motivation to work hard, not to mention the effect on one's physical and mental health. Concern about uneven productivity growth, product quality, and declining employee satisfaction has persuaded managers to consider two job design strategies.

Strategy One: Fitting People to Jobs

For technological or economic reasons, work sometimes must be divided into routine and repetitive tasks. Imagine, for example, doing Paula Villalta's job at Chung's Gourmet Foods in Houston, Texas:

Quickly wrapping one egg roll after another, Paula Villalta becomes rapt herself.

Her fingers move with astonishing speed, placing a glutinous vegetable mixture on a small sheet of pastry before rolling it closed in one smooth stroke. But the secret to her swiftness lies not just in her nimble hands.

The real key, says Ms. Villalta, pointing to her head, is staying completely focused throughout an eight-hour shift. . . .

The results are stunning. The average wrapper at Chung's Gourmet churns out about 4,000 shrimp, pork, vegetable, or chicken egg rolls per shift. Ms. Villalta typically tops 6,000.

In routine-task situations, steps can be taken to avoid chronic dissatisfaction and bolster motivation. Three proven alternatives include realistic job previews, job rotation, and limited exposure. Each involves adjusting the person rather than the job in the person-job equation. Hence, each entails creating a more compatible fit between an individual and a routine or fragmented job. (In line with this approach is the use of mentally disadvantaged workers often in sheltered workshops.)

Realistic Job Previews. Unrealized expectations are a major cause of job dissatisfaction, low motivation, and turnover. Managers commonly create unrealistically high expectations in job applicants to entice them to accept a position. This has proved particularly troublesome with regard to routine tasks. Dissatisfaction too often sets in when lofty expectations are brought down to earth by dull or tedious work. **Realistic job previews** (RJPs), honest explanations of what a job actually entails, have been successful in helping to avoid employee dissatisfaction resulting from unrealized expectations. On-the-job and laboratory research have demonstrated the practical value of giving a realistic preview of both positive and negative aspects to applicants for highly specialized and/or difficult jobs.

A recent statistical analysis of 40 different RJP studies revealed these patterns: fewer dropouts during the recruiting process, lower initial expectations, and lower turnover and higher performance once on the job. The researcher recommended a contingency approach regarding the form and timing of Ribs. *Written* RJPs are better for reducing the dropout rate during the recruiting process, whereas *verbal* RJPs more effectively reduce post-hiring turnover (quitting). "RJPs given just *before* hiring are advisable to reduce attrition [dropouts] from the recruitment process and to reduce . . . turnover, but organizations wishing to improve employee performance should provide RJPs *after* job acceptance, as part realistic socialization effort."

Job Rotation. As the term is used here, **job rotation** involves periodically moving people from one specialized job to another. Such movement prevents stagnation. Other reasons for rotating personnel include compensating for a labor shortage, safety, training, and preventing fatigue. *Carpal tunnel syndrome* and other painful and disabling injuries stemming from repetitive motion tasks can be reduced significantly through job rotation. (The FBI rotates its agents off the drug squad periodically to discourage corruption.) If highly repetitive and routine jobs are unavoidable, job rotation, by introducing a modest degree of novelty, can help prevent boredom and resulting alienation. Of course, a balance needs to be achieved—people should be rotated often enough to fight boredom and injury but not so often that they feel unfairly manipulated or disoriented.

realistic job previews Honest explanations of what a job actually entails

job rotation Moving people from one specialized job to another

Limited Exposure. Another way of coping with the need to staff a highly fragmented and tedious job is to limit the individual's exposure to it. A number of organizations have achieved high productivity among routine-task personnel by allowing them to earn an early quitting time. This technique, called **contingent time off** (CTO) or earned time off, involves establishing a challenging yet fair daily performance standard, or quota, and letting employees go home when it is reached. The following CTO plan was implemented at a large manufacturing plant where the employees were producing about 160 units a day with 10 percent rejects:

> If the group produced at 200 units with three additional good units for each defective unit, then they could leave the work site for the rest of the day. Within a week of implementing CTO intervention, the group was producing 200+ units with an average of 15 percent rejects. These employees, who had formerly put in an 8-hour day, were now working an average of 6.5 hours per day and, importantly, they increased their performance by 25 percent.

Some employees find the opportunity to earn eight hours of pay for six hours of steady effort extremely motivating.

Companies using contingent time off report successful results. Impressive evidence comes from a large-scale survey of 1,598 U.S. companies employing about 10 percent of the civilian workforce. Among nine nontraditional reward systems, "earned time off" ranked only eighth in terms of use (5 percent of the companies). But among those using it, earned time off ranked second in terms of positive impact on job performance—an 85 percent approval rating. Thus, the use of contingent time off has not yet reached its excellent potential as a motivational tool.

Strategy Two: Fitting Jobs to People

The second job-design strategy calls for managers to consider changing the job instead of the person. Two job-design experts have proposed that managers address the question, "How can we achieve a fit between persons and their jobs that fosters *both* high work productivity and a high-quality organizational experience for the people who do the work?" Two techniques for moving in this direction are job enlargement and job enrichment.

Job Enlargement. As used here, **job enlargement** is the process of combining two or more specialized tasks in a work flow sequence into a single job. Aetna used this technique to give some of its office employees a measure of relief from staring at a video display terminal (VDT) all day:

> Aetna Life & Casualty in Hartford . . . reorganized its payroll department to combine ten full-time data-entry jobs with ten jobs that involve paperwork and telephoning. Now nobody in the department spends more than 70 percent of [the] day on a VDT. Morale and productivity have gone up dramatically since the change, says Richard Assunto, Aetna's payroll services manager.

A moderate degree of complexity and novelty can be introduced in this manner. But critics claim that two or more potentially boring tasks do not necessarily make one challenging job. Furthermore, organized labor has criticized job enlargement as a devious ploy for getting more work for the same amount of money. But if pay

contingent time off
Rewarding people with early time off when they get the job done

job enlargement
Combining two or more specialized tasks to increase motivation

and performance are kept in balance, boredom and alienation can be pushed aside a bit by job enlargement.

Job Enrichment. In general terms, **job enrichment** is redesigning a job to increase its motivating potential. Job enrichment increases the challenge of one's work by reversing the trend toward greater specialization. Unlike job enlargement, which merely combines equally simple tasks, job enrichment builds more complexity and depth into jobs by introducing planning and decision-making responsibility normally carried out at higher levels. Thus, enriched jobs are said to be *vertically loaded,* whereas enlarged jobs are *horizontally loaded.* Managing an entire project can be immensely challenging and motivating due to vertical job loading. Scott Nichols, a home construction foreman, had this to say about his job:

> I find it very rewarding. Just building something, creating something, and actually seeing your work. . . . You start with a bare, empty lot with grass growing up and then you build a house. A lot of times you'll build a house for a family, and you see them move in, that's pretty gratifying. . . . I'm proud of that.

Jobs can be enriched by upgrading five core dimensions of work: (1) skill variety, (2) task identity, (3) task significance, (4) autonomy, and (5) job feedback. Each of these core dimensions deserves a closer look.

- *Skill variety.* The degree to which the job requires a variety of different activities in carrying out the work, involving the use of a number of different skills and talents of the person

- *Task identity.* The degree to which the job requires completion of a "whole" and identifiable piece of work; that is, doing a job from beginning to end with a visible outcome

- *Task significance.* The degree to which the job has a substantial impact on the lives of other people, whether those people are in the immediate organization or in the world at large

- *Autonomy.* The degree to which the job provides substantial freedom, independence, and discretion to the individual in scheduling the work and in determining the procedures to be used in carrying it out

- *Job feedback.* The degree to which carrying out the work activities required by the job provides the individual with direct and clear information about the effectiveness of his or her performance

It is important to note that not all employees will respond favorably to enriched jobs. Personal traits and motives influence the connection between core job characteristics and desired outcomes. Only those with the necessary knowledge and skills plus a desire for personal growth will be motivated by enriched work. Furthermore, in keeping with Herzberg's two-factor theory, dissatisfaction with factors such as pay, physical working conditions, or supervision can neutralize enrichment efforts. Researchers have reported that fear of failure, lack of confidence, and lack of trust in management's intentions can stand in the way of effective job enrichment. But job enrichment can and does work when it is carefully thought out, when management is committed to its long-term success, and when employees desire additional challenge.

Motivation Through Rewards

rewards Material and psychological payoffs for working

All workers, including volunteers who donate their time to worthy causes, expect to be rewarded in some way for their contributions. **Rewards** may be defined broadly as the material and psychological payoffs for performing tasks in the workplace. Managers have found that job performance and satisfaction can be improved by properly administered rewards. Today, rewards vary greatly in both time and scope, depending on one's employer and geographical location. In fact, a popular book among managers is titled *1001 Ways to Reward Employees*.

In this section, we distinguish between extrinsic and intrinsic rewards, review alternative employee compensation plans, and discuss the effective management of extrinsic rewards.

Extrinsic versus Intrinsic Rewards

extrinsic rewards Payoffs, such as money, that are granted by others

intrinsic rewards Self-granted and internally experienced payoffs, such as feeling of accomplishment

There are two different categories of rewards. **Extrinsic rewards** are payoffs granted to the individual by other people. Examples include money, employee benefits, promotions, recognition, status symbols, and praise. The second category is called **intrinsic rewards,** which are self-granted and internally experienced payoffs. Among intrinsic rewards are a sense of accomplishment, self-esteem, and self-actualization. Usually, on-the-job extrinsic and intrinsic rewards are intermingled. For instance, employees often experience a psychological boost when they complete a big project in addition to reaping material benefits. Harvard Business School's Abraham Zaleznik recently offered this perspective:

> I think a paycheck buys you a baseline level of performance. But one thing that makes a good leader is the ability to offer people intrinsic rewards, the tremendous lift that comes from being aware of one's own talents and wanting to maximize them.

Employee Compensation

Compensation deserves special attention at this point because money is the universal extrinsic reward. Moreover, since "labor costs are about two-thirds of total business expenses," compensation practices need to be effective and efficient. Employee compensation is a complex area fraught with legal and tax implications. Although an exhaustive treatment of employee compensation plans is beyond our present purpose, we can identify major types. Table 10.1 lists and briefly describes ten different pay plans. Two are nonincentive plans, seven qualify as incentive plans, and one plan is in a category of its own. Each type of pay plan has advantages and disadvantages. Therefore, there is no single best plan suitable for all employees. Indeed, two experts at the U.S. Bureau of Labor Statistics say the key words in compensation for the next 25 years will be "flexible" and "varied." A diverse workforce will demand an equally diverse array of compensation plans.

TABLE 10.1 Guide to Employee Compensation Plans

Pay Plan	Description/Calculation	Main Advantage	Main Disadvantage
Nonincentive			
Hourly wage	Fixed amount per hour worked	Time is easier to measure than performance	Little or no incentive to work hard
Annual salary	Contractual amount per year	Easy to administer	Little or no incentive to work hard
Incentive			
Piece rate	Fixed amount per unit of output	Pay tied directly to personal output abuses	Negative association with sweatshops and rate-cutting
Sales commission	Fixed percentage of revenue	Pay tied directly to personal volume of business other employees	Morale problem when sales personnel earn more than
Merit pay	Bonus granted for out-standing performance	Gives salaried employees incentive to work harder	Fairness issue raised when tied to subjective appraisals
Profit sharing	Distribution of specified percentage of bottom-line profits	Individual has a personal stake in firm's profitability	Profits affected by more than just performance (for example, by prices and competition)
Gain sharing	Distribution of specified percentage of productivity gains and/or cost savings	Encourages employees to work harder *and* smarter	Calculations can get cumbersome
Pay-for-knowledge	Salary or wage rates tied to degrees earned or skills mastered	Encourages lifelong learning	Tends to inflate training and labor costs
Stock options	Selected employees earn to acquire firm's stock free or at a discount	Gives individual a personal stake in firm's financial performance	Can be resented by ineligible personnel; morale lied to stock price
Other			
Cafeteria compensation (life-cycle benefits)	Employee selects personal mix of benefits from an array of options	Tailored benefits package fits individual needs	Can be costly to administer

Improving Performance with Extrinsic Rewards

Extrinsic rewards, if they are to motivate job performance effectively, need to be administered in ways that (1) satisfy operative needs, (2) foster positive expecta-tions, (3) ensure equitable distribution, and (4) reward results. Let us see how these four criteria can he met relative to the ten different pay plans in Table 10.1.

Rewards Must Satisfy Individual Needs. Whether it is a pay raise or a pat on the back, a reward has no motivational impact unless it satisfies an operative need.

Not all people need the same things, and one person may need different things at different times. Money is a powerful motivator for those who seek security through material wealth. But the promise of more money may mean little to a financially secure person who seeks ego gratification from challenging work. People's needs concerning when and how they want to be paid also vary.

Because cafeteria compensation is rather special and particularly promising, we shall examine it more closely. **Cafeteria compensation** (also called life-cycle benefits) is a plan that allows each employee to determine the makeup of his or her benefit package. Because today's nonwage benefits are a significant portion of total compensation, the motivating potential of such a privilege can be sizable.

> Under these plans, employer provide minimal "core" coverage in life and health insurance, vacations and pensions. The employee buys additional benefits to suit [his or her] own needs, rising credit based on salary service, and age.
>
> The elderly bachelor, for instance, may pass up the maternity coverage he would receive, willy-nilly under conventional plans and "buy" additional pension contributions instead. The mother whose children are covered by her husband's employee health insurance policy may choose legal and dental are insurance instead.

Although some organizations have balked at installing cafeteria compensation because of added administrative expense, the number of programs in effect in the United States has grown steadily. Cafeteria compensation enhances employee satisfaction, according to at least one study, and represents a revolutionary step toward fitting rewards to people, rather than vice versa.

Employees Must Believe Effort Will Lead to Reward. According to expectancy theory, an employee will not strive for an attractive reward unless it is perceived as being attainable. For example, the promise of an expenses-paid trip to Hawaii for the leading salesperson will prompt additional efforts at sales only among those who feel they have a decent chance of winning. Those who believe they have little chance of winning will not be motivated to try any harder than usual. Incentive pay plans, especially merit pay, profit sharing, gain sharing, and stock options, need to be designed and communicated in a way that will foster believable effort-reward linkages.

Rewards Must Be Equitable. Something is equitable if people perceive it to be fair and just. Each of us carries in our head a pair of scales upon which we weigh equity. Figure 10.5 shows one scale for *personal equity* and another for *social equity*. The personal equity scale tests the relationship between effort expended and rewards received. The social equity scale, in contrast, compares our own effort-reward ratio with that of someone else in the same situation. We are motivated to seek personal and social equity and to avoid inequity. An interesting aspect of research on this topic has demonstrated that inequity is perceived by those who are *overpaid* as well as by those who are underpaid. Since perceived inequity is associated with feelings of dissatisfaction and anger, jealousy, or guilt, inequitable reward schemes tend to be counterproductive and are ethically questionable. Record-setting executive pay in recent years of painful downsizings and massive layoffs has been roundly criticized as inequitable and unfair.

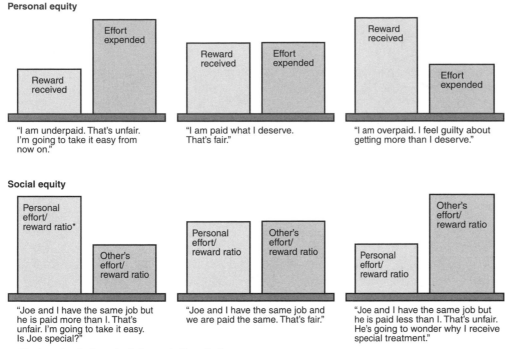

Personal equity

Reward received | Effort expended
"I am underpaid. That's unfair. I'm going to take it easy from now on."

Reward received | Effort expended
"I am paid what I deserve. That's fair."

Reward received | Effort expended
"I am overpaid. I feel guilty about getting more than I deserve."

Social equity

Personal effort/ reward ratio* | Other's effort/ reward ratio
"Joe and I have the same job but he is paid more than I. That's unfair. I'm going to take it easy. Is Joe special?"

Personal effort/ reward ratio | Other's effort/ reward ratio
"Joe and I have the same job and we are paid the same. That's fair."

Personal effort/ reward ratio | Other's effort/ reward ratio
"Joe and I have the same job but he is paid less than I. That's unfair. He's going to wonder why I receive special treatment."

* The lower the effort/reward ratio, the greater the motivation.

FIGURE 10.5
Personal and Social Equity

Rewards Must Be Linked to Performance. Ideally, there should be an if-then relationship between task performance and extrinsic rewards. Traditional hourly wage and annual salary pay plans are weak in this regard. They do little more than reward the person for showing up at work. Managers can strengthen motivation to work by making sure that those who give a little extra get a little extra. In addition to piece-rate and sales-commission plans, merit pay, profit sharing, gain sharing, and stock option plans are popular ways of linking pay and performance. The concept of team-based incentive pay as a way of rewarding teamwork and cooperation has been slow to take hold in the United States for two reasons: (1) it goes against the grain of an individualistic culture; and (2) poorly conceived and administered plans have given team-based pay a bad reputation.

All incentive pay plans should be carefully conceived because undesirable behavior may inadvertently be encouraged. Consider, for example, what the head of Nucor Corporation, a successful minimill steel company, had to say about his firm's bonus system:

> [Nucor's] bonus system . . . is very tough. If you're late even five minutes, you lose your bonus for the day. If you're late more than 30 minutes, or you're absent because of sickness or anything else, you lose your bonus for the week. Now we do have what we call four "forgiveness" days during the year when you can be sick or you have to close on a house or your wife is having a baby. But only four. We have a melter, Phil Johnson, down in Darlington, and one of the workers

came in one day and said that Phil had been in an automobile accident and was sitting beside his car off of Route 52, holding his head. So the foreman asked why didn't you stop and help him?" And the guy said, "And lose my bonus?"

Like goals, incentive plans foster selective perception. Consequently, managers need to make sure goals and incentives point people in ethical directions.

Motivation Through Employee Participation

participative management Empowering employees to assume greater control of the workplace

While noting that the term *participation* has become a "stewpot" into which every conceivable kind of management fad has been tossed, one management scholar has helpfully identified four key areas of participative management. Employees may participate in (1) setting goals, (2) making decisions, (3) solving problems, and (4) designing and implementing organizational changes. Thus, **participative management** is defined as the process of empowering employees to assume greater control of the workplace. When personally and meaningfully involved, above and beyond just doing assigned tasks, employees are said to be more motivated and productive. In fact, a recent study of 164 New Zealand companies with at least 100 employees found lower employee turnover and higher organizational productivity among firms using participative management practices.

This section focuses on three approaches to participation. They are quality control circles, open-book management, and self-managed teams. After taking a closer look at each, we consider four keys to successful employee participation programs.

Quality Control Circles

quality control circles Voluntary problem-solving groups committed to improving quality and reducing costs

Developed in Japan during the early 1960s, this innovation took the U.S. industrial scene by storm during the late 1970s and early 1980s. Today, thousands of quality control circles can be found in hundreds of North American and European companies. **Quality control circles**, commonly referred to as QC circles or simply quality circles, are voluntary problem-solving groups of five to ten employees from the same work area who meet regularly to discuss quality improvement and ways to reduce costs. A weekly one-hour meeting, during company time, is common practice. By relying on *voluntary* participation, QC circles attempt to tap the creative potential every employee possesses. Although QC circles do not work in every situation, benefits such as direct cost savings, improved worker-management relations, and greater individual commitment have been reported.

QC circles should be introduced in evolutionary fashion rather than by management edict. Training, supportive supervision, and team building are all part of this evolutionary development. The idea is to give those who work day in and day out at a specific job the tools, group support, and opportunity to have a say in nipping quality problems in the bud. Each QC circle is responsible not only for recommending solutions but also for actually implementing and evaluating those solutions. According to one observer, "The invisible force behind the success of QC's is its ability to bring the psychological principles of Maslow, McGregor, and Herzberg into the workplace through a structured process."

Open-Book Management

open-book management Sharing key financial data and profits with employees who are trained and empowered

Open-book management (OBM) involves "opening a company's financial statements to all employees and providing the education that will enable them to understand how the company makes money and how their actions affect its success and bottom line." Clearly, this is a bold break from traditional management practice. Many companies claim to practice OBM, but few actually do. Why? OBM asks managers to correct three typical shortcomings by (1) displaying a high degree of trust in employees, (2) having a deep and unwavering commitment to employee training, and (3) being patient when waiting for results.

A four-step approach to OBM is displayed in Figure 10.6. The STEP acronym stands for *share, teach, empower,* and *pay.* Skipping or inadequately performing a step virtually guarantees failure. A systematic process is needed. Experts tell us it takes at least two complete budget cycles (typically two years) to see positive results. In step 1, employees are exposed to eye-catching public displays of key financial data. Sales, expense, and profit data for both the organization and relevant business units are shared in hallways, cafeterias, and on internal Web sites. Of course, without step 2, step 1 would be meaningless. Comprehensive, ongoing training gives all employees a working knowledge of the firm's business model. Here is what Jelly Belly Candy Co. does:

> Through Jelly Belly University, employees from the upper-most management level to administrative support personnel learn the art of candy making, evaluate the results and conduct product evaluations, production scheduling and inventory control.

Thus, Jelly Belly's employees not only learn how to make great jelly beans; they also learn what it takes to make a profit in the process. In OBM companies, finance specialists teach other employees how to read and interpret basic financial documents such as profit-loss statements. Entertaining and instructive business board

FIGURE 10.6

The Four S.T.E.P. Approach to Open-Book Management

SOURCE: Based on Raj Aggarwal and Betty J. Simkins, "Open Book Management—Optimizing Human Capital," *Business Horizons,* 44 (September–October 2001): 5–13.

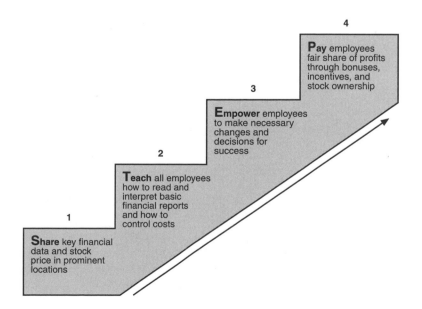

1 **Share** key financial data and stock price in prominent locations

2 **Teach** all employees how to read and interpret basic financial reports and how to control costs

3 **Empower** employees to make necessary changes and decisions for success

4 **Pay** employees fair share of profits through bonuses, incentives, and stock ownership

games and computer simulations have proved effective. Remedial education is provided when needed. Armed with knowledge about the company's workings and financial health, employees are ready for step 3. Managers find it easier to trust empowered employees to make important decisions when the employees are adequately prepared. In step 4, employees enjoy the fruits of their efforts by sharing profits and/or receiving bonuses and incentive compensation. There is no magic to OBM. It simply involves doing *important* things in the *right* way.

Self-Managed Teams

According to the logic of this comprehensive approach to participation, self-management is the best management because it taps people's full potential. Advocates say self-management fosters creativity, motivation, and productivity. **Self-managed teams,** also known as autonomous work groups or high-performance work teams, take on traditional managerial tasks as part of their normal work routine. They can have anywhere from 5 to more than 30 members, depending on the job. Unlike QC circles, which are staffed with volunteers, employees are assigned to self-managed teams. Cross-trained team members typically rotate jobs as they turn out a complete product or service. Any supervision tends to be minimal, with managers acting more as *facilitators* than as order givers.

Vertically Loaded Jobs. In the language of job enrichment, team members' jobs are vertically loaded. This means nonmanagerial team members assume duties traditionally performed by managers. But specifically which duties? A survey of industry practices in *Training* magazine answered this question.

General Mills has extended the idea of self-managed teams to the point that the night shift in its cereal plant in Lodi, California, runs with no managers at all. Other progressive organizations such as General Foods, Texas Instruments, Corning, General Electric, Boeing, Procter & Gamble, and Volvo have operations built around self-managed teams. *Fortune* quoted the head of Texas Instruments as saying, "No matter what your business, these teams are the wave of the future."

Managerial Resistance. Not surprisingly, managerial resistance is the number one barrier to self-managed teams. More than anything else, self-managed teams represent change, and lots of it.

> Adopting the team approach is no small matter; it means wiping out tiers of managers and tearing down bureaucratic barriers between departments. Yet companies are willing to undertake such radical changes to gain workers' knowledge and commitment—along with productivity gains that exceed 30 percent in some cases.

Traditional authoritarian supervisors view autonomous teams as a threat to their authority and job security. For this reason, *new* facilities built around the concept of self-managed teams, so-called greenfield sites, tend to fare better than reworked existing operations.

Managers who take the long view and switch to self-managed teams are finding it well worth the investment of time and money. Self-managed teams even show early promise of boosting productivity in the huge service sector.

Keys to Successful Employee Participation Programs

According to researchers, four factors build the *employee* support necessary for any sort of participation program to work:

1. A profit-sharing or gain-sharing plan
2. A long-term employment relationship with good job security
3. A concerted effort to build and maintain group cohesiveness
4. Protection of the individual employee's rights

Working in combination, these factors help explain motivational success stories such as that of Norsk Hydro in the chapter Closing Case.

It should he clear by now that participative management involves more than simply announcing a new program, such as open-book management. To make sure a supportive climate exists, a good deal of background work often needs to be done. This is particularly important in view of the conclusion drawn by researchers who analyzed 41 participative management studies:

> Participation has . . . [a positive] effect on both satisfaction and productivity and its effect on satisfaction is somewhat stronger than its effect on productivity . . . Our analysis indicates specific organizational factors that may enhance or constrain the effect of participation. For example, there is evidence that a participative climate has a more substantial effect on workers' satisfaction than participation in specific decisions.

In the end, effective participative management is as much a managerial attitude about sharing power as it is a specific set of practices. In some European countries, such as Germany, the supportive climate is reinforced by government-mandated participative management.

Other Motivation Techniques for a Diverse Workforce

Workforce diversity has made "flexibility" a must for managers today. This chapter concludes with a look at ways of accommodating emerging employee needs. For example, a big concern these days involves striking a proper life balance between work and leisure. By meeting these needs in creative ways, such as flexible work schedules, family support services, wellness programs, and sabbaticals, managers hope to enhance motivation and job performance.

Flexible Work Schedules

flextime Allows employees to choose their own arrival and departure times within specified limits

The standard 8 A.M. to 5 P.M., 40-hour workweek has come under fire as dual-income families, single parents, and others attempt to juggle hectic schedules. Taking its place is **flextime**, a work-scheduling plan that allows employees to determine their own arrival and departure times within specific limits. All employees must be present during a fixed core time (see the center portion of Figure 10.7). If

FIGURE 10.7

Flextime in Action

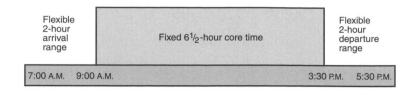

an eight-hour day is required, as in Figure 10.7, an early bird can put in the required eight hours by arriving at 7:00 A.M., taking half an hour for lunch, and departing at 3:30 P.M. Alternatively, a late starter can come in at 9:00 A.M. and leave at 5:30 P.M. When given the choice of "flexible work hours" versus an "opportunity to advance" in a recent survey, 58 percent of the women opted for flexible hours. Forty-three percent of the men chose that option. The growing use of flextime and other alternative work arrangements, such as telecommuting, is partly due to employer self-interest. Employers want to cut the cost of unscheduled absenteeism. A 2001 survey found the average annual cost for each employee's unscheduled absenteeism (68 percent of which was not for illness) to be $775. Flextime can also be used to accommodate the special needs of disabled employees.

Benefits. In addition to many anecdotal reports citing the benefits of flextime, research studies have uncovered promising evidence. Flextime has several documented benefits:

- Better employee-supervisor relations

- Reduced absenteeism

- Selective positive impact on job performance (e.g., a 24 percent improvement for computer programmers over a two-year period but no effect on the performance of data-entry worker)

Flextime, though very popular among employees because of the degree of freedom it brings, is not appropriate for all situations. Problems reported by adopters include greater administrative expense, supervisory resistance, and inadequate coverage of jobs.

Alternatives. Other work-scheduling innovations include *compressed workweeks* (40 or more hours in fewer than five days) and *permanent part-time* (workweeks with fewer than 40 hours). *Job sharing* (complementary scheduling that allows two or more part-timers to share a single full-time job), yet another work-scheduling innovation, is growing in popularity among employers of working parents.

A recent European study suggests employees may be paying a price for the freedom of flexible work scheduling. Compared with a control group of employees on fixed schedules, employees with compressed workweeks, rotating shifts, irregular schedules, and part-time jobs experienced significantly more health, psychological, and sleeping problems.

Family Support Services

With dual-income families and single parents caught between obligations to family and the job, both the government and companies are coming to the rescue. On the federal government front, the Family and Medical Leave Act (FMLA) took effect in the United States in 1993 after years of political debate. FMLA has significant holes and limitations. First, only companies with 50 or more employees are required to comply with the law mandating up to 12 weeks of unpaid leave per year for family events such as births, adoptions, or sickness. Because the vast majority of U.S. businesses (95 percent) employ fewer than 50 people, millions of working Americans (43 percent) are left unprotected by FMLA. Second, employees can be required by their employer to exhaust their sick leave and vacation allotments before taking FMLA leave. Fortunately, states and businesses can plug some of the holes in FMLA.

At least 35 states have equivalent or more generous parental and family leave laws. Eligible employees can choose the more generous option when both federal and state laws apply. Meanwhile, on the business front, a few companies go so far as to grant paid parental and family sickness leaves. Many other exciting corporate family support service initiatives are cropping up. A growing but still very small number of companies in the United States (11 percent in 1999) provide on-site day-care facilities. About 15 percent provide emergency child-care services. Eldercare centers, for employees' elderly relatives who cannot be left home alone, are starting to appear. Some companies have banded together to form reduced-rate day-care cooperatives for their employees. Emergency child care is a welcome corporate benefit for working parents.

Wellness Programs

Stress and burnout are inevitable consequences of modern work life. Family-versus-work conflict, long hours, overload, hectic schedules, deadlines, frequent business travel, and accumulated work-place irritations are taking their toll. Progressive companies are coming to the rescue with *wellness programs* featuring a wide range of offerings. Among them are stress reduction, healthy eating and living clinics, quit-smoking and weight-loss programs, exercise facilities, massage breaks, behavioral health counseling, and health screenings. The ultimate objective is to help employees achieve a sustainable balance between their personal lives and work lives, with win-win benefits all around.

> For example, Citibank experienced decreases in health risks and savings of between $4.36 and $4.73 for each dollar spent on its health education and awareness program. In another example, Glaxo Wellcome's health promotion program saved the company an estimated $1 million in 1998, and has reduced medical leave of absence by 20,000 workdays since 1996.

Sabbaticals

Several companies, including IBM, Wells Fargo, 3Com, and McDonalds, give selected employees paid sabbaticals after a certain number of years of service. Two to six months of paid time off gives the employee time for family, recreation, and travel. Intel offers an eight-week break with pay every seven years. The idea is to refresh long-term employees and hopefully bolster their motivation and loyalty in the process.

Summary

1. Maslow's five-level needs hierarchy, although empirically criticized, makes it clear to managers that people are motivated by emerging rather than fulfilled needs. Assuming that job satisfaction and performance are positively related, Herzberg believes that the most that wages and working conditions can do is eliminate sources of dissatisfaction. According to Herzberg, the key to true satisfaction, and hence motivation, is an enriched job that provides an opportunity for achievement, responsibility, and personal growth. Expectancy theory is based on the idea that the strength of one's motivation to work is the product of perceived probabilities of acquiring personally valued rewards. Both effort-performance and performance-reward probabilities are important to expectancy theory.

2. Goals can be an effective motivational tool when they are specific, difficult, participatively set, and accompanied by feedback on performance. Goals motivate performance by directing attention, encouraging effort and persistence, and prompting goal-attainment strategies and action plans.

3. Managers can counteract the boredom associated with routine-task jobs through realistic job previews, job rotation, and limited exposure. This third alternative involves letting employees earn early time off.

4. Job enrichment vertically loads jobs to meet individual needs for meaningfulness, responsibility, and knowledge of results. Personal desire for growth and a supportive climate must exist for job enrichment to be successful.

5. Both extrinsic (externally granted) and intrinsic (self-granted) rewards, when properly administered, can have a positive impact on performance and satisfaction. There is no single best employee compensation plan. A flexible and varied approach to compensation will be necessary in the coming years because of workforce diversity. The following rules can help managers maximize the motivational impact of extrinsic rewards: (1) rewards must satisfy individual needs, (2) one must believe that effort will lead to reward, (3) rewards must be equitable, and (4) rewards must be linked to performance. Gain-sharing plans have great motivational potential because they emphasize participation and link pay to actual productivity.

6. Participative management programs foster direct employee involvement in one or more of the following areas: goal setting, decision making, problem solving, and change implementation. Quality control circles are teams of volunteers who meet regularly on company time to discuss ways to improve product/service quality. The S.T.E.P. model of open-book management encourages employee participation when managers (1) *share* key financial data with all employees, (2) *teach* employees how to interpret financial statements and control costs, (3) *empower* employees to make improvements and decisions, and (4) *pay* a fair share of profits to employees. Employees assigned to self-managed teams participate by taking on tasks traditionally performed by management. Profit sharing or gain sharing, job security, cohesiveness, and protection of employee rights are keys to building crucial employee support for participation programs.

7. A diverse workforce requires diverse motivational techniques. Flex-time, a flexible work-scheduling scheme that allows employees to choose their own arrival and departure times, has been effective in improving employee-

supervisor relations while reducing absenteeism. Employers are increasingly providing family support services such as child care, elder care, parental leaves, and adoption benefits. Employee wellness programs and sabbaticals are offered by some companies.

◎ Hands-On Exercise

Quality-of-Work-Life Survey

Instructions

Think of your present job, or one you had in the past, and circle one number for each of the following items. Add the circled numbers to get a total quality-of-work-life score. Alternatively, you can use this survey to interview another job-holder to determine his or her quality of work life. (*Note:* This survey is for instructional purposes only because it has not been scientifically validated.)

General Job Satisfaction

■ Most of the time, my job satisfaction is

Very low   *Very high*

1 · · · · · · · 2 · · · · · · · 3 · · · · · · · 4 · · · · · · · 5 · · · · · · · 6 · · · · · · · 7

Quality of Supervision

■ The person I report to respects me, listens to me, and supports me.

Never   *Always*

1 · · · · · · · 2 · · · · · · · 3 · · · · · · · 4 · · · · · · · 5 · · · · · · · 6 · · · · · · · 7

Quality of Communication

■ The organization keeps me well informed about its mission and pending changes.

Never   *Always*

1 · · · · · · · 2 · · · · · · · 3 · · · · · · · 4 · · · · · · · 5 · · · · · · · 6 · · · · · · · 7

Organizational Climate

■ My workplace generally feels like

A cold, rainy day   *A warm, sunny day*

1 · · · · · · · 2 · · · · · · · 3 · · · · · · · 4 · · · · · · · 5 · · · · · · · 6 · · · · · · · 7

Job Design

■ The work I do is

Routine and boring   *Varied and challenging*

1 · · · · · · · 2 · · · · · · · 3 · · · · · · · 4 · · · · · · · 5 · · · · · · · 6 · · · · · · · 7

Unimportant   *Important*

1 · · · · · · · 2 · · · · · · · 3 · · · · · · · 4 · · · · · · · 5 · · · · · · · 6 · · · · · · · 7

Feedback and Compensation

■ I am given timely and constructive feedback.

False   *True*

1 · · · · · · · 2 · · · · · · · 3 · · · · · · · 4 · · · · · · · 5 · · · · · · · 6 · · · · · · · 7

■ I am paid fairly for what I do.

False   *True*

1 · · · · · · · 2 · · · · · · · 3 · · · · · · · 4 · · · · · · · 5 · · · · · · · 6 · · · · · · · 7

Coworkers

■ My coworkers are

Negative and unfriendly   *Positive and friendly*

1 · · · · · · · 2 · · · · · · · 3 · · · · · · · 4 · · · · · · · 5 · · · · · · · 6 · · · · · · · 7

Work Hours and Schedules

■ My work hours and schedules are flexible and accommodate my lifestyle.

Never   *Always*

1 · · · · · · · 2 · · · · · · · 3 · · · · · · · 4 · · · · · · · 5 · · · · · · · 6 · · · · · · · 7

Organizational Identification

■ I have a strong sense of commitment and loyalty to my work organization.

False   *True*

1 · · · · · · · 2 · · · · · · · 3 · · · · · · · 4 · · · · · · · 5 · · · · · · · 6 · · · · · · · 7

Stress

■ The degree of unhealthy stress in my workplace is

Very high   *Very low*

1 · · · · · · · 2 · · · · · · · 3 · · · · · · · 4 · · · · · · · 5 · · · · · · · 6 · · · · · · · 7

Total quality-of-work-life score = _____

SCALE:

12–35 = Warning—this job could be hazardous to your health

36–60 = Why spend half your waking life settling for average?

61–84 = T.G.I.M. (Thank goodness it's Monday)

For Consideration/Discussion

1. Which of these various quality-of-work-life factors is of overriding importance to you? Why? Which are least important? Why?
2. How strongly does your quality-of-work-life score correlate with the amount of effort you put into your job? Explain the connection.
3. How helpful would this survey be in your search for a better job? Explain.
4. How much does your total score reflect your attitude about life in general?
5. What should your managers do to improve the quality-of-work-life scores for you and your coworkers?

6. How important is quality of work life to your overall lifestyle and happiness? Explain.

Internet Exercises

1. **More on open-book management (OBM):** As discussed in this chapter, OBM is an underused way to reap the benefits of participative management. It requires managers to rethink some of their assumptions about managing people. A good place to begin is with a free tutorial at **www.bizcenter.com.** At the home page, click on the box "Open-Book Mgmt." Read the one-page introduction and, at the bottom of the page, click on "To Book Excerpt." Read the clear and concise four-page overview of OBM.

   Learning Points: 1. Name two or three useful insights about OBM you gained from this tutorial. 2. Does OBM appeal to you? Explain. 3. Do you believe OBM has great promise in the business world? Why or why not? 4. What are the major stumbling blocks for OBM in today's typical organizations? How can they be over-come?

2. **Getting the upper hand on stress and heart disease:** According to the American Heart Association, "nearly 62 million Americans have some form of cardiovascular disease, and nearly 1 million die from it each year. . . . Heart disease ranks as the No. 1 killer in the USA, although one-third of those deaths could be prevented if people ate better diets and exercised more." Stress also is a risk factor in this heart disease epidemic. A good place to start your personal battle against heart disease is with a risk assessment. You can do that for free online, thanks to the Medical University of South Carolina at **www.musc.edu.** Click on the tab "Search" at the home page. Enter the words "stress quiz" in the search box and click on "Submit." Select "AA Week 1999 Stress Quiz" and complete and score the ten-item quiz. For a heart disease risk assessment, go back and follow the same procedure, entering the words "risk of heart disease" in the search box. From the list of resources, select "Your Risk of Heart Disease: Quiz." Score your heart disease risk and read about the risk factors you can and cannot control.

   Learning Points: 1. What do you need to do to improve your stress score? (*Tip:* Consult the Skills & Tools box at the end of this chapter for advice on managing stress.) 2. What do you need to do to lower your risk of heart disease?

3. **Check it out:** Are you underpaid? Need supporting evidence to ask for a raise? Want to know how much you could make if you switched jobs or careers? Like to know how much someone else makes? Go online to **www.salary.com** and put the Salary Wizard to work.

CLOSING CASE

Seeking Proper Balance at Norway's Norsk Hydro

On the surface, Norway seems to be a moderate place. The climate can be intemperate, but the people and the lifestyle are just the opposite—the picture of restraint and judiciousness. Oh, there are some unassuming little oddities: Norwegians eat fish for breakfast, and often for lunch and for dinner. Caviar is so common that it comes in tubes, just like toothpaste. Very few people are overweight.

All of which seems charmingly unusual—but hardly alien.

The workplace, too, seems familiar: computers, cubicles, bullet-point slides. Familiar, that is, until you look more closely.

Every weekday at 6:10 A.M., Morten Lingelem boards a train at Sandefjord for the 90-minute ride to his job in Oslo. Lingelem, 42, a process-technology manager, has a standing reservation in the train's "office car," where he can power up his laptop and work in quiet comfort. That office car serves a purpose that's exactly the opposite of what it would be in the United States: It enables Lingelem to hold down a demanding engineering-management job, to spend more than three hours a day commuting, and still to be home by 6 P.M.

Atle Taerum, a colleague of Lingelem's, lives on a farm 90 minutes west of Oslo. And, two days a week, that's where he is, taking care of his 10-month-old daughter. Taerum is never without his cell-phone. On those days, customers—perhaps calling from Africa or from the Middle East—often reach him while he's plowing his fields, or chaperoning his son's kindergarten class.

Norway is, in fact, a sort of alternative universe of work. The inhabitants, the setting, the language, and the profit imperative all seem familiar. But Norwegians have a very different attitude about work—and a singular view of what work can become.

That vision is rooted in the notion that balance is healthy. The argument: work can be redesigned to promote balance. More than that, balance can become a source of corporate and national competitive advantage. Working less can, in fact, mean working better.

Norsk Hydro, the company that employs both Lingelem and Taerum, is one of Norway's dominant institutions. It's the world's second-largest producer of oil from the Norwegian North Sea, and the single-largest salmon farmer. Hydro fertilizer feeds Florida tomatoes and Arizona golf courses. Hydro metals toughen Cadillac Seville bumpers and Nokia cell-phones.

Hydro operates in 70 countries and employs 39,000 people, many of whom live and work outside of Norway. But it remains emphatically Norwegian—an organization not easily understood in American terms. As excess defines American culture, so balance shapes life for Norwegians, who long ago discovered sane responses to the tension between work and family. Norway is a place, after all, where people typically leave work between 4 P.M. and 4:30 P.M. Working women get at least 38 weeks of paid maternity leave; men get as many as 4 weeks of paid leave. Norway's answer to "How much is enough?" is found in the way the nation operates. Balance is the place where conversations about work and life begin.

In its 94 years of operation, "Hydro has created and nurtured industry in Norway," says Roald Nomme, a consultant and former manager at Hydro. "What is deep in the culture of Hydro is to think in the long term, to think more holistically—to think about the connections between employees, the company, and society."

Now Hydro is reexamining these connections. In a series of experiments across the company, it is testing a much more ambitious vision of balance. The two-year-old project, known as Hydrotlex, has given hundreds of employees varying combinations of flexible hours, home offices, new technology, and redesigned office space.

What has Hydro learned?

Hydro believes that it can help employees find a better balance by redesigning physical work spaces—and by redesigning work itself. It can free people from old restrictions on where and when they work. That flexibility makes workers more productive and jobs more appealing, and more appealing jobs attract more talented people.

Linked to the push for flexibility are new notions of diversity. Hydro believes that diversity goes beyond race or gender. Diversity has to do with *perspective*—and it exists *within* individuals: each of us is many different people at different times in our lives. Cultivate that diversity, and greater creativity will follow.

These workplace initiatives come at a critical time for Hydro. Because of weak commodity and oil prices, profits dropped by 4 percent between 1994 and 1998, even as revenues increased by 40 percent. In most American companies, such performance would be enough to end any grand experiments in work redesign, diversity, and balance. But at Hydro, those projects persist and even thrive—because, to Hydro, these initiatives are not indulgences. They are critical strategic elements for survival.

Yes, Hydro must go head-to-head with competitors in the United States—and in Germany, in Singapore, and in Mexico. As it fights these global battles, Hydro is up against relentless freneticism. We Americans pay lip service to sanity, but when the going gets tough, we readily abandon balance and work even harder.

Norwegians believe that such mania is not sustainable. In the end, they say, balance will win out. . . . .

Indeed, Norwegian culture—the prism through which Hydro's efforts at balance must be viewed—takes some fundamental American attitudes about work and turns them upside down.

In the United States, for instance, working long hours is seen as admirable, even heroic. At Hydro, the standard workday, even for professionals, is seven and a half hours. If you're still sitting at your desk at 6 P.M., people wonder why you can't get your work done.

Work in Norway is also shaped by a tradition of cooperation between unions and management that's unheard of in the United States. Labor and management typically work together to change processes and structures for greater efficiency. Unions believe that higher productivity brings more jobs and higher pay. Management wants higher profits—but satisfied employees aren't bad either.

All this allows—and perhaps requires—Norwegians to consider balance in fundamental terms. A rich life is a diverse collection of compelling experiences, some of which involve work. Work that is all-consuming is unhealthy—for the individual, for the organization, and for the community. Time spent away from work is restorative. More to the point: Time spent outside work fuels work itself.

For Discussion

1. How does Herzberg's two-factor theory enter into this case? Explain.
2. How well do you think open-book management would work at Norsk Hydro? Explain.
3. Do you like Norsk Hydro's attempts to promote better work/life balance? Why? How well would this approach work in the United States (or another country of your choice)?
4. What role does work play in your life? What are you doing (or do you plan to do) to achieve a decent balance in your life?

UNDERSTANDING WORK TEAMS

OPENING INCIDENT

"Revolutionize the international advertising world to create and control the buss about brands across borders." That's the bold mission for StrawberryFrog, a small advertising agency with 40 people headquartered in Amsterdam. Yet for Karin Drakenberg, the Swedish chief executive of StrawberryFrog, the goal is not only ambitious, but, she and her employees feel, very achievable. All employees of the organization are absolutely committed to making the mission statement a reality.

StrawberryFrog has never had a traditional hierarchical organizational structure. Instead, it uses a "multicultural, open-room concept." Since its founding on Valentine's Day in 1999, the company depends on a network of about 200 people around the globe who can pitch in when they're needed to work on various projects. For example, the agency's graphic design work is done in Amsterdam, Brussels, San Francisco, and Sydney. With no cumbersome administrative bureaucracy to slow it down, the agency has landed some large ad campaigns—for such companies as Mitsubishi Europe, Sprint, Pharmacia and Upjohn, Sony Ericsson, Credit Suisse, Ikea, and *Elle*. The team at StrawberryFrog feel that good global campaigns are found in big ideas, not in big bureaucracies. The use of sophisti-cated technologies allow StrawberryFrog the same "Knowledge control as any of the big agencies—coupled with its speed, flexibility, and the quality of the work." The 20 or 30 languages spoken by StrawberryFrog employees together enables the company to effectively communicate with anyone in the world.

The key to StrawberryFrog's approach is its model of virtual work teams. By relying on a web of freelancers around the globe, the agency enjoys a network of talent without all the unnecessary overhead and complexity of rigid work arrangements. The inspiration for this approach came from the film and construction industries. If you look at the film industry, workers are essentially "free agents" who move from project to project applying their skills—directing, talent search, costuming, makeup, acting, set design—as needed. And the construction industry has mastered the art of managing multiskilled team all working together on one shared vision. Those are the hallmarks of what Drakenberg is attempting to do. It allows StrawberryFrog to win the attention of big advertisers seeking a twenty-first century image for their twentieth-century products. Given its success in just a few years in existence, it appears that its model of virtual teams is working.

Like Karen Drakenberg, managers today believe that the use of teams will allow their organizations to increase sales or produce better products faster and at lower costs. Although the effort to create teams isn't always successful, well-planned teams can reinvigorate productivity and better position an organization to deal with a rapidly changing environment.

From *Fundamentals of Management*, 4/E by Robbins, Stephen P. and DeCenzo, David, © 2004. Reprinted by permission of Pearson Education, Inc., Upper Saddle River, NJ.

The Popularity of Teams

In the early 1970s, when companies such as Toyota, General Foods, and Volvo introduced teams, it made news because no one else was doing it. "Today, it's just the opposite: It's the organization that doesn't use some form of team that is noteworthy. Pick up almost any business publication, and you will read how teams have become an essential part of work in companies such as Honeywell, General Electric, Saab, John Deere, Imperial Oil, Australian Airlines, Honda, Florida Power and Light, Shiseido, and FedEx. In fact, about 80 percent of all *Fortune* 500 companies are using teams in some part of their organization.

How do we explain the current popularity of teams? The evidence suggests that teams typically outperform individuals when tasks require multiple skills, judgment, and experience. As organizations restructure themselves to compete more effectively and efficiently, they are turning to teams as a better way to utilize employee talents.

Management has found that teams are more flexible and responsive to a changing environment than traditional departments or other forms of permanent work groupings. Teams also can be quickly assembled, deployed, refocused, and disbanded.

Finally teams may offer more that just increased efficiency and enhanced performance for the organization: They can serve as a source of job satisfaction. Because team members are frequently empowered to handle many of the things that directly affect their work, teams serve as an effective means for management to enhance employee involvement, increase employee morale, and promote workforce diversity.

What Are the Stages of Team Development?

Team development is a dynamic process. Most teams find themselves in a continual state of change. But even though teams probably never reach stability, there's a general pattern to most teams' evolution. The five stages of team development, shown in Figure 11.1, are forming, storming, norming, performing, and adjourning.

FIGURE 11.1
Stages of Team Development

Prestage I   Stage I Forming   Stage II Storming

Stage III Norming   Stage IV Performing   Stage V Adjourning

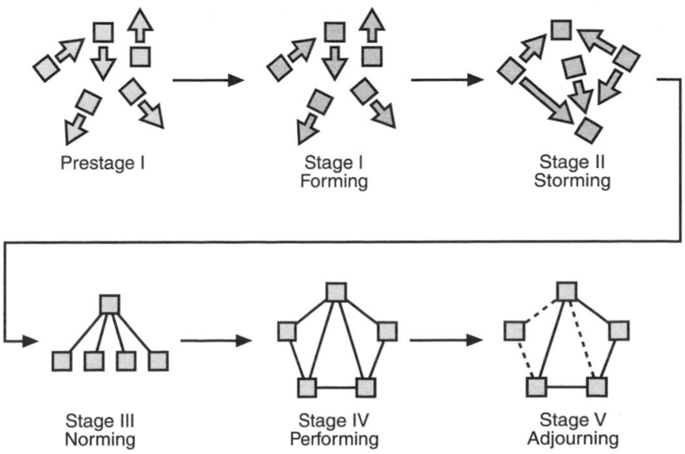

forming The first stage of work team development, characterized by uncertainty about development, purpose, structure, and leadership

storming The second stage of work team development, characterized by intragroup conflict

norming The third stage of work team development, in which close relationships develop and members begin to demonstrate cohesiveness

performing The fourth stage of work team development, in which the structure is fully functional and accepted by team members

adjourning The fifth and final stage of the development of temporary work teams, in which the team prepares for its disbandment

work group A group that interacts primarily to share information and to make decisions that will help each member perform within his or her area of responsibility

The first stage, **forming,** is characterized by a great deal of uncertainty about the group's purpose, structure, and leadership. Members are testing the waters to determine what types of behaviors are acceptable. This stage is complete when members have begun to think of themselves as part of a team.

The **storming** stage is one of intragroup conflict. Members accept the existence of the team but resist the control that the group imposes on individuality. Further, there is conflict over who will control the team. When stage II is complete, there will be relatively clear leadership within the team.

The third stage is one in which close relationships develop and members begin to demonstrate cohesiveness. There is now a stronger sense of team identity and camaraderie. This **norming** stage is complete when the team structure solidifies and members have assimilated a common set of expectations of appropriate work behavior. The fourth stage is **performing.** The structure is fully functional and accepted by team members. Their energy is diverted from getting to know and understand each other to performing the necessary tasks. For permanent teams, performing is the last stage of their development. For temporary teams—those that have a limited task to perform—there is an **adjourning** stage. In this stage, the team prepares for its disbandment. A high level of task performance is no longer the members' top priority. Instead, their attention is directed toward wrapping up activities.

Recognizing that teams progress through these stages, one can pose an obvious question: Do they become more effective as they progress through each stage? Some researchers argue that the effectiveness of work units does increase at advanced stages, but it's not that simple. Although that assumption may be generally true, what makes a team effective is complex. Under some conditions, high levels of conflict are conducive to high levels of group performance. We might expect, then, to find situations in which teams in Stage II outperform those in Stage III or V. Similarly, teams do not always proceed clearly from one stage to the next. Sometimes, in fact, several stages are going on simultaneously—as when teams are storming and performing at the same time. Therefore, one should not always assume that all teams precisely follow this developmental process or that stage IV is always most preferable. Instead, it is better to think of these stages as a general framework, which should remind you that teams are dynamic entities, and can help you better understand the issues that may surface in a teams life.

Aren't Work Groups and Work Teams the Same?

At this point, you may be asking yourself where this discussion is going. Aren't teams and groups the same thing? No. In this section, we define and clarify the difference between a work group and a work team.

In the last chapter, we defined a group as two or more individuals who have come together to achieve certain objectives. A **work group** interacts primarily to share information and to make decisions that will help each group member perform within his or her area of responsibility. Work groups have no need or opportunity to engage in collective work that requires joint effort. Consequently, their performance is merely the summation of all the group members' individual contributions. There is no positive synergy that would create an overall level of performance greater than the sum of the inputs.

work team A group that engages in collective work that requires joint effort and generates a positive synergy

A **work team**, on the other hand, generates positive synergy through a coordinated effort. Their individual efforts result in a level of performance that is greater than the sum of those individual inputs. Figure 11.2 highlights the main differences between work groups and work teams.

These descriptions should help to clarify why so many organizations have restructured work processes around teams. Management is looking for that positive synergy that will allow the organization to increase performance. The extensive use of teams creates the potential for an organization to generate greater outputs with no increase in (or even fewer) inputs. For example, at Wachovia Asset Management Division of Wachovia Bank, mutual funds investment teams have significantly improved investment performance since its team structure was implemented in the late 1990s. As a result, Wachovia's teams have helped the bank improve its Morningstar financial rating—placing it in the 31st percentile; this is up from its place in the 76th percentile three years earlier.

Recognize, however, that such increases are simply "potential." Nothing inherently magical in the creation of work teams guarantees that this positive synergy and its accompanying productivity will occur. Accordingly, merely calling a group a team doesn't automatically increase its performance. As we show later in this chapter, successful or high-performing work teams have certain common characteristics. If management hopes to gain increases in organizational performance—like those at Wachovia—it will need to ensure that its teams possess those characteristics.

Types of Work Teams

Work teams can be classified on the basis of their objectives. The four most common forms of teams in an organization are functional teams, problem-solving teams, self-managed teams, and cross-functional teams (see Figure 11.3). A technology-based model for the twenty-first century, the virtual team, will also be discussed.

What Is a Functional Team?

functional teams A work team composed of a manager and the employees in his or her unit and involved in efforts to improve work activities or to solve specific problems within the particular functional unit

Functional teams are composed of a manager and the employees in his or her unit. Within this functional team, issues such as authority, decision making, leadership, and interactions are relatively simple and clear. Functional teams are often involved

FIGURE 11.2
Comparing Work Teams and Work Groups

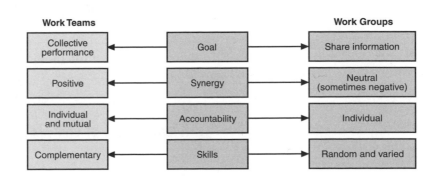

FIGURE 11.3

Types of Work Teams

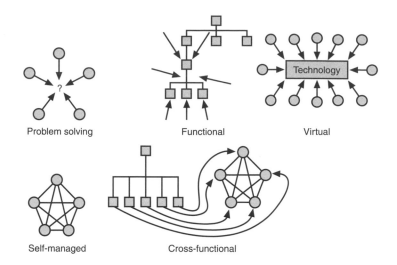

Problem solving

Functional

Virtual

Self-managed

Cross-functional

in efforts to improve work activities or to solve specific problems within a particular functions unit. For example, at the Marque, Inc., headquarters in Goshen, Indiana (manufacturers of emergency squad trucks), employees in all departments in the organization participate on teams, making decisions to "make their products faster, cheaper, and better."

How Does a Problem-Solving Team Operate?

problem-solving teams Work teams typically composed of 5 to 12 hourly employees from the same department who meet each week to discuss ways of improving quality, efficiency, and the work environment

quality circles Work teams composed of 8 to 10 employees and supervisors who share an area of responsibility and who meet regularly to discuss quality problems investigate the causes of the problem, recommend solution, and take corrective actions but who have no authority

self-managed work team A formal group of employees that operates without a manager and is responsible for a complete work process or segment that delivers a product or service to an external or internal customer

Almost 25 years ago, teams were just beginning to grow in popularity, and the form they took was strikingly similar. These teams typically were composed of 5 to 12 hourly employees from the same department who met for a few hours each week to discuss ways of improving quality, efficiency, and the work environment. We call these **problem-solving teams.** In problem-solving teams, members share ideas or offer suggestions on how work processes and methods can be improved. Some of the most widely practiced applications of problem-solving teams witnessed during the 1980s were **quality circles,** which are work teams of 8 to 10 employees and supervisors who share an area of responsibility. They meet regularly to discuss their quality problems, investigate causes of the problems, recommend solutions, and take corrective actions. They assume responsibility for solving quality problems, and they generate and evaluate their own feedback. Rarely, however, are these teams given the authority to unilaterally implement any of their suggestions. Instead, they make a recommendation to management, which usually makes the decision about the implementation of recommended solutions. Jo Egbert, general manager of Kimball Manufacturing in Boise, Idaho—makers of cables and electronic and electomechanical assemblies—recognized that her company needed to improve production operations and reduce "work-in-process" inventory. After several months of implementing and supporting problem-solving teams, Kimball Manufacturing employees reduced production time by 50 percent, and reduced work-in-process inventory from 14 to 3.5 days.

What Is a Self-Managed Work Team?

Another type of team commonly being used in organizations is the self-directed or self-managed team. A **self-managed work team** is a formal group of employees that operates without a manager and is responsible for a complete work process or segment that delivers a product or service to an external or internal customer. Nearly 70 percent of the *Fortune* 1000 organizations have implemented self-managed work teams. Typically, this kind of team has control over its work pace, determines work assignments and when breaks are taken, and inspects is own work. Fully self-managed work teams even select their own members and have the members evaluate each other's performance. As a result, supervisory positions take on decreased importance and may even be eliminated.

How Do Cross Functional Teams Operate?

cross-functional work team A team composed of employees from about the same hierarchical level but from different work areas in an organization who are brought together to accomplish a particular task

The next type of team we will identify is the **cross-functional work team**, which consists of employees from about the same hierarchical level but from different work areas in the organization. Workers are brought together to accomplish a particular task.

Many organizations have used cross-functional teams for years. For example, in the 1960s, IBM created a large team made up of employees from across departments in the company to develop the highly successful System 360. However, the popularity of cross-functional work teams exploded in the late 1980s. All the major automobile manufacturers—including Toyota, DaimlerChrysler, Nissan, General Motors, Ford, Honda, and BMW have turned to this form of team in order to coordinate complex projects. For example, Hewlett-Packard's Medical Products Group has used cross-functional teams to decrease product development times and optimize their organizational resources.

Cross-functional teams are also an effective way to allow employees from diverse areas within an organization to exchange information, develop new ideas, solve problems, and coordinate complex tasks. But cross-functional teams can be difficult to manage. The early stages of development (e.g., storming) are very often time-consuming as members learn to work with diversity and complexity. This difficulty with diversity, however, can be turned into an advantage. One of the tenets of a group decision-making process is that groups provide more complete information and are more creative than individuals. The diversity of a work team can help identify creative or unique solutions. Furthermore, the lack of a common perspective caused by diversity usually means that team members will spend more time discussing relevant issues, which decreases the likelihood that a weak solution will be selected. However, keep in mind that the contribution that diversity makes to teams probably will decline over time. As team members become more familiar with one another, they form a more cohesive group, but the positive aspect of this decline in diversity is that a team bond is built. It takes time to build trust and teamwork. Later in this chapter are the present ways managers can help facilitate and build trust among team members.

Are Virtual Teams a Reality in the New Millennium?

virtual team A team that meets electronically; allows groups to meet without concern for space or time

A **virtual team** is an extension of the electronic meetings. A virtual team allows groups to meet without concern for space or time and enables organizations to link workers together in a way that would have been impossible in the past. Team members use computer technology to link physically dispersed members in order to achieve a common goal—using technological advances like conference calls, video conferencing, or e-mail to solve problems even though they may be geographically dispersed or several time zones away. The advertising project teams at StrawberryFrog would be an example of a virtual team. So, too, are some of the team structures at Heineken, manufacturers of Heineken Beer. Heineken uses virtual teams in many aspects of its advertising activities. For example, in an effort to increase Heineken sales, the company brought together people from "local and international companies with expertise in retailing, music, Web design, and advertising." By taking the best talent from each component, Heineken officials were better able to produce an advertising campaign that would lead to the company's goals—increasing the brand awareness, and sales of Heineken Beer.

Why Do Entrepreneurs Use Teams?

Employee work teams tend to be extremely popular in entrepreneurial ventures, and three types of teams appear to be common. These include empowered functional teams (teams that have authority to plan and implement process improvements); self-directed teams (teams that are nearly autonomous and responsible for many activities that were once the jurisdiction of manager); and cross-functional teams (teams that include a hybrid grouping of individuals who are experts in various specialties and who work together on various tasks).

Entrepreneurial firms use teams because they facilitate the technology and market demands the organization is facing. Teams, entrepreneurs find, help the organization to make products faster, cheaper, and better. Additionally teams permit entrepreneurs to tap into the collective wisdom of the venture's employees. Entrepreneurs have found that empowering employees to make decisions is one of the best ways for them to adapt to change. Additionally, the team culture can improve the overall workplace environment and worker morale.

For team efforts to work, however, entrepreneurs must shift from the traditional command-and-collaboration style. Entrepreneurs must recognize that individual employees can understand the business and can innovate just as effectively as they can. For example, at Marque, Inc., CEO Scott Jessup recognized that he wasn't the smartest person in the company when it came to production problems. But he was smart enough to recognize that if his company wanted to expand its market share in manufacturing its medical emergency-squad vehicles, new levels of productivity needed to be reached. While the organization had enjoyed success with its functional teams, he decided to form a cross-functional team—bringing together people from production, quality assurance, and fabrication—who could spot production bottlenecks and other problems. More importantly, he gave the team the authority to resolve the constraints.

Characteristics of High-Performance Work Teams___

Teams are not automatic productivity enhancers. We know that they can also be disappointments for management. What common characteristics, then, do effective teams have? Research provides some insight into the primary characteristics associated with high-performance work teams. Let's take a look at these characteristics as summarized in Figure 11.4.

High-performance work teams have both a *clear understanding* of the goal and a belief that the goal embodies a worthwhile or important result. Moreover, the importance of these goals encourages individuals to redirect energy away from personal concerns and toward team goals. In high-performing work teams, members are committed to the team's goals; they know what they are expected to accomplish and understand how they will work together to achieve those goals. Effective teams are composed of competent individuals. They have the relevant technical skills and abilities to achieve the desired goals and the personal characteristics required to achieve excellence while working well with others. These same individuals are also capable of readjusting their work skills—called job morphing—to fit the needs of the team. It's important not to overlook the personal characteristics. Not everyone who is technically competent has the skills to work well as a team member. High-performing team members possess both technical and interpersonal skills.

Effective teams are characterized by *high mutual trust* among members. That is, members believe in the integrity, character, and ability of one another. But, as you probably know from your own personal relationships, trust is fragile. Members of an effective team exhibit intense loyalty and dedication to the team. They are willing to do anything that has to be done to help their team succeed. We call this loyalty and dedication *unified commitment*. Studies of successful teams have found that members identify with their teams. Members redefine themselves to include membership in the team as an important aspect of the self. Unified commitment, then, is characterized by dedication to the team's goal and a willingness to expend extraordinary amounts of energy to achieve them.

Not surprisingly, effective teams are characterized by *good communication*. Members are able to convey messages in a form that is readily and clearly understood. This includes nonverbal as well as spoken messages. Good communication

FIGURE 11.4

Characteristics of High-performing Work Teams

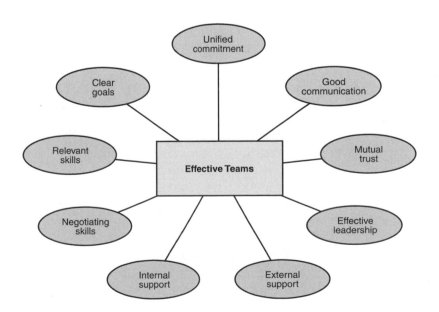

is characterized by a healthy dose of feedback from team members and management. This helps to guide team members and to correct misunderstandings. Like two individuals who have been together for many years, members of high-performing teams are able to quickly and effectively share ideas and feelings.

When jobs are designed around individuals, job descriptions, rules and procedures, and other types of formalized documentation clarify employee roles. Effective teams, on the other hand, tend to be flexible and continually make adjustments, so team members must possess adequate negotiating skills. Because problems and relationships are regularly changing in teams, the members have to be able to confront and reconcile differences.

Effective leaders can motivate a team to follow them through the most difficult situations. How? Leaders help clarify goals. They demonstrate that change is possible by overcoming inertia. And they increase the self-confidence of team members, helping them to realize their potential more fully. The best leaders are not necessarily directive or controlling. Increasingly, effective team leaders are taking the roles of coach and facilitator. They help guide and support the team, but they don't control it. This description obviously applies to self-managed teams, but it also increasingly applies to problem-solving and cross-functional teams in which members themselves are empowered. For some traditional managers, changing their role from boss to facilitator—from giving orders to working for the team—is a difficult transition. Although most managers relish the newfound shared authority, or come to understand its advantages through leadership training, some hard-nosed, dictatorial managers are just ill suited to the team concept and must be transferred or replaced.

The final condition for an effective team is a *supportive climate*. Internally, the team should be provided with a sound infrastructure. This includes proper training, an understandable measurement system with which team members can evaluate their overall performance, an incentive program that recognizes and rewards team activities, and a supportive human resources system. The infrastructure should support members and reinforce behaviors that lead to high levels of performance. Externally, management should provide the team with the resources needed to get the job done.

Turning Individuals into Team Players

So far, we have made a strong case for the value and growing popularity of work teams, but not every worker is inherently a team player. Some people prefer to be recognized for their individual achievements. In some organizations, too, work environments are such that only die strong survive. Creating teams in such an environment may meet some resistance. Finally, countries differ in terms of how conducive they are to individualism and collectivism. Teams fit well in countries that score high on collectivism. But what if an organization wants to introduce teams into an individualistic society (like that of the United States)? As one writer stated, regarding teams in the United States, Americans don't grow up learning how to function in teams. In school they don't get a team report card, or learn the names of the team of sailors who traveled with Columbus to America. This limitation apparently would apply to Canadians, British, Australians, and others from individualistic societies.

What Are the Management Challenges of Creating Team Players?

The points raised are meant to dramatize that one substantial barrier to work teams is the individual resistance that may exist. Employees' success, when they are part of teams, is no longer defined in terms of individual performance. Instead, success is a function of how well the team as a whole performs. To perform well as team members, individuals must be able to communicate openly and honestly with one another, to confront differences and resolve conflicts, and to place lower priority on personal goals for the good of the team. For many employees, these are difficult, and sometimes impossible assignments.

The challenge of creating team players will be greatest where the national culture is highly individualistic and the teams are being introduced into an established organization that has historically valued individual achievement. This describes, for instance, the environment that faced managers at AT&T, Ford, Motorola, and other large U.S. companies. These firms prospered by hiring and rewarding corporate stars, and they bred a competitive work climate that encouraged individual achievement and recognition. Employees in these types of organizations can experience culture shock caused by a sudden shift in the focus to teamwork.

In contrast, the challenge for management is less demanding when teams are introduced in places in which employees have strong collectivist values—such as Japan or Mexico. The challenge of forming teams will also be less in new organizations that use teams as their initial form of structuring work. Saturn Corporation, for instance, is an American Organization. Although owned by General Motors, the company was designed around teams from its start. Everyone at Saturn was hired on the understanding that they would he working in teams, and the ability to be a good team player was a hiring prerequisite.

What Roles Do Team Members Play?

High-performing work teams carefully match people to various roles. One stream of research has identified nine potential roles that work team members often can play: creator-innovator, explorer-promoter, assessor-developer, thrust-organizer, concluder-producer, controller-inspector, upholder-maintainer, reporter-adviser, and linker (see Figure 11.5). Let's briefly review each team role.

Creator-innovators are usually imaginative and good at initiating ideas or concepts. They are typically very independent and prefer to work at their own pace on their own—and very often on their own time. *Explorer-promoters* like to take new ideas and champion their cause. These individuals are good at picking up ideas from the creator-innovators and finding the resources to promote those ideas. However, they often lack the patience and control skills to ensure that the ideas are followed through in detail. *Assessor-developers* have strong analytical skills. They're at their best given several different options to evaluate and analyze before a decision is made. *Thruster-organizers* like to set up procedures to turn ideas into

FIGURE 11.5
Team Member Roles

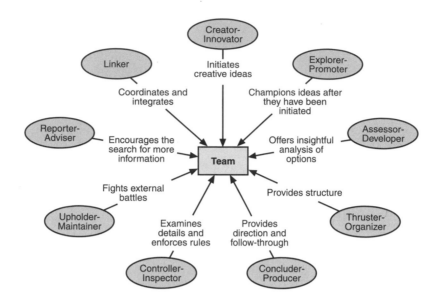

reality and get things done. They set goals, establish plans, organize people, and establish systems to ensure that deadlines are met. And, somewhat like thruster-organizers, *concluder-producers* are concerned with result. Only their role focuses on keeping to deadlines and ensuring that all commitments are followed through. Concluder-producers take pride in producing a regular output to a standard.

Controller-inspectors have a high concern for establishing and enforcing rules and policies. They are good at examining details and making sure that inaccuracies are avoided. They want to check all the facts and figures to make sure they're complete. *Upholder-maintainers* hold strong convictions about the way things should be done. They will defend the team and fight its battles with outsiders while, at the same time, strongly supporting fellow team members. Accordingly, these individuals provide team stability. *Reporter-advisers* are good listeners and tend not to press their point of view on others. They tend to favor getting more information before making decisions. As such, they perform an important role in encouraging the team to seek additional information before making decisions and discouraging the team from making hasty decisions.

The last role—the *linkers*—overlaps the others. This role can be assumed by any actors of the previous eight roles. Linkers try to understand all views. They are coordinators and integrators. They dislike extremism and try to build cooperation among all team members. They also recognize the various contributions that other team members make and try to integrate people and activities despite differences that might exist.

If forced to, most individuals can perform any of these roles. However, most have two or three they strongly prefer. Managers need to understand the strengths that each individual can bring to a team, they need to select team members on the basis of an appropriate mix of individual strengths and allocate work assignments that fit each member's preferred style. By matching individual preferences with team role demand, managers increase the likelihood that the team members will work well together. Unsuccessful teams may have an unbalanced portfolio of individual talents, with too much energy being expended in one area and not enough in other areas.

How Can a Manager Shape Team Behavior?

There are several options available for managers who are trying to turn individuals into team players. The three most popular ways include proper selection, employee training, and rewarding the appropriate team behaviors. Let's look at each of these.

What Role Does Selection Play? Some individuals already possess the interpersonal skills to be effective team players. When hiring team members, in addition to checking on the technical skills required to successfully perform the job, the organizations should ensure that applicants can fulfill team roles.

As we have mentioned before, some applicants have been socialized around individual contributions and, consequently, lack team skills, as might some current employees who are restructuring into teams. When faced with such candidates, a manager can do several things. First, and most obvious, if team skills are woefully lacking, don't hire that candidate. If successful performance requires interaction, rejecting such a candidate is appropriate. On the other hand, a candidate who has only some basic skills can be hired on a probationary basis and required to undergo training to shape him or her into a team player. If the skills aren't learned or practiced, the individual may have to be separated from the company for failing to achieve the skills necessary for performing successfully on the job.

Can We Train Individuals to Be Team Players? Performing well in a team involves a set of behaviors. As we discussed in the preceding chapter, new behaviors can he learned. Even a large portion of people who were raised on the importance of individual accomplishment can be trained to become team players. Training specialists can conduct exercises that allow employees to experience the satisfaction that teamwork can provide. The workshops usually cover such topics as team problem solving, communications, negotiations, conflict resolution, and coaching skills. It's not unusual, too, for these individuals to be exposed to the five stages of team development that we discussed earlier. At Bell Atlantic, for example, trainers focus on how a team goes through various stages before it gels. And employees are reminded of the importance of patience, because teams take longer to do some things—such as make decisions—than do employees acting alone.

What Role Do Rewards Play in Shaping Team Players? Organization's reward system needs to encourage cooperative efforts rather than competitive ones. For instance, Lockheed Martin's Aeronautics company has organized its 20,000-plus employees into teams. Rewards are structured to return a percentage increase in the bottom line to the team members on the basis of achievements of the team's performance goals.

Promotions, pay raises, and other forms of recognition should be given to employees who are effective collaborative team members. This doesn't mean that individual contribution is ignored, but rather that it is balanced with selfless contributions to the team. Examples of behaviors that should be rewarded include training new colleagues, sharing information with teammates, helping resolve team conflicts, and mastering new skills in which the team is deficient. Finally, managers cannot forget the inherent rewards that employees can receive from teamwork. Work teams provide camaraderie. It's exciting and satisfying to be an

Does Everyone Have To Be a Team Player?

You're a production manager at the Saturn plant. One of your newest employees is Barbara Petersen, who has a bachelor's degree in engineering and a master's in business. You recently hired Barbara out of college for a position in supply chain management.

You've recently been chosen to head up a cross-functional team to look at ways to reduce inventory costs. This team would essentially be a permanent task force. You've decided to have team members come from supplier relations, cost accounting, transportations, and production systems. You've also decided to include Barbara on the team. While she has only been at Saturn for four months, you've been impressed with her energy, smarts, and industriousness. You think this would be an excellent assignment for her to increase her visibility in the company and expand her understanding of the company's inventory system.

When you called Barbara into your office to give her the good news, you were quite surprised by her response. "I'm not a team player," she said, "I didn't join clubs in high school. I was on the track team and I did well, but track is an individual sport. We were a team only in the sense that we rode together in the same bus to away meets. In college, I avoided the whole sorority thing. Some people may call me a loner. I don't think that's true. I can work well with others, but I hate meetings and committees. To me, they waste so much time. And anything you're working on with a group, you've got all these different personalities that you have to adjust for. I'm an independent operator. Give me a job and I'll get it done. I work harder than anyone I know—and I give my employer 150 percent. But I don't want my performance to be dependent on the other people in my group. They may not work as hard as I will. Someone is sure to shirk some of their responsibilities. I just don't want to be a team player."

What do you do? Should you give Barbara the option of joining the inventory cost reduction team? Is it unethical for you to require someone like Barbara to do his or her job as part of a team?

integral part of a successful team. The opportunity to engage in personal development and to help teammates grow can be a very satisfying and rewarding experience for employees.

How Can a Manager Reinvigorate a Mature Team?

The fact that a team is performing well at any given point in time is no assurance that it will continue to do so. Effective teams can become stagnant. Initial enthusiasm can give way to apathy. Time can diminish the positive value from diverse perspectives as cohesiveness increases. In terms of the five-stage development model, teams don't automatically stay at the performing stage. Familiarity and team success can lead to contentment and complacency. And, as that happens, the team may become less open to novel ideas and innovative solutions. Mature teams, also, are particularly prone to suffer from groupthink as team members begin to believe they can read everyone's mind and assume that they know what the others are thinking. Consequently, team members become reluctant to express their thoughts and are less likely to challenge one another.

Another source of problems for mature teams is that their early successes are often due to having taken on easy tasks. It's normal for new teams to begin by taking on those issues and problems they can most easily handle. But as time passes, the easy problems are solved, and the team has to begin to tackle the more difficult issues. At this point, the team has frequently established its processes and routines, and team members are often reluctant to change the workable system they have developed. When that happens, problems arise. Internal team processes no longer work smoothly. Communication bogs down, and conflict increases because problems are less likely to have obvious solutions. All in all, team performance may dramatically drop.

What can a manager do to reinvigorate mature teams—especially ones that are encountering the problems described above? We offer the following suggestions (see Figure 11.6). Prepare team members to deal with the problems of team maturity. Remind them that they are not unique. All successful teams eventually have to address maturity issues: Members shouldn't feel let down or lose their confidence in the team concept when the initial excitement subsides and conflicts begin to surface. When teams get into ruts, it may help to provide them with refresher training in communication, conflict resolution, tears processes, and similar skills. This training can help team members regain their confidence and trust in each other. Offer advanced training. The skills that worked well with easy problems may be insufficient for some of the more difficult problems the team is addressing. Mature teams can often benefit from advanced training to help members develop stronger problem-solving, interpersonal, and technical skills. Encourage teams to treat their development as a constant learning experience. Just as organizations use continuous improvement programs, teams should approach their own development as part of a search for continuous improvement. Teams should look for ways to improve, to confront member and frustrations, and to use conflict as a learning opportunity.

Contemporary Team Issues

As we close this chapter, we will address two issues related to managing teams—continuous process improvement programs and diversity in teams.

FIGURE 11.6

How to Reinvigorate Mature Teams

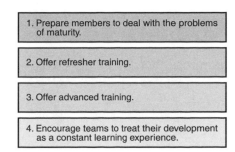

1. Prepare members to deal with the problems of maturity.

2. Offer refresher training.

3. Offer advanced training.

4. Encourage teams to treat their development as a constant learning experience.

Why Are Teams Central to Continuous Process Improvement Programs?

One of the central characteristics of continuous process improvement programs is the use of teams. Why teams? Teams provide the natural vehicle for employees to share ideas and implement improvements. The essence of continuous improvement is process improvement, and employee participation is the linchpin of process improvement. In other words, continuous improvement requires management to encourage employees to share ideas and to act on what the employees suggest. As one author put it, "None of the various processes and techniques will catch on and be applied except in work teams. All such techniques and processes require high levels of communication and contact, response, adaptation, and coordination and sequencing. They require, in short, the environment that can be supplied only by superior work teams."

How Does Workforce Diversity Affect Teams?

Managing diversity on teams is a balancing act. Diversity typically provides fresh perspectives on issues, but it makes it more difficult to unify the team and reach agreements. The strongest case for diversity on work teams arises when these teams are engaged in problem-solving and decision-making tasks. Heterogeneous teams bring multiple perspectives to the discussion, thus increasing the likelihood that the team will identify creative or unique solutions. Additionally, the lack of a common perspective usually means diverse teams spend more time discussing issues, which decreases the chances that a weak alternative will be chosen. However, keep in mind that the positive contribution that diversity makes to decision-making teams undoubtedly declines over time. As we pointed out in the previous chapter, diverse groups have more difficulty working together and solving problems, but this problem dissipates with time. Expect the value-added component of diverse teams to increase as members become more familiar with each other and the team becomes more cohesive.

Studies tell us that members of cohesive teams have greater satisfaction, lower absenteeism, and lower attrition from the group. Yet cohesiveness is likely to be lower on diverse teams. So here is a potential negative of diversity: It can be detrimental to group cohesiveness. But again, the relationship between cohesiveness and group productivity is moderated by performance-related norms. We suggest that if the norms of the team are supportive of diversity, a team can maximize the value of heterogeneity while achieving the benefits of high cohesiveness. This makes a strong case for having team members participate in diversity training.

☺ Comprehension and Application

Reading for Comprehension

1. Contrast (1) self-managed and cross-functional teams and (2) virtual and face-to-face teams.

2. What problems might surface in teams during each of the five stages of team development?
3. How do virtual teams enhance productivity?
4. In what ways can management invigorate stagnant teams?
5. Why do you believe mutual respect is important to developing high-performing work teams?

Linking Concepts to Practice

1. How do you explain the rapidly increasing popularity of work teams in countries such as the United States and Canada, whose national cultures place a high value on individualism?
2. "All work teams are work groups, but not all work groups are work teams." Do you agree or disagree with the statement? Discuss.
3. Would you prefer to work alone or as part of a team? Why? Support your response with data from your self-assessments.
4. Describe a situation in which individuals, acting independently, outperform teams in an organization.
5. Contrast the pros and cons of diverse teams.

VIDEO CASE APPLICATION

Engenia Software, Inc: Keeping Work Teams Productive 24/7

In 1999, as a result of his own frustration while working at IBM, CEO Jeffrey Crigler launched Eugenia Software. Inc., based in Reston, VA. He was fascinated by the potential for network applications that would enable people to swap ideas, but was impatient with the slow pace of development at a large company like IBM. With the introduction of Unity, Engenia has created a desktop that allows people inside and outside a corporation to collaborate across space and time. Jeffrey Crigler likens it to "having a very sophisticated beeper system" that allows users to keep track of every detail of a team project from a very high level. "It lets you concentrate on the underlying issues rather than running around and gathering up status," he says.

Joseph Rhyne is senior vice president of technology at Thompson Corporation, one of the world's largest online publishing companies. Regardless of where his travels take him, Rhyne uses Unity's digital "dashboard" to check on the exact status of the projects his teams are running without so much as an e-mail. "I can see if things are falling behind or need help," he says. Everything related to a project including documents, activities, and people shows up on the same customized, secured Web page. Any team member working anywhere in the world, at any time of day or night can be synchronized from his or her desktop to view the same page in real time.

Team members no longer have to worry about finding documents or about whose computer the files are on. "Even if the information is distributed all over the place," says Jeff Kay, chief technology officer, Engenia Software, Inc., Unity will bring it together. A user can access a workspace for a corporate project, get the latest changes made by co-workers and continue working online or off-line.

However, not even a sophisticated knowledge management tool like Unity can turn human beings into team players automatically. In our individualistic American culture, many ambitious people have long assumed that protecting knowledge is the path to power in the workplace. According to Ben Gottesman, executive editor, *PC Magazine,* "the Internet has made it very apparent that it is by exposing knowledge" within the context of teamwork that will give today's companies a competitive advantage. "But," says Gottesman, "it is taking time for individuals to realize that success lies in collaboration."

"Teams that we depend on to get our work done in most businesses are more and more becoming teams between companies," according to Jeffrey Crigler. "Businesses need to work with suppliers, outside contractors, consultants, and even people that might be competitors." Eugenia's Unity uses intelligent "software agents" to help both virtual and brick-and-mortar companies coordinate the planning, execution, and reporting functions of complex projects.

Eugenia Software, Inc.'s corporate literature describes Unity software as an innovative package that never sleeps, and is never distracted by meetings, travel, or other responsibilities. It is a software solution that does exactly what you would do if you had nothing else to do in life but spend 24 hours a day monitoring every step in your IT project. The software reacts to obstacles in real-time and takes actions you want it to take as soon as the action is needed.

The header on Engenia's home page reads: "Always Current. Always Aware." Depending on your perspective, this could conjure up the quintessential butler who anticipates your every need or Big Brother watching your every move. As high-performing work teams become key to sustaining competitive advantage, businesses in all sectors will demand access to 'round the clock control. For as long as we still need to sleep, we will need software programs like Unity.

Questions

1. Briefly compare and contrast the advantages of Unity software to the manager of a virtual team like StawberryFrog, with its benefits to the manager of a cross-functional team within a large corporation like General Electric.
2. Do you think that Unity's digital dashboard can help executives like Joseph Rhyne, senior vice president of technology, Thompson Corporation, to be more effective leaders? Explain.
3. According to Ben Gottesman, executive editor, *PC Magazine,* it is taking time for individuals to realize that success lies in collaboration or teamwork. What are some of the methods managers can use to ensure that their employees will perform well as members of a team?
4. If you are a fan of *PC Week,* you might have read a profile of Patrick Savage, a graduate of Virginia Polytechnic Institute and State University with a computer science degree. After six months of searching, he found his dream job as a software engineer at Engenia Software, Inc. He wanted a small innovative company where he could learn quickly, have access to new technologies, and a chance to make a difference. The article includes a picture of Patrick Savage

riding a mountain bike against a beautiful sky and the following quote: "Engenia has a lot going for it. But I could also see myself moving on in a few years—there are just so many opportunities out there." In your opinion, will Patrick Savage make a good team player? Explain.

Developing Your Coaching Skill

Coaching Others

About the Skill. Effective managers are increasingly being described as coaches rather than bosses. Just like coaches, they're expected to provide instruction, guidance, advice, and encouragement to help team members improve their job performance.

Steps in Practicing the Skill

1. *Analyze ways to improve the team's performance and capabilities.* A coach looks for opportunities for team members to expand their capabilities and improve performance. How? You can use the following behaviors. Observe your team members' behaviors on a day-to-day basis. Ask questions of them: Why do you do a task this way? Can it be improved? What other approaches might be used? Show genuine interest in team members as individuals, not merely as employees. Respect them individually. Listen to each employee.

2. *Create a supportive climate.* It's the coach's responsibility to reduce barriers to development and to facilitate a climate that encourages personal performance improvement. How? You can use the following behaviors. Create a climate that contributes to a free and open exchange of ideas. Offer help and assistance. Give guidance and advice when asked. Encourage your team. Be positive and upbeat. Don't use threats. Ask, "What did we learn from this that can help us in the future?" Reduce obstacles. Assure team members that you value their contribution to the team's goals. Take personal responsibility for the outcome, but don't rob team members of their full responsibility. Validate the team members' efforts when they succeed. Point to what was missing when they fail. Never blame team members for poor results.

3. *Influence team members to change their behavior.* The ultimate test of coaching effectiveness is whether an employee's performance improves. You must encourage ongoing growth and development. How can you do this? Try the following behaviors. Recognize and reward small improvements and treat coaching as a way of helping employees to continually work toward improvement. Use a collaborative style by allowing team members to participate in identifying and choosing among improvement ideas. Break difficult tasks down into simpler ones. Model the qualities that you expect from your team. If you want openness, dedication, commitment, and responsibility from your team members, you must demonstrate these qualities yourself.

Practicing the Skill. Collaborative efforts are more successful when every member of the group or team contributes a specific role or task toward the completion of the goal. To improve your skill at nurturing team effort, choose two of the following activities and break each one into at least six to eight separate tasks or steps. Be sure to indicate which steps are sequential, and which can be done simultaneously with others. What do you think is the ideal team size for each activity you choose?

a. Making an omelet
b. Washing the car
c. Creating a computerized mailing list
d. Designing an advertising poster
e. Planning a ski trip
f. Restocking a supermarket's produce department

Developing Your Diagnostic and Analytical Skills

Tape Resources

Tape Resources is what many individuals would consider a classic small company. Headquartered in Virginia Beach, Virginia, Tape Resources sells blank videotapes and audiotapes to businesses like television stations and production companies. Some of its most popular tapes—from manufacturers such as Sony, Fuji, Maxell, and Panasonic—carry price tags ranging from $10 to $25. The company doesn't try to compete on price. Rather, its strategy is to offer superior customer service, or as company officials call it, "Legendary Customer Service." For many of its customers, this means that Tape Resources provides a guaranteed in-stock program and speedy delivery.

The company has about 15 employees and annual sales approaching the $20 million mark. Its early sales grew more than 700 percent in just six short years. The company's owner, Seph Barnard, wanted that trend to continue. So he implemented a plan that he thought would excite his sales staff and promote teamwork among them. Salespeople at Tape Resources fill orders from repeat customers as well as from new ones who contact the company as a result of advertising campaigns. Once the sale is completed, it goes to the shipping department for packaging and delivery. Barnard added a commission incentive on top of the sales staff's salaries, but the new program was met with almost immediate resistance. Tension among staff became rampant. That's because the salespeople worked in the same offices as everyone else, but now they had an opportunity to make significantly more money than other employees. Employees who had been excluded from the incentive program—like those in shipping—became resentful.

Somewhat surprisingly, even the salespeople who would benefit from the added income started to have difficulties. Whereas once the salespeople cooperated and covered for one another, they now became reluctant to spend time away from the phones or to help others on specific tasks. They also didn't like it when another salesperson served a customer they had helped earlier—thereby taking away their commission. As a result of Barnard's "great incentive program," nearly all of the company's employees had become territorial and began looking out for "number one." Within six months, Barnard realized that he had made a mistake. All he wanted to do was to increase sales. Instead, his incentive plan increased resentment among team members.

While Barnard has since given up much of the control of his company to his chief operating officer, and takes frequent sabbaticals from work, his efforts have not been a waste of time. Employees took it upon themselves to recognize the importance of a team concept where all employees can benefit as the company benefits. For example, many of the employees formed a special team to win a sales contest sponsored by a tape manufacturer, which earned them an all-expenses-paid trip to Cancun, Mexico. It appears that when they, as a group, saw the benefit for all employees and not a select few, the team camaraderie and company good that Barnard had hoped for came to fruition—with annual sales increases in the 24 percent range.

Questions

1. Why do you believe the sales team incentive system failed? Cite specific examples to support your position.
2. While the initial "team concept" failed, employees later used many of the team concepts that ultimately worked for them—and made the organization grow. Why do you believe the "employee-formed" team was successful?
3. Using the nine characteristics of a high-performing work team, describe each of the nine elements as they relate to this case. Use examples where appropriate. If a characteristic was not specifically cited in the case, describe how it may have been witnessed in this situation.

Enhancing Your Communication Skills

1. Teams create conflict among their members, and conflict can lead to lower productivity. Management, then, should not support the concept of teams. Build one argument to support his statement and another to show why the statement is false. Then, take a position on one side of the controversy and support your opinion.
2. Describe why work teams are more acceptable in Japan than in the United States or Canada. Explain how Japanese firms in the United States can still use teams even though the cultural dimensions are different.
3. Develop a presentation explaining whether you would prefer to work alone or as part of a team. What does your response indicate in terms of organizational cultures in which you might work? Explain.

COMMUNICATION AND INFORMATION TECHNOLOGY

A MANAGER'S DILEMMA

Semifreddi's is an artisan-bread bakery (bakers of specialty bread and bread shaped in unusual and artistic ways) in Emeryville, California. Semifreddi is an Italian word meaning "half-cold" and refers to partially frozen desserts. Customers love the name and the hand-shaped specialty breads. CEO Tom Frainier (a Berkeley M.B.A. who left the corporate world after seven successful years in management) runs the company, whose annual revenues are over $7 million. He describes himself as an "accessible, available, communicative guy." However, language barriers have been a challenge for Tom and his workers, most of whom are from Mexico, Laos, China, Peru, Cambodia, and Vietnam. Even though his workers have limited English-language skills, Tom feels that he communicates sufficiently well with his diverse workforce because no major problems have arisen—at least yet.

When customers began making comments about the lack of parking on one side of the bakery, Tom called an employee meeting, just as he did anytime there were issues to be discussed. He asked workers not to park in the spaces reserved for customers. Some employees misunderstood and thought he was telling them not to drive to work. Tom later said that his mistake was talking slowly and loudly and assuming that by doing so his employees would understand him. However, the miscommunication over the parking issue was minor in comparison to another of his communication challenges.

Tom is a strong believer in open-book management, an approach in which the "books," or company financial statements, are shared with employees in order to help them better understand the business and make them feel more like a partner in it. To show his commitment to sharing information, he recently gathered together employees from different work shifts and shared a long list of financial numbers with them. When Tom asked them if they understood, all heads nodded in agreement. Tom said later, "I didn't realize that they were just being polite." His desire to involve his employees by sharing the financial results wasn't working.

Put yourself in Tom's position. What could he do to improve the effectiveness of his communications?

What would you do?

Tom Frainier of Semifreddi's recognizes the importance of effectively communicating with his employees. Communication between managers and employees provides the information necessary to get work done effectively and efficiently in organizations. As such, there's no doubt that communication is fundamentally linked to managerial performance. In this chapter, well present basic concepts in managerial communication. We'll explain the interpersonal communication process, methods of communicating, barriers to effective communication, and ways to overcome those barriers. We'll also look at organizational communication issues including communication flow and communication networks. And, because managerial communication is so greatly influenced by information technology, we'll look at it as well. Finally, we'll discuss several contemporary communication issues facing managers.

Understanding Communication

Unlike the character Bill Murray plays in *Groundhog Day,* Neal L. Patterson, CEO of Cerner Corporation, a health care software development company based in Kansas City, probably wishes he *could* do over one day. Upset with the fact that employees didn't seem to be putting in enough hours, he sent an angry and emotional e-mail to about 400 company managers that said, in part:

> We are getting less than 40 hours of work from a large number of our K.C.—based EMPLOYEES. The parking lot is sparsely used at 8 A.M.; likewise at 5 P.M. managers, you either do not know what your EMPLOYEES are doing, or you do not CARE. You have created expectations on the work effort which allowed this to happen inside Cerner, creating a very unhealthy environment. In either case, you have a problem and you will fix it or I will replace you . . . I will hold you accountable. You have allowed things to get to this state. You have two weeks. Tick, tock.

Although the e-mail was meant only for the company's managers, it was leaked and posted on a Yahoo! discussion site. The tone of the e-mail surprised industry analysts, investors, and of course, Cerner's managers and employees. The company's stock price dropped 22 percent over the next three days. Patterson apologized to his employees and acknowledged, "I lit a match and started a firestone." This is a good example of why its important for managers to understand the impact of communication.

The importance of effective communication for managers can't be overemphasized for one specific reason: Everything a manager does involves communicating. Not *some* things, but everything! A manager can't make a decision without information. That information has to be communicated. Once a decision is made, communication must again take place. Otherwise, no one would know that a decision was made. The best idea, the most creative suggestion, the best plan, or the most effective job redesign can't take shape without communication. Managers need effective communication skills. We aren't suggesting that good communication skills alone make a successful manager. We can say, however, that ineffective communication skills can lead to a continuous stream of problems for the manager.

What Is Communication?

communication The transfer and understanding of meaning

Communication is the transfer and understanding of meaning. The first thing to note about this definition is the emphasis on the *transfer* of meaning. This means that if no information or ideas have been conveyed, communication hasn't taken place. The speaker who isn't heard or the writer who isn't read hasn't communicated.

More importantly, however, communication involves the *understanding* of meaning. For communication to be successful, the meaning must be imparted and understood. A letter written in Portuguese addressed to a person who doesn't read Portuguese can't be considered communication until its translated into a language the person does read and understand. Perfect communication, if such a thing existed, would be when a transmitted thought or idea was perceived by the receiver exactly as it was envisioned by the sender.

Another point to keep in mind is that *good* communication is often erroneously defined by the communicator as *agreement* with the message instead of clearly understanding the message. If someone disagrees with us, many of us assume that the person just didn't fully understand our position. In other words, many of us define good communication as having someone accept our views. But I can clearly understand what you mean and just not agree with what you say. In fact, many times when a conflict has gone on for a long time, people will say its because the parties aren't communicating effectively. That assumption reflects the tendency to think that effective communication equals agreement.

The final point we want to make about communication is that it encompasses both **interpersonal communication**—communication between two or more people—and **organizational communication**—all the patterns, networks, and systems of communication within an organization. Both these types of communication are important to managers in organizations.

Functions of Communication

Why is communication important to managers and organizations? It serves four major functions: control, motivation, emotional expression, and information.

Communication acts to control member behavior in several ways. Organizations have authority hierarchies and formal guidelines that employees are required to follow. For instance, when employees are required to communicate any job-related grievance first to their immediate manager, or to follow their job description, or to comply with company policies, communication is being used to control. But informal communication also controls behavior. When work groups tease or harass a member who's working too hard or producing too much (making the rest of the group look bad), they're informally controlling the member's behavior.

Communication encourages *motivation* by clarifying to employees what is to be done, how well they're doing, and what can be done to improve performance if it's not up to par. As employees set specific goals, work toward those goals, and receive feedback on progress toward goals, communication is required.

For many employees, their work group is a primary source of social interaction. The communication that takes place within the group is a fundamental mechanism by which members share frustrations and feelings of satisfaction. Communication, therefore, provides a release for *emotional expression* of feelings and for fulfillment of social needs.

Finally, individuals and groups need information to get things done in organizations. Communication provides that *information*.

No one of these four functions is more important than the others. For groups to work effectively, they need to maintain some form of control over members,

interpersonal communication Communication between two or more people

organizational communication All the patterns, networks, and systems of communication within an organization

motivate members to perform, provide a means for emotional expression, and make decisions. You can assume that almost every communication interaction that takes place in a group or organization is fulfilling one or more of these four functions.

Interpersonal Communication

message A purpose to be conveyed

encoding Converting a message into symbols

channel The medium a message travels along

decoding Retranslating a sender's message

communication process The seven elements involved in transferring meaning from one person to another

noise Any disturbances that interfere with the transmission, receipt, or feedback of a message

Before communication can take place, a purpose, expressed as a **message** to be conveyed, must exist. It passes between a source (the sender) and a receiver. The message is converted to symbolic form (called **encoding**) and passed by way of some medium (**channel**) to the receiver, who retranslates the sender's message, (called decoding). The result is the transfer of meaning from one person to another. Figure 12.1 illustrates the seven elements of the **communication process**: the communication source, the message, encoding, the channel, decoding, the receiver, and feedback. In addition, note that the entire process is susceptible to **noise**—disturbances that interfere with the transmission, receipt, or feedback of a message. Typical examples of noise include illegible print, phone static, inattention by the receiver, or background sounds of machinery or co-workers. Remember that anything that interferes with understanding can be noise, and noise can create distortion at any point in the communication process. Let's look at how distortions can happen with the sender, the message, the channel, the receiver, and the feedback loop.

A *sender* initiates a message by *encoding* a thought. Four conditions influence the effectiveness of that encoded message: the skills, attitudes, and knowledge of the sender, and the social-cultural system. How? We'll use ourselves, as your textbook authors, as an example. If we don't have the requisite skills, our message won't reach you, the reader, in the form desired. Our success in communicating to you depends on our writing skills. In addition, any preexisting ideas (attitudes) that we may have about numerous topics will affect how we communicate. For instance, our attitudes about managerial ethics or the importance of managers to organizations influence our writing. Next, the amount of knowledge we have about a subject affects the message(s) we are transferring. We can't communicate what we don't know; and if our knowledge is too extensive, it's possible that our writing won't be understood by the readers. Finally, the social-cultural system in which we live influences us as communication senders. Our beliefs and values (all part of culture) act to influence what and how we communicate. Think back to our chapter-opening "Manager's Dilemma" and how Tom Frainier wants to be an effective

FIGURE 12.1
The Interpersonal Communication Process

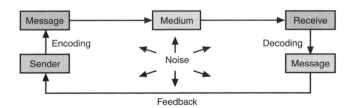

communicator. As he encodes his ideas into messages when communicating with employees, he needs to reflect on his skill, attitudes, knowledge, and the social-cultural system (of both the United States and his employees' countries of origin) in order to reduce any possible noise.

The *message* itself can distort the communication process, regardless of the kinds of supporting tools or technologies used to convey it. A message is the actual physical product encoded by the source. It can be the written document, the oral speech, and even the gestures and facial expressions we use. The message is affected by the symbols used to transfer meaning (words, pictures, numbers, etc.), the content of the message itself, and the decisions that the sender makes in selecting and arranging both the symbols and the content. Noise can distort the communication process in any of these areas.

The *channel* chosen to communicate the message also has the potential to be affected by noise. Whether it's a face-to-face conversation, an e-mail message, or a company-wide memorandum, distortions can, and do, occur. Managers need to recognize that certain channels are more appropriate for certain messages. (Think back to how Cerner's CEO chose to communicate his frustration with his manager by e-mail and whether that was an appropriate choice.) Obviously, if the office is on fire, a memo to convey the fact is inappropriate! And if something is important, such as an employee's performance appraisal, a manager might want to use multiple channels—perhaps an oral review followed by a written letter summarizing the points. This decreases the potential for distortion.

The *receiver* is the individual to whom the message is directed. Before the message can be received, however, the symbols in it must be translated into a form that the receiver can understand. This is the *decoding* of the message. Just as the sender was limited by his or her skills, attitudes, knowledge, and social-cultural system, so is the receiver. And just as the sender must be skillful in writing or speaking, the receiver must be skillful in reading or listening. A person's knowledge influences his or her ability to receive. Moreover, the receiver's attitudes and social-cultural background can distort the message.

The final link in the communication process is a *feedback loop*. Feedback returns the message to the sender and provides a check on whether understanding has been achieved. Because feedback can be transmitted along the same types of channels as the original message, it faces the same potential for distortion.

Methods of Communicating Interpersonally

You need to communicate to your employees the organization's new policy on sexual harassment; you want to compliment one of your workers on the extra hours she's put in to help your work group complete a customer's order; you must tell one of your employees about changes to her job; or you would like to get employees' feedback on your proposed budget for next year. In each of these instances, how would you communicate this information? Managers have a wide variety of communication methods from which to choose.

These include face-to-face, telephone, group meetings, formal presentations, memos, traditional mail, fax machines, employee publications, bulletin boards, other company publications, audio- and videotapes, hotlines, electronic mail, computer conferencing, voice mail, teleconferences, and videoconferences. All of these communication channels include oral or written symbols, or both. How do you know which to use? Managers can use 12 questions to help them evaluate the various communication methods.

1. *Feedback*—How quickly can the receiver respond to the message?
2. *Complexity capacity*—Can the method effectively process complex messages?
3. *Breadth potential*—How many different messages can be transmitted using this method?
4. *Confidentiality*—Can communicators be reasonably sure their messages are received only by those for whom they're intended?
5. *Encoding ease*—Can sender easily and quickly use this channel?
6. *Decoding ease*—Can receiver easily and quickly decode messages?
7. *Time-space constraint*—Do senders and receivers need to communicate at the same time and in the same space?
8. *Cost*—How much does it cost to use this method?
9. *Interpersonal warmth*—How well does this method convey interpersonal warmth?
10. *Formality*—Does this method have the needed amount of formality?
11. *Scanability*—Does this method allow the message to be easily browsed or scanned for relevant information?
12. *Time of consumption*—Does sender or receiver exercise the most control over when the message is dealt with?

Figure 12.2 provides a comparison of the various communication methods on these 12 criteria. Which method a manager ultimately chooses should reflect the needs of the sender, the attributes of the message, the attributes of the channel, and the needs of the receiver. For instance, if you need to communicate to an employee the changes being made in her job, face-to-face communication would be a better choice than a memo since you want to be able to address immediately any question and concerns that she might have.

We can't leave the topic of interpersonal communication methods without looking at the role of **nonverbal communication**—that is, communication transmitted without words. Some of the most meaningful communications are neither spoken nor written. A loud siren or a red light at an intersection tells you something without words. When a college instructor is teaching a class, she doesn't need words to tell her that her students are bored when their eyes are glassed over or they begin to read the school newspaper in the middle of class. Similarly, when students start putting their papers, notebooks, and book away, the message is clear: Class time is about over. The size of a person's office or the clothes he or she wears also convey messages to others. These are all forms of nonverbal communication. The best-known types of nonverbal communication are body language and verbal intonation.

Body language refers to gestures, facial expressions, and other body movements that convey meaning. A person frowning "says" something different from one who's smiling. Hand motions, facial expressions, and other gestures can communicate emotions or temperaments such as aggression, fear, shyness, arrogance, joy, and anger. Knowing the meaning behind someone's body moves and learning how to put forth your best body language can help you personally and professionally.

nonverbal communication Communication transmitted without words

body language Gestures, facial configurations, and other movements of the body that convey meaning

CRITERIA

Channel	Feedback Potential	Complexity Capacity	Breadth Potential	Confidentiality	Encoding Ease	Decoding Ease	Space Constraint	Cost	Personal Warmth	Formality	Scam ability	Consumption Time
Face-to-face	1	1	1	1	1	1	1	2	1	4	4	S/R
Telephone	1	4	2	2	1	1	3	3	2	4	4	S/R
Group meetings	2	2	2	4	2	2	1	1	2	3	4	S/R
Formal presentations	4	2	2	4	3	2	1	1	3	3	5	Sender
Memos	4	4	2	3	4	3	5	3	5	2	1	Receiver
Postal mail	5	3	3	2	4	3	5	3	4	1	1	Receiver
Fax	3	4	2	4	3	3	5	3	3	3	1	Receiver
Publications	5	4	2	5	5	3	5	2	4	1	1	Receiver
Bulletin boards	4	5	1	5	3	2	2	4	5	3	1	Receiver
Audio/ videotapes	4	4	3	5	4	2	3	2	3	3	5	Receiver
Hotlines	2	5	2	2	3	1	4	2	3	3	4	Receiver
E-mail	3	4	1	2	3	2	4	2	4	3	4	Receiver
Computer conference	1	2	2	4	3	2	3	2	3	3	4	S/R
Voice mall	2	4	2	1	2	1	5	3	2	4	4	Receiver
Tele-conference	2	3	2	5	2	2	2	2	3	3	5	S/R
Video-conference	3	3	2	4	2	2	2	1	2	3	5	S/R

FIGURE 12.2

Comparison of Communication Methods

NOTE: Ratings are on a 1–5 scale where 1 = high and 5 = low. Consumption time refers to who controls the reception of communication. S/R means the sender and receiver share control.

SOURCE: P. G. Clampitt, *Communicating for Managerial Effectiveness* (Newbury Park. CA: Sage Publications, 1991), p. 136.

verbal intonation An emphasis given to words or phrases that conveys meaning

Verbal intonation refers to the emphasis someone gives to words or phrases that conveys meaning. To illustrate how intonations can change the meaning of a message, consider the student who asks the instructor a question. The instructor replies, "What do you mean by that?" The student's reaction will vary, depending on the tone of the instructor's response. A soft, smooth vocal tone conveys interest and creates a different meaning from one that is abrasive and puts a strong emphasis on saving the last word. Most of us would view the first intonation as coming from someone sincerely interested in clarifying the student's concern, whereas the second suggests that the person is defensive or aggressive.

The fact that every oral communication also has a nonverbal message can't be overemphasized. Why? Because the nonverbal component usually carries the greatest impact. "Its not *what* you said, but *how* you said it." People respond to *how* something is said as well as *what* is said. Managers should remember this as they communicate.

Barriers to Effective Interpersonal Communication

In our discussion of the interpersonal communication process, we noted the continual potential for distortion. What causes distortion? In addition to the general distortions identified in the communication process, managers face other barriers to effective communication.

filtering The deliberate manipulation of information to make it appear more favorable to the receiver

Filtering. **Filtering** is the deliberate manipulation of information to make it appear more favorable to the receiver. For example, when a person tells his or her manager what the manager wants to hear, that individual is filtering information. Does this happen much in organizations? Yes, it does! As information is communicated up through organizational levels, its condensed and synthesized by senders so those on top don't become overloaded with information. Those doing the condensing filter communications through their personal interests and perceptions of what is important.

The extent of filtering tends to be a function of the number of vertical levels in the organization and the organizational culture. The more vertical levels there are in an organization, the more opportunities there are for filtering. As organizations become less dependent on strict hierarchical arrangements and instead use more collaborative, cooperative work arrangements, information filtering may become less of a problem. In addition, the ever-increasing use of e-mail to communicate in organizations reduces filtering because communication is more direct as intermediaries are bypassed. Finally, the organizational culture encourages or discourages filtering by the type of behavior it rewards. The more that organizational rewards emphasize style and appearance, the more managers will be motivated to filter communications in their favor.

Emotions. How a receiver feels when a message is received influences how he or she interprets it. You'll often interpret the same message differently, depending on whether you're happy or upset. Extreme emotions are most likely to hinder effective communication. In such instances, we often disregard our rational and objective thinking processes and substitute emotional judgments. It's best to avoid reacting to a message when you're upset because you're not likely to be thinking clearly.

Information Overload. A marketing manager goes on a week-long sales trip to Spain, where he doesn't have access to his e-mail and is faced with 1,000 messages on his return. It's not possible to fully read and respond to each and every one of those messages without facing **information overload**—when the information we have to work with exceeds our processing capacity. Today's typical executive frequently complains of information overload. Statistics show that the average business e-mail user devotes 90 minutes a day to "organizing" e-mail. Other statistics show that employees send and receive an average of 204 e-mail messages every day. The demands of keeping up with e-mail, phone calls, faxes, meetings, and professional reading create an onslaught of data that is nearly impossible to process and assimilate. What happens when individuals have more information than they can sort and use? They tend to select out, ignore, pass over, or forget information. Or, they may put off further processing until the overload situation is over. Regardless, the result is lost information and less effective communication.

information overload
The information we have to work with exceeds our processing capacity

Defensiveness. When people feel that they're being threatened, they tend to react in ways that reduce their ability to achieve mutual understanding. That is, they become defensive—engaging in behaviors such as verbally attacking others, making sarcastic remarks, being overly judgmental, and questioning others' motives. When individuals interpret another's message as threatening, they often respond in ways that hinder effective communication.

Language. Words mean different things to different people. Age, education, and cultural background are three of the more obvious variables that influence the language a person uses and the definitions he or she gives to words. Author/journalist William F. Buckley Jr., and rap artist Nelly both speak English. But the language each uses is vastly different.

In an organization, employees typically come from diverse backgrounds (think back to our chapter-opening "Manager's Dilemma") and have different patterns of speech. Even employees who work for the same organization but in different departments often have different **jargon**—specialized terminology or technical language that members of a group use to communicate among themselves.

jargon Specialized terminology or technical language that members of a group use to communicate among themselves

Keep in mind that while we may speak the same language, our use of that language is far from uniform. Senders tend to assume that the words and phrases they use mean the same to the receiver as they do to them. This, of course, is incorrect and creates communication barriers. Knowing how each of us modifies the language would help minimize those barriers.

National Culture. As the chapter-opening "Managers Dilemma" pointed out, communication differences can also arise from the different languages that individuals use to communicate and the national culture they're part of. Interpersonal communication isn't conducted the same way around the world. For example, let's compare countries that place a high value on individualism (such as the United States) with countries where the emphasis is on collectivism (such as Japan).

In the United States, communication patterns tend to be oriented to the individual and clearly spelled out. U.S. managers rely heavily on memoranda, announcements, position papers, and other formal forms of communication to state their positions on issues. U.S. supervisors may hoard information in an attempt to make themselves look good and as a way of persuading their employees

The Communication Styles of Men and Women

"You don't understand what I'm saying, and you never listen!" "You're making a big deal out of nothing." Have you said (or heard) these statements or ones like them to friends of the opposite sex? Most of us probably have! Research shows us that men and women tend to have different communication styles. Let's look more closely at these differing styles and the problems that can arise, and try to suggest ways to minimize the barriers.

Deborah Tannen has studied the ways that men and women communicate, and reports some interesting differences. The essence of her research is that men use talk to emphasize status, while women use it to create connection. She states that communication between the sexes can be a continual balancing act of juggling our conflicting needs for intimacy, which suggests closeness and commonality, and independence, which emphasizes separateness and differences. It's no wonder, then, that communication problems arise! Women hear and speak a language of connection and intimacy. Men hear and speak a language of status and independence. For many men, conversations are merely a way to preserve independence and maintain status in a hierarchical social order. Yet for many women, conversations are negotiations for closeness and seeking out support and confirmation. Let's look at a few examples of what Tannen has described.

Men frequently complain that women talk on and on about their problems. Women, however, criticize men for not listening. What's happening is that when a man hears a woman talking about a problem, he frequently asserts his desire for independence and control by offering solutions. Many women, in contrast, view conversing about a problem as a way to promote closeness. The woman talks about a problem to gain support and connection, not to get the male's advice.

Here's another example: Men are often more direct than women in conversation. A man might say, "I think you're wrong on that point." A woman might say, "Have you looked at the marketing department's research report on that issue?" The implication in the woman's comment is that the report will point out the error. Men frequently misread women's indirectness as "covert" or "sneaky," but women aren't as concerned as men with the status and one-upmanship that directness often creates.

Finally, men often criticize women for seeming to apologize all the time. Men tend to see the phrase "I'm sorry" as a sign of weakness because they interpret the phrase to mean the woman is accepting blame, when he may know she's not to blame. The woman also knows she's not at fault. Yet she's typically using "I'm sorry" to express regret: "I know you must feel bad about this and I do, too."

Because effective communication among the sexes is important in *all* organizations, how can we manage these differences in communication styles? To keep gender differences from becoming persistent barriers to effective communication requires acceptance, understanding, and a commitment to communicate adaptively with each other. Both men and women need to acknowledge that there are differences in communication styles, that one style isn't better than the other, and that it takes real effort to "talk" with each other successfully.

to accept decisions and plans. And for their own protection, lower level employees also often engage in this practice.

In collectivist countries, such as Japan, there's more interaction for its own sake and a more informal manner of interpersonal contact. The Japanese manager, in contrast to the U.S. manager, engages in extensive verbal consultation with subordinates over an issue first, and draws up a formal document later to outline the agreement that was made. The Japanese value decisions by consensus, and open communication is an inherent part of the work setting. Also, face-to-face communication is encouraged.

Cultural differences can affect the way a manager chooses to communicate. And these differences undoubtedly can be a barrier to effective communication if not recognized and taken into consideration.

Overcoming the Barriers

On average, an individual must hear new information seven times before he or she truly understands. In light of this fact and the barriers to communication, what can managers do to overcome these barriers? The following suggestions should help make your interpersonal communication more effective.

Use Feedback. Many communication problems can be directly attributed to misunderstanding and inaccuracies. These problems are less likely to occur if the manager uses the feedback loop in the communication process, either verbally or nonverbally.

If a manager asks a receiver, "Did you understand what I said?" the response represents feedback. Good feedback should include more than yes-and-no answers. The manager can ask a set of questions about a message to determine whether or not the message was received and understood as intended. Better yet, the manager can ask the receiver to restate the message in his or her own words. If the manager hears what was intended, understanding and accuracy should improve. Feedback includes subtler methods than directly asking questions or having the receiver summarize the message. General comments can give a manager a sense of the receiver's reaction to a message.

Of course, feedback doesn't have to be conveyed in words. Actions *can* speak louder than words. A sales manager sends an e-mail to his or her staff describing a new monthly sales report that all sales representatives will need to complete. If some of them don't turn in the new report, the sales manager has received feedback. This feedback suggests that the sales manager needs to clarify further the initial communication. Similarly, when you're talking to people, you watch their eyes and look for other nonverbal clues to tell whether they're getting your message or not.

Simplify Language. Because language can be a barrier, managers should choose words and structure their messages in ways that will make those messages clear and understandable to the receiver. Remember, effective communication is achieved when a message is both received and *understood*. Understanding is improved by simplifying the language used in relation to the audience intended. This means, for example, that a hospital administrator should always try to communicate in clear, easily understood terms and that the language used in messages to the surgical staff should be purposefully different from that used with office employees. Jargon can facilitate understanding when it's used within a group of those who know what it means, but it can cause many problems when used outside that group.

Listen Actively. When someone talks, we hear. But too often we don't listen. Listening is an active search for meaning, whereas hearing is passive. In listening, two people are engaged in thinking: the sender *and* the receiver.

Many of us are poor listeners. Why? Because it's difficult and usually more satisfying to be on the offensive. Listening, in fact, is often more tiring than talking. It demands intellectual effort. Unlike hearing, **active listening**, which is listening for full meaning without making premature judgments or interpretations, demands total concentration. The average person normally speaks at a rate of about 125 to 200 word per minute. However, the average listener can comprehend up to 400 words per minute. The difference obviously leaves lots of idle time for the brain and opportunities for the mind to wander.

Active listening is enhanced by developing empathy with the sender—that is, by placing yourself in the sender's position. Because senders differ in attitudes, interests, needs, and expectations, empathy makes it easier to understand the actual content of a message. An empathetic listener reserves judgment on the message's content and carefully listens to what is being said. The goal is to improve your ability to receive the full meaning of a communication without having it distorted by premature judgments or interpretations. Other specific behaviors that active listeners demonstrate are listed in Figure 12.3.

Constrain Emotions. It would be naive to assume that managers always communicate in a rational manner. We know that emotions can severely cloud and distort the transference of meaning. A manager who is emotionally upset over an issue is more likely to misconstrue incoming messages and fail to communicate his or her outgoing messages clearly and accurately. What can the manager do? The simplest answer is to refrain from communicating until he or she has regained composure.

Watch Nonverbal Cues. If actions speak louder than words, then its important to watch your actions to make sure they align with and reinforce the words that go along with them. The effective communicator watches his or her nonverbal cues to ensure that they convey the desired message.

active listening
Listening for full meaning without making premature judgment or interpretations

FIGURE 12.3
Active Listening Behaviors

Source: Based on P. L. Hunsaker, *Training in Management Skills* (Upper Saddle River, NJ: Prentice Hall, 2001).

Organizational Communication

An understanding of managerial communication isn't possible without looking at the fundamentals of organizational communication. In this section, we look at several important aspects of organizational communication, including formal versus informal communication, the flow patterns of communication, and formal and informal communication networks.

Formal versus Informal Communication

formal communication Communication that follows the official chain of command or is required to do one's job.

Communication within an organization is often described as formal or informal. **Formal communication** refers to communication that follows the official chain of command or is part of the communication required to do one's job. For example, when a manager asks an employee to complete a task, he or she is communicating formally. So is the employee who brings a problem to the attention of his or her manager. Any communication that takes place within prescribed organizational work arrangements would be classified as formal.

informal communication Communication that is not defined by the organization's structural hierarchy

Informal communication is organizational communication that is not defined by the organization's structural hierarchy. When employees talk with each other in the lunch room, as they pass in hallways, or as they're working out at the company exercise facility, that's informal communication. Employees form friendships and communicate with each other. The informal communication system fulfills two purposes in organizations: (1) it permits employees to satisfy their need for social interaction, and (2) it can improve an organization's performance by creating alternative, and frequently faster and more efficient, channels of communication.

Direction of Communication Flow

Organizational communication can flow downward, upward, laterally, or diagonally. Let's look at each.

downward communication Communication that flows downward from a manager to employees

Downward. Any communication that flows downward from a manager to employees is **downward communication**. Downward communication is used to inform, direct, coordinate, and evaluate employees. When managers assign goals to their employees, they're using downward communication. Managers are also using downward communication by providing employees with job descriptions, informing them of organizational policies and procedures, pointing out problems that need attention, or evaluating their performance. Downward communication can take place through any of the communication methods we described earlier.

upward communication Communication that cuts across work areas and organizational levels

Upward Communication. Managers rely on their employees for information. Reports are given to managers to inform them of progress toward goals and any current problems. **Upward communication** is communication that flows upward from employees to managers. It keeps managers aware of how employees feel about their jobs, their co-workers, and the organization in general. Managers also rely on upward communication for ideas on how things can be improved. Some examples of upward communication include performance reports prepared by employees, suggestion boxes, employee attitude surveys, grievance procedures, manager-employee discussions, and informal group sessions in which employees have the opportunity to identify and discuss problems with their manager or even representatives of top-level management.

The extent of upward communication depends on the organizational culture. If managers have created a climate of trust and respect and use participative decision making or empowerment, there will be considerable upward communication as employees provide input to decisions. For example, FedEx CIO Robert Carter holds town hall meetings with his staff about every six weeks and sits down once a month with eight randomly selected employees to talk over issues and concerns. He has created an environment where employees want to share information and has found these communication encounters to be prime opportunities for finding out what's going on with his employees. In a highly structured and authoritarian environment, however, upward communication still takes place, but will be limited in both style and content.

Lateral Communication. Communication that takes place among employees on the same organizational level is called **lateral communication.** In today's often chaotic and rapidly changing environment, horizontal communications are frequently needed to save time and facilitate coordination. Cross-functional teams, for instance, rely heavily on this form of communication interaction. However, it can create conflicts if employees don't keep their managers informed about decisions they've made or actions they've taken.

Diagonal Communication. **Diagonal communication** is communication that cuts across both work areas *and* organizational levels. When an analyst in the credit department communicates directly with a regional marketing manager—note the different department and different organizational level—about a customer problem, that's diagonal communication. In the interest of efficiency and speed, diagonal communication can be beneficial. And the increased use of e-mail facilitates diagonal communication. In many organizations, any employee can communicate by e-mail with any other employee, regardless of organizational work area or level. However, just as with lateral communication, diagonal communication has the potential to create problems if employees don't keep their managers informed.

Organizational Communication Networks

The vertical and horizontal flows of organizational communication can be combined into a variety of patterns called **communication networks.** Figure 12.4 illustrates three common communication networks.

Types of Communication Networks. In the *chain* network, communication flows according to the formal chain of command, both downward and upward. The *wheel* network represents communication flowing between a clearly identifiable and strong leader and others in a work group or team. The leader serves as the hub through whom all communication passes. Finally in the *all-channel* network, communication flows freely among all members of a work team.

As a manager, which network should you use? The answer depends on your goal. Figure 12.4 also summarizes the effectiveness of the various networks

lateral communication Communication that takes place among any employees on the same organizational level

diagonal communication Communication that cuts across work areas and organizational levels

communication networks The variety of patterns of vertical and horizontal flows of organizational communication

FIGURE 12.4

Three Common Organizational Communication Networks and How They Rate on Effectiveness Criteria

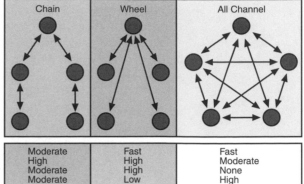

Criteria	Chain	Wheel	All Channel
Speed	Moderate	Fast	Fast
Accuracy	High	High	Moderate
Emergence of leader	Moderate	High	None
Member satisfaction	Moderate	Low	High

grapevine The informal organizational communication network

according to four criteria: speed, accuracy, the probability that a leader will emerge, and the importance of member satisfaction. One observation is immediately apparent: No single network is best for all situations. If you're concerned with high member satisfaction, the all-channel network is best; if having a strong and identifiable leader is important, the wheel facilitates this; and if accuracy is most important, the chain and wheel networks work best.

The Grapevine. We can't leave our discussion of communication networks without discussing the **grapevine**—the informal organizational communication network. The grapevine is active in almost every organization. Is it an important source of information? You bet! One survey reported that 75 percent of employees hear about matters first through rumors on the grapevine.

What are the implications for managers? Certainly, the grapevine is an important part of any group or organization communication network and well worth understanding. It identifies for managers those bewildering issues that employees consider important and anxiety producing. It acts as both a filter and a feedback mechanism, picking up on the issues employees consider relevant. More importantly, from a managerial point of view, it is possible to analyze what is happening on the grapevine—what information is being passed, how information seems to flow along the grapevine, and what individuals seem to be key conduits of information on the grapevine. By being aware of the grapevine's flow and patterns, managers can stay on top of issues that concern employees, and, in turn, can use the grapevine to disseminate important information. Since the grapevine can't be eliminated, managers should "manage" it as an important information network.

Rumors that flow along the grapevine also can never be eliminated entirely. What managers can do, however, is minimize the negative consequences of rumors by limiting their range and impact. How? By communicating openly, fully, and honestly with employees, particularly in situations where employees may not like proposed or actual managerial decisions or actions. Open and honest communication with employees can impact the organization in various ways. A study of employee attitudes by Watson Wyatt Worldwide concluded that open communication had a significant positive impact on employee attitudes, but only one out of three employees surveyed rated their company as favorable in this area. But for those companies that scored high on communication, this study showed that total returns to shareholders were three times higher than at companies that had poor communication.

Understanding Information Technology

Technology is changing the way we live and work. Take the following four examples: Japanese employees and managers, housewives, and teens use wireless interactive Web phones to send e-mail, surf the Web, swap photos, and play computer games. At Postnet, the Swedish postal service's Internet subsidiary, employees work at tables with electrical and data-connection cables to plug in their laptop computers. Postnet's CEO spends her days walking around the office carrying her mobile phone which is connected to the postal system's main switchboard. Over 75 percent of IBM's 355,000 employees regularly use instant messaging software for communicating and for workplace collaboration. And at ChevronTexaco's worldwide headquarters in San Francisco, employees often meet to share information and to exchange ideas in "visualization centers" where data and graphics can be displayed on enormous screens.

The world of communication isn't what it used to be! Managers are challenged to keep their organizations functioning smoothly while continually improving work operations *and* staying competitive even though both the organization and the environment are changing rapidly. Although changing technology has been a significant source of the environmental uncertainty facing organizations, these same technological advances have enabled managers to coordinate the work efforts of employees in ways that can lead to increased efficiency and effectiveness. Information technology now touches every aspect of almost every company's business. The implications for the ways managers communicate are profound.

How Technology Affects Managerial Communication

Technology, and more specifically information technology, has radically changed the way organizational members communicate. For example, it has significantly improved a manager's ability to monitor individual or team performance, it has allowed employees to have more complete information to make faster decisions, and it has provided employees more opportunities to collaborate and share information. In addition, information technology has made it possible for people in organizations to be fully accessible, any time, regardless of where they are. Employees don't have to be at their desks with their computers on to communicate with others in the organization. Two developments in information technology seem to be having the most significant impact on current managerial communication: networked computer systems and wireless capabilities.

Networked Computer System. In a networked computer system, an organization links its computers, creating an organizational network. Organizational members can then communicate with each other and tap into information whether they're down the hall, across town, or halfway across the world. Although we won't get into the mechanics of how a network system works, we will address some of its communication applications including e-mail, instant messaging, voice mail, fax, electronic data interchange, teleconferencing and videoconferencing, and intranets and extranets.

Pogo.com reported that in a single month over 1 million people at work visited its game site, and the average workplace player spent more than 2 hours and 34 minutes per visit glued to a Pogo.com game. Funny stories, jokes, and pictures make their way from one employee's e-mail inbox to another's, to another's, and so forth. An elf bowling game sent by e-mail was a favorite diversion during the holiday season.

Although these may seem like fun and harmless activities, it's estimated that such Internet distractions cost businesses over $54 billion annually. While there's a high dollar cost associated with using the Internet at work for other than business reasons, is there a psychological benefit to be gained by letting employees do something to relieve the stress of pressure-packed jobs? What are the ethical issues associated with widely available Internet access at work for both employees and for organizations?

e-mail The instantaneous transmission of written messages on computers that are linked together

instant messaging (IM) Interactive real-time communication that takes place among computer users logged on the computer network at the same time

voice mail A communication system that digitizes a spoken message, transmits it over a network, and stores the message on disk for the receiver to retrieve later

fax Communication through machines that allow the transmission of documents containing both text and graphics over ordinary telephone lines

electronic data interchange (EDI) A way for organizations to exchange standard business transaction documents using direct computer-to-computer

E-mail, the instantaneous transmission of written messages on linked computers, is a quick and convenient way for organizational members to share information and communicate.

Some organizational members who find e-mail slow and cumbersome are using **instant messaging (IM).** This is interactive real-time communication that takes place among computer users who are logged onto the computer network at the same time. IM first became popular among teens and preteens who wanted to communicate online with their friends. Now, it's moving to the workplace. With IM, there's no waiting for a colleague to read e-mail. Whatever information needs to be communicated can be done so instantaneously. However, there are a couple of drawbacks to instant messaging. It requires users to be logged on to the organization's computer network at the same time. This leaves the network open to security breaches. Also, the most popular versions of IM software are currently incompatible with each other. However, as new versions of IM software are created, these drawbacks are likely to be addressed.

A **voice mail** system digitizes a spoken message, transmits it over the network, and stores the message for the receiver to retrieve later. Voice mail allows information to be transmitted even though a receiver may not be physically present to take the information. Receivers can choose to save the message for future use, delete it, or route it to other parties.

Fax machines allow the transmission of documents containing both text and graphics over ordinary telephone lines. A sending fax machine scans and digitizes the document. A receiving fax machine reads the scanned information and reproduces it in hard copy form. Information that is best viewed in printed form can be easily and quickly shared by organizational members.

Electronic data interchange (EDI) is a way for organizations to exchange standard business transaction documents, such as invoices or purchase orders, using direct computer-to-computer networks. Organizations often use EDI with vendors, suppliers, and customers because it saves time and money. How? Information on transactions is transmitted from one organization's computer system to another through a telecommunications network. The printing and handling of paper documents at one organization are eliminated as is the inputting of data at the other organization.

Meetings—one-on-one, team, divisional, or organization-wide—have always been one way to share information. The limitations of technology used to dictate that meetings take place among people in the same physical location, but that's no longer the case! **Teleconferencing** allows a group of people to confer simultaneously using telephone or e-mail group communications software. If meeting participants can see each other over video screens, the simultaneous conference is called **videoconferencing.** Work groups, large and small, that might be in different locations, can use these communication network tools to collaborate and share information. During the SARS virus outbreak, several companies used videoconferencing to communicate with customers and employees. Although videoconferencing allowed communication to continue, it still lacked that personal touch. For instance, Dale Fuller, CEO of Borland, who was scheduled to go to China to talk with officials about economic development and possible software sales, wondered whether not being there for the face-to-face meetings and having to communicate via videoconference instead would result in missed sales.

Networked computer systems have allowed the development of organizational intranets and extranets. An **intranet** is an organizational communication network that uses Internet technology and is accessible only by employees. Many organizations are using intranets as ways for employees to share information and collaborate on documents and projects from different locations. For example, Buckman Laboratory, a manufacturer of specialty chemicals based in Memphis, Tennessee, uses an intranet so employees can easily find information about products, markets, and customers. Employees contribute information to and get information from this knowledge network known as K'Netix®. An **extranet** is an organizational communication network that uses Internet technology and allows authorized users inside the organization to communicate with certain outsiders such as customers or vendors. For instance, Harley-Davidson has developed an extranet that allows faster and more convenient communications with dealers.

Wireless Capabilities. At Seattle-based Starbucks Corporation, 600 district managers have been outfitted with mobile technology, allowing them to spend more time in the company's stores. Anne Saunders, vice president of Starbucks Interactive, says, "These are the most important people in the company. Each has between 8 and 10 stores that he or she services. And while their primary job is outside of the office—and in those stores—they still need to be connected." While the communication possibilities for a manager in a networked world are exciting, the real potential is just beginning! Networked computer systems require organizations (and employees) to be connected by wires. Wireless communication depends on signals sent through air or space without any physical connection, using things such as microwave signals, satellites, radio waves and radio antennas, or infrared light rays. The latest twist in wireless capability is Internet access made possible by "hot spots," which are simply locations where users gain wireless access

teleconferencing
Communication system that allows a group of people to confer simultaneously using telephone or e-mail group communications software

videoconferencing A simultaneous communication conference where participants can see each other

intranet An organizational communication network that uses Internet technology and is accessible only by organizational employees

extranet An organizational communication network that uses Internet technology and allows authorized users inside the organization to communicate with certain outsiders to the Internet. At the end of 2002 in the United States alone, there were about 4,000 of these hot spots, and projections for their number over the next couple of years ranged from 30,000 to the hundreds of thousands. Since nearly 21 million U.S. workers are on the move on any given day, wireless smart phones, notebook computers, and other pocket communication devices have spawned a whole new way for managers to "keep in touch." And the number of worldwide mobile users keeps increasing. In the Asia-Pacific region alone, there are over 206 million mobile users. Employees don't have to be at their desks with their phones or computers wired in and turned on to communicate with others in the organization. As technology continues to improve in this area, we'll see more and more organizational members using wireless communication as a way to collaborate and share information.

How Information Technology Affects Organizations

Employees—working in teams or as individuals—need information to make decisions and do their work. After describing the communications capabilities managers have at their disposal, it's clear that technology *can* significantly affect the way that organizational members communicate, share information, and do their work.

Communication and the exchange of information among organizational members are no longer constrained by geography or time. Collaborative work efforts among widely dispersed individuals and teams, sharing of information, and integration of decisions and work throughout an entire organization have the potential to increase organizational efficiency and effectiveness. And while the economic benefits of information technology are obvious, managers must not forget to address the psychological drawbacks. For instance, what is the psychological cost of an employee always being accessible? Will there be increased pressure for employees to "check in" even during their off hours? How important is it for employees to separate their work lives and their personal lives? While there are no easy answers to these questions, these are issues that managers will have to face. In the next section, we're going to look at other important communication issues that managers in today's organizations must face.

Communication Issues In Today's Organizations

"Pulse lunches." That's what managers at Citibank's offices throughout Malaysia used to address pressing problems with declining customer loyalty and staff morale and increased employee turnover. By connecting with employees and listening to their concerns—that is, taking their "pulse"—during informal lunch settings, managers were able to make changes that boosted both customers locally and employee morale by over 50 percent and reduced employee turnover to nearly zero.

Being an effective communicator in today's organizations means being connected—most importantly to employees and customers, but actually to any of the organization's stakeholders. In this section, we want to examine four communication issues that are of particular significance to today's managers, including managing Internet gripe sites, managing the organization's knowledge resources, communicating with customers, and using politically correct communication.

Managing Internet Gripe Sites

"Upper management was clueless." "I have never seen a finer example of the 'upward failure' model." "I saw people cry at work regularly." These were just a few of the messages posted anonymously on a discussion board at Vault.com by individuals identifying themselves as employees of Agency.com. After logging on and reading some of the gripes, Agency's co-founder and former CEO Kyle Shannon e-mailed his employees saying, "I can assure you that we take the messages on these boards very seriously." He apologized, acknowledged the company's growing pains, and promised he would "listen to the issues and address them as quickly as possible."

In addition to employee gripe sites, other Internet gripe sites feature customers' complaints. Although our focus isn't on the customer gripe sites, many of them criticize organizations for alleged shortcomings such as lousy service or unreasonable policies—information that managers should make note of and evaluate as to what action needs to be taken.

A manager's first reaction to these public forum complaints about organizational decisions or actions is likely to be anger or denial. Yet, managers shouldn't be so fast to condemn these gripe sites. Instead, they should view them as a source of information. What can be learned from the information—accurate or inaccurate—that's posted on these sites?

A recent study of employee Internet gripe sites provided a "unique insight into the expression of employee and public grievances about companies." The researchers concluded that company managers have been slow to recognize the value of this resource. What value would these sites have? In monitoring them, managers can instantly uncover employees' "hot-button" issues. As employees vent their frustration over perceived injustices, managers have the opportunity to tap into what they are feeling, even if employees' interpretations of situations may be inaccurate or incomplete. In addition, it's also a way for a manager to judge the mood of the workforce, especially in large, geographically dispersed organizations. In these organizations where employees may not have easy access to upper-level managers to discuss issues and concerns, the Internet gripe site can be viewed as another means of upward communication.

So what can managers do to "manage" these gripe sites? First, as we just discussed, recognize them as a source of valuable information. Then, just as he or she would do with information received in more traditional ways, a manager can either ignore it or respond to it. Some possible responses might include posting messages on the gripe site to clarify misinformation or taking actions to correct whatever problems have been written about. In addition, managers might set up an anonymous *internal* forum such as an intranet and encourage employees to post gripes there, rather than on the public Internet. Finally, managers should continue to monitor the Web sites. By keeping their fingers on the pulse of concerns important to employees, they can choose the best course of action.

Managing the Organization's Knowledge Resources

Pam Johnson is a materials expert at product design firm IDEO. To make finding the right materials easier, she's building a master library of samples linked to a database that explains their properties and manufacturing processes. What Johnson is doing is managing knowledge and making it easier for others at IDEO to "learn" and benefit from her knowledge. That's what today's managers need to do with the organization's knowledge resources—make it easy for employees to communicate.

MANAGING ORGANIZATIONAL CHANGE

THE MANAGEMENT CHALLENGE

Ghosn Arrives to Save Nissan

At the time, Renault's 1999 decision to plow $5.5 billion into buying part of Nissan motors seemed a ridiculously risky bet. In 1999 alone, Nissan had lost $5.7 billion, had debts of about $11 billion, and had watched its share of the Japanese car market fall for 25 years. In 2000, Nissan sold 80% of its cars at a loss. The situation wasn't helped by the nature of the task facing Carlos Ghosn, the person Renault sent to Japan to turn Nissan around.

He knew the only way to save Nissan was to take some decidedly un-Japanese steps: Close 5 domes-tic plants, cut 21,000 jobs, sell assets, and impose merit-based pay. As he said, "There were no sacred cows, no constraints, no taboos . . ." Yet, as a French citizen flying in to save a Japanese company, Ghosn faced a particularly tricky dilemma. How could he implement the widespread cuts and changes he knew were required, when doing so might trigger resentment and resistance on the part of the firm's Japanese workers and customers? Ghosn could only succeed by applying everything he knew about how to change an organization. The question was, how should he do that and what should he do first?

Carlos Ghosn knew, managers usually don't have the luxury of just dictating the changes that must be made. They have to size up what needs to be changed, and then implement those changes in a way that minimizes employee resistance. The purpose of this chapter is to show you how to successfully implement an organizational change. The main topics we'll focus on include how to decide what to change and how to change it, a nine-step process for implementing organizational change and managing interpersonal conflict.

An Overview of the Organizational Change Process

Leading an organizational change can be treacherous, even for CEOs with lots of clout. The change may require the cooperation of dozens or even hundreds of managers and supervisors, resistance may be considerable, and the manager will probably have to complete the change while the firm continues to serve its customer base. In 2000–2001, Ford CEO Jacques Nasser tried to press through changes aimed at making Ford "one of the world's best-run companies." He tried to change how the firm produced and marketed its cars, and how it evaluated, trained, and rewarded its employees. As CEO Nasser had enormous clout. However, it wasn't enough to overcome the resistance of the firm's managers, employees, and dealers. His board forced him out in less than a year.

Not all organizational changes are as broad or complex as those facing Carlos Ghosn or Jacques Nasser. For example, you may just want to stop two departments from bickering, install a new computer, or get your employees to be less risk-averse.

However, whether the required change is simple or complex, the basic organizational change process remains basically the same. Figure 13.1 presents an overview of this process. As illustrated, the "change agent" (usually the manager leading the change) needs to ask him- or herself three basic questions.

1. *What are the forces acting upon me?* In other words, what are the pressures I should take into consideration as I decide what to change and how I should change it? For example, what are the external pressures prompting the change—such as lackluster financial performance, inadequate new product development, or new competitors gaining market share—and how quickly must we respond to them? In terms of internal pressures, how am I usually inclined to lead a change? For example, am I normally more collaborative/people-oriented or more unilateral/task-oriented in my approach to doing things? Will my usual approach work in this case?

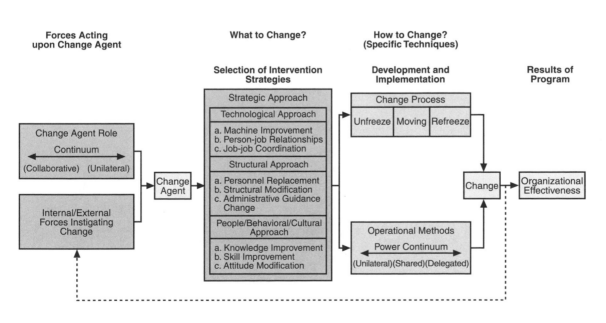

FIGURE 13.1
Model for Planned Organizational Change

SOURCE: Adapted from Larry Short, "Planned Organizational Change," *MSU Business Topics,* Autumn 1973, pp. 53–61; ed. Theodore Herbert, *Organizational Behavior: Readings and Cases* (New York: McMillan, 1976), p. 351.

2. *What should we change?* Should the changes be strategic and companywide or relatively limited? Sometimes, the firm needs a strategic, organization-wide change. As at Nissan, this meant reformulating the firm's strategy (what business are we in, and how should we compete?) as well as changing Nissan's organization structure, production technologies, and the "people side" of the company—it's employees' knowledge, skills, and attitudes. But, often, the required change can be more limited in scope. Perhaps one department needs reorganizing, or the firm just needs to install a new technology. We'll discuss how to decide what to change in the following section.

3. *How should we change it?* The next question is, "How should we actually implement the change?" The manager's basic concern here is making sure that the change is both successful and timely. No manager wants the nightmare Nasser ran into at Ford. Overcoming employee resistance will, therefore, loom large in the implementation decision. "Should 1 force through the change or get the employees involved, and (if the latter) how involved should they be?" We'll see later in the chapter that the basic approach generally involves a process psychologist Kurt Lewin called "unfreeze, moving, refreeze." It underscores the importance of provoking the employees out of their traditional ways of doing things. However, before turning to deciding how to implement the change, let us look at how managers decide what to change.

Deciding What to Change

The manager's change program can aim to alter one of four basic things: The firm's strategy, technology, structure, and people/behavior/culture. We'll look at each in this section. However, remember that in practice, such changes are rarely compartmentalized. Instead, the manager needs to take a coordinated view of the change and its implications. Thus, a recent decision by Aetna Insurance to change its strategy and downsize also prompted changes in the firm's structure and in how it trains the sales force.

Strategic Change

Changing the firm's strategy is one option. For example, faced with declining profits, Aetna Insurance recently pulled back from its high-growth strategy. The firm had emphasized adding more policyholders. Its new strategy is to emphasize fewer but more profitable ones. Management reduced policyholders from 22 million to 14.4 million. By focusing on more profitable policyholders, Aetna was able to boost profits by 10 times—to $108 million in one recent quarter. Similarly, faced with surprising competition from digital cameras, Kodak's former CEO refocused the company, redeploying assets to build the firm's competencies in digital photography.

strategic change A change in a firm's strategy

While often unavoidable and required for survival, **strategic changes** like these are risky. This is especially true when the firm faces what researchers call discontinuous change. This is an unexpected change that triggers a crisis, as when digital photography suddenly started crowding conventional film off the shelves. Changes like these have companywide impact, frequently (as at Aetna) prompting changes in the firm's structure, technology, and people. They're often made under short time constraints. They are usually reactions to uncontrollable outside events like deregulation, intensified global competition, and dramatic technological innovations such as the Internet. Managers faced with the need to make such a change would do well to keep the research evidence in mind:

1. *Strategic changes are usually triggered by factors outside the company.* External threats or challenges, such as deregulation, intensified global competition, and dramatic technological innovations like the Internet usually prompt organizations to embark on companywide, strategic changes.
2. *Strategic changes are often required for survival.* Researchers found that making a strategic change did not guarantee success, but that firms which didn't change failed to survive. This was especially true when discontinuous environmental change—change of an unexpected nature—required quick and effective strategic change, such as when the Internet suddenly made bookselling more competitive.
3. *Strategic changes implemented under crisis conditions are highly risky.* Strategic changes made under crisis conditions and with short time constraints were the riskiest and most prone to fail. Changes like these eventually trigger changes companywide—for instance, to the firm's structure, technologies, people, and culture and core values. Core values (such as "don't make any risky moves") are especially hard to change, so trying to change them tends to trigger the most employee resistance—as Ford's Jacques Nasser discovered.

Technological Change

technological change
Changing the way the company creates and markets its products or services

Technological change is a second basic approach. Technological change means changing the way the company creates and markets its products or services. Here, for example, the manager might want to improve operations by (1) installing or modifying the firm's computer systems or machinery, (2) modifying the relationship between the employees and their physical environment, or (3) modifying the interface of the employees with the technology itself—for instance, improving the workflow or reducing the discomfort caused by bending over a machine. The following Management in Action feature illustrates technological change.

Structural Change: How to Reorganize

structural change
Changing one or more aspects of the company's organization structures

Structural change means changing one or more aspects of the company's organization structures. Structural changes may involve several things. Managers may *reorganize*—change the firm's organization chart and structural elements. (Thus, GE's new CEO, Jeffrey Immelt, recently reorganized his firm's huge GE Capital division. He broke it into four divisions, with their four managers reporting directly to him rather than to the former GE Capital head.) Managers may also change the structure by simply replacing, dismissing, or adding personnel. Or they may

When Bill Zollars became CEO at Yellow Freightways, the firm was just coming off an appalling year. It had just lost about $30 million, laid off workers, and had a Teamsters union strike. Previously a senior vice president at Ryder Corp., Zellers had built its high-tech integrated logistics unit into a $1.5 billion business. He believed that saving Yellow Freightways would require extensive technological change.

One of Zollars' biggest changes, therefore, involved upgrading the firm's technology. Yellow has now spent over $80 million per year in the past few years on new integrated information systems. Now, for instance, when customers call 1-800-go-yellow, the service representative automatically sees the profile corresponding to that caller's phone number. That automatically tells the sales representative where the customer's company is located, what kind of shipments it typically makes, what sort of loading dock it has, and the firm's previous shipping destinations. This dramatically reduced the time it took to process an order—to as little as 15 seconds in most cases.

Zollars and his team also equipped each dockworker with a wireless "mobile data terminal." Now, even before the truck arrives, the worker can see what's on board and when its pulling into the dock. And, if the worker takes longer to unload the pallets than the system estimates it should take given the amount of freight, an alert is sent to the mobile data terminal. Managers back at headquarters can monitor progress, and send in additional employees if help is required.

As is usually the case with changes like these, changing the technology needs to go hand in glove with changing the people. It's futile to install a new system that employees cannot or will not use properly. Before making his changes, Zollars, therefore, carefully explained his plan to all the employees. With 25,000 people in hundreds of locations around the country, Zollars spent over a year going from terminal to terminal, standing on loading docks and explaining the changes. The new technology gives the employees the information they need to solve problems quickly. But this meant Zollars had to make sure that the employees got the additional decision-making authority they required, as well as training on the new equipment. Another effect of all these changes has been to change Yellow's culture. Linking employees with the new technology and giving them the authority to make fast, on-the-spot decisions (empowering them) helped to win their commitment and dedication to getting the job done fast.

change the firm's infrastructure by changing its policies, procedures, and rules (such as the firm's performance appraisal system).

In any case, structural changes tend to trigger resistance. New structures mean new reporting relationships, so some may view the change as a demotion. New structures may also mean new tasks and job descriptions ("task redesign") for employees. For example, Kodak assigned new tasks to its new Digital Photo division employees. People often have an affinity for predictability and the status quo. Not everyone welcomes new tasks.

Reorganizing is a familiar organizational change technique in today's fast-changing times. For example, after dismissing thousands of employees, Lucent needed a new organization design. Former CEO Richard McGinn had organized the company around 31 different businesses. When the board of directors dismissed McGinn, his successor, Harry Schacht, argued that the 11-division structure was too unwieldy; he chopped the design down to five units. More recently (as Lucent continues to downsize), it announced it was reorganizing from five units down to two main units (and laying off 80 executives in the process). One unit, Integrated Network Solutions, will handle landline-based businesses, such as optical networks and phone-call switching. Mobility Solutions will focus on Lucent's wireless products.

Reorganizations confront the manager with two basic questions: (1) Do we really need a new structure? (2) How exactly should the new structure look?

Is a New Structure Really Required? An organizational problem doesn't necessarily mean that a dramatic structural overhaul is required. The current structure may simply need some fine-tuning. Figure 13.2 helps the manager make this determination. Start by determining if just fine-tuning is in order. For example, ask if it might be sufficient to just clarify employees' responsibilities or reporting relationships.

When you identify a problem with your design, first look for ways to fix it without substantially altering it. If that doesn't work, you'll have to make fundamental changes. Here's a step-by-step process for resolving problems:

STEPS NOT INVOLVING MAJOR DESIGN CHANGE

Modify without changing the units.
- Refine the allocation of responsibilities (for example, clarify powers and responsibilities).
- Refine reporting relationships and processes.
- Refine lateral relationships and processes (for example, define coordination mechanisms).
- Refine accountabilities (for example, define more appropriate performance measures).

Redefine Skill Requirements and Incentives.
- Modify criteria for selecting people.
- Redefine skill development needs.
- Develop incentives.

Shape Informal Context.
- Clarify the leadership style needed.
- Define norms of behavior, values, or social context.

STEPS INVOLVING MAJOR DESIGN CHANGE

Make Substantial Changes in the Units.
- Make major adjustments to unit boundaries.
- Change unit roles (for example, turn functional units into business units or shared services).
- Introduce new units or merge units.

Change the Structure.
- Change reporting lines.
- Create new divisions.

FIGURE 13.2
Is a New Structure Really Required?

Source: Adapted from Michael Goold and Andrew Campbell, "Do You Have a Well-Designed Organization?" *Harvard Business Review*, March 2002, p. 124.

How Exactly Should the New Structure Look? Fine tuning is not always sufficient. As at GE or Lucent, an entirely new organization structure and chart—a major organizational redesign—may be required. How does the manager decide what the structural problem is, and what the new structure should look like? In general, of course, the guidelines in Chapters 6 and 7 apply. For example, fast-changing *environments* tend to require more adaptive, organic, networked "learning organization"-type structures. Mass production technologies favor mechanistic structures. Also consider the firm's *strategy and goals*. When INS and Customs goals evolved after 9/11 from taxes to security, that goal virtually mandated reorganizing those two department's enforcement units into a single, more powerful unit. We also saw that managers have to use *logic* and *common sense* when organizing.

To help managers enhance their use of logic and common sense, two researchers developed several tests the manager can apply to better gauge (1) the problem with the current structure, and (2) what the new organization structure should look like. These nine tests are as follows.

1. *The market advantage test.* Does your design direct sufficient management attention to your sources of competitive advantage in each market? "The first and most fundamental test of a design . . . is whether it fits your company's market strategy." The firm's strategy must identify both the markets in which the company will compete, and what the firm's competitive advantages will be. The organization structure must then support that strategy. For example, if the strategy involves expanding overseas, an organization structure that had no provision for addressing the markets abroad should raise a red flag. The two experts say that the rule of thumb here is this: "If a single unit is dedicated to a single segment, the segment is receiving sufficient attention. If no unit has responsibility for the segment, the design is fatally flawed and needs to be revamped." Smaller firms or those facing other strategic concerns may not be able to afford the duplication inherent in creating a structure that addresses multiple markets. However, the basic test remains: "Does your design direct sufficient management attention to your sources of competitive advantage in each market?"

   For example, Volkswagen recently considered reorganizing its nine brands into three operational divisions—one for premium cars, one for mass-market cars, and one for commercial vehicles. One intent of this reorganization is to enable the firm to better focus on what it increasingly sees as VW's three separate market segments. These are premium brands (Audi, Bugatti, Bentley, and Lamborghini), mass brands (Volkswagen), and commercial vehicles.

2. *The parenting advantage test.* Does your design help the corporate parent add value to the organization? For example, GE is a highly diverse conglomerate. So some might ask, "Would it not be more efficient for each of GE's separate divisions to spin off and run themselves rather than to remain part of GE's overall structure?" GE says, "No." It argues that the GE corporate parent brings enormous additional value to each subsidiary. For example, the current structure helps ensure that modern management techniques (such as using the Internet to build a boundaryless supply chain) devised in one unit quickly spread to the others. Suppose ensuring that such sharing of management know-how is an advantage the parent

firm expects to provide. Then, to pass the *parenting advantage test,* the firm's structure should facilitate such sharing.

3. *The people test.* Does your design reflect the strengths, weaknesses, and motivations of your people? The point is that "if an organization is not suited to the skills and attitudes of its members the problem lies with the design, not the people." The basic question here is whether the organization structure provides the appropriate responsibilities and relationships and wins employee commitment. For example, after PepsiCo purchased Quaker Oats Co., PepsiCo reorganized some business units partly because of the strengths of some executives it inherited with the Quaker purchase. For example, Robert Morrison, Quaker's CEO, quickly assumed responsibility for PepsiCo's Tropicana juice unit, while continuing to oversee the original Quaker business.

4. *The feasibility test.* Have you taken into account all the obstacles that may impede the implementation of your design? The basic question here is, "What could stand in the way of successfully implementing my new organization design?" Constraints may include government regulations, the interests of the company stakeholders (including its employees and unions), the firm's information systems, and its corporate culture. For example, in terms of culture, "[3M] is a homegrown place with a collegial atmosphere where the emphasis on being nice to each other means issues haven't always surfaced in an honest way" says one 3M senior vice president. That could have meant resistance on the part of employees to making the hard-nosed structural decisions its new CEO had to make, including consolidating purchasing units and moving some manufacturing abroad. However, he anticipated the potential constraints and dealt with them successfully.

5. *The specialist culture test.* Does your design protect units that need distinct cultures? For example, 3M is known for the number of new products its engineers produce (including Scotch tape, and Post-it notes). Reorganizing R&D, therefore, required addressing its special cultural needs. As its new CEO says, "3M people wake up every morning thinking about what new product they can bring to market. Innovation is in their DNA—and if I kill that entrepreneurial spirit, I will have failed. My job is to build on that strength, corral it, and focus it."

6. *The difficult-links test.* Does your design provide coordination solutions for the unit-to-unit links that are likely to be a problem? In other words, have you addressed the hard-to-coordinate relationships?

7. *The redundant-hierarchy test.* Does your design have too many levels and units? For example, when he became CEO of GE, Jack Welch (now former CEO) found that GE had a hierarchy of what he believed were redundant "parent units." There was a corporate headquarters staff; and then below that, there were various group-level executive vice president staffs; and below that, there were business-level groups. One of the first steps Welch took was to pare the corporate staff, eliminate division groupings, and let most of the heads of the largest independent business units report directly to him and his team.

8. *The accountability test.* Does your design support effective controls? For example, is the company organized in such a way that if a problem arose

(such as a dramatic sales decline) for a particular product line, you could quickly identify the manager responsible?

9. *The flexibility test.* Does your design facilitate the development of new strategies and provide the flexibility required to adapt to change? The question here is whether your organization structure "provides ways for a company to pursue innovation and allows for adaptability to changing circumstances." The aim is to make sure the organization structure doesn't become an impediment to identifying opportunities and pursuing them. For example, several years ago, the magazine publisher Emap saw that new media and Internet-based publishing could be a significant new publishing opportunity. Management knew the firm's current magazine-focused business units might not want to risk diluting their own efforts by pursuing new digital opportunities. Emap management, therefore, created a new digital business function to deal with these opportunities.

People/Behavioral/Cultural Change

Strategic, technical, and structural changes invariably trigger various changes in the behavioral side of the firm, including the employees' attitudes, values, and skills. Sometimes, employees simply don't have the *knowledge* or *skills* to do the job. Here, managers such as Yellow Freightways Bill Zollars call on training and development techniques to improve employees' skills. At other times, the "people" problems stem from *misunderstanding* or *conflict.* Here, organizational development interventions or conflict-resolution efforts (like those discussed shortly) may be in order.

Finally, the manager may want to change the firm's organizational or corporate culture—the *basic values* its employees share and the ways in which these values manifest themselves in behavior. For example, some attribute Motorola's recent lackluster performance to the company's culture, which one writer describes as "stifling bureaucracy, snail-paced decision making, . . . engineering bigotry that subordinates customer focus, and internal competition so fierce that [CEO] Galvin himself has referred to it as a 'culture of warring tribes.' "

The first step in changing the culture is to understand what it is now. Checklist 13.1 can be of use here.

The Basics of Changing Culture. You know from your own experience that changing someone's values entails more than just talk. Parents might tell their children to eat only healthy foods. But suppose the children see their parents saying one thing and doing another? Chances are that the parents' actions will mold their children's values about what's right or wrong when it comes to food.

The same is true of cultural change at work: You have to send the right signals. When he decided to transform Kodak, for instance, the former CEO knew he had to do more than talk. Top executives who weren't performing were replaced and new incentive plans and more results-oriented appraisal systems were instituted. The net effect was to send a strong signal to employees throughout the firm. It said, "The values of being efficient, effective, and responsive are a lot more important today than they were the week before."

HOW TO READ AN ORGANIZATION'S CULTURE

☑ *Observe the physical surroundings.* Look at how the employees are dressed, the degree of openness among offices, the pictures and photographs on the walls, the type of furniture and its placement, and any signs (such as a long list of activities that are "prohibited here"!).

☑ *Sit in on a team meeting.* How do the employees treat each other? Are there obvious differences in how each rank of employee is treated? Are the communications open or decidedly one-sided?

☑ *Listen to the language.* Is there a lot of talk about "quality," "perfection," and "going the extra mile?" Or is there more emphasis on "don't rock the boat," "don't tell those people what we're doing," or "be nice."

☑ *Note to whom you are introduced and how they act.* Is the person casual or formal, laid-back or serious? Does it seem that you're only being introduced to a limited number of people—or to everyone in the unit?

☑ *Get the views of outsiders, including vendors, customers, and former employees.* What do they think of the firm? Do you get responses like "they're so bureaucratic that it takes a year to get an answer"? Or do they say things like "they're open and flexible and always willing to accommodate?"

Creating and Sustaining the Right Corporate Culture. The board makes you CEO of a struggling company. The firm is known for its culture of backbiting, bureaucratic behavior, and disdain for clients. What steps would you take to change the company's culture? Experts suggest the following broad tactics:

1. *Make it clear to your employees what you pay attention to, measure, and control.* For example, direct your employees' attention toward controlling costs or serving customers if those are the values you want to emphasize. Use management policies and practices to send strong signals about what is or is not acceptable. At Toyota, for example, "quality and teamwork" are desirable values. It therefore makes sense that Toyota's employee selection and training process emphasizes the candidate's quality and teamwork orientation.
2. *React appropriately* to critical incidents and organizational crises. For example, if you want to emphasize the value that "we're all in this together," don't react to declining profits by laying off operating employees and middle managers while giving top managers a raise.

3. *Use "signs, symbols, stories, rites, and ceremonies"* to signal your values. At Ben & Jerry's, signs and symbols help sustain the company's culture. The "joy gang" team distributes awards to worthy B&J teams. The team's existence is a concrete symbol of the firm's values, which emphasize charity, fun, and goodwill. At JC Penney, loyalty and tradition are values. To support this, the firm inducts new management employees into the "Penney Partnership" at formal conferences, where they commit to the firm's core values of "honor, confidence, service, and cooperation."

4. *Deliberately role model, teach, and coach the values you want to emphasize.* For example, Wal-Mart founder Sam Walton lived the values "hard work, honesty, neighborliness, and thrift" that he wanted Wal-Mart employees to follow. He was one of the richest men in the world, but he drove a pickup truck. He explained this by saying, "If I drove a Rolls Royce, what would I do with my dog?"

5. *Communicate your priorities by how you allocate rewards.* Leaders communicate their priorities by how they link raises and promotions to particular behaviors. For example, General Foods decided several years ago to reorient its strategy from cost control to diversification and sales growth. It therefore revised the firm's pay plan. Management linked bonuses to sales volume and to new-product development rather than just to increased earnings.

6. *Make your HR procedures and criteria consistent* with the values you espouse. When he became chairman and CEO of IBM, Louis Gerstner instituted new appraisal systems and pay plans to reinforce his focus on performance.

Lawrence Weinbach's efforts to change the culture at Unisys are a good example of how to create the right corporate culture.

Deciding How to Implement Change

After deciding what to change, the manager must decide, "How should we actually implement the change?" As noted earlier, the manager's basic concern is to ensure that the change is both successful and timely. The basic issue here is how to deal with and minimize employee resistance. Functionally, the manager's options range from unilaterally ramming through the change to having the employees themselves decide what to change and how to change it.

Why Do People Resist Change?

Overcoming resistance is often the hardest part of leading a change. Niccolo Machiavelli, a shrewd observer of 16th-century Italian politics, put it this way: "There is nothing so difficult to implement as change, since those in favor of the change will often be small in number while those opposing the change will be numerous and enthusiastic in their resistance to change."

The fact that a change is advisable or even mandatory doesn't mean employees will accept it. In fact, even the company's key people—perhaps including some top and middle managers—may (perhaps slyly) resist it. They may just prefer the status quo.

Lawrence Weinbach, chairman and CEO of Unisys, took many steps to change the culture of that firm—and particularly to focus employees on performance and execution. For example, ". . . We've moved to a pay-for-performance approach, to make sure that we're properly recognizing the people who are doing things right. . . . in some cases, we've needed to tell people to seek opportunities elsewhere where they will be happier. . . . we've invested in training and education and created Unisys University, where employees can find courses and programs on a range of . . . business related topics. We've also spent a lot of time communicating and educating people about the importance of execution. I think we've done pretty well at getting everyone here to understand what we're good at, what our core competencies are, and then driving home the fan that you have to deliver every single day."

Application Example. It's easy to see how such resistance might arise. Take a personal example. Suppose you've been attending a management class with the college's best professor. Several weeks into the semester, the dean comes in and announces that some students will have to move. They must move to another professor and class because the fire marshal says the lecture hall is overcrowded.

The dean asks you to move. What would go through your mind? Probably several things: that moving might adversely affect your grade; that you don't want to leave the friends you've made here and start all over again; that it might be just a tad embarrassing to have to get up and leave (although obviously it's not your fault); and that it's no fair you should be one of those singled out. The change makes sense—and indeed is quite benign. But in spite of that, you don't want to go!

Years ago, Professor Paul Lawrence said it's usually not the technical aspects of a change employees resist, but its social consequences—"the changes in their human relationships that generally accompany the technical change." Thus, they may see in the change diminished responsibilities for themselves and, therefore, lower status in the organization and less job security. Sometimes, it's not fear of the obvious consequences but rather apprehension about the unknown consequences that produces resistance. For example, how much do you know about the professor who'll be teaching that new class you're being moved to—and about the new classmates? Not much, unfortunately.

Sources of Resistance

Resistance has many sources. For example, in his book *Beyond the Wall of Resistance,* consultant Rick Maurer says resistance like this can stem from two main sources. What he calls *Level 1* resistance stems from lack of information or honest disagreement over the facts. *Level 2* resistance is more personal and emotional. Here, people are afraid—that the change may cost them their jobs, or to lose face, for instance. Maurer says that treating all resistance as if it were Level 1 can undermine the manager's change efforts. For example, using "slick visual presentations to explain change with nice neat facts, charts, and time lines, when what people really want to hear is: 'What does this mean to them?' " can be a recipe for disaster.

Furthermore, some people are more resistant to change than others—they always seem to be fighting the system. As you might imagine, they are usually not the sorts of employees who contribute in a positive way to organizational change. One study focused on six organizations—two European companies, two Australian banks, a U.S. university, and a Korean manufacturing firm. Its aim was to determine how managers' personality traits influenced their reactions to change. Three personality traits—tolerance for ambiguity, having a positive self-concept, and being more tolerant of risk—significantly predicted effectiveness in coping with change. Managers with the lowest self-image, least tolerance for ambiguity, and least tolerance for risk appeared, as expected, to be the most resistant.

Sometimes, employees say they want to change (and may actually mean it), and yet they resist the program. What accounts for this? Two organizational psychologists recently suggested that this resistance may be the result of "competing commitments." In other words, the employees say they want to change (and may even think they do), but in fact, a competing commitment makes them resist it.

Figure 13.3 provides a few examples. For example, "Helen" says and may believe that she is committed to the new initiative. However, she has an unstated competing commitment: "Do not upset my relationship with my boss by leaving the [mentored] role." She's therefore actually not pushing her team to implement the new initiative.

Uncovering competing commitments like these requires a diagnostic process. First, notice and record the person's actual, current behavior (since it's not what they say they *want* to do but what they're *actually* doing that is important to you as a manager). Second, speak with the person and lead him or her to understand what the competing commitments really are.

Overcoming Resistance to Change

Psychologist Kurt Lewin proposed a famous model to summarize the basic process for implementing a change with minimal resistance. To Lewin, all behavior in organizations was a product of two kinds of forces: those striving to maintain the status quo, and those pushing for change. Implementing change thus meant either reducing the forces for the status quo or building up the forces for change. Lewin's process consists of three steps: unfreezing, moving, and refreezing.

Unfreezing means reducing the forces pressing for the status quo. The usual way to accomplish this is by presenting a provocative problem or event. The goal is to get employees to recognize the need for change and to search for new solutions. Attitude surveys, interview results, or participatory informational meetings often provide such provocative events. As we'll see in a moment, some managers accomplish this by creating a crisis—such as by suggesting that bankruptcy might be imminent if things don't change fast.

Once you have employees' attention, you must move them in the desired direction. Lewin's second step, *moving*, aims to shift or alter the behavior of the employees. **Moving** means developing new behaviors, values, and attitudes by applying

unfreezing A step in psychologist Kurt Lewin's model of change that involves reducing the forces for the status quo, usually by presenting a provocative problem or event to get people to recognize the need for change and to search for new solutions

moving A step in psychologist Kurt Lewin's model of change aimed at using techniques and actually altering the behaviors, values, and attitudes of the individuals in an organization

Stated commitment I am committed to . . .	What am I doing, or not doing, that is keeping my stated commitment from being fully realized?	Competing commitments	Big assumptions
Helen . . . the new initiative.	I don't push for top performance from my team members or myself; I accept mediocre products and thinking too often; I don't prioritize.	I am committed to not upsetting my relationship with my boss by leaving the [mentored] role.	I assume my boss will stop supporting me if I move toward becoming his peer; I assume that I don't have what it takes to successfully carry out a cutting-edge project.
Bill . . . being a team player.	I don't collaborate enough; I make unilateral decisions too often; I don't really take people's input into account.	I am committed to being the one who gets the credit and to avoiding the frustration or conflict that comes with collaboration.	I assume that no one will appreciate me if I am not seen as the source of success; I assume nothing good will come of my being frustrated in conflict.
Jane . . . turning around my department.	Too often, I let things slide; I'm not proactive enough in getting people to follow through with their tasks.	I am committed to not setting full sail until I have a clear map of how we get our department from here to there.	I assume that if I take my group out into deep waters and discover I am unable to get us to the other side, I will be seen an an incompetent leader who is undeserving of trust or responsibility.

FIGURE 13.3

How Immune Is the Person to Change?

SOURCE: Robert Kegan and Lisa Lahey, "The Real Reason People Won't Change," *Harvard Business Review*, November 2001, p. 89.

one or more organizational change techniques. We discuss organizational change technique options later in this chapter.

Lewin was shrewd enough to know that just making a change is not enough. People and organizations tend to revert to their old ways of doing things unless management reinforces the new ways. Whether it's a new diet, a new saving plan, or a new organizational procedure, Lewin knew you had to reinforce the change. If you did not, you run the risk that the change won't be permanent. That's what Lewin meant by **refreezing.** He said you had to institute new systems and procedures that would support and maintain the changes that you made.

Companies' experiences with reengineering help illustrate the importance of applying an effective organizational change process. Many such programs have been successful but failure rates run as high as 70%. When reengineering does fail, it is often due to behavioral factors. Sometimes, employees resist and undermine the new procedures. Reengineering without considering the new skill requirements, training, and reporting relationships can aggravate the situation. As John Champs, a long-time reengineering proponent, has said, "In short, reducing hierarchy, bureaucracy, and the rest of it is not just a matter of rearranging the furniture to face our customers and markets. It is [also] a matter of rearranging the quality of people's attachments—to their work and to each other. These are *cultural* matters."

refreezing A step in psychologist Kurt Lewin's model of change aimed at preventing a return to old ways of doing things by instituting new systems and procedures that reinforce the new organizational changes

BUSINESS PROCESS REENGINEERING

One firm's experience reengineering its processes illustrates some of the issues involved in implementing a successful change. **Business reengineering** is "the radical redesign of business processes, combining steps to cut waste and eliminate repetitive, paper-intensive tasks in order to improve cost, quality, and service, and to maximize the benefits of information technology." The basic approach is to (1) identify a business process to be redesigned (such as approving a mortgage application); (2) measure the performance of the existing processes; (3) identify opportunities to improve these processes; and (4) redesign and implement a new way of doing the work, usually by (5) assigning ownership of formerly separate tasks to an individual or team that use new computerized systems to support the new arrangement.

A system installed at Bank One Mortgage provides an example. As illustrated in Figure 13.4, Bank One redesigned its mortgage application process so that it required fewer steps and reduced processing time from 17 days to 2. In the past, a mortgage applicant completed a paper loan application that the bank then entered in its computer system. A series of specialists such as credit analysts and underwriters evaluated the application individually as it moved through eight different departments.

Bank One replaced the sequential operation with a work-cell, a team, approach. Loan originators in the field now entered the mortgage application directly into laptop computers, where software checked it for completeness. The information then went electronically to regional production centers. Here, specialists (like credit analysts and loan underwriters) convened electronically, working as a team to review the mortgage together—at once. After they formally closed the loan, another team of specialists took on the task of servicing the loan.

The basic need is to prepare employees for the change, both to reduce resistance and to provide them with the knowledge, skills, and attitudes they need to do their new jobs.

A Nine-Step Process for Leading Organizational Change

Lewin's unfreeze-moving-refreeze model provides a powerful framework for making a change, but the devil, of course, is in the details. In particular, what specific

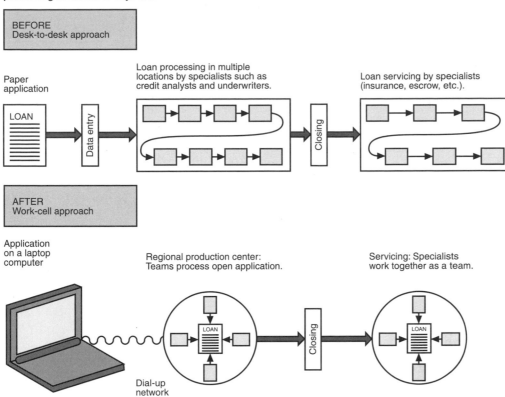

Shifting from a traditional approach helped Bank One Mortgage slash processing time from 17 days to 2

BEFORE
Desk-to-desk approach

Paper application

LOAN

Data entry

Loan processing in multiple locations by specialists such as credit analysts and underwriters.

Closing

Loan servicing by specialists (insurance, escrow, etc.).

AFTER
Work-cell approach

Application on a laptop computer

Dial-up network

Regional production center: Teams process open application.

LOAN

Closing

Servicing: Specialists work together as a team.

LOAN

FIGURE 13.4

Redesigning Mortgage Processing at Bank One

By redesigning its mortgage processing system and the mortgage application process, Bank One will be able to handle the increased paperwork as it moves from processing 33,000 loans per year to processing 300,000 loans per year.

steps should a manager use to carry out the change? Experts have proposed many multistep models. Change experts Wendel French and Cecil Bell Jr. describe six such multistep models, for instance. The following nine-step list provides a useful change process for managers.

Create a Sense of Urgency

You know something's wrong. What do you do now? Do you just paper over the problems? Or do you take remedial action? Most experienced leaders instinctively know that before taking action, they have to unfreeze the old habits. They have to create a sense of urgency.

Creating a sense of urgency has a double-barreled benefit. For those who might want to resist the change, it can convince them of the need for the change. And it may jar those who might simply be neutral (or who simply don't care) out of their complacency. Techniques managers use to create a sense of urgency include:

- *Create a crisis* by allowing a financial loss or exposing managers to major weaknesses relative to competitors.
- *Eliminate examples of excess* such as company-owned country club facilities, numerous aircraft, or gourmet executive dining rooms.
- *Set targets* for revenue, income, productivity, customer satisfaction, and product development cycle time so high that they can't be reached by those conducting business as usual.
- *Send more data* about customer satisfaction and financial performance to more employees, especially information that demonstrates weaknesses relative to competitors.

Decide What to Change

You've just taken over as CEO of a troubled company. You know you have to make changes. What are your options—what is it about the company that you can change? In practice, as explained earlier, you can change the firm's strategy, technologies, and structure, as well as the culture, attitudes, and skills of its people.

Create a Guiding Coalition and Mobilize Commitment

Leading a change is one thing. Trying to do it all by yourself is another. Major transformations—such as the one CEO McNerney achieved by transforming 3M—are often associated with one highly visible leader. But no leader can accomplish a major change alone. That's why most leaders create a *guiding coalition* of influential people. Such individuals become the vanguard—the missionaries and implementers of change. The coalition should work as a team and should include people with enough power to lead the change effort.

You must choose the right lieutenants. One reason is to gather political support. The leader therefore has to ensure that there are enough key players "on board," so that those left out can't easily block progress. The coalition should also have the expertise, credibility, and leadership skills required to explain and implement the change. One option is to create one or more broad, employee-based task forces to diagnose the company's problems. Doing so can produce a shared understanding of and commitment to what the company can and must improve. Leaders can also be trained to lead change, as the following Management in Action feature shows.

Develop and Communicate a Shared Vision

Beyond the guiding coalition, the firm's other employees also need a vision they can rally around, a signpost on which to focus. A vision is "a general statement of the organization's intended direction that evokes emotional feelings in organization members." When Barry Gibbons became CEO of a struggling Spec's Music retail chain, its employees, owners, and bankers—all of its stakeholders—required a vision around which to rally. Gibbons's vision of a leaner Spec's offering both concerts and retail music helped to provide the needed sense of direction.

Power, respect, and influence drive coalition-member choice, but some otherwise logical candidates may lack the leadership skills to play a forceful role. Can you train these employees to be better leaders of change? The answer, based on one recent study, is yes.

This study focused specifically on training the employees to be transformational leaders. Such leaders tend to act charismatic, stimulating, and inspirational. The study took place at a large bank in Canada. The trainers randomly assigned managers of the 20 branches in one region to receive transformational leadership training—or not to receive it.

The first part of the two-part training program consisted of a one-day training session that familiarized participants with the meaning of transformational leadership. The trainers explained and illustrated how to implement transformational leadership in the managers' branches. The second part consisted of several one-on-one booster sessions. Here a trainer met individually with each of the managers to go over the latter's leadership style. The two developed personal action plans for the manager, to enable him or her to become more of a goal-oriented, transformational leader.

The results were quite positive. For example, the subordinates of the transformation-trained managers subsequently perceived their managers as higher on intellectual stimulation and charisma than did subordinates of managers in the no-training group. Supporting otherwise qualified change-coalition members to be more effective at taking leadership roles in the change thus seems quite feasible.

Having a vision is useless unless the employees share that vision. Change expert John Kotter says, "The real power of a vision is unleashed only when most of those involved in an enterprise or activity have a common understanding of its goals and direction." Key steps in communicating a vision include:

- *Keep it simple.* Here is an example of a good statement of vision: "We are going to become faster than anyone else in our industry at satisfying customer needs."
- *Use multiple forums.* Try to use every channel possible—big meetings and small, memos and newspapers, formal and informal interaction—to spread the word.
- *Use repetition.* Ideas sink in deeply only after people have heard them many times.
- *Lead by example.* "Walk the talk" so that your behaviors and decisions are consistent with the vision you advocate.

Empower Employees To Make the Change

Some leaders then confront a dilemma. They need the active assistance of their employees to implement the change. But the employees haven't the tools, skills, authority or freedom to do what's needed to help. For example, in a study of change in major companies like Sears Roebuck & Co., Royal Dutch Shell, and the U.S. Army, the researchers found that employees were rarely able or willing to do what it took to carry out the change if they thought they lacked the power to do so. Therefore, ask "Do employees believe they can affect organ national performance? Do they believe they have the power to make things happen?"

There are many potential barriers to empowerment—and, therefore, many ways to remove them. Allied Signal (now Honeywell), CEO Lawrence Bossidy put all of his 80,000 people through quality training. He also created area "councils" (for instance, for Asia). These councils allowed employees who were undertaking initiatives in those areas to get together, share market intelligence, and compare notes.

Generate Short-Term Wins

Most people can't wait years before deciding if they're going in the right direction. They need periodic feedback: what some call "short-term wins." The guiding coalition in one company set its sights on producing one highly visible and successful new product about 20 months after the start of its organizational renewal effort. It selected the new product in part because the coalition knew that the introduction was doable. Accomplishing it sent a strong signal that the broader, longer-term change was also doable.

Consolidate Gains and Produce More Change

The challenge, now, is to capitalize on the short-term wins. This is the time to press ahead and extend your gains. You have increased credibility from the short-term wins. Use it to change all of the systems, structures, and policies that don't fit well with the company's new vision.

Anchor the New Ways of Doing Things in the Company Culture

As you consolidate and extend the gains, remember that you will need a parallel change in the company's values and culture. Perhaps you want a "team-based, quality-oriented, adaptable organization." However, that is not going to happen if the firm's shared values still emphasize "selfishness, mediocrity, and bureaucratic behavior." Changing the culture is, therefore, crucial. It is one of the manager's most challenging jobs. We discussed cultural change earlier in the chapter.

Monitor Progress and Adjust the Vision as Required

Finally, monitor the effectiveness of the change. Continually compare results to goals. One firm appointed an oversight team composed of managers, a union representative, an engineer, and several others. They monitored the functioning of

The approach used by Carlos Ghosn in his dramatic turnaround of Nissan Motors illustrates how a manager can use his firm's employees to devise and implement the change. When the Renault executive agreed to head up the turnaround at Renault's new strategic partner, Nissan had lost billions of dollars, and it had billions more in debts. It was utilizing only about 53% of its auto producing capacity, and it was losing $1,000 on every car it sold in the United States. Purchasing costs were 15–25% higher than at Renault.

Ghosn knew he had to make big changes—and fast. Another CEO (especially one with such extensive experience in the auto business) might have assumed that the way to go was to formulate and force through the changes. However, as Ghosn puts it, "I knew that if I had tried simply to impose the changes from the top, I would have failed. Instead, I decided to use as the centerpiece of the turnaround effort a set of cross-functional teams."

Figure 13.5 summarizes Ghosn's approach. As you can see, he organized cross-functional teams, each with responsibilities for the main tasks required for Nissan to have a successful turnaround. He appointed teams for business development, purchasing, manufacturing and logistics, research and development, sales and marketing, general and administrative, financing costs, phaseout of products, and organization. (The figure shows 5 of the teams.) Each team had a set of executive leaders, a day-to-day operational 'pilot,' and specific assignments. Each consisted of about 10 members, all middle managers with line responsibilities (except for the "executive leaders").

Based on recent results, the changes designed and pushed through by Nissan's teams were quite successful. For example, net profit rose from a loss of $5.7 billion in fiscal year 1999 to a profit of about $2.8 billion in fiscal year 2001. Automotive debt dropped from $11.2 billion in 1999 to $5.8 billion in 2002.

the firm's new self-managing teams. Another firm used morale surveys to monitor employees' reactions to the changes. The Management in Action feature above describes what Carlos Ghosn did at Nissan.

A Special Kind of Change: Becoming an E-Business

Every business is becoming an e-business today. For example, Bank One sponsored an Immersion Day in New York City to introduce its new Internet bank, **wingspanbank.com.** As *Fortune* recently put it, "e or be eaten": Either link your business to the Web, or say goodbye to your business.

The problem is that "blending old business and e-business—'clicks and mortar'—is for the most part a difficult, awkward process." The merger of AOL and Time Warner is one striking example. Here Time-Warner's more buttoned-down, conservative culture sometimes clashed with AOL's entrepreneurial values. And consider Sears's Internet operation. Most Sears headquarters employees are housed in comfortable offices in the firm's Chicago tower. Over at their Internet division in Hoffman Estates, Illinois, Sears's e-employees, including its former treasurer, have small cubicles. "Boxes lie everywhere."

Team	Purchasing	Manufacturing & Logistics	Sales & Marketing	Phaseout of Products & Parts Complexity Management	Organization
CFT Leaders	• executive VP of purchasing • executive VP of engineering	• executive VP of manufacturing • executive VP of product planning	• executive VP of overseas sales & marketing • executive VP of domestic sales & marketing	• executive VP of domestic sales & marketing • executive VP of product planning	• executive VP of finance (CFO) • executive VP of manufacturing
CFT Pilot	• general manager of purchasing	• deputy general manager of manufacturing	• manager of overseas sales & marketing	• manager of product planning	• manager of human resources
Functions Represented	• purchasing • engineering • manufacturing • finance	• manufacturing • logistics • product planning • human resources	• sales & marketing • purchasing	• product planning • sales & marketing • manufacturing • engineering • finance • purchasing	• product planning • sales & marketing • manufacturing • engineering • finance • purchasing
Team Review Focus	• supplier relationships • product specifications and standards	• manufacturing efficiency and cost effectiveness	• advertising structure • distribution structure • dealer organization • incentives	• manufacturing efficiency and cost effectiveness	• organizational structure • employee incentive and pay packages
Objectives Based on Review	• cut number of suppliers in half • reduce costs by 20% over three years	• close three assembly plants in Japan • close two power-train plants in Japan • improve capacity utilization in Japan from 53% in 1999 to 82% in 2002	• move to a single global advertising agency • reduce SG&A costs by 20% • reduce distribution subsidiaries by 20% in Japan • close 10% of retail outlets in Japan	• reduce number of plants in Japan from seven to four by 2002 • reduce number of platforms in Japan from 24 to 15 by 2002 • reduce by 50% the variation in parts (due to differences in engines or cars).	• create a worldwide corporate headquarters • create regional management committees • empower program directors • implement performance-oriented compensation.

FIGURE 13.5
Some of Nissan's Cross-Functional Teams (CFTs)

SOURCE: Adapted from Carlos Ghosn, "Saving the Business Without Losing the Company," *Harvard Business Review*, January 2002, pp. 40–41.

What changes can you expect when moving from a conventional to an Internet-based business? "Entering the e-commerce realm is like managing at 90 mph. E-business affects finance, human resources, training, supply-chain management, customer-resource management, and just about every other corporate function. This puts the managers of these departments in a new light," says the chief strategist for one e-business.

As at AOL/Time Warner, how to structure the new enterprise is a big issue. For one thing, you'll have to decide whether to blend the new e-business into the company's current structure or organize it as a separate entity. If you blend the two entities, what role should the e-business play? Some argue for assigning one manager responsibility for the e-business initiative. Others say that "it's far better to develop an organizational structure that puts the Web and e-business at the central focus of a cross-departmental business group, rather than merely adding Web responsibilities to a preexisting task list." Greg Rogers heads up Whirlpool Corporation's e-commerce operation. He says that the company's strategy will have to change too: "Internet strategy is really business strategy." The company's new business strategy will have to reflect the tact that the company now embraces e-commerce as part of its competitive advantage.

Using Organizational Development to Change Organizations

organizational development An approach to organizational change in which the employees themselves formulate the change that's required and implement it, usually with the aid of a trained consultant

action research The process of collecting data from employees about a system in need of change, and then feeding that data back to the employees so that they can analyze it, identify problems, develop solutions, and take action themselves

human process interventions Organizational change techniques aimed at enabling employees to develop a better understanding of their own and others' behaviors for the purpose of improving that behavior such that the organization benefits

Organizational development (OD) is a special approach to organizational and cultural change, in which the employees formulate and implement the change, usually with the aid of a trained facilitator. OD has three distinguishing characteristics:

1. It is based on **action research,** which means collecting data about a group, department, or organization, and then feeding that data back to the employees. Then the group members themselves analyze the data and develop hypotheses about what the problems in the unit might be.
2. It applies behavioral science knowledge in order to improve the organization's effectiveness.
3. It changes the organization in a particular direction—toward improved problem solving, responsiveness, quality of work, and effectiveness.

The range of OD applications (also called OD interventions or techniques) has increased over the years. OD got its start with **human process interventions.** These aimed to help employees better understand and modify their own and others attitudes, values, and beliefs—and thereby improve the company.

Today (see Table 13.1), OD practitioners aren't just involved in changing participants' attitudes, values, and beliefs. Now, they also directly alter the firm's structure, practices, strategy, and culture. However, OD's distinguishing characteristic has stayed the same: to have the employees themselves analyze the situation and develop the solutions. Let's look at the four main types of OD interventions: human process, technostructural, HR management, and strategic.

TABLE 13.1 Examples of OD Interventions and the Organizational Levels They Affect

Interventions	Primary Organizational Level Affected		
	Individual	Group	Organization
Human Process			
T-groups	x	x	
Process consultation		x	
Third-party intervention	x	x	
Team building		x	
Organizational confrontation meeting		x	x
Intergroup relations		x	x
Technostructural			
Formal structural change			x
Differentiation and integration			x
Cooperative union-management projects	x	x	x
Quality circles	x	x	
Total quality management		x	x
Work design	x	x	
Human Resource Management			
Goal setting	x	x	
Performance appraisal	x	x	
Reward systems	x	x	x
Career planning and development	x		
Managing workforce diversity	x		
Employee wellness	x		
Strategic			
Integrated strategic management			x
Culture change			x
Strategic change			x
Self-designing organizations		x	x

Human Process Applications

Human process applications aim at improving employees' human relations skills. The goal is to provide employees with the insight and skills they need to analyze their own and others' behavior more effectively. With this new insight, they should be able to solve interpersonal and intergroup problems more intelligently. *Sensitivity training, team building,* and *survey research* are three classic techniques here.

Sensitivity training (aka laboratory or t-group training) was one of the earliest OD techniques. It aims to increase the participant's insight into his or her own behavior and the behavior of others by encouraging an open expression of feelings in the training group. Typically, 10 to 15 people meet, usually away from the job. The focus is on the feelings and interactions of group members. Participants are encouraged to portray themselves as they are now, in the group, rather than in

sensitivity training Also called laboratory or t-group training, the basic aim of this organizational development technique is to increase participants' insight into their own behavior and that of others by encouraging an open expression of feelings in a trainer-guided group

team building The process of improving the effectiveness of a team through action research or other techniques

terms of past experiences. T-group training is obviously very personal in nature, so it's not surprising that it is controversial and that its use has diminished markedly.

OD's action research emphasis is perhaps most evident in **team building.** This is a special process for improving the effectiveness of a team. The facilitator collects data concerning the team's performance and then feeds it back to the members of the team. The participants examine, explain, and analyze the data. They then develop specific action plans or solutions for solving the team's problems.

Before the meeting, the consultant interviews each group member. He or she asks what their problems are, how the group functions, and what obstacles are preventing the group from performing better. The consultant might then categorize the interview data into themes and present the themes to the group at the beginning of the meeting. (Themes like lack of cohesion might be culled from statements such as, "I can't get any cooperation around here.") The group then explores and discusses the themes, examines the underlying causes of the problems, and works on solutions.

survey research The process of collecting data from attitude surveys filled out by employees of an organization, then feeding the data back to workgroups to provide a basis for problem analysis and action planning

Some firms use **survey research** to create a sense of urgency. Here, the facilitator/consultant has employees throughout the company fill out attitude surveys. He or she then feeds back the data to top management and to the appropriate group or groups. The survey data provide a convenient method for unfreezing an organization's management and employees. It provides a lucid, comparative, graphic illustration of the fact that the organization has problems.

Technostructural Applications

formal structure change An intervention technique in which employees collect information on existing formal organizational structures and analyze it for the purpose of redesigning and implementing new organizational structures

As noted above, OD practitioners no longer limit themselves to human process applications (such as team-building). Instead, they are increasingly involved in efforts to change the structures, methods, and job designs of firms. Compared with human process interventions, technostructural interventions (as well as HR management interventions and strategic interventions) focus directly on productivity improvement and efficiency. For example, in a **formal structure change program,** employees collect data on existing structures and analyze them. The purpose is to jointly redesign and implement new organizational structures. OD practitioners also assist in implementing employee-involvement programs, including quality circles and job redesign.

strategic interventions An organization development application aimed at effecting a suitable fit among a firm's strategy, structure, culture, and external environments

HR Management Applications

OD practitioners use action research to help employees analyze and change personnel practices. Targets of change include the performance appraisal system and reward system. Another typical effort involves using action research to institute workforce diversity programs. These aim to boost cooperation among a firm's diverse employees.

integrated strategic management An organizational development program to create or change a company's strategy by analyzing the current strategy, choosing a desired strategy, designing a strategic change plan, and implementing the new plan

Strategic Applications

Strategic interventions are companywide OD programs aimed at achieving a better fit among a firm's strategy, structure, culture, and external environments. **Integrated strategic management** is one example. It involves four steps:

1. *Analyze strategy and organizational design.* Senior managers and other employees utilize models such as the SWOT matrix to analyze the firm's current strategy and organizational design.
2. *Choose a desired strategy* and organizational design. Based on the analysis, senior management formulates a strategic vision, objectives, and plan, and an organizational structure for implementing them.
3. *Design a strategic change plan.* The group designs a strategic change plan. This "is an action plan for moving the organization from its current strategy and organizational design to the desired future strategy and design." The plan explains how management will implement the strategic change. It includes specific activities as well as the costs and budgets associated with them.
4. *Implement the strategic change plan.* The final step is to implement the strategic change plan and then measure and review the results.

The Global Manager. OD practices such as sensitivity training that may be acceptable in one context may be frowned upon in another. Managers thinking of using OD interventions abroad, therefore, need to consider the cultural context.

A recent study of OD usage by U.S., Japanese, and European Multination Corporations and local Chinese firms in Hong Kong illustrates this. Although these firms were all operating in the same Hong Kong environment, the results suggest that OD usage was largely a function of the firms' countries of origin. In particular, there were distinct differences in OD usage between Western and Asian firms. For example, Chinese and Japanese firms generally practiced all types of OD interventions less frequently than did Western firms. In this study, the researchers also found that the individual development types of intervention (like sensitivity training) were least used even for the American firms, and that the Chinese firms were even less open to individual and personal level interventions like these than were European and U.S. firms.

The researchers concluded that the Chinese tended to be more skeptical of personal and confrontation-type interventions then were the European and U.S. firms. On the other hand, local Chinese firms used HR-type, system-level OD interventions, for instance to strengthen their reward systems and personnel and succession planning. These HR activities "have a long-term orientation, [and] are [therefore] more often practiced in local Chinese firms. This phenomenon is consistent with the cultural perspective that Chinese have long-term and collective values."

Managing Interpersonal Conflict

Few things are potentially as deadly for a company's performance as uncontrolled conflict among employees or departments. Opposing parties put their own aims above those of the organization, and the organization's effectiveness suffers. Time that they could have used productively evaporates, as people hide information and jockey for position. Opponents may become so angry that their health suffers. Managing conflicts like these is a major part of all managers' organizational change responsibilities.

Sometimes these conflicts are structural in nature, sometimes not. Where conflicts stem from structural sources like interdepartmental differences and points of view, structural solutions include exchanging personnel and minimizing interdependencies. However, many (or most) conflicts require the manager's personal intervention. It is at this point that the manager must become something of a diplomat. He or she must size up the situation and decide what conflict-resolution style to use.

Every diplomat knows that there are different ways ("conflict-resolution styles") to settle an argument—and that some are better than others, depending on the situation. For example, having both parties meet to confront the facts and hammer out a solution is usually better than simply smoothing over the conflict by pushing problems under a rug. Yet there are undoubtedly times when letting things just cool down is advisable. Knowing which approach to use—and when—is an art.

Interpersonal Conflict-Resolution Styles

Different conflict experts have slightly different ways of describing the conflict resolution styles a person can use. One popular approach involves thinking of conflict resolution styles in terms of a *dual concern model*. This approach views conflict resolution styles as based on two things—the individual's concern for his or her *own* outcomes and for the outcomes of *others*. This produces a matrix, as in Figure 13.6, and four (or five) styles (depending on the expert).

Accommodators are high in concern for others and low in concern for self. They tend to sacrifice their own goals and to satisfy the needs of others. *Avoiders* are low in concern for both self and others. They "allow conflicts to go unresolved or permit others to take responsibility for solving the problem." *Competitors* maximize their own outcomes while disregarding the effects on others. For them, conflict is always a win-lose situation. *Collaborators* pursue a win-win style. They are high in their concern for self and for others. They ". . . try to integrate the needs of both parties into a solution that will maximize the interests of both." Compromisers fall in the middle of both sides.

Figure 13.7 provides a self-assessment exercise for sizing up your own conflict-resolution style, using a similar list of styles. One thing to remember is that

FIGURE 13.6
Conflict Handling Styles

SOURCE: Kenneth W. Thomas, "Organizational Conflict," ed., Steven Kerr, *Organizational Behavior* (Columbus, OH: Grid Publishing, 1979), in Andrew DuBrin, *Applying Psychology* (Upper Saddle River, NJ: Prentice Hall, 2000), p. 223.

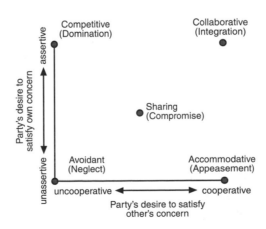

Indicate how often you do the following when you differ with someone.

WHEN I DIFFER WITH SOMEONE	Usually	Sometimes	Seldom
1. I explore our differences, not backing down, but not imposing my view either.	❏	❏	❏
2. I disagree openly, then invite more discussion about our differences.	❏	❏	❏
3. I look for a mutually satisfactory solution.	❏	❏	❏
4. Rather than let the other person make a decision without my input, I make sure I am heard and also that I hear the other out.	❏	❏	❏
5. I agree to a middle ground rather than look for a completely satisfying solution.	❏	❏	❏
6. I admit I am half wrong rather than explore our differences	❏	❏	❏
7. I have a reputation for meeting a person halfway.	❏	❏	❏
8. I expect to get out about half of what I really want to say.	❏	❏	❏
9. I give in totally rather than try to change another's opinion.	❏	❏	❏
10. I put aside any controversial aspects of an issue.	❏	❏	❏
11. I agree early on rather than argue about a point.	❏	❏	❏
12. I give in as soon as the other party gets emotional about an issue.	❏	❏	❏
13. I try to win the other person over.	❏	❏	❏
14. I work to come out victorious, no matter what.	❏	❏	❏
15. I never back away from a good argument.	❏	❏	❏
16. I would rather win than end up compromising.	❏	❏	❏

Scoring Key and Interpretation

Total your choices as follows: Give yourself 5 points for "Usually"; 3 points for "Sometimes"; and 1 point for "Seldom." Then total them for each set of statements, grouped as follows:

Set A: items 13–16	Set C: items 5–8
Set B: items 9–12	Set D: items 1–4

Treat each set separately.

A score of 17 or above on any set is considered high;

Scores of 8 to 16 are moderate;

Scores of 7 or less are considered low.

Sets A, B, C, and D represent conflict-resolution strategies:

A = Forcing/domination. I win, you lose.

B = Accommodation. I lose, you win.

C = Compromise. Both win some, lose some.

D = Collaboration. I win, you win.

Everyone has a basic or underlying conflict-handling style. Your scores on this exercise indicate the strategies you rely upon most.

FIGURE 13.7
Your Conflict Resolution Style

SOURCE: Thomas J. Von de Embse, *Supervision: Managerial Skills for a New Era* (New York: Macmillan Publishing Company, 1987), in Stephen Robbins and Philip Hunsaker, *Training in Interpersonal Skills* (Upper Saddle River, NJ: Prentice Hall, 1996), pp. 217–19.

people seem to be capable of adapting their style to the situation and of using several styles at once.

A Study of Interpersonal Conflict Styles

In practice, people usually don't rely on a single conflict-resolution mode; they use several simultaneously. A study of supervisors and subordinates illustrates this.

The researchers studied how supervisors used several possible conflict-resolution styles. The researchers' basic question was this: Is some combination of these styles more effective at resolving conflicts than others? They analyzed videotapes of 116 male police sergeants handling a standardized, scripted conflict with either a subordinate or a superior. The possible styles in this study (with examples) included:

- *Confrontation.* In recent meetings we have had a thrashing around about our needs. At first, we did not have much agreement. However, we kept thrashing the issues around, and we finally agreed on the best solution." Confronting the issue head-on is often the best approach. This is especially so when the parties are willing to confront and air their differences in a civil, problem-solving manner.

- *Forcing.* "If I want something very badly and I am confronted by a road-block, I go to top management for the backing I need to get the decision made. If there is a conflict, then I take the decision to somebody higher up." Forcing can be effective as a brute show of power. However, remember the old saying: "The person convinced against his will is of the same opinion still." Forcing compliance can backfire if the person you're forcing can wiggle out of the deal later.

- *Avoidance.* "I'm not going to discuss that with you." **Avoidance** or **smoothing over** usually won't resolve a conflict. In fact, doing so may actually make it worse if bad feelings fester. However, some problems—especially small ones—sometimes do go away by themselves. And avoidance may be your only option if one or both parties are highly emotional.

- *Process controlling.* "We're going to follow my agenda for this meeting, and solve this problem my way." Process controlling means dominating the conflict resolution process to one's own advantage.

- *Compromise and collaboration.* "I'm sure we can figure out a way to solve this together." "We're all in the same boat." **Compromise** means each person gives up something in return for reaching agreement. This approach can work well. However, it assumes a high level of maturity and willingness on both parties' parts. And it can leave one or both parties feeling that they could have done better if they'd bargained harder. **Collaboration** meant both sides work together to achieve agreement.

- *Accommodating.* "Calm down so we can work this out." **Accommodation** can help calm an opponent who is not uncontrollably irate. However, this is a stop-gap measure. You'll have to take up the issue again later, since the matter remains unresolved.

avoidance Moving away from or refusing to discuss a conflict issue

smoothing over In conflict management, diminishing or avoiding a conflict issue

process controlling Dominating the conflict resolution process to one's own advantage

compromise Settling a conflict through mutual concessions

collaboration A conflict-management style in which both sides work together to achieve agreement

accommodation Giving in to the opponent in an attempt to end a conflict

It was obvious that to resolve the conflict, the sergeant had to use several styles simultaneously. For example, problem solving tended to enhance the sergeant's effectiveness, especially if he or she combined it with some forcing. However, process controlling—dominating the conflict-resolution process to one's own advantage, for instance, by not letting the conversation stray off track—was even more effective. It was better than trying to force the issue by insisting that the adversary follow orders. Some sergeants also boosted their conflict-management effectiveness by being somewhat accommodating.

The bottom line seems to be this: At least for these police sergeants, using three styles together—*problem solving* while being moderately *accommodating* and still maintaining a strong hand in controlling the conflict-resolution process—was an especially effective combination. Multiple styles seems to be the way to go.

Summary

1. Whatever the change, the basic organizational change process remains basically the same. The change agent (usually the manager leading the change) needs to ask him- or herself three basic questions: What are the forces acting upon me? What should we change? How should we change it?
2. The manager's change program can aim to alter one of four basic things: The firm's strategy, technology, structure, and people/behavior/culture. In practice, such changes are rarely compartmentalized. Instead, the manager needs to take a systems view of the change and it's implications.
3. The hardest part of leading a change is overcoming resistance. Resistance stems from several sources: habit, resource limitations, threats to power and influence, fear of the unknown, and altering employees' personal compacts.
4. Methods of dealing with resistance include education and communication, facilitation and support, participation and involvement, negotiation and agreement, manipulation and co-optation, and coercion. Lewin suggests unfreezing the situation, perhaps by using a dramatic event to get people to recognize the need for change.
5. A nine-step process for actually leading organizational change includes creating a sense of urgency; deciding what to change; creating a guiding coalition and mobilizing commitment to change through a joint diagnosis of business problems; developing and then communicating a shared vision; removing barriers to the change and empowering employees; generating short-term wins; consolidating gains and producing more change: anchoring the new ways of doing things in the company's culture; and monitoring progress and adjusting the vision as required.
6. Organizational development (OD) is a special approach to organizational change that basically involves letting the employees themselves formulate and implement the change that's required, often with the assistance of a trained consultant. Types of OD applications include human process applications, technostructural interventions, HR management applications, and strategic applications.

7. Different conflict experts have slightly different ways of describing the conflict resolution styles a person can use. One popular approach involves thinking of conflict resolution styles in terms of a "dual concern model." This approach views conflict resolution styles as based on two things—the individual's concern for his or her own outcomes and for the outcomes of others. This produces a matrix and four (or five) styles (depending on the expert): *accommodators, avoiders, competitors,* and *collaborators.*

Experiential Exercises

1. In teams of 4–5 students, use what you learned about organizational culture in this chapter to describe the organizational culture in this class. List the specific things that you believe contributed to creating that culture and what specifically you would do to fine-tune the culture.

2. You are the professor in a management class, and you have a problem. Classes started last week, and the class did not get off to a good start. You arrived late, were snappy with the students, and gave them the impression that you'd be running a tough, dictatorial classroom. Several students dropped the course, and most of the others probably stayed only because the other sections are full. You don't want to spend a miserable semester. Form teams of 4–5 students, and write out an outline, using the nine-step change process from this chapter that shows what exactly you would change in your class (if you were the professor) and how you would change it, to have a more pleasant and productive class.

3. Working in teams of 4–5 students, explain specifically how you would apply each of the three steps in Lewin's change process to overcome resistance to change in the following situations: (1) Your brother is 200 pounds overweight. How would you get him to go on a diet? (2) Your professor gave you an A-minus instead of an A, because you compiled a 91.9 average instead of the required 92, and you want the grade changed to A. (3) You want to go to France on vacation this year, but your significant other is concerned with the risks of flying and of being out of the United States. How can you get that person to change his or her mind? (4) You just applied for a job as marketing manager for a local department store. The head of HR says that you seem like a very good candidate but that you don't have quite enough experience. How would you overcome his or her resistance?

CLOSING CASE

Immelt Splits GE Capital

In his first major reorganization since taking over as CEO of General Electric, Jeffrey Immelt said he was splitting GE's huge GE capital finance division into four major parts. GE Capital produces about 40% of all of GE's earnings, and the heads of its individual insurance, consumer finance, commercial finance, and equipment units formally reported to GE capital chief executive Denis Hayden. He, in turn, reported to Jeffrey Immelt, along with the heads of GE's various other businesses, including NBC, appliances, and medical equipment. Under the new organization, Immelt eliminated the position of GE Capital chief executive, and the heads of GE Capital's four main insurance, consumer finance, commercial finance, and equipment units will now report directly to Immelt.

In making the change, Immelt basically said he wanted more direct day-to-day control over GE Capital's huge financial services businesses. He said, "This will create a clearer line of sight on how our financial services businesses operate and enhance growth." The reorganization will, therefore, give him the same direct control over each of the GE capital divisions that he now has with respect to GE's other businesses, such as appliances and jet engines.

Another benefit of the change, according to GE, is that "our external reporting will mirror this organizational structure, providing greater clarity for investors." In other words, investors will now receive financial reports on each of the four GE Capital businesses rather than on just GE Capital as a whole.

While the reorganization seems to make sense, several observers have criticized it. The range of businesses and the number of people reporting to Immelt is already quite large, and the new organization means he'll have three additional people reporting directly to him. Furthermore, there are some obvious synergies among the four separate GE Capital divisions; therefore, it's now going to be up to Immelt to ensure that he provides the required coordination so that those synergies take place. Others point out that the sorts of improvements that Immelt says he wants—such as giving him a clearer idea of what each of the four divisions is doing—could have been accomplished without a major reorganization. In the past, for instance, GE's former CEO, Jack Welch, routinely personally reviewed major GE Capital transactions. Another analyst pointed out that ". . . Whenever a high-level executive [such as Nayden] departs, you have to be a little bit skeptical, and it raises a red flag that perhaps there may be another shoe."

Questions

1. Use Figure 13.2 to answer this question: Was this reorganization really necessary? What other knowledge that you have about how to reorganize would you apply to answering that question, and what conclusions would you arrive at?

2. Use the nine "test" questions (such as the market advantage test) in this chapter both to analyze the organization that Immelt decided upon and to answer this question: How would you have reorganized GE Capital?

YOU BE THE CONSULTANT

Fine-Tuning an Effective Organizational Culture at JetBlue

Anyone who's flown in the past few years (including the industry's most experienced, "elite-status" flyers) knows how frustrating flying can be, because of the long security lines, testy employees, and (when you finally get on the plane) lack of food. It hasn't been pleasant, and David Neeleman knew that building JetBlue meant putting "pleasant" back into flying. He also knows there's more to building a great airline than buying brand-new planes and offering low fares and seatback TVs (although that certainly helps). Great companies have great cultures, values, and expected behaviors that guide everything employees do. As he says in his "Welcome from our CEO" memo to passengers on JetBlue's Web site, ". . . We set out to bring humanity back to air travel and to make traveling more enjoyable." That's why Neeleman and his team have worked so hard to create the right culture at JetBlue.

In building the right culture, he and his team have taken several tangible steps. The Culture page on its Web site lays out the company's five values: safety, caring, integrity, fun, and passion. The Diversity page follows up with management's commitment to "encourage a diverse environment where teamwork prevails over cultural or ethnic differences." Creating the right culture means hiring people who have the sorts of values and behavior patterns JetBlue is looking for. If you browse through JetBlue's online job listings, you will, therefore, find numerous references to values and behavior. For example, the customer service crew needs to be "[a]ble to demonstrate a Passion for taking Care of customers with Integrity while having Fun and doing it all Safely." Its people should "find a way to say 'YES' to the customer." Other job listings—such as that for the manager of operations—similarly stress the need to exhibit a passion for the work of that position. JetBlue's online employment application form requires applicants to "[t]ell us your 'shining moment' story . . . ," when you've "gone out of your way to meet the needs of a customer or fellow employees." It also asks the applicant to describe an instance when he or she had "FUN on the job."

Neeleman and his team also take other culture-building steps. For example, you will often find him or members of his top-management team on the planes, speaking with passengers and crew to judge the level of service. They also pitch in with the ground crews, helping them load and unload planes and sort baggage.

Assignment

You and your team are consultants to Mr. Neeleman, who is depending on your management expertise to help him navigate the launching and management of JetBlue. Here's what he wants to know from you now:

1. Develop a form we can use to "read" how employees see our culture now. Could we use the same form to measure our passengers' perceptions of our culture? Tell us how we should go about doing the latter.

2. Write a brief (one-paragraph) summary of the sort of culture we are shooting for now. Then tell us what you would do to fine-tune that target culture, to delete aspects you think are unwise, or to add aspects you believe are necessary. Explain your changes, please.

3. Based on anything you know about JetBlue, list at least five other tangible things the company does (other than those in the case above) to create JetBlue's culture.

FOUNDATIONS
OF CONTROL

CASE STUDY

The management process is fairly straightforward. You plan to set your goals and you obtain and organize the necessary resources to make the plans a reality. You hire employees who possess the skills, knowledge, and abilities to successfully perform the often complex required tasks. Then you monitor the activities making sure you are on target. Where goals are not being met, you make the necessary changes. These are the fundamentals of management that serve as the foundation for operating an effective and efficient organization. In some organizations—like Enron, Adelphia, WorldCom, and Tyco International—these fundamentals have been ignored or abused. Executives in these organizations sadly have demonstrated that these fundamentals can be misused, especially when the controls that exist to protect the enterprise become dysfunctional. The fall of the Enron empire is a clear example of this situation.

Enron executives distorted internal financial data and released misleading profit reports through the use of complex accounting transactions. For instance, through some clever accounting maneuvers, Enron simply kept hundreds of millions of dollars in debt off its balance sheets. And by the creative use of partnerships, Enron executives created financial obligations that never showed up on the books. Although such a practice was in accordance with generally accepted accounting principles, had Enron executives classified the partnerships as subsidiaries, they would have had to account for the losses incurred by a number of them.

Compounding these potential problematic partnerships, Enron executives also engaged in bartering activities. By swapping telecommunications network capabilities with other companies, Enron recorded the barter sales as revenues, even though no cash ever changed hands. Furthermore, through another creative accounting practice—called derivatives—Enron hid losses it incurred on its investments in financing unsuccessful businesses.

Should Enron executives have been able to get away with these financial shenanigans? Not if proper controls had been established. Part of those controls are independent audits. And Enron had one of the largest U.S. accounting firms, Arthur Andersen, vouching for its accounting practices. Unfortunately for Enron investors and Arthur Andersen (this fiasco eventually led to the demise of Arthur Andersen as a going concern and the loss of 70,000 jobs), Andersen either never knew about Enron's financial manipulations or chose to ignore them.

The controls that had been established to protect investors in publicly held organizations were not working properly at the least—or worse, stretched to their limits by greed. As investigations continue into the Enron debacle, with criminal charges being brought, and convictions achieved, one thing is certain—the control systems failed. This once giant energy company is gone, as well as the livelihoods and retirements of thousands of employees and investors. The fact that this string of events could reach such epic proportions is a lesson in controlling and ethics for all of us!

From *Fundamentals of Management*, 4/E by Robbins, Stephen P. and DeCenzo, David, © 2004. Reprinted by permission of Pearson Education, Inc., Upper Saddle River, NJ.

The Enron example illustrates how dysfunctional control systems can be detrimental to an organization's performance. As we show in this chapter, effective management requires a well-designed control system—one that assists the organization in achieving its strategic goals.

What Is Control?

control The process of monitoring activities to ensure that they are being accomplished as planned and of correcting any significant deviations

Control is the management function involving the process of monitoring activities to ensure that they are being accomplished as planned and correcting any significant deviations. Managers cannot really know whether their units are performing properly until they have evaluated what activities have been done and have compared the actual performance with the desired standard. An effective control system ensures that activities are completed in ways that lead to the attainment of the organization's goals. The effectiveness of a control system is determined by how well it facilitates goal achievement The more it helps managers achieve their organization's goals, the better the control system.

When we introduced organizations, we stated that every organization attempts to effectively and efficiently reach its goals. Does that imply, however, that the control systems organizations use are identical? In other words, would Nokia, Royal Dutch Shell, France Telecom, and Wal-Mart all have the same type of control system? Probably not. Although similarities may exist, there are generally three different approaches to designing control systems. These are market, bureaucratic, and clan controls as summarized in Figure 14.1.

market control An approach to control that emphasizes the use of external market mechanisms such as price competition and market share

Market control emphasizes the use of external market mechanisms. Controls are built around such criteria as price competition or market share. Organizations

Type of Control	Characteristics
Market	Uses external market mechanisms, such as price competition and relative market share, to establish standards used in system. Typically used by organizations with clearly specified and distinct products or services and that face considerable marketplace competition.
Bureaucratic	Emphasizes organizational authority. Relies on administrative and hierarchical mechanisms, such as rules, regulations, procedures, policies, standardization of activities, well-defined job descriptions, and budgets to ensure that employees exhibit appropriate behaviors and meet performance standards.
Clan	Regulates employee behavior by the shared values, norms, traditions, rituals, beliefs, and other aspects of the organization's culture. Often used by organizations in which teams are common and technology is changing rapidly.

FIGURE 14.1
Characteristics of Three Approaches to Control Systems

using a market control approach usually have clearly specified and distinct products and services and considerable competition. Under these conditions, the various divisions of the organization are typically turned into profit centers and evaluated by the percentage of total corporate profits each generates. For instance, at Matsushita, each of the various divisions—which produces such products as videos, home appliances, and industrial equipment—is evaluated according to its contribution to the company's total profits. Using these measures, managers make decisions about future resource allocations, strategic changes, and other work activities that may need attention.

bureaucratic control
An approach to control that emphasizes authority and relies on administrative rules, regulations, procedures, and policies

A second approach to control systems is **bureaucratic control,** a control approach that emphasizes authority and relies on administrative rules, regulations, procedures, and policies. This type of control depends on standardization of activities, well-defined job descriptions to direct employee work behavior, and other administrative mechanisms—such as budgets—to ensure that organizational members exhibit appropriate work behaviors and meet established performance standards. At BP Amoco, managers of various divisions are allowed considerable autonomy and freedom to run their units as they see fit. Yet they are expected to stick closely to their budgets and stay within corporate guidelines.

clan control An approach to designing control systems in which employee behaviors are regulated by the shared values, norms, traditions, rituals, beliefs, and other aspects of the organization's culture

Clan control is an approach to designing control systems in which employee behaviors are regulated by the shared values, norms, traditions, rituals, beliefs, and other aspects of the organization's culture. In contrast to bureaucratic control, which is based on strict hierarchical mechanisms, clan control depends on the individual and the group (the clan) to identify appropriate and expected work-related behaviors and performance measures. Clan control is typically found in organizations in which teams are widely used and technologies change often. For instance, organizational members at SAS Institute (the Cary, NC-based software company), employees are well aware of the expectations regarding appropriate work behavior and performance standards. The organizational culture—through the shared values, norms, and stories about the company's founder, Jim Goodnight—conveys to individuals what's really important in the organization as well as what is not. Rather than relying on prescribed administrative controls, SAS employees are guided and controlled by the clan's culture.

It is important to recognize that most organizations do not totally rely on just one of these three approaches to design an appropriate control system. Instead, an organization typically chooses to emphasize either bureaucratic or clan control and then add some market control measures. The key, however, in any of the approaches is to design an appropriate control system that helps the organization effectively and efficiently reach its goals.

The Importance of Control

Planning can be done; an organization structure can be created to efficiently facilitate the achievement of objectives, and employees can be directed and motivated. Still, as we saw with Enron, there is no assurance that activities are going as planned and that the goals are, in fact, being attained. Control is the final link in the functional chain of management. However, the value of the control function lies predominantly in its relation to planning and delegating activities.

Objectives are the foundation of planning. Objectives give specific direction to mangers. However, just stating objectives or having employees accept your objectives is no guarantee that the necessary actions have been accomplished. The effective manager needs to follow up to ensure that the actions others are supposed to take and the objectives they are supposed to achieve are, in fact, being taken and achieved.

The Control Process

The control process consists of three separate and distinct steps: (1) measuring actual performance, (2) comparing actual performance against a standard, and (3) taking managerial action to correct deviations or inadequate standards (see Figure 14.2). Before we consider each step in detail, you should be aware that the control process assumes that standards of performance already exist, having been created in the planning function. If managers use some variation of mutual goal setting, then the objectives set are, by definition, tangible, verifiable, and measurable. In such instances, those objectives are the standards against which progress is measured and compared. If goal setting is not practiced, then standards are the specific performance indicators that management uses. Our point is that these standards are developed in the planning function; planning must precede control.

What Is Measuring?

To determine actual performance, a manager must acquire information about it. The first step in control, then, is measuring. Let's consider how we measure and what we measure.

FIGURE 14.2
The Control
Process

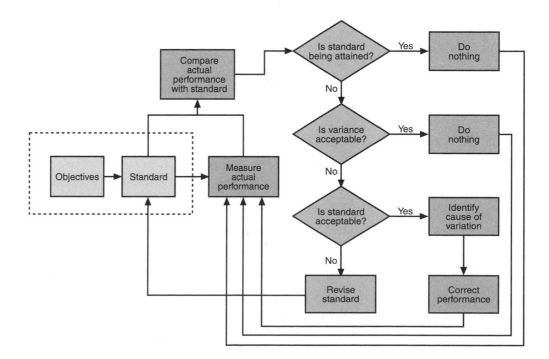

How Do Managers Measure? Four common sources of information frequently used to measure actual performance are personal observation, statistical reports, oral reports, and written reports. Each has particular strengths and weaknesses; however, use of a combination of them increases both the number of input sources and the probability of receiving reliable information.

Personal observation provides first-hand, intimate knowledge of the actual activity—information that is not filtered through others. It permits intensive coverage because minor as well as major performance activities can be observed, and it provides opportunities for the manager to read between the lines. **Management by walking around (MBWA)** is a phrase that is used to describe when a manager is out in the work area, interacting directly with employees, and exchanging information about what's going on. MBWA can pick up factual omissions, facial expressions, and tones of voice that may be missed by other sources. Unfortunately, in a time when quantitative information suggests objectivity, personal observation is often considered an inferior information source. It is subject to perceptual biases; what one manager sees, another might not. Personal observation also consumes a good deal of time. Finally, this method suffers from obtrusiveness. Employees might interpret a manager's overt observation as a sign of a lack of confidence or of mistrust.

The widespread use of computers has led managers to rely increasingly on *statistical reports* for measuring actual performance. This measuring device, however, isn't limited to computer outputs. It also includes graphs, bar charts, and numerical displays of any form that managers can use for assessing performance. Although statistical information is easy to visualize and effective for showing relationships, it provides limited information about an activity. Statistics report on only a few key areas and may often ignore other important, often subjective, factors.

Information can also be acquired through *oral reports*—that is, through conferences, meetings, one-to-one conversations, or telephone calls. In organizations in which employees work in a cultural environment, this approach may be the best way to keep tabs on work performance. For instance, at the Ken Blanchard Companies in Escondido, California, managers are expected to hold one-on-one meetings with each of their employees at least once every two weeks. The advantages and disadvantages of this method of measuring performance are similar to those of personal observation. Although the information is filtered, it is fast, allows for feedback, and permits expression and tone of voice as well as words themselves to convey meaning. Historically, one of the major drawbacks of oral reports has been the problem of documenting information for later reference. However, our technological capabilities have progressed in the past couple of decades to the point where oral reports can be efficiently taped and become as permanent as if they were written.

Actual performance may also be measured by *written reports*. Like statistical reports, they are slower yet more formal than first- or second-hand oral measures. This formality also often gives them greater comprehensiveness and conciseness than is found in oral reports. In addition, written reports are usually easy to catalog and reference.

Given the varied advantages and disadvantages of each of these four measurement techniques, managers should use all four for comprehensive control efforts.

management by walking around (MBWA) A phrase used to describe when a manager is out in the work area interacting with employees

What Do Managers Measure? What managers measure is probably more critical to the control process than how they measure. Why? The selection of the wrong criteria can result in serious dysfunctional consequences. Besides, what we measure determines, to a great extent, what people in the organization will attempt to excel at. For example, assume that your instructor has required a total of 10 writing assignments from the exercises at the end of each textbook chapter. But, in the grade computation section of the syllabus, you notice that these assignments are not scored. In fact, when you ask your professor about this, she replies that these writing assignments are for your own enlightenment and do not affect your grade for the course; grades are solely a function of how well you perform on the three exams. We predict that you would, not surprisingly, exert most, if not all, of your effort toward doing well on the three exams.

Some control criteria are applicable to any management situation. For instance, because all managers, by definition, direct the activities of others, criteria such as employee satisfaction or turnover and absenteeism rates can be measured. Most managers have budgets for their area of responsibility set in monetary units (dollars, pounds, francs, lire, and so on). Keeping costs within budget is, therefore, a fairly common control measure. However, any comprehensive control system needs to recognize the diversity of activities among managers. For example, a production manager in a paper tablet manufacturing plant might use measures of the quantity of tablets produced per day, tablets produced per labor hour, scrap tablet rate, or percentage of rejects returned by customers. On the other hand, the manager of an administrative unit in a government agency might use number of document pages produced per day, number of orders processed per hour, or average time required to process service calls. Marketing managers often use measures such as percent of market held, number of customer visits per salesperson, or number of customer impressions per advertising medium.

> "What we measure is probably more critical to the control process than how we measure. The selection of the wrong criteria can result in a seriously dysfunctional consequence."

As you might imagine, some activities are more difficult to measure in quantifiable terms. It is more difficult, for instance, for a manager to measure the performance of a medical researcher or a middle school counselor than of a person who sells life insurance. But most activities can be broken down into objective segments that allow for measurement. The manager needs to determine what value a person, department, or unit contributes to the organization and then convert the contribution into standards.

Most jobs and activities can be expressed in tangible and measurable terms. When a performance indicator cannot be stated in quantifiable terms, managers should look for and use subjective measures. Certainly, subjective measures have significant limitations. Still, they are better than having no standards at all and ignoring the control function. If an activity is important, the excuse that it is difficult to measure is inadequate. In such cases, managers should use subjective performance criteria. Of course, any analysis or decisions made on the basis of subjective criteria should recognize the limitations of the data.

How Do Managers Compare Actual Performance to Planned Goals? The comparing step determines the degree of discrepancy between actual performance and the standard. Some variation in performance can be expected in all activities; it is therefore critical to determine the acceptable **range of variation** (see Figure 14.3). Deviations beyond this range become significant and should receive the manager's attention. In the comparison stage, managers are particularly concerned with the size and direction of the variation. An example should help make this clearer.

Pat Welsh is the sales manager for South Atlantic Distributors. The company distributes imported beers in several states in the South. Welsh prepares a report during the first week of each month that summarizes sales for the previous month, classified by brand name. Figure 14.4 displays both the standard and actual sales figures (in hundreds of cases) for the month of July.

Should Pat be concerned about the July performance? Sales were a bit higher than originally targeted, but does that mean there were no significant deviations? Even though overall performance was generally quite favorable, several brands might need to he examined more closely by Pat. However, the number of brands that deserve attention depends on what Pat believes to be *significant*. How much variation should Welsh allow before corrective action is taken?

The deviation on several brands is very small and undoubtedly not worthy of special attention. These include Molson, Moosehead, and Amstel Light. Are the shortages for Corona and Dos Equis brands significant? That's a judgment Pat must make. Heineken sales were 15 percent below the goal. This brand needs attention. Welsh should look for a cause. In this case, Pat attributes the loss to aggressive advertising and promotion programs by the big domestic producers, Anheuser-Busch and Miller. Because Heineken is the best-selling import, it is most vulnerable to the promotion clout of the big domestic producers. If the decline in Heineken is more than a temporary slump, Welsh will need to cut back on inventory stock.

An error in understating sales can be as troublesome as an overstatement. For instance, is the surprising popularity of Tecate (up 68 percent) a one-month aberration, or is this brand increasing its market share? Our South Atlantic example illustrates that both overvariance and undervariance require managerial attention.

range of variation The acceptable parameters of variance between actual performance and the standard

FIGURE 14.3
Defining an Acceptable Range of Variation

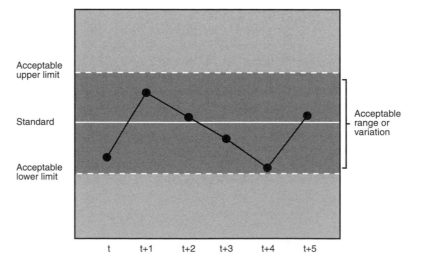

Brand	Standard	Actual	Over (Under)
Heineken	1,075	913	(162)
Molson	630	634	4
Beck's	800	912	112
Moosehead	620	622	2
Labatt's	540	672	132
Corona	160	140	(20)
Amstel light	225	220	(5)
Dos Equis	80	65	(15)
Tecate	170	286	116
Total cases	4,300	4,464	164

FIGURE 14.4

Mid-Western Distributors' Sales Performance for July (hundreds of cases)

What Managerial Action Can Be Taken?

The third and final step in the control process is managerial action. Managers can choose among three courses of action: They can do nothing, they can correct the actual performance, or they can revise the standard. Because doing nothing is fairly self-explanatory, let's look more closely at the latter two choices.

Correct Actual Performance. If the source of the variation has been deficient performance, the manager will want to take corrective action. Examples of such corrective action might include changes in strategy, structure, compensation practices, or training programs; the redesign of jobs; or the replacement of personnel.

A manager who decides to correct actual performance has to make another decision: Should he or she take immediate or basic corrective action? **Immediate corrective action** corrects problems at once and gets performance back on track. **Basic corrective action** asks how and why performance has deviated and then proceeds to correct the source of deviation. It is not unusual for managers to rationalize that they do not have the time to take basic corrective action and therefore must be content to perpetually put out fires with immediate corrective action. Effective managers, however, analyze deviations and, when the benefits justify it, take the time to permanently correct significant variances between standard and actual performance.

To return to our example of South Atlantic Distributors, Pat Welsh might take basic corrective action on the negative variance for Heineken. He might increase promotion efforts, increase the advertising budget for this brand, or reduce future orders with the manufacturer. The action Welsh takes will depend on the assessment of each brand's potential sales.

Revise the Standard. It is also possible that a variance was a result of an unrealistic standard—that is, the goal may have been too high or too low. In such cases the standard needs corrective attention, not the performance. In our example, the

immediate corrective action Correcting a problem at once to get performance back on track

basic corrective action Determining how and why performance has deviated and then correcting the source of deviation

sales manager might need to raise the standard for Tecate to reflect its increasing popularity, much as, in sports, athletes adjust their performance goals upward during a season if they achieve their season goal early.

The more troublesome problem is the revising of a performance standard downward. If an employee or unit falls significantly short of its target, the natural response is for the employee or unit to blame the standard. For instance, students who make a low grade on a test often attack the grade cutoff points as too high. Rather than accept the fact that their performance was inadequate, the students argue that the standards were unreasonable. Similarly, salespeople who fail to meet their monthly quota may attribute the failure to an unrealistic quota. It may be true that standards are too high, resulting in a significant variance and demotivating those employees being assessed against it. However, keep in mind that if employees or managers don't meet the standard, the first thing they are likely to attack is the standard itself. If you believe that the standard is realistic, hold your ground. Explain your position, reaffirm to the employee or manager that you expect future performance to improve, and then take the necessary corrective action to turn that expectation into reality.

Types of Control

Management can implement controls before an activity commences, while the activity is going on, or after the activity has been completed. The first type is called feedforward control; the second is concurrent control, and the last is feedback control (see Figure 14.5).

What Is Feedforward Control?

feedforward control
Control that prevents anticipated problems

The most desirable type of control—**feedforward control**—prevents anticipated problems because it takes place in advance of the actual activity. It's future-directed. For instance, when McDonald's opened its first restaurant in Moscow, it sent company quality control experts to help Russian farmers learn techniques for growing high-quality potatoes, and sent bakers to teach the processes for baking high-quality breads. Why? Because McDonald's strongly emphasizes product quality no matter what the geographical location. It wants a cheeseburger in Moscow to taste like one in Hartford, Connecticut. Another example of feedforward control is the scheduled aircraft maintenance programs clone by the major airlines. These are designed to detect, and its hoped, prevent structural damage that might lead to an airline disaster.

The key to feedforward control, therefore, is taking managerial action before a problem occurs. Feedforward controls allow management to prevent problems rather than having to cure them later. Unfortunately, these controls require timely and accurate information that is often difficult to develop. As a result, managers frequently have to use one of the other two types of control.

FIGURE 14.5
Types of Control

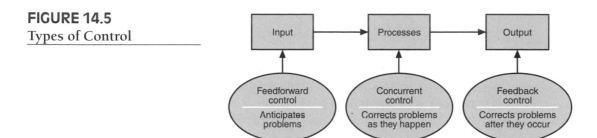

When Is Concurrent Control Used?

concurrent control
Control that takes place while an activity is in progress

Concurrent control, as its name implies, takes place while an activity is in progress. When control is enacted while the work is being performed, management can correct problems before they become too costly.

The best known form of concurrent control is direct supervision. When a manager directly oversees the actions of an employee, the manager can concurrently monitor the employee's actions and correct problems as they occur. Although there is obviously some delay between the activity and the manager's corrective response, the delay is minimal. Technical equipment (such as computers and computerized machine controls) can be designed to include concurrent controls. For example, you may have experienced concurrent control when using a computer program such as word-processing that alerts you to a misspelled word or incorrect grammatical usage. In addition, many organizational quality programs rely on concurrent controls to inform workers of whether their work output is of sufficient quality to meet standards.

Why Is Feedback Control So Popular?

The most popular type of control relies on feedback. The control takes place after the action. The control report that Pat Welsh (from our South Atlantic Distributors example) used for assessing beer sales is an example of **feedback control.**

feedback control
Control that takes place after an action

The major drawback of this type of control is that by the time the manager has the information the damage has already been done. It's analogous to locking the barn door after the horse has been stolen. But for many activities, feedback is the only viable type of control available. For example, financial statements are an example of feedback controls. If, for instance, the income statement shows that sales revenues are declining, the decline has already occurred. So at this point, the manager's only option is to try to determine why sales decreased and to correct the situation.

Feedback has two advantages over feedforward and concurrent control. First, feedback provides managers with meaningful information on the effectiveness of their planning effort. Feedback that indicates little variance between standard and actual performance is evidence that planning was generally on target. If the deviation is great, a manager can use that information to make new plans more effective. Second, feedback control can enhance employee motivation. People want information on how well they have performed. Feedback control provides that information.

Control Implications for Managers

A $165 million NASA Mars Polar Lander probe disappears without a trace. Marriott International implements its First Ten program, setting a standard for hassle-free guest check-in (based on the belief that guests ideally should be in their rooms within the first ten minutes of their arrival). Better financial controls implemented by CEO Pamela D. A. Reeve improve the financial results of Lightbridge, a Massachusetts-based company that helps telecommunications carriers acquire new clients and retain them. As these examples illustrate, controlling plays an important role in results and is an important function of managing. Without controls, managers would have insufficient information to resolve problems, make decisions, or take appropriate actions. How can managers perform the control function effectively and efficiently? To answer this question, we're going to look at the qualities of an effective control system, the contingency factors that affect the design of control systems, and how controls need to be adjusted for national differences.

What Are the Qualities of an Effective Control System?

Effective control systems tend to have certain qualities in common. The importance of these qualities varies with the situation, but we can generalize that the following characteristics should make a control system effective.

- **Accuracy**   A control system that generates inaccurate information can result in management's failing to take action when it should or responding to a problem that doesn't exist. An accurate control system is reliable and produces valid data.

- **Timeliness**   Controls should call management's attention to variations in time to prevent serious infringement on a unit's performance. The best information has little value if it is dated. Therefore, an effective control system must provide timely information.

- **Economy**   A control system must be economically reasonable. Any system of control has to justify the benefits that it gives in relation to the costs it incurs. To minimize costs, management should try to impose the least amount of control necessary to produce the desired results.

- **Flexibility**   Controls must be flexible enough to adjust to problems or to take advantage of new opportunities. Few organizations face environments so stable that there is no need for flexibility. Even highly mechanistic structures require controls that can be adjusted as times and conditions change.

- *Understandability*   Controls that cannot be understood have no value. It is sometimes necessary, therefore, to substitute less complex controls for sophisticated devices. A control system that is difficult to understand can cause unnecessary mistakes, frustrate employees, and eventually be ignored.

- *Reasonable criteria*   Control standards must be reasonable and attainable. If they are too high or unreasonable, they no longer motivate. Because most employees don't want to risk being labeled incompetent by accusing superiors of asking too much, employees may resort to unethical or illegal shortcuts. Controls should, therefore, enforce standards that challenge and stretch people to reach higher performance levels without demotivating them or encouraging deception.

- *Strategic placement*   Management can't control everything that goes on in an organization. Even if it could, the benefits couldn't justify the costs. As a result, managers should place controls on factors that are strategic to the organization's performance. Controls should cover the critical activities, operations, and events within the organization. That is, they should focus on places at which variations from standard are most likely to occur or at which a variation would do the greatest harm. If a department's labor costs are $100,000 a month and postage costs are $150 a month, a 5 percent overrun in the former is more critical than a 20 percent overrun in the latter. Hence, we should establish controls for labor and a critical dollar allocation, whereas postage expenses would not appear to be critical.

- *Emphasis on the exception*   Because managers can't control all activities, they should place their strategic control devices where those devices can call attention only to the exceptions. An exception system ensures that a manager is not overwhelmed by information on variations from standard. For instance, if management policy gives supervisors the authority to give annual raises up to $500 a month, approve individual expenses up to $1,500, and make capital expenditures up to $10,000, then only deviations above those amounts require approval from higher levels of management. These checkpoints become controls that are part of the authority constraints and free higher levels of management from reviewing routine expenditures.

- *Multiple criteria*   Managers and employees alike will try to look good on the criteria that are controlled. If management controls by using a single measure such as unit profit, effort will be focused only on looking good on that standard.

Multiple measures of performance widen this narrow focus. Multiple criteria have a dual positive effect. Because they are more difficult to manipulate than a single measure, they can discourage employee efforts to merely look good. In addition, because performance can rarely be objectively evaluated from a single indicator, multiple criteria make possible more accurate assessments of performance.

■ *Corrective action*   An effective control system not only indicates when a significant deviation from standard occurs but also suggests what action should be taken to correct the deviation. That is, it ought to both point out the problem and specify the solution. This form of control is frequently accomplished by establishing if–then guidelines; for instance, if unit revenues drop more than 5 percent, then unit costs should be reduced by a similar amount.

What Factors Affect Control?

Although our generalizations about effective control systems provide guidelines, their validity is influenced be situational factors. What types of contingency factors will affect the design of an organization's control system? These include size of the organization, one's position in the organization's hierarchy, degree of decentralization, organizational culture, and importance of an activity (see Figure 14.6).

Control systems should vary according to the size of the organization. A small business relies on informal and more personal control devices. Concurrent control

FIGURE 14.6
Contingency Factors in the
Design of Control Systems

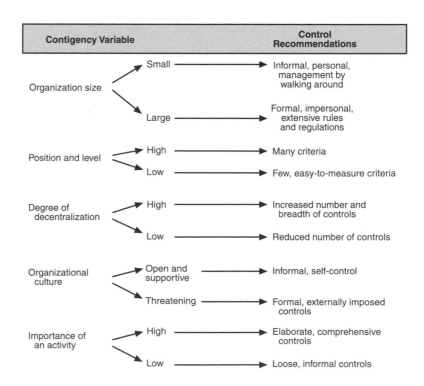

through direct supervision is probably most cost-effective. As organizations increase in size, direct supervision is likely to be supported by an expanding formal system. Very large organizations will typically have highly formalized and impersonal feedforward and feedback controls.

The higher one moves in the organization's hierarchy, the greater the need for multiple sets of control criteria, tailored to the unit's goals. This reflects the increased ambiguity in measuring performance as a person moves up the hierarchy. Conversely, lower-level jobs have clearer definitions of performance, which allow for a narrower interpretation of job performance.

The greater the degree of decentralization, the more managers will need feedback on the performance of their employees' decisions. Because managers who delegate authority are ultimately responsible for the actions of those to whom it is delegated, they will want proper assurances that their employees' decisions are both effective and efficient.

The organizational culture may be one of trust, autonomy, and openness, or one of fear and reprisal. In the former, we can expect to find informal self-control and, in the latter, externally imposed and formal control systems to ensure that performance is within standards. As with leadership styles, motivation techniques, organizational structuring, conflict management techniques, and the extent to which organizational members participate in decision making, the type and extent of controls should be consistent with the organization's culture.

Finally, the importance of an activity influences whether, and how, it will be controlled. If control is costly and the repercussions from error small, the control system is not likely to be elaborate. However, if an error can be highly damaging to the organization, extensive controls are likely to be implemented—even if the cost is high.

Do Controls Need to Be Adjusted for Cultural Differences?

The concepts of control that we've discussed are appropriate for organizational units that aren't geographically distant or culturally distinct. But what about global organizations? Would control systems be different, and what should managers know about adjusting controls for national differences?

Methods of controlling employee behavior and operations can be quite different in different countries. In fact, the differences in organizational control systems of global organizations are primarily in the measurement and corrective action steps of the control process. In a global corporation, for instance, managers of foreign operations tend not to be closely controlled by the home office if for no other reason than that distance keeps managers from being able to observe work directly. Because distance creates a tendency for formalized controls, the home office of a global company often relies on extensive, formal reports for control. The global company may also use the power of information technology to control work activities. For instance, IYG Holding Company (a wholly-owned subsidiary of Ito-Yokado Co., Ltd., and Seven-Eleven Japan Co., Ltd, that own the 7-Eleven convenience store chain) uses automated cash registers not only to record sales and monitor inventory, but also to schedule tasks for store managers and to track their use of the built-in analytical graphs and forecasts. If managers don't use them enough, they're told to increase their activities.

Technology's impact on control is most evident in comparisons of technologically advanced nations with more primitive countries. Organizations in technologically advanced nations such as the United States, Japan, Canada, Great Britain, Germany, and Australia use indirect control devices—particularly computer-related reports and analyses—in addition to standardized rules and direct supervision to ensure that activities are going as planned. In less technologically advanced countries, direct supervision and highly centralized decision making are the basic means of control.

Also, constraints on what corrective action managers can take may affect managers in foreign countries because laws in some countries do not allow managers the option of closing facilities, laying off employees, or bringing in a new management team from outside the country. Finally, another challenge for global companies in collecting data is comparability. For instance, a company's manufacturing facility in Mexico might produce the same products as a facility in Scotland. However, the Mexican facility might be much more labor intensive than its Scottish counterparts (to take advantage of lower labor costs in Mexico). If the top-level executives were to control costs by, for example, calculating labor costs per unit or output per worker, the figures would not be comparable. Managers in global companies must address these types of global control challenges.

The Dysfunctional Side of Control

Have you ever noticed that some of the people who work in the college registrar's office don't seem to care much about students' problems? At times they appear to be so fixated on ensuring that every rule is followed that they lose sight of the fact that their job is to help students, not to hassle them.

At the Chronic Fatigue and Immune Dysfunction Syndrome Association of America, executives were spending thousands of dollars each year on research. As the association's CEO, Kim Keeney stated, "we're in this business to go out of business." That's why they kept funding research projects. They would raise money, and use the monies for research support—making available millions of dollars for research. While the association's executives were excited about the opportunity to raise awareness of the disease and pursue a cure, they recognized one thing: They had no idea where their money was being spent. Without controlling for research outcomes, they believe more than $12 million was misspent by one of the organizations to whom they had given money.

"Some employees may manipulate measures to give the appearance they are performing well."

This example illustrates what can happen when controls are lacking. Similar results occur when controls are inflexible or control standards are unreasonable, too. That's because people lose sight of the organization's overall goals. Instead of the organization running the controls, the controls can sometimes run the organization.

Because control systems don't monitor everything, problems can occur when individuals or organizational units attempt to look good exclusively on control measures. The result again is something that is dysfunctional. More often than not, this dysfunctionality is caused by incomplete measures of performance. If the control system evaluates only the quantity of output, people will ignore quality. Similarly, if the system measures activities rather than results, people will spend their time attempting to look good on the activity measures.

To avoid being reprimanded by managers, people may engage in behaviors that are designed solely to influence the information system's data output during a given control period. Rather than actually performing well, employees may manipulate measures to give the appearance that they are performing well. That's precisely one of the key factors in the Enron scandal. Evidence indicates that the manipulation of control data is not a random phenomenon. It depends on the importance of an activity. Organizationally important activities are likely to make a difference in a person's rewards; therefore, there is a great incentive to look good on those particular measures. When rewards are at stake, individuals tend to manipulate data to appear in a favorable light by, for instance, distorting actual figures, emphasizing successes, and suppressing evidence of failures. On the other hand, only random errors have been found to occur when the distribution of rewards is unaffected.

Our conclusion is that controls have both an upside and a downside. Failure to design flexibility into a control system can create problems more severe than those the controls were implemented to prevent.

Contemporary Issues in Control

There are issues that can arise as managers design efficient and effective control systems. Technological advances in computer hardware and software, for example, have made the process of controlling much easier. But these advances in technology brought with them difficult questions regarding what managers have the right to know about employees and how far they can go in controlling employee behavior. In this section, we're going to look at two contemporary issues in control—workplace privacy and employee theft.

Is My Work Computer Really Mine?

If you work, do you think you have a right to privacy at your workplace? What can your employer find out about you and your work? You might be surprised by the answers. Employers can (and most often do), among other things, read your e-mail (even those marked personal or confidential), tap your phone, and monitor your computer work. And these actions aren't all that uncommon. Today, nearly 80 percent of all businesses surveyed by the American Management Association indicate they monitor employees.

Why do managers feel they must monitor what employees are doing? A big reason is that employees are hired to work, not to surf the Web checking stock prices, placing bets at online casinos, or shopping for presents for family or friends. Recreational on-the-job Web surfing has been said to cost a billion dollars in wasted computer resources and billions of dollars in lost work productivity annually. That's a significant cost to businesses.

Technological advances have made the process of managing an organization much easier. But technological advancements have also provided employers a means of sophisticated employee monitoring. Although most of this monitoring is designed to enhance worker productivity, it could, and has been, a source of concern over worker privacy. These advantages have also brought with them difficult questions regarding what managers have the right to know about employees and how far they can go in controlling employee behavior, both on and off the job.

What can your employer find out about you and your work? You might be surprised by the answers! Consider the following:

- The mayor of Colorado Springs, Colorado, reads the electronic mail messages that city council members send to each other from their homes. He defended his actions by saying he was making sure that e-mail to each other was not being used to circumvent his state's "open meeting" law that requires most council business to be conducted publicly.

- The U.S. Internal Revenue Service's internal audit group monitors a computer log that shows employee access to taxpayers' accounts. This monitoring activity allows management to check and see what employees are doing on their computers.

- American Express has an elaborate system for monitoring telephone calls. Daily reports are provided to supervisors that detail the frequency and length of calls made by employees, as well as how quickly incoming calls are answered.

- Managements in several organizations require employees to wear badges at all times while on company premises. These badges contain a variety of data that allow employees to enter certain locations in the organization. Smart badges, too, can transmit where the employee is at all times!

Just how much control should a company have over the private lives of its employees? Where should an employer's rules and controls end? Does the boss have the right to dictate what you do on your own free time and in your own home? Could, in essence, your boss keep you from engaging in riding a motorcycle, skydiving, smoking, drinking alcohol, or eating junk food? Again, the answers may surprise you. What's more, employer involvement in employees' off-work lives has been going on for decades. For instance, in the early 1900s, Ford Motor company would send social workers to employees' homes to determine whether their off-the-job habits and finances were deserving of year-end bonuses. Other firms made sure employees regularly attended church services. Today, many organizations, in their quest to control safety and health insurance costs, are once again delving into their employees' private lives.

Although controlling employees' behaviors on and off the job may appear unjust or unfair, nothing in our legal system prevents employers from engaging in these practices. Rather, the law is based on the premise that "if employees don't like the rules, they have the option of quitting."

Managers, too, typically defend their actions in terms of ensuring quality, productivity, and proper employee behavior. For instance, an IRS audit of its southeastern regional offices found that 166 employees took unauthorized looks at the tax returns of friends, neighbors, and celebrities.

When does management's need for information about employee performance cross over the line and interfere with a worker's right to privacy? Is any action by management acceptable as long as employees are notified ahead of time that they will be monitored? And what about the demarcation between monitoring work and nonwork behavior? When employees do work-related activities at home during evenings and weekends, does management's prerogative to monitor employees remain in force? What's your opinion?

Another reason that managers monitor employee e-mail and computer usage is that they don't want to risk being sued for creating a hostile workplace environment because of an offensive message or inappropriate images displayed on a co-worker's computer. Establish what actually happened and can help managers react quickly. Consider what happened at Chevron. They settled a sexual harassment lawsuit for $2.2 million because offensive e-mails—like "25 reasons why beer is better than women"—were readily circulated on the company's e-mail system. Organizations like Citigroup and Morgan Stanley Dean Ritter have also been taken to court by employees for racist e-mail proliferating on their systems. As one researcher pointed out, federal law views a company's e-mail no differently than if offensive materials were circulated on a company's letterhead.

Finally managers want to ensure that company secrets aren't being leaked. Although protecting intellectual property is important for all businesses, it's especially important in high-tech industries. Managers need to be certain that employees are not, even inadvertently, passing along information to others who could use that information to harm the company.

The consequences of inappropriate workplace computer usage also can be serious for employees and companies. For instance, shortly before Christmas in 1999, 23 workers at a *New York Times* administrative center in Norfolk, Virginia, were fired, and a number of other employees were reprimanded for violating the company's policy that prohibits using the corporate e-mail system to "create, forward, or display any offensive or disruptive messages, including photographs, and audio material." A number of Xerox employees were dismissed for spending as much as eight hours a day browsing X-rated and e-shopping Web sites during work hours. Two executives at Salomon Smith Barney were fired after a routine check of corporate e-mail turned up pornographic material. And Lockheed Martin's e-mail system crashed for six hours after an employee sent 60,000 co-workers an e-mail (asking them to respond back using an attached e-receipt) about a national prayer day. Since Lockheed depended heavily on its internal e-mail communication system, this crash cost the company hundreds of thousands of dollars.

Even with all the workplace monitoring that managers can do, employees in the United States do have some protection from the Federal Electronic Communications Privacy Act of 1986 (EPCA). The ECPA prohibits unauthorized interception of electronic communication. Although this law gives employees some privacy protection, it doesn't make workplace electronic monitoring illegal, as employers are allowed to monitor communications for business reasons or when employees have been notified of this practice. A similar law, the Data Protection Act of 1998, permits much of the same for companies in the United Kingdom. Although employees may think that it's unfair for a company to monitor their work electronically and to fire them for what they feel are minor distractions, the courts have ruled that since the computer belongs to the company, it has a right to monitor anything on its system. The point here is that there needs to be a balance between management's need to know and the effect employee monitoring may have on employee morale.

One interesting facet to the employee monitoring debate centers around protecting the enterprise. Since September 11, 2001, many government agencies and private organizations have been increasing their computer surveillance in an effort to support "homeland security." Because computer systems can and have been hacked, significant data can be lost. Moreover, a terrorist attack on U.S. computer systems could prove extremely damaging to the U.S. economy. As such, we can anticipate even more system monitoring and significantly more surveillance of many of the "normal" activities in our daily lives.

Is Employee Theft on the Rise?

Would it surprise you to find out that nearly 85 percent of all organizational theft and fraud is committed by employees—not outsiders? And it's costly. It's estimated that U.S. companies lose about $29 billion annually from employee theft and fraud. **Employee theft** is defined as any unauthorized taking of company property by employees for their personal use. It can range from embezzlement to fraudulent filing of expense reports to removing equipment, parts, software, and office supplies from company premises. Although retail businesses have long faced particularly serious potential losses from employee theft, loose financial controls at start-ups and small companies and the ready availability of information technology have made employee stealing an escalating problem in all kinds and sizes of organizations. In fact, a recent survey of U.S. businesses indicated that more than 35 percent of employees admitted to stealing from their employers. That number is even higher when you include theft by employees who have been laid off. It's a control issue that managers need to educate themselves about and with which they must be prepared to deal.

Why do employees steal? The answer depends on whom you ask. Experts in various fields—industrial security, criminology, clinical psychology—all have different perspectives. The industrial security people propose that people steal because the opportunity presents itself through lax controls and favorable circumstances. Criminologists say its because people have financial-based pressures (such as personal financial problems or vice-based pressures (such as gambling debts). And the clinical psychologists suggest that people steal because they can rationalize whatever they're doing as being correct and appropriate behavior ("everyone does it," "they had it coming," this company makes enough money and they'll never miss anything this small," "I deserve this for all that I put up with," and so forth). Although each of these approaches provides compelling insights into employee theft and has been instrumental in programs designed to deter it, unfortunately, employees continue to steal.

What can managers do? Under certain circumstances as part of a theft investigation in the organization an employer could require an employee to submit to a polygraph (lie detector test). There are also other means available. Lets look at some suggestions for managing employee theft. We can use the concepts of feedforward, concurrent, and feedback control to identify measures for deterring or reducing employee theft. We've presented this in Figure 14.7.

Entrepreneurs and Control

Entrepreneurs must look at controlling their ventures' operations in order to prosper in both the short and the long run. Those unique control issues that face entrepreneurs include managing growth, managing downturns, and exiting the venture.

Feedforward	Concurrent	Feedback
Careful prehiring screening.	Treat employees with respect and dignity.	Make sure employees know when theft or fraud has occurred—not naming names but letting people know this is not acceptable.
Establish specific policies defining theft and fraud and discipline procedures.	Openly communicate the costs of stealing.	Use the services of professional investigators.
Involve employees in writing policies.	Let employees know on a regular basis about their successes in preventing theft and fraud.	Redesign control measures.
Educate and train employees about the policies.	Use video surveillance equipment if conditions warrant.	Evaluate your organization's culture and the relationships of managers and employees.
Have professionals review your internal security controls.	Install "lock-out" options on computers, telephones, and e-mail. Use corporate hot lines for reporting incidences. Set a good example.	

FIGURE 14.7

Control Measures for Deterring or Reducing Employee Theft or Fraud

SOURCES: Based on A. H. Bell and D. M.Smith, "Protecting the Company Against Theft and Fraud," *Workforce Online* (www.workforce.com), December 3, 2000; J. D. Hansen, "To Catch a Thief," *Journal of Accountancy,* March 2000, pp. 43–46; and J. Greenberg, The Cognitive Geometry of Employee Theft," in *Dysfunctional Behavior in Organizations: Nonviolent and Deviant Behavior* (Stamford, CT: JAI Press, 1998), pp. 147–93.

How Must the Entrepreneur Control for Growth?

William Williams, cofounder of Glory Foods, has taken an unusual approach to managing growth—slow down the process. His company, based in Columbus, Ohio, sells "down-home-tasting" Southern specialities that are quick and easy to prepare. These items are an alternative to the traditional Southern cooking that takes hours of preparation. Glory Foods has successfully cornered a market niche by following a conservative path to growth. Williams' decision to move slowly was based mostly on the fact that he didn't want to dilute the founders' equity positions down to minority levels in order to acquire the increased financing needed to grow. Although the slow growth approach may have taken more time, Williams and his partners felt it was worth it because they still have total control over what happens in the company.

Growth is a natural and desirable outcome for entrepreneurial ventures. In fact, it's part of our definition of entrepreneurship. Entrepreneurial ventures pursue growth. However, growth doesn't have to be frantic and chaotic. Growing slowly can be just as successful, as William Williams discovered at Glory Foods.

Growth doesn't occur just randomly or by luck. Successfully pursuing growth typically requires an entrepreneur to manage all the challenges associated with growing. This entails planning, organizing, and controlling for growth.

Planning for Growth. As we said earlier in this chapter, controlling is tied closely to planning. And the best growth strategy is a well-planned one. Ideally, the decision to grow doesn't come about spontaneously, but instead is part of the venture's overall business goals and plans. Rapid growth without planning can be disastrous. Entrepreneurs need to address growth strategies as part of their business planning but shouldn't be overly rigid in that planning. The plans should be flexible enough to exploit unexpected opportunities that arise. With plans in place, the successful entrepreneur must then organize for growth.

Organizing for Growth. The key challenges for an entrepreneur in organizing for growth include finding capital, finding people, and strengthening the organizational culture.

Having enough capital is a major challenge facing growing entrepreneurial ventures. The money issue never seems to go away. It does take capital to expand. The process of finding capital to fund growth is much like going through the initial financing of the venture. However, this time, hopefully, the venture has a successful track record to back up the request. If it doesn't, it may be extremely difficult to acquire the necessary capital. That's why we said earlier that the best growth strategy is a planned one. Part of that planning should be how growth will be financed. For example, the Boston beer company which produces Samuel Adams grew 30 percent to 60 percent a year for 12 years by focusing almost exclusively on increasing its top-selling product line. However, the company was so focused on increasing market share that it had few financial controls and an inadequate financial infrastructure. During periods of growth, cash flow difficulties would force company president and brew master Jim Koch to tap into a pool of unused venture capital funding. However, when a chief financial officer joined the company in the late 1980s, he developed a financial structure that enabled the company to manage its growth more efficiently and effectively by setting up a plan for funding growth.

Another important issue that a growing entrepreneurial venture needs to address is finding people. Even if the venture is growing quickly, this challenge may be intensified because of the time constraints. It's important to plan, as much as possible, the number and types of employees needed to support the increasing workload as the venture grows. Also, it may be necessary to provide additional training and support to employees to help them handle the increased pressures associated with a growing organization.

Finally, when a venture is growing, it's important to create a positive, growth-oriented culture that enhances the opportunities to achieve success, both organizationally and individually. This sometimes can be difficult to do, particularly when changes are occurring rapidly. However, the values, attitudes, and beliefs that are established and reinforced during these times are critical to the entrepreneurial ventures, continued and future success. Figure 14.8 lists some suggestions that entrepreneurs might use to ensure that their venture's culture is one that embraces and supports a climate in which organizational growth is viewed as desirable and important. Keeping employees focused and committed to what the venture is doing is critical to the ultimate success of its growth strategies. If employees don't buy into the direction in which the entrepreneurial venture is headed, it's unlikely the growth strategies will be successful.

- Keep the lines of communication open—inform employees about major issues.
- Establish trust by being honest, open, and forthright about the challenges and rewards of being a growing organization.
- Be a good listener—find out what employees are thinking and facing.
- Be willing to delegate duties.
- Be flexible—be willing to change your plans if necessary.
- Provide consistent and regular feedback by letting employees know the outcomes—good and bad.
- Reinforce the contributions of each person by recognizing employees' efforts.
- Continually train employees to enhance their capabilities and skills.
- Maintain the focus on the venture's mission even as it grows.
- Establish and reinforce "we" spirit since a successful growing venture takes the coordinated efforts of all the employees.

FIGURE 14.8
Suggestions for Achieving a Supportive Growth-Oriented Culture

Controlling for Growth. Maintaining good financial records and financial controls over cash flow, inventory, customer data, sales orders, receivables, payables, and costs should be a priority of every entrepreneur—whether pursuing growth or not. However, its particularly important to reinforce these controls when the entrepreneurial venture is expanding. It's all too easy to let things "get away" or to put off doing them when there's an unrelenting urgency to get things done. Rapid growth, or even slow growth, does not excuse the need to have effective controls in place. In fact, it's particularly important to have established procedures, protocols, and processes and to use them. Even though mistakes and inefficiencies can never be entirely eliminated, at least an entrepreneur should ensure that every effort is being made to achieve high levels of productivity and organizational effectiveness. For example, at Green Gear Cycling, CEO Alan Scholz recognized the importance of controlling for growth. How? By following a "customer for life" strategy. By continually monitoring customer relationships and orienting organizational work decisions around their possible impacts on customers, Green Gears employees hope to keep customers for life. That's significant because they figure that if they could keep a customer for life, the value would range from $10,000 to $25,000 per lifetime customer.

How Does the Entrepreneur Manage Downturns?

Although organizational growth is a desirable and important goal for entrepreneurial ventures, what happens when things turn sour—when the growth strategies don't result in the intended outcomes and, in fact, result in a decline in performance? Nobody likes to fail, especially entrepreneurs. However, when an entrepreneurial venture faces times of trouble, what can be done? The first step is recognizing that a crisis is brewing.

"The first step in managing a downturn is recognizing that a crisis is brewing."

Recognizing Crisis Situations. An entrepreneur should be alert to the warning signs of a business in trouble. Some signals of potential performance decline include inadequate cash flow, excess number of employees, unnecessary and cumbersome administrative procedures, fear of conflict and taking risks, tolerance of work incompetence, lack of a clear mission or goals, and ineffective or poor communication within the organization.

"boiled frog phenomenon" A classical psychological response experiment

Another perspective on recognizing performance declines revolves around what is known as the **"boiled frog phenomenon."** The "boiled frog" is a classic psychological response experiment. In one case, a live frog that's dropped into a boiling pan of water reacts instantaneously and jumps out of the pan. But, in the second case, a living frog that's dropped into a pan of mild water that is gradually heated to the boiling point, fails to react and dies. A small firm may be particularly vulnerable to the boiled frog phenomenon because the entrepreneur may not recognize the "water heating up"—that is, the subtly declining situation. When changes in performance are gradual, a serious response may never be triggered or may come too late to do anything about the situation. So what does this teach us? That entrepreneurs need to be alert to the signals that the venture's performance may be worsening. Entrepreneurs cannot wait until the water has reached the boiling point to react.

When Things Turn for the Worse. Although an entrepreneur hopes never to have to deal with the organizational downturns, declines, or crises, there may come a time when he or she must do just that. After all, nobody likes to think about things going bad or taking a turn for the worse. But that's exactly what the entrepreneur needs to do—think about it before it happens, using feedforward control. It's important to have an up-to-date plan for covering bad times. It's just like mapping out exit routes from your home in case of a fire. An entrepreneur wants to be prepared before an emergency hits. This plan should focus on providing specific details for controlling the most fundamental and critical aspects of running the business—things like revenues, costs, and debt. Beyond having a plan for controlling the venture's critical financial inflows and outflows, other actions would involve identifying specific strategies for cutting costs and restructuring the venture.

How Does the Entrepreneur Exit the Venture?

Getting out of an entrepreneurial venture might seem a strange thing for an entrepreneur to do. However, there may come a point when the entrepreneur decides it's time to move on. That decision may be based on the fact that the entrepreneur hopes to cash out on the investment in the venture—called **harvesting**—or that the entrepreneur is facing serious organizational performance problems and wants to get out. It may even be the entrepreneur's desire to focus on other pursuits (either personal or business related). The issue involved with exiting the venture includes choosing a proper business valuation method and knowing what's involved in the process of selling a business.

harvesting When an entrepreneur hopes to cash out on the investment he or she made in the business

Business Evaluation Method. Valuation techniques generally fall into three categories: (1) asset valuations; (2) earnings valuations; and (3) cash flow valuations. Setting a value on a business can be a little tricky. In many cases, the entrepreneur has sacrificed much for the business and sees it as his or her "baby" Calculating the value of the "baby" based on objective standards such as cash flow or some multiple of net profits can sometimes be a shock. That's why it's important for an entrepreneur who wishes to exit a venture to get a comprehensive business valuation prepared by professionals.

Other Exiting Considerations. Although the hardest part of preparing to exit a venture is valuing it, other factors also should be considered. This includes such matters as deciding who sells the business, determining the tax implications of the venture's sale, establishing how potential buyers are to be screened, and determining when to tell employees about the sale. The process of exiting the entrepreneurial venture should be approached as carefully as the process of launching it. If the entrepreneur is selling the venture on a positive note, he or she wants to realize the value built up in the business. If the venture is being exited because of declining performance, the entrepreneur wants to maximize the potential return.

◎ Comprehension and Application

Reading for Comprehension

1. What is the role of control in management?
2. Name four methods managers can use to acquire information about actual organizational performance.
3. Contrast immediate and basic corrective action.
4. What are the advantages and disadvantages of feedforward control?
5. What can management do to reduce the dysfunctionality of controls?

Linking Concepts to Practice

1. How are planning and control linked? Is the control function linked to the organizing and leading functions of management? Explain.
2. Why do you believe feedback control is the most popular type of control? Justify your response.
3. Why is what is measured probably more critical to the control process than how it is measured?
4. "Organizations have the right to monitor employees—both on and off the job." Build an argument supporting this statement and an argument disagreeing with the statement.

VIDEO CASE APPLICATION

YOUpowered: Safeguarding the Consumer's Online Privacy in the Name of Good Business

For lawyers and ethicists, privacy issues revolving around Internet use in the workplace and at home are just heating up. Consumers are increasingly wary of security problems in cyberspace and reluctant to have personal information fall into the wrong hands. YOUpowered gives both businesses and consumers an ethical solution to their needs through permission-based personalization, by detecting and blocking cookies.

These aren't the kind of cookies you enjoy with your milk. According to David Zimmerman, Ph.D., chief technology officer, YOUpowered, there are "good" cookies and "bad" cookies, cookies being the invisible software dropped on your hard drive by nearly every company with a Web site.

The "bad" cookies record and track your every move, and may be used by organizations to send you unwanted promotions and clutter your home computer screen with ads. Dr. Zimmerman believes that giving consumers control over their personal Internet profiles is the best response to the surreptitious, seemingly unstoppable, use of cookies by the e-business community. Using ORBY, individuals create their own digital profiles including name, password, address, job, and credit card numbers. They are notified on-screen about what information is being collected and can opt in or out of sharing their personal responses.

YOUpowered benefits the business community as well, by compiling online behavior information about surfer's Web activities and habits. YOUpowered's Orby software enables companies to build a strong customer base of people whose privacy preferences are compatible with the company's Web site. Orby's goal is to support a closer relationship between businesses and clients based on consumer confidence.

Two e-businesses that have integrated ORBY are MaxManager, a service that stores and organizes on-line shopping orders and receipts, and @once.com, an online marketer for companies like Nintendo, Egghead, and J.Crew. Both companies are committed to the idea that being open with Web site visitors will foster consumer trust *and* repeat business.

"A consumer should have access to their information," says Matthew Ellice, privacy officer, @once.com. "They should know exactly what their on-site experience will entail and what they can expect." Orby works together with an application called Consumer Trust to disclose what a firm would like to know, what they will use the data for, how long they plan to keep it, and whether they intend to do future "e-mailings.'"

Do you think that being observed silently by invisible bits of software while making online Christmas purchases in your own living room is an invasion of your privacy? No one seems to know the answer. The ethical and legal issues surrounding organizational monitoring of people at home and at work remain murky. Yet, the use of electronic surveillance monitoring devices have become commonplace in American businesses. In the face of soaring Internet crime, it is certainly defensible. Cyber thieves, among them many rank and file employees, are stealing millions if not billions of dollars a year from businesses in the United States and abroad. According to the *New York Times,* "thieves are not just diverting cash from company bank accounts, they are pilfering valuable information like business development strategies, new product specifications, or contract bidding plans and selling the data to competitors."

Founded in 1997, New York City based YOU-powered is the leading provider of Web-wide Smart Personalization solutions for today's e-business community. Here in America, where defending one's right to privacy is endemic to the national character, YOUpowered's Orby is likely to be in demand.

Questions

1. How might the manager of a small virtual advertising business use ORBY to help him or her improve feedforward control, concurrent control, or feedback control? Explain.
2. When asked about MaxManager's decision to implement ORBY, Dan Berg, vice president of business development replied: "Those of us who have started these online and Internet companies are consumers and users of the Internet as well. I don't want my information disseminated in ways I don't know about." Analyze his answer from an entrepreneurial viewpoint, as well as a personal stance.
3. As an employee at @once, would you expect the organizational culture to dictate concern for employee privacy? Explain. Under these circumstances would you feel it was an invasion of your privacy for @once management to have accessed your personal health information upon filing your insurance claim after an unplanned hospital stay or would you reason that human resource personnel are accustomed to dealing with these issues and not take action? Explain. If you chose not to let the incident go, what form of action would you take?

Developing Your Performance Feedback Skill

About the Skill

In this chapter, we introduced several suggestions for providing feedback. One of the more critical feedback sessions will occur when you, as a manager, are using feedback control to address performance issues.

Steps in Practicing the Skill

1. *Schedule the feedback session in advance and be prepared.* One of the biggest mistakes you can make is to treat feedback control lightly. Simply calling in an employee and giving feedback that is not well organized serves little purpose for you and your employee. For feedback to be effective, you must plan ahead. Identify the issues you wish to address and cite specific examples to reinforce what you are saying. Furthermore, set aside the time for the meeting with the employee. Make sure that what you do is done in private and can be completed without interruptions. That may mean closing your office door (if you have one), holding phone calls, and the like.

2. *Put the employee at ease.* Regardless of how you feel about the feedback, you must create a supportive climate for the employee. Recognize that giving and getting this feedback can be an emotional event even when the feedback is positive. By putting your employee at ease, you begin to establish a supportive environment in which understanding can take place.

3. *Make sure the employee knows the purpose of this feedback session.* What is the purpose of the meeting? That's something any employee will be wondering. Clarifying what you are going to do sets the appropriate stage for what is to come.

4. *Focus on specific rather than general work behaviors.* Feedback should be specific rather than general. General statements are vague and provide little useful information—especially if you are attempting to correct a problem.

5. *Keep comments impersonal and job related.* Feedback should be descriptive rather than judgmental or evaluative, especially when you are giving negative feedback. No matter how upset you are, keep the feedback job related and never criticize someone personally because of an inappropriate action. You are censuring job-related behavior, not the person.

6. *Support feedback with hard data.* Tell your employee how you came to your conclusion on his or her performance. Hard data help your employees to identify with specific behaviors. Identify the "things" that were done correctly and provide a detailed critique. And, if you need to criticize, state the basis of your conclusion that a good job was not completed.

7. *Direct the negative feedback toward work-related behavior that the employee controls.* Negative feedback should be directed toward work-related behavior that the employee can do something about. Indicate what he or she can do to improve the situation. This practice helps take the sting out of the criticism and offers guidance to an individual who understands the problem but doesn't know how to resolve it.

8. *Let the employee speak.* Get the employee's perceptions of what you are saying, especially if you are addressing a problem. Of course, you're not looking for excuses, but you need to be empathetic to the employee. Get his or her side. Maybe there's something that has contributed to the issue. Letting the employee speak involves your employee and just might provide information you were unaware of.

9. *Ensure that the employee has a clear and full understanding of the feedback.* Feedback must be concise and complete enough so that your employee clearly and fully understands what you have said. Consistent with active listening techniques, have your employee rephrase the content of your feedback to check whether it fully captures your meaning.

10. *Detail a future plan of action.* Performing doesn't stop simply because feedback occurred. Good performance must be reinforced, and new performance goals set. However, when there are performance deficiencies, time must be devoted to helping your employee develop a detailed, step-by-step plan to correct the situation. This plan includes what has to be done, when, and how you will monitor the activities. Offer whatever assistance you can to help the employee, but make it clear that it is the employee, not you, who has to make the corrections.

Practicing the Skill

Think of a skill you would like to acquire or improve, or a habit you would like to break. Perhaps you would like to learn a foreign language, start exercising, quit smoking, ski better, or spend less. For the purpose of this exercise, assume you have three months to make a start on your project and all the necessary funds. Draft a plan of action that outlines what you need to do, when you need to do it, and how you will know that you have successfully completed each step of your plan. Be realistic, but don't set your sights too low either.

Review your plan. What outside help or resources will you require? How will you get them? Add these to your plan.

Could someone else follow the steps you've outlined to achieve the goal you set? What modifications would you have to make, if any?

Developing Your Diagnostic and Analytical Skills

SiloCaf

At the Port of New Orleans, the largest coffee port in the United States, one company is handling an old-fashioned product in a new-fashioned way. Frederico Pacorini's SiloCaf, a fully computerized bulk-coffee storage, handling, and processing facility, is a place where tradition meets technology and where control is taking on a new perspective.

SiloCaf was founded in 1933 as a freight-forwarding company that moved products from one location to another. Today, however, the company primarily moves coffee, and the way that it controls and monitors its entire processing operation is about as technologically advanced as possible. Why has SiloCaf invested in technology for such a seemingly simple product? The primary reason is that consumers want the same flavor each time they purchase a can of coffee. However, coffee is a natural product, and coffee beans may vary from crop to crop. Getting consistent flavor is difficult without some way to control the coffee blend. That's crucial to a big company like Folger's, that demands consistency in taste. Nearly one-third of all coffee processed in the United States comes through the New Orleans facility. Without the technology, the company simply could not meet customer demands. As a result, SiloCaf is addressing these challenges by using information systems and computer technology.

Massimo Toma is SiloCaf's systems and resources manager. He is responsible for overseeing the coffee-blending process. Each week, several million pounds of coffee beans come into SiloCaf's warehouse from all over the world. More than 2 million pounds of coffee are processed in every 12-hour shift. Once the coffee has been processed, it's loaded into standard one-pound bags, larger bulk packages, or into 2,000-pound super-sacks, and shipped to a coffee-roasting company. At any one time, SiloCaf has from 35 to 40 million pounds of coffee in its facility for processing. If you consider the price of a pound of coffee, SiloCaf has an extremely valuable resource in its possession. Actually, SiloCaf never owns the coffee. Rather, it's owned by the roasting company or the dealer who delivers the coffee to the roasting company.

All the mechanical parts in SiloCaf's New Orleans facility have been brought from Italy, where the company first developed its technology. Frederico Pacorini, the son of the founder and manager of the New Orleans facility, says that technology in a business like theirs is important because it allows them to make all the blends they need for the coffee roasters and to optimize the process of making the various coffee blends. SiloCaf's employers receive continually updated statistical reports for each one of the scales used to blend coffee. The reports enable them to check the consistency of the scales' performance, which is important for achieving the consistency that the coffee drinker wants. In addition, the technology also helps employees to oversee the cleaning, sorting, and bagging of raw coffee beans before they are shipped to roasters.

You might think that this high-tech control would be expensive. It's not! SiloCaf's solution to the blend-consistency challenge is to use technology that is relatively simple and inexpensive. In fact, the company's investment was a mere 1 percent of all plant investment expenditures.

Enhancing Your Communication Skills

1. "Controls have to be sophisticated for them to be effective." Present both sides of the argument (for and against) this statement. Conclude your presentation with a persuasive statement of why you agree or disagree.
2. Describe how you can use the concepts of control in your own personal life. Be specific in your examples and think in terms of the feedforward, concurrent, and feedback controls that you use for different parts of your life.
3. Visit the Society of Human Resource Management's Web site for HR News, <www.shrm.org/hrnews>, and research the latest information on privacy issues and employee monitoring. Describe the pros and cons of having employees monitored and the latest technology that is used to enhance monitoring activities for the organization.

INDEX

BMW, 315
Body language, 337
Boeing, 155
Boiled frog phenomenon, 410
Bossidy, Larry, 249, 250t
Bounded discretion, 86
Brainstorming, 99–100, 101t
Breuer, Rolf, 223
Bribery, government standards on, 52
Buckman Laboratory, 349
Buffering, 63, 64–65
Bureaucracy
    adapting to environment and, 63
    Weber and, 32, 33fig., 233
Bureaucratic control, 389fig., 390
Burnham, David, 238
Business Development Bank of Canada, 196
Business ecosystems, 123–24
Business function, departmentalization by, 220
Business reengineering, 130, 367, 368
Business Week, 135

C
Cafeteria compensation, 294
Campbell, Andrew, 359fig.
Canada, entrepreneurship and, 189
Canadian Federation of Independent Business, 189
Capability profile, 129–30
Care perspective, 147
Carlstrom, Tina, 84
Carpal tunnel syndrome, 289
Carrefour, 170, 171
Case, Steve, 214
Cash flow, management of, 207
Castaneda, Maureen, 146
Centralization, 227–28
Certain decisions, 75
Chain communication network, 345–46
Channel, 335, 336
Charismatic leadership
    methods of transforming followers under, 261–63
    research on, 263–64
    transactional leadership vs., 260–61
Charles Schwab, 127
Chevron, 405
Chief executive officer (CEO), 4
    jointly held by two persons, 238–39
China
    economic system of, 157
    organizational development in, 378
    World Trade Organization and, 159–60
Chronic Fatigue and Immune Dysfunction Syndrome

Association of America, 402
Chrysler, 121, 135–36
Circuit City, 35
Cisco Systems, 133–34
Citibank, 129, 350
Citigroup, 239, 405
Clan control, 390
Classical management perspective, 10–12
Classical organization theories, 232–37
Closed system, 16, 37
Coaching skills, 327–28
Coalition formation, 65
Coastal Physician Group Inc., 262
Coca-Cola, 76t, 161, 172–73
Code law system, 160
Code of ethics, 148
Colgate-Palmolive, 221, 222fig.
Collaboration (conflict resolution), 379, 380fig., 381
Collectivism, individualism vs., 174, 318–19, 340–42
Command economy, 157
Commercial News USA, 153
Commoditization, 116–17
Common law legal system, 160
Common market, 158
Communication, 332–43
    current issues in, 350–52
    defined, 333–34
    functions of, 334–35
    gender differences in, 341
    in a multicultural environment, 177, 332
    information technology, 347–51
    interpersonal, 335–43
    manager's skills in, 7, 23–25, 333
    organizational, 343–46
    work teams and, 317–18, 329
Communication networks, 345–46
Communication process, 335
Compatability test, 87
Competitive advantage, 122
Competitive environment, 51–52, 55–60
    competitors, 56–57
    customers and, 59–60
    product suppliers and, 58–59
    threat of new entrants and, 57
    threat of product substitutes and, 57–58
Competitive scope, 122
Competitors, 56–57
Competitors model of conflict resolution, 379
Compressed workweeks, 300
Compromise (conflict resolution), 380fig., 381
Computer-assisted communication, 108–9
Computerized information systems, 173